The Music of
Luigi Dallapiccola

Eastman Studies in Music

Ralph P. Locke, Senior Editor
Eastman School of Music

(ISSN 1071–9989)

The Poetic Debussy: A Collection of His Song Texts and Selected Letters
(Revised Second Edition)
Edited by Margaret G. Cobb

Concert Music, Rock, and Jazz since 1945: Essays and Analytical Studies
Edited by Elizabeth West Marvin and Richard Hermann

Music and the Occult: French Musical Philosophies, 1750–1950
Joscelyn Godwin

"Wanderjahre of a Revolutionist" and Other Essays on American Music
Arthur Farwell, edited by Thomas Stoner

French Organ Music from the Revolution to Franck and Widor
Edited by Lawrence Archbold and William J. Peterson

Musical Creativity in Twentieth-Century China: Abing, His Music, and Its Changing Meanings (includes CD)
Jonathan P.J. Stock

Elliott Carter: Collected Essays and Lectures, 1937–1995
Edited by Jonathan W. Bernard

Music Theory in Concept and Practice
Edited by James M. Baker, David W. Beach, and Jonathan W. Bernard

Music and Musicians in the Escorial Liturgy under the Habsburgs, 1563–1700
Michael Noone

Analyzing Wagner's Operas: Alfred Lorenz and German Nationalist Ideology
Stephen McClatchie

The Gardano Music Printing Firms, 1569–1611
Richard J. Agee

"The Broadway Sound": The Autobiography and Selected Essays of Robert Russell Bennett
Edited by George J. Ferencz

Theories of Fugue from the Age of Josquin to the Age of Bach
Paul Mark Walker

The Chansons of Orlando di Lasso and Their Protestant Listeners: Music, Piety, and Print in Sixteenth-Century France
Richard Freedman

Berlioz's Semi-Operas: Roméo et Juliette *and* La damnation de Faust
Daniel Albright

The Gamelan Digul and the Prison Camp Musician Who Built It
Margaret J. Kartomi

"The Music of American Folk Song" and Selected Other Writings on American Folk Music
Ruth Crawford Seeger

Portrait of Percy Grainger
Malcolm Gillies and David Pear

Berlioz: Past, Present, Future
Edited by Peter Bloom

The Musical Madhouse (Les Grotesques de la Musique)
Hector Berlioz
Translated by Alastair Bruce

The Music of Luigi Dallapiccola
Raymond Fearn

The Music of Luigi Dallapiccola

Raymond Fearn

Ⓡ University of Rochester Press

Copyright © 2003 Raymond Fearn

All Rights Reserved. Except as permitted under current legislation, no part of this work may be photocopied, stored in a retrieval system, published, performed in public, adapted, broadcast, transmitted, recorded, or reproduced in any form or by any means, without the prior permission of the copyright owner.

First published 2003
Reprinted in paperback 2010
Transferred to digital printing 2012

University of Rochester Press
668 Mt. Hope Avenue, Rochester, NY 14620, USA
www.urpress.com
and Boydell & Brewer Limited
PO Box 9, Woodbridge, Suffolk IP12 3DF, UK
www.boydellandbrewer.com

ISSN: 1071-9989
Cloth ISBN-13: 978-1-58046-078-1
Cloth ISBN-10: 1-58046-078-X
Paperback ISBN-13: 978-1-58046-347-8

Library of Congress Cataloging-in-Publication Data

Fearn, Raymond, 1944–
   The music of Luigi Dallapiccola / Raymond Fearn
      p. cm. — (Eastman studies in music, /ISSN 1071-9989 ; v. 23)
   Includes bibliographical references and index.
   ISBN 1-58046-078-X (hardcover: alk. paper)
    1. Dallapiccola, Luigi, 1904–1975. 2. Dallapiccola, Luigi, 1904–1975—Criticism and interpretation. 3. Composers—Italy—Biography.
I. Title. II. Series.

ML410.D138 F43 2003
780'.92—dc21

                                                  2003007367

A catalogue record for this title is available from the British Library.

This publication is printed on acid-free paper.
Printed in the United States of America

In memory of Laura Dallapiccola, Muse and Companion of the composer, whose altissima luce *brought so much of his work into existence*

Luigi Dallapiccola at the piano in his house at Via Romana 34, Florence, in 1958. Photograph by Foto Levi, Florence; courtesy of the Dallapiccola Archive.

Contents

List of Music Examples	ix
List of Tables and List of Figures	xiii
Preface and Acknowledgments	xv
Abbreviations	xix

1. The Beginnings: 1904–1938 1
   Childhood and Youth 1
   Due liriche del Kalevala 10
   Partita 11
   Estate 13
   Divertimento in quattro esercizi 17
   Musica per tre pianoforti (Inni) 22
   Sei cori di Michelangelo Buonarroti il Giovane 28
   Tre laudi 33
   Volo di notte 38

2. Self-Exile and Discovery: 1939–1945 50
   The Discovery of Webern 50
   Piccolo concerto per Muriel Couvreux 53
   Canti di prigionia 56
   Marsia 66
   Editing Monteverdi's *Ulisse* 72
   Sonatina canonica 74
   Encounter with Webern 81
   Liriche greche 84

3. Towards the Light of Freedom: 1945–1948 97
   Ciaccona, intermezzo e adagio 99
   Due studi 105
   Rencesvals 110
   Il prigioniero 115

4. The Serial Idea: 1948–1953 128
   The Principles of Serialism 128
   Quattro liriche di Antonio Machado 131
   Tre poemi 134
   Job 140
   Tartiniana 152
   Quaderno musicale di Annalibera 157
   Goethe-Lieder 171

5. Text and Symbol: 1954–1964	179
Piccola musica notturna	180
Canti di liberazione	185
An Mathilde	193
Tartiniana seconda	197
Cinque canti	200
Concerto per la notte di Natale dell'anno 1956	204
Requiescant	206
Dialoghi	212
Preghiere	216
Parole di San Paolo	221
Three Questions with Two Answers	224
6. Ulysses, Wanderer and Discoverer: 1965–1975	232
Ulisse	232
Sicut umbra	252
Tempus destruendi—Tempus aedificandi	258
Commiato	265
Journeyings and Returns: The Nature of Dallapiccola's Art	269
Appendix: List of Compositions	273
Notes	278
Selected Bibliography	291
Index	297

Music Examples

1.1.	*Frammento del Kalevala,* mm.1–22	11
1.2.	*Partita.* Passacaglia theme, mm.1–8	12
1.3.	*Partita.* Naenia B.M.V., fig.77	13
1.4.	*Estate,* mm. 31–42	15
1.5 (a).	*Divertimento.* Siciliana, mm. 202–5.	18
1.5 (b).	*Canti di prigionia,* row	18
1.6.	*Divertimento.* Bourrée, mm. 156–62	19
1.7.	*Inni.* I, mm. 1–7	23
1.8.	*Inni.* I, mm. 50–55	25
1.9.	*Inni.* II, mm. 61–64	26
1.10.	*Inni.* III, mm. 1–9	27
1.11.	"Coro delle Malmaritate," mm. 57–60	29
1.12.	"Coro dei lanzi briachi," opening	31
1.13.	"Coro degli Zitti," principal themes	32
1.14.	"Coro degli Zitti," conclusion	32
1.15.	*Tre laudi,* mm.1–9	35
1.16.	*Tre laudi,* mm. 59–62	36
1.17.	*Tre laudi,* mm. 92–98	37
1.18.	*Tre laudi,* mm. 156–60	37
1.19.	*Volo di notte,* mm. 71–74	47
1.20.	*Volo di notte,* mm. 695–98	48
2.1.	*Piccolo concerto per Muriel Couvreux.* I, opening measures	54
2.2.	*Piccolo concerto per Muriel Couvreux.* II, cadenza: conclusion	55
2.3.	*Canti di prigionia.* I, mm. 1–4	60
2.4.	*Canti di prigionia.* III, mm. 1–7	63
2.5.	*Canti di prigionia.* III, mm. 32–41	64
2.6.	*Marsia,* opening measures	69
2.7.	*Marsia,* fig. 36	69
2.8.	*Marsia,* fig. 59	70
2.9.	*Marsia,* rows	70
2.10.	*Marsia,* fig. 92	71
2.11 (a).	*Sonatina canonica.* I, mm. 1–16	76
2.11 (b).	Paganini. Capriccio No. 20, mm. 1–9	77
2.12 (a).	*Sonatina canonica.* II, mm. 1–6	78
2.12 (b).	Paganini. Capriccio No. 19, mm. 1–4	78
2.13.	*Sonatina canonica.* II, mm. 7–12	79
2.14.	*Sonatina canonica.* III, entire movement	79–80
2.15.	*Cinque frammenti di Saffo.* I, mm. 1–7	88
2.16.	*Cinque frammenti di Saffo.* IV, rows	89
2.17.	*Cinque frammenti di Saffo.* IV, mm. 68–74	90
2.18.	*Due liriche di Anacreonte,* mm. 1–7	91

2.19.	*Due liriche di Anacreonte*, mm. 37–44	92
2.20.	*Sex carmina Alcaei*. I, opening measures	93
2.21.	*Sex carmina Alcaei*. IV, opening measures	95
3.1 (a).	*Ciaccona*, mm. 1–8	100
3.1 (b).	*Ciaccona*, row	100
3.2.	*Ciaccona*, mm. 84–92	101–102
3.3.	*Intermezzo*, mm. 93–100	102
3.4 (a).	*Intermezzo*, rhythmic cell	103
3.4 (b).	Berg. *Wozzeck*, rhythmic cell	103
3.5 (a).	*Adagio*, mm. 201–13	103–104
3.5 (b).	*Adagio*, row	104
3.6.	*Adagio*, mm. 262–75	104–105
3.7.	*Due studi*, rows A and B	106
3.8.	*Due studi*. Fuga, mm. 108–16	106–107
3.9.	*Due studi*. Sarabanda, mm. 1–9	107
3.10.	*Due studi*. Fuga, mm. 150–57	108–109
3.11 (a).	*Rencesvals*, mm. 1–2	112
3.11 (b).	*Rencesvals*, mm. 6–12	112
3.11 (c).	*Rencesvals*, serial derivation	112–113
3.12 (a).	*Il prigioniero*, mm. 360–70	117–118
3.12 (b).	*Il prigioniero*, "Liberty" row	118
3.13.	*Il prigioniero*, mm. 1–4	119
3.14 (a).	*Il prigioniero*, mm. 240–44	119
3.14 (b).	*Il prigioniero*, "Prayer" row	120
3.15 (a).	*Il prigioniero*, mm. 198–203	120–121
3.15 (b).	*Il prigioniero*, "Hope" row	121
3.16.	*Il prigioniero*, mm. 806–15	122
4.1 (a).	*Quattro liriche di Antonio Machado*. I, mm. 1–8	131–132
4.1 (b).	*Quattro liriche di Antonio Machado*. I, row	132
4.2 (a).	*Quattro liriche di Antonio Machado*. II, mm. 46–51	133
4.2 (b).	*Quattro liriche di Antonio Machado*. II, row	133
4.3.	*Quattro liriche di Antonio Machado*. III, row	133
4.4.	*Quattro liriche di Antonio Machado*. IV, mm. 91–96	134
4.5 (a).	*Tre poemi*. I, mm.1–3	135
4.5 (b).	*Tre poemi*. I, row	135
4.6.	*Tre poemi*. II, mm. 1–9	137
4.7.	*Tre poemi*. III, mm. 1–3	138
4.8 (a).	*Job*, row	144
4.8 (b).	*Job*. VI, mm. 1–10	144–145
4.9.	*Job*. I, mm. 8–22	146–147
4.10.	*Job*. VII, mm. 4–13	147–148
4.11.	*Job*. IV, mm. 47–50	149
4.12.	*Tartiniana*. II, mm. 1–7	155
4.13 (a).	Tartini. *Sonata 2/7*, mm. 1–2	155
4.13 (b).	Tartini. *Sonata 2/7*, mm. 7–8	156

Music Examples

4.14.	*Tartiniana.* III, fig. 33	156
4.15 (a).	*Quaderno musicale di Annalibera,* I, mm. 1–6	159
4.15 (b).	*Quaderno musicale di Annalibera,* row	159
4.16.	*Quaderno musicale di Annalibera.* II, mm. 1–6	160
4.17.	*Quaderno musicale di Annalibera.* III, mm. 1–8	161
4.18.	*Quaderno musicale di Annalibera.* IV, mm. 1–5	162
4.19.	*Quaderno musicale di Annalibera.* V, mm. 1–4	163
4.20.	*Quaderno musicale di Annalibera.* VI, mm. 1–6	164
4.21.	*Quaderno musicale di Annalibera.* VII, mm. 1–9	165
4.22.	*Quaderno musicale di Annalibera.* VIII, mm. 1–9	166
4.23.	*Quaderno musicale di Annalibera.* VIII, mm. 24–30	166
4.24.	*Quaderno musicale di Annalibera.* IX, mm. 8–19	167
4.25.	*Quaderno musicale di Annalibera.* X, mm. 1–7	168
4.26.	*Quaderno musicale di Annalibera.* XI, mm. 10–18	169–170
4.27.	Schoenberg. *Six Little Piano Pieces,* Op. 19, no. 6, conclusion	170
4.28.	*Goethe-Lieder,* row	172
4.29.	*Goethe-Lieder.* I, mm. 1–10	173
4.30.	*Goethe-Lieder.* I, mm. 11–13	174
4.31.	*Goethe-Lieder.* I, mm. 14–20	174
4.32.	*Goethe-Lieder.* II, entire movement	175–176
4.33.	*Goethe-Lieder.* V, mm. 1–10	177
4.34.	*Goethe-Lieder.* VII, mm. 1–5	177–178
5.1.	*Piccola musica notturna,* mm. 57–63	181–182
5.2.	*Piccola musica notturna,* rows A and B	183
5.3 (a).	Bartók. *Music for Strings, Percussion, and Celesta,* opening measures	183
5.3 (b).	*Piccola Music Notturna,* opening measures	184
5.4 (a).	*Canti di liberazione,* row	188
5.4 (b).	*Canti di liberazione,* mm. 20–26	188
5.5.	*Canti di liberazione.* II, mm. 1–6	189
5.6.	*Canti di liberazione.* II, mm. 39–47	190
5.7.	*Canti di liberazione.* II, mm. 113–17	191
5.8.	*Canti di liberazione.* II, conclusion	192
5.9 (a).	*An Mathilde,* mm. 1–3	194
5.9 (b).	*An Mathhilde,* row	194
5.9 (c).	*An Mathilde,* row fragments	194
5.10.	*An Mathilde.* III, mm. 1–2	195
5.11.	Bach. Three-Part Invention (Sinfonia) in F Minor, mm. 1–3	196
5.12.	*Tartiniana seconda.* I, fig. 1	198
5.13.	*Tartiniana seconda.* IV: Maestoso, mm. 1–8	199
5.14.	*Tartiniana seconda.* IV: Doloroso, mm. 1–4	200
5.15.	*Cinque canti,* row	201
5.16.	*Cinque canti.* III, mm. 55–59	202
5.17.	*Concerto per la notte di Natale dell'anno 1956.* IV, mm. 23–26	205

5.18.	*Requiescant.* III, mm. 4–10	208
5.19.	*Requiescant.* III, mm. 41–45	208–209
5.20.	*Requiescant.* V, mm. 1–7	210
5.21.	*Requiescant.* V, conclusion	211
5.22.	*Dialoghi,* row	213
5.23.	*Dialoghi,* mm. 1–13	214–215
5.24.	*Preghiere,* row	217
5.25.	*Preghiere.* I, mm. 1–4	218
5.26.	*Preghiere.* II, mm. 65–70	219
5.27.	*Preghiere.* III, mm. 126–33	220
5.28 (a).	*Parole di San Paolo,* row	223
5.28 (b).	*Parole di San Paolo,* opening measures	223
5.29.	*Three Questions with Two Answers,* "Question" motif	226
5.30.	*Three Questions with Two Answers.* I, two rows	227
5.31.	*Three Questions with Two Answers.* II, mm. 34–44 (flute solo)	227
5.32.	*Three Questions with Two Answers.* IV, mm. 11–17	228–229
5.33 (a).	*Three Questions with Two Answers.* V, cell	229
5.33 (b).	*Three Questions with Two Answers.* V, mm. 10–13	230
6.1.	*Ulisse.* I, mm. 1–2	236
6.2.	*Ulisse,* rows: Sea 1, 2, 3	238
6.3.	*Ulisse,* "Female" rows	239
6.4.	*Ulisse.* I, mm. 23–29	240
6.5.	*Ulisse.* II, mm. 855–58	241
6.6.	*Ulisse.* "Stars" motif: II, mm. 952–54	243–244
6.7.	*Ulisse.* I, mm. 678–83	246
6.8.	*Ulisse.* I, mm. 698–701	247–248
6.9.	*Ulisse,* "Hades" row	249
6.10.	*Ulisse.* I, mm. 990–92	250
6.11.	*Sicut umbra.* I, entire movement	254
6.12.	*Sicut umbra.* IV, mm. 142–50	255–256
6.13.	*Sicut umbra,* sketch for ". . . hay que buscar . . ."	256–257
6.14.	*Tempus destruendi—Tempus aedificandi.* "Ploratus," mm. 1–7	260
6.15.	*Tempus destruendi—Tempus aedificandi.* "Ploratus," mm. 48–55	261
6.16 (a).	*Tempus destruendi—Tempus aedificandi.* "Exhortatio," row	261
6.16 (b).	*Tempus destruendi—Tempus aedificandi.* "Exhortatio," mm. 1–8	262–263
6.17.	*Tempus destruendi—Tempus aedificandi.* "Exhortatio," mm. 18–22	263–264
6.18.	*Tempus destruendi—Tempus aedificandi.* "Exhortatio," mm. 39–42	264
6.19.	*Commiato.* I, mm. 1–8	267
6.20.	*Commiato.* III, mm. 93–96	268

Tables

1.1. The incorporation of closed musical forms within *Volo di notte* and the provenance of various musical sections of the opera from the earlier *Tre laudi*.   45
4.1. *Quaderno musicale di Annalibera*: the four distinct phrases, each constructed from a duality of rows in melody and accompaniment.   169
5.1. *Piccola musica notturna*: the ternary pattern revolving around the use of the two rows A and B.   185
5.2. *Dialoghi*: the numerical ratio between the metronome indications.   214
6.1. *Ulisse*: allusions in the Epilogue.   245
6.2. *Sicut umbra*: the canonic form of the first movement.   253

Figures

4.1 *Tre poemi*: correspondence of the elements of the row-structure in the first song.   136
6.1. Symmetrical structural shape of *Ulisse*.   236

Preface and Acknowledgments

To write the first book in English about a composer is often hazardous. When that composer is widely acknowledged to have been one of the most important Italian composers of the twentieth century, the hazards become more acute. Nonetheless, this book attempts to give a balanced assessment of the work of Luigi Dallapiccola (1904–75) through an examination of all his creative *oeuvre*. It takes into account all previous studies of the composer's work, but in addition it is based upon examination of the sketches, plans, and other materials housed in the Dallapiccola Archive of the Gabinetto Vieusseux in Florence.

It is astonishing that this should be the first book in English. While the music of other figures of comparable stature in twentieth-century music has received a good deal of critical examination in the English-speaking world, that of Dallapiccola, as will be seen at once from a glance at the bibliography in this book, has not received the kind of attention that it deserves. This by no means belittles those thorough and often inspired studies of aspects of his work that have appeared in English-language journals at various times during recent decades. The work of Rudy Shackelford, Rosemary Brown, John Waterhouse, Michael Eckert, and Hans Nathan has remedied to some extent the lack of a more comprehensive study of the composer in English. The groundwork for studying Dallapiccola's music was set out just a few years after the composer's death by Dietrich Kämper of the University of Cologne, and all subsequent scholars working in this field must feel profound gratitude to him, not only for the thoroughness of his work, but also for the inspiration and musicality of his approach to the composer's work.

Dallapiccola's name appears in every music dictionary and guide to twentieth-century music, however small and inadequate; it is almost invariably linked with phrases such as "Italianate lyricism," "the first Italian serial composer," or, in more general terms, "Mediterranean sensuousness." With a composer whose music is not performed as frequently as it deserves, commentators on twentieth-century music, even some of the more informed and perceptive, can sometimes be forgiven for resorting to such labels. Once the labels have been attached, it is almost impossible to present the composer without the accompanying label, which, despite the kernel of truth it contains, sometimes makes it difficult to approach the composer's work in a fresh and engaging way. The present study, if it had no loftier aims, attempts to place Dallapiccola's work within contexts other than those suggested by the usual clichés.

Any critical examination of the work of a composer of Dallapiccola's stature must begin with a love of the music itself. In the case of Dallapiccola, the universal admiration afforded his work by a large body of performers is a constant inspiration to anyone attempting to assess his work as a whole. There can sometimes come a point at which one's interest in studying, playing, or listening to the same scores over an extended period can wane, but this has never happened in my own case with Dallapiccola. Indeed, further acquaintance seems to produce greater inquisitiveness, and one is almost tempted to adapt the old saying, "familiarity breeds contempt," to something like "familiarity breeds an awareness of unfamiliarity." As one gains an understanding and appreciation of the music, one becomes aware that other aspects of the composer's art await discovery, and this is without doubt an ideal basis for research.

This book owes its final form and contents entirely to the author. However, without the help, advice, and enlightenment offered by a large number of individuals and organizations, it would have struggled slowly towards the light. I would therefore like to acknowledge the help given to me, in different ways, by the following:

First of all, Timothy Madigan and Molly Cort of the University of Rochester Press, and Ralph Locke and Louise Goldberg of the Eastman School of Music, for their patience and advice.

The University of Keele, for the provision of research leave in order to complete the book, and to the Department of Music of that institution, particularly Chris King and Julie Hibbs, for endlessly patient practical assistance.

The British Academy, who generously provided funds enabling me to visit the Dallapiccola Archive in Florence.

The institutions that kindly invited me to present papers on aspects of my research, thus enabling me to hone my ideas and approaches to the music: Saint Patrick's College, Maynooth, Ireland, in particular Harry Smith and Patrick Devine; the Gesellschaft für Musikforschung, in particular Wolfgang Ruf; and the Società Italiana di Musicologia.

The Gabinetto Vieusseux of Florence, in particular Mila De Santis and Caterina Del Vivo, as well as its Director, Enzo Siciliano, for the opportunity on several occasions to study the materials of Dallapiccola housed in the beautiful and inspiring surroundings of the Bonsanti Contemporary Archive in Via Maggio.

Annalibera Dallapiccola, for an immensely inspiring and fruitful discussion of the work of her father.

Carolyn Gianturco of the University of Pisa, for the opportunity to discuss my research with members of the Associazione per la Ricerca delle Fonti Musicali in Toscana.

Dietrich Kämper, for many words of encouragement and support that he gave me at various points during my research.

Fiamma Nicolodi and Pierluigi Petrobelli, for helpful information and advice.

Lastly but perhaps most importantly, I would like to record my most humble and profound gratitude to the late Laura Dallapiccola, widow of the composer. On only one occasion did I have the privilege of spending a few hours with her, just a few months before her death, in the apartment in Via Romana in Florence which had been home to the composer for many years. However, during that conversation I was put in touch with the very center of Dallapiccola's life, indeed with a center of European culture which, I believe, has had a deep influence upon my work on his music. Our conversations about the composer, and in particular about the literary aspect of his compositions in which Laura played a major role, were indeed unforgettable, and I hope that the dedication of this book to her memory will go some way to express the gratitude I feel.

I thank the following publishers and other organizations that have given permission for the use of material whose copyright is held by them:

Gabinetto Vieusseux, Florence, for the quotations of diary entries of Dallapiccola, as well as letters from Dallapicccola to various people, and letters written to him, and for the use of a sketch for one of his works which is housed at the Archive in Florence.

Annalibera Dallapiccola, for permission to use letters, part of an unpublished piece, and a musical sketch from the Florence Archive.

Il Saggiatore, Milan, for parts of the book *Parole e Musica,* a collection of the composer's writings.

Faber and Faber, London, for extracts from Anthony Beaumont's book on Ferruccio Busoni, as well as parts of the journal *Music Survey* and an article by Dallapiccola originally published in that journal.

Mr. Stephen James Joyce, grandson of the writer, for permission to quote from James Joyce's *Pomes Penyeach.*

Gruppo Editoriale Bramante, for part of Zanetti's *La musica italiana nel novecento.*

Oklahoma University Press, for part of *The Composer Speaks* (edited by R. S. Hines).

Toccata Press, for parts of Rudy Shackelford's collection of Dallapiccola's writings.

Fondazione Cini, Venice, in particular its Music Director, Professor Giovanni Morelli, for part of a letter from Dallapiccola to Malipiero.

PFD (Peters Fraser and Dunlop) Agency for permission, on behalf of Harvey Sachs, to quote part of Harvey Sachs's *Music in Fascist Italy.*

Penguin Books, for parts of Antoine de Saint-Exupéry's *Night Flight* and André Gide's preface to the English translation.

Perspectives of New Music, for part of an article by Michael Eckert.

For permission for the music examples quoted in the book, I am pleased to thank the following publishers:

  Carisch, Milan: *Divertimento, Inni, Cori di Michelangelo il Giovani, Tre laudi, Piccolo concerto per Muriel Couvreux, Canti di prigionia, Marsia.*
  Ricordi: *Volo di notte.*
  Schott/Ars Viva: *Piccola musica notturna, Tre poemi*
  Universal Edition: *Ciaccona, intermezzo e adagio*
  Zanibon, Padua: *Estate.*
  Suvini Zerboni, Milan: the rest of Dallapiccola's works not listed above.

All translations of documents originally in languages other than English, unless otherwise indicated, have been made by the author.

Raymond Fearn
Convento di Monteripido
Perugia, Italy
June 2002

Abbreviations

Appunti: Luigi Dallapiccola. *Appunti incontri meditazioni*. Milan: Suvini Zerboni, 1970.
Kämper, *GF*: Dietrich Kämper. *Gefangenschaft und Freiheit: Leben und Werk des Komponisten Luigi Dallapiccola*. Cologne: Gitarre und Laute, 1984.
LD: Luigi Dallapiccola.
Nicolodi, *Saggi*: Fiamma Nicolodi, ed. *Luigi Dallapiccola: Saggi, testimonianze, carteggio, biografia e bibliografia*. Milan: Suvini Zerboni, 1975.
PM: Luigi Dallapiccola. *Parole e Musica*. Milan: Il Saggiatore, 1980.
Shackelford, *DO*: Rudy Shackelford, ed. *Dallapiccola on Opera*. London: Toccata Press, 1987.

I

The Beginnings: 1904–1938

In 1946 Luigi Dallapiccola was asked to compose music for a planned documentary film on the Renaissance painter Piero della Francesca. He set about the task so enthusiastically that, when the film project was abandoned a few weeks later, he had already composed some of the music, based upon scenes depicted in the famous cycle of Piero's frescoes in Arezzo, "The Legend of the True Cross." This film music was to find its way into another composition, but given the speed with which Dallapiccola had responded to the commission, it is tempting to ask whether his evident enthusiasm was prompted by the film's subject, rather than simply because the commission came when he was most in need of it. It seems that he felt a bond with Piero that went much deeper than simply an admiration of that most "Tuscan" of artists and touched upon some essential qualities shared by both composer and painter. In the work of both Piero and Dallapiccola, there can certainly be found a seriousness of theme and a vibrant sense of coloration, but it is above all in the powerful combination of poetry and rationality that the two artists share common ground. That sense of an expressivity founded upon a rational structure within the work of art can also be found in many creators whose work impinged at various points upon Dallapiccola's music: Dante, Bach, Joyce, Berg, and Webern. Such a rational conception of artistic design and purpose did not arise suddenly, but, along with other characteristics of the composer's work, grew from a host of experiences and influences, many of which had their origins in the composer's early years.

Childhood and Youth

Dallapiccola was born in 1904, not in one of the historic cities of Italy, but in Pazin (Pisino), a small town at the centre of the Istrian peninsula, that often-disputed triangle of land jutting out into the northern Adriatic, and this birthplace was judged by the composer himself as of considerable importance in the formation of his artistic personality. He described the place of his birth as a "microcosm."

> Psychology maintains the dominant, almost unique importance that childhood and adolescent experiences have in the formation of personality in general, and in particular that of the artist . . . it should not be forgotten that the little peninsula called Istria, where I was born, was located at the crossroads of three cultures. When the train stopped at the station in my home town, the stationmaster would shout out "Mitterburg-Pisino-Pazin!" It is well known how much frontier lands contribute to the jumble of races and cultures; in addition, the mentality to be found in borderlands is very different from that generally to be found in the interior parts of countries. How can this mentality be defined? Perhaps by calling it "restless".[1]

Dallapiccola wrote these words when attempting to explain the origins of two of his most heartfelt and passionate compositions—*Canti di prigionia* and *Il prigioniero*—in which his emotional reaction to contemporary events found potent expression. But perhaps the adjective he uses to describe the "borderland mentality"—*inquieta*—suggests that a general sense of unease had affected the composer during his formative years. This no doubt came from being a member of an Italian-speaking minority living in a foreign land (Istria, at the time of Dallapiccola's birth in 1904, was a part of the Austrian Empire), and consequently being detached from the mainstream of Italian cultural life. The composer's early years were spent in a rather strange situation: the ties he had with the mainland of Italy were predominantly linguistic and religious, while in other respects his birthplace was at a considerable cultural remove from Italy. Two factors in particular, the distance from an Italian cultural center and the precarious political and national situation of the borderland, contributed to the formation of Dallapiccola's mental horizons. This was one of the reasons why, when he had to decide where to spend his student years, he chose Florence, not only a city with a long cultural and artistic history, but one in which he might immerse himself in those strands of cultural and intellectual life from which he had earlier felt isolated.

Other influences on Dallapiccola in his youth also contributed to the formation of some characteristics of the mature artist. These included a strong awareness of the multiplicity of cultures, a sense of the cruelty of oppression, and a desire for freedom, all of which were to become important threads in the fabric of his later creativity. Pisino was at a politically sensitive point, in a corner of the Austrian Empire uneasily suspended between Italian, Germanic, and Slav cultures. His father, a teacher of classical languages and head of the only school allowed in the area for the Italian-speaking minority, occupied a position of considerable instability and worked in an atmosphere of political distrust. The Austrian authorities were quick to suppress any irredentist movements within the Italian community, and for a while during the First World War, his father was declared "politically untrustworthy." The high school was closed down, and the whole family sent into exile in the Austrian city of Graz for eighteen months in 1917–18. Between the two world wars, Istria became a part of Italy, but the tensions remained: after 1945 it was annexed to Yugoslavia, and now forms a part of the Republic of Croatia.

Dallapiccola had begun piano lessons at the age of eight, first of all with a local teacher by the name of Pischiutta. The child's gifts were such that his teacher began to harbor musical ambitions for his pupil, but his parents were skeptical about the wisdom of such an idea. Dallapiccola's childhood years were intensely happy ones, and the composer was to remember with great affection his family holidays in Ala, in the Adige valley north of Verona, the childhood home of his mother, Domitilla Alberti. He remembered in particular seeing an early silent film there called *The Odyssey of Homer,* made by Giuseppe de Liguoro. The artistic quality of this early film experiment was not high: Dallapiccola remembered in particular its "excessive miming" and its "exaggeratedly declamatory style of recitation,"[2] but the seed from which the composer's last opera and most profound work would eventually grow had been sown.

The musical limitations of the region in which Dallapiccola grew up were considerable, and without any possibility of contact with either operatic or orchestral life, he could only slowly extend the horizons of his musical culture beyond the piano music he studied at home. However, during the enforced exile of the Dallapiccola family in Graz, between March 1917 and November 1918, the horizons of his musical culture broadened. In the opera house there he saw not only *The Flying Dutchman* and *Die Meistersinger,* but also the entire cycle of *The Ring of the Nibelungs* (whose leitmotifs he sketched into a musical notebook), as well as Mozart's *Don Giovanni* and Weber's *Der Freischütz.* Thus, the first operas that Dallapiccola saw were those forming the kernel of German rather than Italian musical culture: Wagner and Mozart were revealed to him as musical dramatists well before Verdi and Puccini. It was in Graz that he finally decided upon a musical career, and he dated this decision from his attendance at a performance of *The Flying Dutchman.* The significance of his first experiences of Wagner's music during his stay in Graz was made clear in a letter he wrote many years later to Wagner's grandson Wolfgang, who had requested an article for the program book for the centenary production of *Die Meistersinger* in 1968:

> Write about *Die Meistersinger?* How could I do this? In the Opera House in Graz, in May 1917, when I was thirteen years old, it was *The Flying Dutchman* that made me make the decision to dedicate myself to music. A month later, on St John's day (a coincidence? I could not possibly say), I had the opportunity to hear *Die Meistersinger* for the first time.

> For years this opera seemed to me the very pinnacle of Richard Wagner's operas (*Parsifal* is obviously not an opera for adolescents); I loved it, and I still love it, deeply. How can I forget, on stage at Graz in Act 2, the entrance of Pogner and Eva, from the far end of the street, while the music darkens and fades? And it would have been obvious that the evening was falling, even if the lights on stage had not been extinguished one by one. I first realized on that evening what landscape could be in music, and I realized that the protagonist of the second act is St John's Eve. (Some time later I began to think that the protagonist of the third act of *Tristan* is the sea). And at the doorway of the theater, after the musical miracle, another miracle, but this time one of nature. The full moon was shining, not on stage any longer but in the sky. (I dare not believe that the Theatre Director, whose name I still remember, Julius Grevenberg, had arranged this).[3]

In the light of some musical and dramatic images to be found in three of Dallapiccola's stage works, this account of the composer's first encounter with Wagner seems to be significant. In particular, Dallapiccola's vivid memory of the "miracle" of the appearance of the full moon at the end of the performance of *Die Meistersinger* is of some importance, and not only because of the revelation of Wagner's art to the thirteen-year-old Dallapiccola. In each of his own operas, *Volo di notte*, *Il prigioniero*, and *Ulisse*, the climax is reached when a revelatory shaft of unearthly light brings to the main character a powerful symbol of his destiny. This is particularly evident in his final opera, *Ulisse*, as Ulysses goes to meet his end alone in a boat in the ocean, and receives a strangely unifying vision of the Maker when he contemplates the stars above (just as Dante had recounted the final all-absorbing vision of stars at the end of his journey in *La Divina Commedia*). As we observe at later points in this study, these visions, and the symbolisms with which they are connected, were to play a crucial role in each of these operas.

After his return to Istria, he studied piano with Alice Andrich Florio in Trieste and harmony and composition with the Trieste composer Antonio Illersberg while he continued as a pupil in his father's high school. Under Illersberg's guidance, he began to discover some of the moderns, particularly Debussy, but Illersberg, who was conductor of a madrigal choir in the city, also introduced his pupil to polyphonic vocal music of the sixteenth and seventeenth centuries. Dallapiccola made his first attempts at composition at this time, under Illersberg's guidance, but he later destroyed them. Illersberg was a man of the widest musical culture, and in his vast music library he demonstrated examples from modern scores as well as from the earlier music of which he was so fond (Dallapiccola later remembered Illersberg pointing out details in Schoenberg's *Gurrelieder* and Ravel's *L'Heure espagnole*). However, the limitations of the region in which he had grown up became increasingly irksome to the young musician, and when his secondary education was completed, he decided to continue his musical studies in Florence. This decision, which was to prove momentous for him, was apparently made in part because of his enormous love of Dante, the image of whose presence he felt throughout the city.

In May 1922, Dallapiccola moved to Florence to study, and he later recorded how the first Florence performance of *Tristan und Isolde,* which took place during the same month, was almost his first musical experience in the city. At the Florence Conservatory he studied piano with Ernesto Consolo, who introduced him to a wider range of modern music, including Bartók and Ravel. He also studied theoretical subjects with Roberto Casiraghi and Corrado Barbieri, two of Ildebrando Pizzetti's pupils, and it was in an essay written by Pizzetti[4] that Dallapiccola first encountered the name of Arnold Schoenberg. Writing of Schoenberg's *Harmonielehre* as well as of his music, Pizzetti had described them in the most pejorative terms possible, calling the music "not yet art." He was not the only Italian who reacted in this way to Schoenberg at that time: his feelings of distaste for the Viennese composer's music were shared by Gian Francesco Malipiero, who had expressed much the same sentiments in an article in 1917.[5]

For Dallapiccola, reading Schoenberg's *Harmonielehre* in Trieste in 1921, prompted at least in part by curiosity after reading Pizzetti's abusive attack, was fundamental in his development, and he later described it (in English) as "How life begins," but Dallapiccola's acquaintance with Schoenberg's music was not to begin until three years after this. In fact, the only Italian musician who might have been of value to Dallapiccola in encouraging his curiosity about Schoenberg's music at that time was Alfredo Casella, who was based in Rome, not Florence. Casella had been forcibly struck by what he sensed was a highly important composer of the most advanced music when he heard such works as *Gurrelieder*; Three Piano Pieces, Opus 11; the first Chamber Symphony; the second String Quartet; and *Pierrot Lunaire* in Paris. It was, however, only when Casella returned to Italy in 1915 that he was able to bring some of his passion for more advanced musical trends into the Italian arena. As a composer, Casella had absorbed a great variety of influences in Paris: having studied with Fauré, he became a close friend of Ravel and Debussy (with whom he performed *Iberia* on two pianos in 1915), but he also took part as pianist or conductor in performances of music by Georges Enescu, Rimsky Korsakov, Balakirev, and Mahler. When he returned to Italy, his immense program of performing activities continued, and he was also very active in the reform of Italian musical education. He continued his pianistic and conducting work, and amongst other things gave the first Italian performance of Stravinsky's *Petrushka*. His most important work as an organizer of musical life immediately on his return to Italy was his foundation of the Società Nazionale di Musica (National Music Society) in 1917–19. Here, he introduced an enormous amount of new music by foreign composers, including Satie, Ravel, Granados, Albeniz, De Falla, Beach, Skriabin, Dukas, and Stravinsky.[6] Casella was without doubt the most active and influential musician in Italy during the 1920s and 1930s, and although his own composition became strongly neoclassical in character during those years, he was nonetheless open in his attitude to, and promotion of, the many strands of contemporary music. Dallapiccola's personal contact with Casella did not begin until 1930, but from that point on the two remained in touch by letter and met on many occasions, right up to Casella's death in 1947. The extreme political differences between the two composers in the late 1930s, with Casella strongly espousing fascism and Dallapiccola becoming equally strongly anti-fascist, eventually caused a great tension between them,[7] but Dallapiccola nonetheless always held the older composer in the highest esteem as a musician. When Dallapiccola arrived in Florence in 1922, he had no opportunity to gain from Casella's wide acquaintance with modern music, but on at least two occasions, as will shortly be reported, the performing and promotional activities of Casella had some influence upon Dallapiccola's compositional outlook.

In Florence, Dallapiccola's gifts as a pianist quickly became evident, and he graduated in piano after little more than two years, in November 1924. He began to appear as pianist in many concerts from this time onwards, and he was particularly known for his interpretation of Mussorgsky's *Pictures at an Exhibition* and the late piano sonatas of Beethoven. However, despite the broadening of his musical horizons in Florence, he later admitted that, as far as composition was concerned, his formal studies at the Conservatory had little or no bearing upon his development. Nonetheless, his student years were not without significant events: foremost among these was the Florence performance of Schoenberg's *Pierrot Lunaire* under the composer's direction in Palazzo Pitti in 1924, as part of a tour of Italian cities that Casella had organized. Dallapiccola recalled this performance many years later, when he wrote to Schoenberg in 1949:

> I had seen you in Florence at the time of the first Italian tour of *Pierrot Lunaire,* but how could I, a Conservatory student, find the courage on that evening to come and shake your hand ? In any case, I have never forgotten the attitude of Puccini with regard to you on that 1 April 1924, and since that evening I have considered the popular Italian composer to be of an intelligence and a humanity that I had not suspected.[8]

From the moment of first hearing *Pierrot Lunaire*, Dallapiccola decided to devote himself to composition, and he began a period of study with Vito Frazzi[9] in Florence that extended for six years, from 1925 until 1931. According to Dallapiccola himself, Frazzi was an able and inspiring teacher, and he was later to write that "[Frazzi] had the rare gift of being able to treat his pupils and himself as on the same mental and cultural level, exposing his many doubts to us, suggesting to us various solutions to the problems he came across, and almost inviting us to collaborate with him."[10]

The most important aspect of the influence of Frazzi's approach to composition upon Dallapiccola may be found in Frazzi's concern with "alternating scales," those in which whole and half steps alternate, and this concern can be seen reflected at several points in Dallapiccola's very earliest unpublished compositions. Frazzi's theoretical exposition of the idea of alternating scales, based upon his examination of examples of such scales in the works of Beethoven, Wagner, Pizzetti, and others, appeared in *Scale alternate* and *Studio dell'armonia cromatica ultratonale* published by Forlivesi in Florence as studies for piano, but which were intended as much for the composer as for the pianist. In an accompanying essay, Frazzi explained how the "alternating scales" in two forms could be constructed upon the dominant rather than the tonic of a tonality, and would serve as he said as "the basis of a system which would tend to bring together all the diatonic tonalities." He applied this theory above all in his opera *Re Lear* (King Lear), composed between 1922 and 1928, which was performed in Florence in 1939, but it received little critical attention. It is, however, remarkable how much Frazzi's ideas on such scales prefigured and to some extent paralleled those of Olivier Messiaen on various "modes," the theory of which appeared only in his *Technique de mon langage musical*, published in Paris in 1944.[11] Michael Eckert investigated the possible relationship of Frazzi's theoretical ideas to elements in Dallapiccola's early music in his study of octatonic elements in these early compositions.[12]

Much of Dallapiccola's music up to the end of the 1930s, when serialism began to emerge as an element in his musical language, was grounded in modal writing, and was thus to a large extent free of the chromatic saturation that had been evident in the pre-serial music of the Viennese composers. The influence of Frazzi was obviously dominant in many of these very early works from Dallapiccola's apprentice period, but some characteristics that are relevant to the composer's later compositions can also be seen. Fiamma Nicolodi pointed to several details of these pieces,[13] and in particular to Dallapiccola's tendency to create symmetrical structures, such as the reprise of the first verse of *La Canzone del Quarnaro* in the last verse, or the symmetrical dynamic shaping of the ninth verse of the same piece, building by gradual stages from *ppp* to *fff* and back within the whole verse.

Other cultural influences of a broader kind also came to bear upon Dallapiccola during the 1920s, notably the writers, artists, and musicians he met at the Giubbe Rosse Café in Piazza della Repubblica in Florence, and those working for the Florentine literary journal *Solaria*. Of particular importance in these literary and intellectual circles were the writers Alessandro Bonsanti and Arturo Loria, and the painters Guido Peyron and Baccio Maria Bacci (who was later to make the stage designs for the 1940 Florence performance of Dallapiccola's first opera, *Volo di notte*). *Solaria*, founded in 1926, was one of the most progressive literary journals in Italy at that time, and it was particularly important for the composer in that it was in the pages of *Solaria* that he first became acquainted with the work of major contemporary writers such as Marcel Proust, James Joyce, Rainer Maria Rilke, T. S. Eliot, and Franz Kafka, translations of whose writings appeared from time to time. The presence of the poet Eugenio Montale in Florence from 1927, where he had originally gone to work for the publisher Bemporad and later worked as Director of the Gabinetto Vieusseux, was also instrumental in Dallapiccola first encountering the work of the three major poets of twentieth-century Italy, Giuseppe Ungaretti, Salvatore Quasimodo, and Montale himself.

Despite this contact with contemporary Italian literature, Dallapiccola seems almost to have avoided any attempt to engage creatively with the work of any of these poets, and it was with more limited, indeed less significant literature that he broached his first original compositions. His earliest attempts were settings of poems in dialect by the Istrian poet Biagio Marin (1891–1985), a friend of the composer who had also made his home in Florence. Dallapiccola was later to consider these works quite unrepresentative of his creativity, leaving instructions that they should be available only for limited perusal even after his death. These were *Fiuri de tapo* (1924–26), *Caligo* (1926) and *Due canzoni di Grado* (1927), the first two for voice and piano, the last for female chorus and small orchestra. When his publisher later requested these works for publication, Dallapiccola declined, saying, "It is a fact that I found my way (or if you prefer, my personality) relatively quickly for our times, I mean between the ages of twenty-nine and thirty. But believe me, there is no reason on earth to let today's public know of certain attempts I made."[14]

Dallapiccola's apprentice years as a composer extended, by his own admission, until around his thirtieth year, but despite the powerful influence generally exerted by Casella's neoclassicism in Italy at that time, there is an almost complete lack of any neoclassical strain in Dallapiccola's early music. He certainly admired Stravinsky's *Les noces* (1917/1923) when he attended a performance conducted by Casella in 1927, but the imprint of this experience was to extend no further than the sonority of multiple pianos he employed in his *Musica per tre pianoforti (Inni)* in 1935 and *Canti di prigionia* in 1938–41. The composer himself did admit to the influence of Debussy, Ravel, and De Falla on some of his early unpublished compositions, but denied emphatically that they contained any hint of an "Istrian folkishness" or "Slav nationalism."

By the end of the 1920s, Dallapiccola's literary horizons expanded to incorporate rather wider sources than the dialect poetry with which he had begun. In his *Due laudi di Iacopone da Todi* in 1929, there appeared for the first time that medieval literary element which was to assume great importance in his subsequent composition. A visit he made to Berlin and Vienna in 1930, when he was engaged as accompanist to an American dancer who went by the name of "La Méri," gave him a further opportunity to enlarge his musical horizons. In Berlin, he heard Strauss's *Elektra* and *Salome,* and Mahler's first symphony, and he saw Verdi's *Simon Boccanegra,* all of which left a deep impression upon him. He was, however, afraid to call upon Schoenberg, who had been living in Berlin since 1926, fearing that he had insufficient experience to enable him to present himself to the older composer. Many years later, when Dallapiccola finally wrote to him in Los Angeles in 1949, Schoenberg expressed regret that he had not made the acquaintance of the younger man in Florence at that earlier date.[15]

Also at this time, Dallapiccola had begun to appear regularly as pianist, and he formed a duo with the violinist Sandro Materassi that would become a regular part of his musical activity for many years. But very few of his own works were performed, and it was not until 1932 that any of his music was published. He began to teach piano at the Florence Conservatory in 1931 when his own teacher, Ernesto Consolo, died, but he never taught more than secondary piano, and he taught composition only occasionally and in a private capacity from 1945 onwards. His daily life in the earlier years was somewhat precarious, and the conservatism of musical attitudes in Florence, influenced in this respect by Pizzetti, meant that progress in bringing his music before the public was very slow. The notorious "Manifesto of Italian Musicians for the Tradition of Nineteenth-Century Romantic Art," which was published in all the country's major newspapers on 17 December 1932—headed by Pizzetti and signed also by Respighi, Zandonai and seven others—attempted to block compositional trends they saw as representative of "modernity":

> In the field of music, more than anywhere else, a Tower of Babel really reigns at the present time. For twenty years now, the most diverse and disparate tendencies have conspired to form a chaotic revolution. We are still surrounded by "tendencies" and "experimentations", and nobody can say to what definite end or secure pathways they will all lead. . . . Gabrieli, Monteverdi, Palestrina, Frescobaldi, Corelli, Scarlatti, Paisiello, Cimarosa, Rossini, Verdi, and Puccini: these are the varied branches of the same tree, and they represent the clamorous and many-voiced flowering of Italian musicality. Yes, friends, we would like to think of ourselves as the direct descendants of Verdi and of Puccini. . . . We are

against any art which does not aim to have, and indeed does not have, any human content, any art which does not aim to be anything more than a mechanical game or a cerebral amusement.[16]

If the aim of the authors of the "Manifesto" was to stem the tide of the modernism they saw as irrelevant to the "traditions" of Italian music, they also raised objections to what they called the "ruminations from our distant musical past" (i.e., Malipiero) and "so-called objective music" (i.e., Casella). Both Malipiero and Casella, of course, took exception to the attack made upon them in the "Manifesto," and in this they were supported by intellectuals and writers such as Massimo Bontempelli and Luigi Pirandello.[17] However, the object of fiercest attack by the polemicists of the "Manifesto" was not really represented in Italy at all at that time: this was what they described as "atonal and polytonal honking."

Due liriche del Kalevala

Dallapiccola belonged neither to the Malipiero nor to the Casella sphere of influence, nor did he indulge in what the authors of the "Manifesto" had called "atonal and polytonal honking." His relationship to the two older composers was nonetheless a close one, as the correspondence he maintained with them testifies. We can judge the extent to which he was able to find an independent compositional voice in a relatively short time, by comparing a musical fragment composed at the end of 1930 with a more substantial work composed over the next two years. *Due liriche del Kalevala* (Two Songs from the Kalevala) has remained unpublished, but a fragment appeared with the title *Frammento del Kalevala* (Fragment of the Kalevala) in the *Revue Internationale de Musique,* published in Brussels in March-April 1938. This is a setting of texts taken from the great Finnish epic which Elias Lönnrot had published in 1835/1849 as a poetic and mythological stimulus to the Finnish nationalist movement, and which had afforded Sibelius some of his most powerful inspiration. In the Dallapiccola fragment, an influence of Pizzetti is detectable in its modalism and gentle pastoralism, and this is the only occasion on which the influence of Pizzetti is present in Dallapiccola's work. A baritone soloist sings to the accompaniment of vocalizations from a group of four sopranos and four contraltos, and the contrapuntal writing is very characteristic of the young composer, although not reaching the more complex varieties of canon that would appear later in his music. Nonetheless, the polyphony is already an important part of the style of this music, creating the gentlest of clashes between the melodic lines (Example 1.1).

Example 1.1. *Frammento del Kalevala*, mm. 1–22.

Partita

In comparison with the Kalevala fragment, the language and style of the *Partita* composed in 1930–32 are altogether more confident. This piece, performed in Florence in 1933, bears a title that might at first glance appear to place it within the orbit of Casella, whose own orchestral *Partita*, composed in 1925, had set the trend for other Italians to follow. Giorgio Federico Ghedini, Antonio Veretti, and Goffredo Petrassi had all followed suit by composing orchestral works called "Partita," all in several movements and all similarly "objective" in character. But Dallapiccola's was, as it were, the cuckoo in the neoclassical nest. His *Partita* is in four movements (a Passacaglia, Burlesca, Recitative and Fanfare, and "Naenia B.M.V." sung by a soprano), but it represented what the composer was later to describe as music that "fell from a planet in which Stravinsky was unknown".[18] The theme on which the opening Passacaglia is based is of a Baroque solemnity and restraint, and has the feel of a Baroque dance, but its freely modal harmony incorporates possibilities that are gradually exploited as the movement progresses (Example 1.2).

Example 1.2. *Partita*. Passacaglia theme, mm.1–8.

The energetic Burlesca second movement, with its positive optimism, is not so far removed from the style of the neoclassical orchestral movements that some of his compatriots were composing at that time. However, the third movement—Recitative and Fanfare—heralds a finale in which Dallapiccola is clearly exploring territory far removed from the world occupied by Casella and Petrassi. This "Naenia B.M.V." is a lullaby of the Virgin sung by a solo soprano, and here once again the composer had found the text in a medieval source, a collection of popular religious poems known as the *Quinquaginta Carmina Medii Aevi*. Here, a certain influence from Respighi's *Lauda per la Natività del Signore* (1929) may be detected in the pastoral simplicity of the melodic line and accompaniment at the beginning of the movement. What is perhaps more intriguing is the possibility that Dallapiccola, in placing a simple movement on an ancient religious text in the final movement of his *Partita,* had been influenced by Mahler's fourth symphony. Mahler was a composer who hardly impinged upon the consciousness of most Italian musicians at that time (although his influence was felt by Casella in some of the works he had written in Paris before the war), but, as we saw earlier, Dallapiccola had encountered Mahler's music during his visit to Vienna and Berlin in 1930. It is not certain whether Dallapiccola had studied the score of Mahler's fourth symphony by this point, but it is possible. The possibility of an influence of Mahler upon Dallapiccola must, therefore, remain speculative, and the nature of the two texts is rather different, that from *Des Knaben Wunderhorn* being a naïve and childish vision of heavenly delights, whereas the text Dallapiccola chose is of a simple, folkish religiosity. Nonetheless, the incorporation of a female voice in the final movement of the work does seem to invite this comparison (Example 1.3).

Example 1.3. *Partita*. Naenia B.M.V., fig.77.

Dallapiccola's mature musical language was permeated so thoroughly by twelve-tone technique that commentators have inevitably devoted a good deal of attention to tracing the emergence of this technique, or at least of twelve-tone figurations, in his work during the early period. What is important to bear in mind, however, is that the incorporation of dodecaphonic techniques and elements in his music was completely natural, growing as it did from expressive needs. It also came about rather slowly, over several years; Dallapiccola did not use a single, all-embracing row as the sole material for any of his compositions until after 1945. In any case, the assimilation of twelve-tone principles by other composers, beyond the immediate circle of Schoenberg's pupils, was by no means as widespread in the 1920s and 1930s as might be inferred from its subsequent importance. In Italy, a composer had to go to very considerable pains to gain any understanding of twelve-tone techniques, since the relevant scores were difficult to obtain and theoretical studies non-existent. Beyond these practical difficulties, any attempt to delve into the "atonal and polytonal honking" of the 1932 "Manifesto" would have been considered eccentric, if not downright perverse, in Italy at that time. In his desire to investigate such music, Dallapiccola had some advantages over many of his compatriots through his extensive contacts abroad and his ability to read German. However, it would be only in the late 1930s that he was able to complete his absorption of twelve-tone ideas, particularly through the advice given him by the Russo-German composer Wladimir Vogel, which will be examined later.

Estate

Dallapiccola's *Partita* was first performed in January 1933, and this was also the first of his compositions to be published, by Carisch in Milan (the third of the four songs in *Dalla mia terra* for mezzo soprano, mixed chorus and orchestra (1928) was to appear in the Turin magazine *Agorà* in 1946, and as noted earlier the first of the *Liriche del Kalevala* was also published in a music magazine in 1938). However, Dallapiccola entered a short piece for male voice choir in a competition organized by the Sindacato Nazionale di Musicisti (National Musicians' Union) in 1932, the prize for which was publication of the work by Zanibon in Padova, as well as performance in Rome. The piece he wrote, *Estate* (Summer), a setting of a fragmentary text by Alcaeus in an Italian translation by E. Romagnoli, won the prize. The rules of the competition had stated that the work had to be composed "in a contemporary style, but easy to sing, capable of performance by a workers' choir": in the event, the choir chosen to performed the piece in Rome was so poorly prepared that Dallapiccola could not bear to stay for the performance, but the work was published by Zanibon. It lasts about four minutes and was written in the space of just a few days, and it would be absurd to speculate on the basis of this isolated and occasional example about Dallapiccola's musical personality at that time, but some features of the piece are perhaps worth considering. The choice of a text from classical antiquity reflected a literary sensibility that, while it hardly accorded with the intentions of the competition's organizers, was to become an important element in much of the composer's later work. In addition, if the evocation of the classical past in the text is evidence of the future composer of the *Liriche Greche,* the harmonic and rhythmic language of the piece already to some extent prefigures his *Cori di Michelangelo*. What is most evident in this short piece, however, is the elegant contrapuntalism of Dallapiccola's language, the utterly natural and unforced manner in which polyphonic imitations occur. This can be heard, for example, as the choral voices imitate the echoing of cicadas from branch to branch (Example 1.4).

It is clear that such vocal imitations, as much else in the piece, derive from the Renaissance Italian madrigal to which Dallapiccola's first teacher, Antonio Illersberg, had earlier introduced him, but a further source of influence upon this contrapuntal inclination in Dallapiccola's work is almost certainly to be found in the work of Ferruccio Busoni. Dallapiccola knew a good deal of Busoni's piano music at that time, including the well-known *Fantasia Contrappuntistica* and Sonatina, both dating from 1910. Busoni's comment on the nature of polyphony, published in the preface to his edition of Bach's *Well-Tempered Clavier,* may well have had a resonance in Dallapiccola's conception of musical expressivity: "A thought process that strives for the heights (vertical) brought into effect through the services of an art with four strands (horizontal)."[19]

Even during the early 1930s, Dallapiccola began to think about a possible stage work, and despite the incomplete and immature nature of the ideas he had at that time, they point in some ways towards the future. His thoughts in this direction are to be found in a literary sketch he made late in 1932, an idea for a libretto and scenario, but one that never resulted in the composition of more than a few measures of music. This was to have been called *Rappresentazione di Anima e di Corpo* (Representation of Body and Soul), taking its title, but only its title, from the morality play Emilio de' Cavalieri had set to music for the Florentine Camerata in 1600. The

Example 1.4. *Estate*, mm. 31–42 (Used by kind permission of Casa Ricordi-BMG Ricordi S.p.A.)

importance of this abortive plan lies not only in being the first occasion on which Dallapiccola wrote his own libretto (he was to be responsible for the libretti of all his stage works), but also in the fact that, like the libretto of *Ulisse* some thirty years later, he called upon a very wide range of literary sources for elements in the text. Among these sources we find Goethe's *Faust*, Nietzsche's *Also sprach Zarathustra* ("O Mensch ! Gib Acht!," as set by Mahler in his third symphony), Gabriele d'Annunzio, Ibsen's *Peer*

Gynt, La Chanson de Roland, Iacopone da Todi, and Dante. Some elements in this libretto were to reappear in different guise in *Ulisse*: for example, the 1932 sketch links together the figure of the Mother with that of Death, based upon the death of the hero's mother in *Peer Gynt,* while in *Ulisse* the final disappearance of the ghost of Ulysses' mother presages the end of the hero's own life. Throughout his life, such symbols and images were to recur in almost cyclic fashion in Dallapiccola's work, whether as poetic images embedded in literary texts or musical emblems and constellations. These elements are constantly transformed into new guises, but nonetheless remain recognizable, and this is the case with the poetic images in this first tentative dramatic sketch. Dallapiccola began to mention to friends plans he had for an opera based on Ulysses as early as 1936, only four years after the *Rappresentazione* sketch had been made, and before either *Volo di notte* or *Il prigioniero* had been penned, but the idea was not taken further for many years.

Dallapiccola's knowledge of the music of Schoenberg during this period hardly extended beyond *Pierrot Lunaire,* heard in Florence, and the earlier sets of piano pieces, Opus 11 and Opus 19. His acquaintance was to grow, chiefly through the efforts of such Italian musicians as Guido Gatti and Alfredo Casella to maintain contacts with musical influences from abroad, at a time when others in the country were in favor of closing off such cultural links. But whereas Dallapiccola's knowledge of Schoenberg's music was limited, the music of both Berg and Webern was to come strongly to the center of his attention within the space of the following year, and this would eventually have a profound effect upon the future direction of his own music. In April-May 1933 an International Music Congress was held in Florence in conjunction with the Maggio Musicale Fiorentino, at which many important musicians from abroad were present, including Bartók, Kodály, and Milhaud. It was on this occasion that Dallapiccola first saw Alban Berg, who had come with Willi Reich and Egon Wellesz, and together with these three and others Dallapiccola made an excursion to Torre del Lago. Some years later he recounted an incident on the journey, and his impressions of Berg's personality:

> Our bus broke down half way, and the passengers all had to get out. The sun was blazing over the highway and the countryside. Alban Berg also got out, with Egon Wellesz and Willi Reich. Berg seemed interested in the breakdown of the engine and, leaning over the hood, was scrutinising the mechanic's movements, with a very amused expression. He seemed to be very curious, as though he had never seen an automobile engine from close up. In recent years he had regularly been attending football matches at the Vienna Stadium, in company with Reich, who assured me that through all those years, Berg had never managed to fathom out just how the rules of the game worked.[20]

In the Maggio Musicale Fiorentino, Dallapicola heard Schoenberg's first string quartet performed by the Kolisch Quartet, and a year later, in April 1934, he heard the same ensemble perform three movements from Berg's *Lyric Suite* in Florence. His first acquaintance with *Wozzeck* had been made in 1928, through reading an article by Guido Gatti, and he studied the score closely in the years that followed.[21] He bought a copy of Berg's Four Pieces for clarinet and piano, Opus 5, at this time, and during rehearsals for the performance of Berg's concert aria *Der Wein* at the Venice Festival of Contemporary Music on 11 September 1934, Dallapiccola was able to speak to Berg. The performance of *Der Wein* was a revelation to Dallapiccola: he was struck not only by its melancholic qualities, but also by the vivid character of its orchestral colorations. He was to write about this, particularly the final part of the cycle *Der Wein der Einsamen*:

> When Hanna Schwarz began to intone "Du gibst ihm Hoffnung, Liebe, Jugendkraft und Stolz", cultural reminiscences began to proliferate in great number in my memory: *L'Absinthe* above all, with its nameless melancholy. It seemed to me as though I were hearing for the first time horns mixed together with strings pizzicato: at that moment the gong transformed everything. One of those miraculous and extremely rare moments that are imprinted in one's memory.[22]

It is worth noting that Dallapiccola's reaction to this first hearing of the music of Berg, as related in this comment, was not dominated by the serial nature of Berg's writing in *Der Wein*, but rather by the hypnotic qualities of Berg's orchestral writing. In this, Dallapiccola joined those many musicians, both at that time and since, who have been similarly entranced not by the compositional techniques but by the magical sound qualities of Berg's work. Dallapiccola had submitted a recent work, *Rapsodia (Studio per la morte del Conte Orlando)*, (Rhapsody [Study for the Death of Count Roland]) for a composition prize whose jury included Berg and Webern; the work had received favorable comment and was also heard in Venice.

Divertimento in quattro esercizi

Dallapiccola later said that he found his artistic personality between the ages of 29 and 31, that is to say between 1933 and 1935, when he composed his *Divertimento in quattro esercizi* for soprano and chamber ensemble and *Musica per tre pianoforti (Inni)*, and these can be regarded as his first characteristic works. While the employment of texts taken from medieval sources in the *Divertimento*, a group of thirteenth-century popular songs, is not new in his work—he had already set a medieval text in *Due laudi di Iacopone da Todi* in 1929—it does represent his first use of a chamber ensemble as accompaniment to the voice, a characteristic feature of many of his later compositions. However, despite the impact of the performance of Schoenberg's *Pierrot Lunaire* he had heard a few years earlier, this does not appear to have influenced the writing for chamber ensemble in the *Divertimento*. The ensemble itself is very differently constituted from that of *Pierrot Lunaire*—no piano is used, nor does the clarinet double with bass clarinet—so the possibilities for creating the searing instrumental lines characteristic of *Pierrot Lunaire* are limited, and in any case the work lacks the chromaticisms of Schoenberg's polyphony. The composer appears to have been influenced more at this stage by Ravel's *Chansons madécasses* (Madagascan Songs) composed in 1925–27, since both works share a flexible, harmonically rich vocabulary and a limpid sense of melodic line. The *Divertimento* also contains many features that point toward the future in the composer's work, including some occasional canonic writing. Despite the absence of any of Schoenberg's chromaticisms in the work, it was noted by Dietrich Kämper that the melodic line of the final movement, Siciliana, not only encompasses a degree of chromatic tension new in Dallapiccola's writing, but also contains a pre-echo of the row later used in *Canti di prigionia*,[23] a characteristic unit of ascending minor thirds culminating in a perfect fourth. This melody is accompanied by a perfect-fourth ostinato at the opening of the movement, but is fully harmonized by the end of the piece (Example 1.5 (a) and (b)).

Example 1.5 (a). *Divertimento*. Siciliana, mm. 202–5.

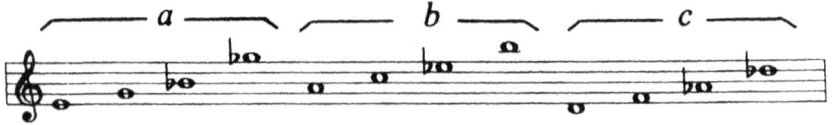

Example 1.5 (b). *Canti di prigionia*, row.

The composer's somewhat strange, antique-sounding denomination of this piece—*in quattro esercizi* (in four exercises)—points to an important characteristic of the work, the element Dallapiccola referred to as "researches in sound," with each of the four movements (Introduzione, Arietta, Bourrée, Siciliana) exploring different timbral possibilities of the ensemble. The composer's skill in light touches of word and mood painting is frequently in evidence: in the expression of the bitter pangs of love in the first song, ending in an unresolved half-step clash between the instrumental lines; in the excited pounding of a young girl's heart as she waits in the garden for her lover to appear (Arietta, mm. 70–80); and in the intricate interweaving of melodic lines as a girl pleads with her mother to let her marry the young man whose look and manner so please her (Siciliana, mm. 225–33).

The "researches in sound" to which the composer referred are to be found in almost every page of the work. It was not until the following year that Dallapiccola broached the composition of his first purely instrumental piece, but in the *Divertimento* we can already see the composer taking pleasure in the instrumental writing to a much greater extent than in any previous work. This is always done in an attempt to create the kind of bright, luminous sound images that would complement the clarity and simplicity of the medieval texts. This imaginative sense of sound and texture is heard most clearly in the third movement, Bourrée, in which the lines of the opening instrumental *fugato* give way to somewhat tipsy dance music as the soprano sings that "this dance is not going well." The offbeat accents in the oboe and clarinet parts, joining in the short modal canon with the soprano, and set against a somewhat aggressive ostinato in the viola and cello, together create a rather "folksy" cheerfulness (Example 1.6), in

Example 1.6. *Divertimento*. Bourrée, mm. 156–62.

a manner that would be explored much later by Dallapicola's pupil Berio in his *Folk Songs.*

Beyond the intrinsic importance of the *Divertimento* as a document of Dallapiccola's emerging musical personality, it had a further significance. It was during a visit he made to Prague for a performance of this work at the I.S.C.M. Festival in 1935 that he was for the first time able to immerse himself in some of the currents of contemporary music he had not previously had the opportunity to study. It was here, for example, that he heard the *Variations for Orchestra,* Opus 31, of Schoenberg, and the *Lulu Symphony* of Berg. He wrote about these in a review for an Italian magazine:

> From the mysterious Introduction, to the Theme (a marvel!), to the nine Variations, to the Finale, it is all so human, so coherent, so right in tone (how can one describe the Adagio, the seventh variation, the culmination of the work, a worthy "pendant" to the twenty-fifth of the *Goldberg Variations*?), and I cannot think about this work I have so recently heard without emotion, perhaps the greatest creation that has been heard for some years.
>
> The Alban Berg that appears in the *Symphonic Fragments from the Opera "Lulu"* [called his *Lulu Symphony*] is very different from the Alban Berg of the *Lyric Suite* for quartet. Here his style is completely theatrical and connects directly with that of the concert aria *Der Wein* that was admired so greatly a year ago in Venice.
>
> The five fragments (Rondo, Ostinato, Lulu's Aria, Variations, Adagio) bring us face to face with a fifty-year-old artist who has achieved a maturity of language and a perfect equilibrium. The Ostinato is a gust of music that makes one's hair stand on end; the Aria carries us into an atmosphere of somewhat resigned sensuality; but the greatest emotion is reserved for the Adagio.
>
> The catastrophe falls. Lulu's shout is something unheard of. And when at the end the voice returns and pronounces the words "Lulu, my angel!—I shall stay near you into eternity," one can think only of the pure and serene flight of the last pages of *Otello* or of *Tristan and Isolde* as something equivalent in the recent history of the theatre.[24]

In the same review of events at the Festival, Dallapiccola wrote admiringly of two works by Czech composers: a chorus from Aloys Hába's opera *Matka* (The Mother) and Janacek's *Jenufa,* but the most important experience of his visit to Prague was recorded, not in a public review, but in the more intimate pages of the composer's diary. Although this diary will not be available for general viewing for many years after the composer's death, he published one diary entry in an article recalling his first memories of Webern's music. This was his very first hearing of Webern's music, when he attended a performance of the Concerto, Opus 24, in Prague, and the effect upon him was immediate, disturbing, and not a little puzzling:

This evening, Heinrich Jalowetz gave the world première of the Concerto, Opus 24, of Anton Webern, a work of unique brevity (barely six minutes of music) and of an absolutely singular concentration. Every decorative element is eliminated. Nine instruments take part in the performance: three woodwinds, three brass, and two strings plus piano.

I could not get an exact idea of the work, too difficult for me; however, it seems to me to be beyond dispute that it represents a whole world. One finds oneself face to face with a man who expresses the greatest number of ideas with the fewest imaginable number of words. Even without having understood the work it seemed to me to reveal an aesthetic and stylistic unity that I could not have wished greater.[25]

One can detect echoes here of the note Schoenberg had written in 1924 as a preface to the score of Webern's *Six Bagatelles* for string quartet ("to express a novel in a single gesture, a joy in a breath—such concentration can only be present in proportion to the absence of self-pity"), and this suggests that Dallapiccola might possibly have seen the score of the *Six Bagatelles* by this point. The influence of Webern appeared in Dallapiccola's music only in a much later period (specifically, after the only personal meeting he had with Webern in March 1942). Dallapiccola did, however, remain in contact with Berg after the end of the Prague visit: at the suggestion of Willi Reich, he sent Berg a copy of an Italian edition of Georg Büchner's *Woyzeck* in 1935, and received a grateful reply and congratulations on the success that he had had in Prague.[26] As a further sign of the importance to Dallapiccola of his visit to Prague in 1935, it was on this occasion that he first met the Russo-German composer Wladimir Vogel, who would be an important guiding figure in the gradual introduction of dodecaphonic ideas that was to take place in Dallapiccola's music over the next few years.[27]

There would indeed appear to have been hardly anything in the music Dallapiccola had composed up to that point to suggest that the 31-year-old would be attracted to the twelve-tone technique. There had been no hint of the Expressionism from which so much of the music of the Viennese composers had gained its emotional intensity, and hardly more than a whisper of the complex chromaticisms that had drawn them towards serial organization. In any case, as has already been noted, it was all but impossible to become acquainted with the music of Schoenberg, Berg, and Webern in Italy during the 1930s. The isolation of Italy from the "Schoenberg Circle" was not a unique phenomenon: Benjamin Britten's wish to study with Berg after the completion of his studies in London in 1933, and the refusal of the Royal College of Music to support such an idea, point to a somewhat similar situation of incomprehension in England at that time. The attraction Dallapiccola felt to the music of the Viennese serialists during that period was visceral and to a large extent intuitive. He found in their way of composing, among many other things, possibilities through which the rational elements of his musical form-building—and also the naturally polyphonic tendency in all his music—might find a logical completion. But for the moment at least his music moved only hesitantly in this direction, not simply because of the lack of any opportunity to study the twelve-tone method in depth, but more significantly because the urgent expressive impetus that would lead him towards serialism was not yet in place. This impetus would eventually come, partly through a desire to find a way of holding together the disparate elements of his musical language, but even more potently through the need for a musical means that would enable him to express the most powerful emotion in the most incisive and direct way.

Musica per tre pianoforti (Inni)

Dallapiccola's first purely instrumental composition, one of the remarkably small number of works he wrote that do not involve the voice, also dates from this time. This was *Musica per tre pianoforti (Inni)*, and it was largely penned before the composer made that crucial visit to Prague in September 1935. The musical language of the work demonstrates the point Dallapiccola's music had reached at this time, but it also indicates how the impact of his acquaintance with the music of the Viennese serialists would clarify rather than profoundly alter his approach to manipulating musical ideas. Here, for the first and, indeed, only time in Dallapiccola's work, we find the influence of Stravinsky, an influence limited to its layout for the percussive medium of multiple pianos that had struck Dallapiccola so forcibly when he heard *Les Noces* some eight years earlier. His eagerness to work with this kind of sonority seems to have stemmed from a wish to create an effect of bellringing in the piece, influenced by the name of the commissioning body of the work—the Carillon Music Society of Geneva. The character of *Inni* could hardly be at a greater distance from the expressive sound world inhabited by the Viennese composers whose music was just then coming to his attention. The bell-like, percussive piano writing, the limitation of its timbre to a single tone color, and the arrangement of material in nondevelopmental blocks all point in directions other than that of the Viennese composers. In fact, the composer himself pointed out in an interview many years later how, in making the themes of *Inni* pass from one instrument to another with the same timbre, he had been "aiming, perhaps for the first time this century, at a return to the stereophony of the Gabrielis."[28]

If the influence of *Les Noces* is detectable in the instrumental layout of the piece, other more diverse influences can be observed in details of its musical language. For example, we can see right at the start the imprint of the "Promenade" theme from Mussorgsky's *Pictures at an Exhibition*—a work Dallapiccola frequently performed at that time, and of which he was to prepare an edition for publication some years later—combined with a momentary suggestion of the bitonality of Milhaud in the stabbed octaves that punctuate the end of each phrase (Example 1.7).

The Beginnings: 1904–1938

Example 1.7. *Inni.* I, mm. 1–7.

The language of *Inni* is predominantly modal, and it is by the constant, obsessive repetition of short rhythmic-melodic motives that the composer creates the atmosphere of ecstatic celebration to which the sub-title—"Hymns"—would seem to refer. Fiamma Nicolodi detected in the various characteristics of the work—its symmetrical structures, modal textures, contrapuntal writing, and "stereophonic" effects between the instruments, all of which tend to recall the Gabrielis—a desire to create a certain *italianità*, a characteristically Italianate freshness, vitality, and clarity.[29]

In the first movement, a compressed 88-measure rondo, the composer seems at times almost wilful in his desire to extract the greatest contrapuntal advantage from the relatively simple theme he had set out at the opening of the piece. In mm. 53–55, for example, the first piano initiates a *stretto* of the motif shown as B in Example 1.7, which is followed through in the second and third pianos, while the bass line is formed from a version of the motif A, rhythmically altered and a full step lower than before. The effect of this dense polyphonic imitation is to enhance the ecstatic and vibrant "hymning" of the movement (Example 1.8).

In the slow central movement, Dallapiccola writes music that is indebted to the examples of nocturnal music that Bartók had frequently penned. As in the Bartók models, this movement is conceived in an arch form, reaching its apogee in an episode in which a varied reprise of the opening music appears (mm. 43–76). Here, the gradually accumulating tensions suggest a barely suppressed violence, itself almost Bartókian in character (Example 1.9).

At the opening of the third movement, the percussive theme given out by the first piano (mm. 1–9) is clearly enunciated in four cells, the first of 11 notes, (E–E), the second of 12 (E–E), the third again of 12 (D–D), and the fourth of 11 (E–E), a reprise of the first (Example 1.10).

This obsessive rhythmic figure is carried through virtually the whole movement, subjected to many variations, but again the composer's predilection for canonic writing comes to the fore. In mm. 59–65 a thematic idea from the second movement reappears, while in a later passage, at a reprise of music from the first movement (mm. 72–77), the composer again indulges in close polyphonic imitations in the manner of a *stretto,* building towards the climax of the movement.

A somewhat curious "motto" Dallapiccola attached to the score of *Inni* for its first performance at the Carillon Festival in Geneva in January 1936 reveals an aspect of his thinking during that period that few other documents make explicit. He spoke about this motto in a letter he wrote to Paola Ojetti the day after the performance, saying that the motto, of which he was very proud, was the "Islamic-Mussolinian" phrase *Il paradiso è all'ombra delle spade* (Paradise is in the shadow of the sword).[30] This accords with a comment about the composer's leaning towards the "ideals" of fascism during that period, to which Goffredo Petrassi referred when he recalled his memories of Dallapiccola at that time (see page 41). Dallapiccola

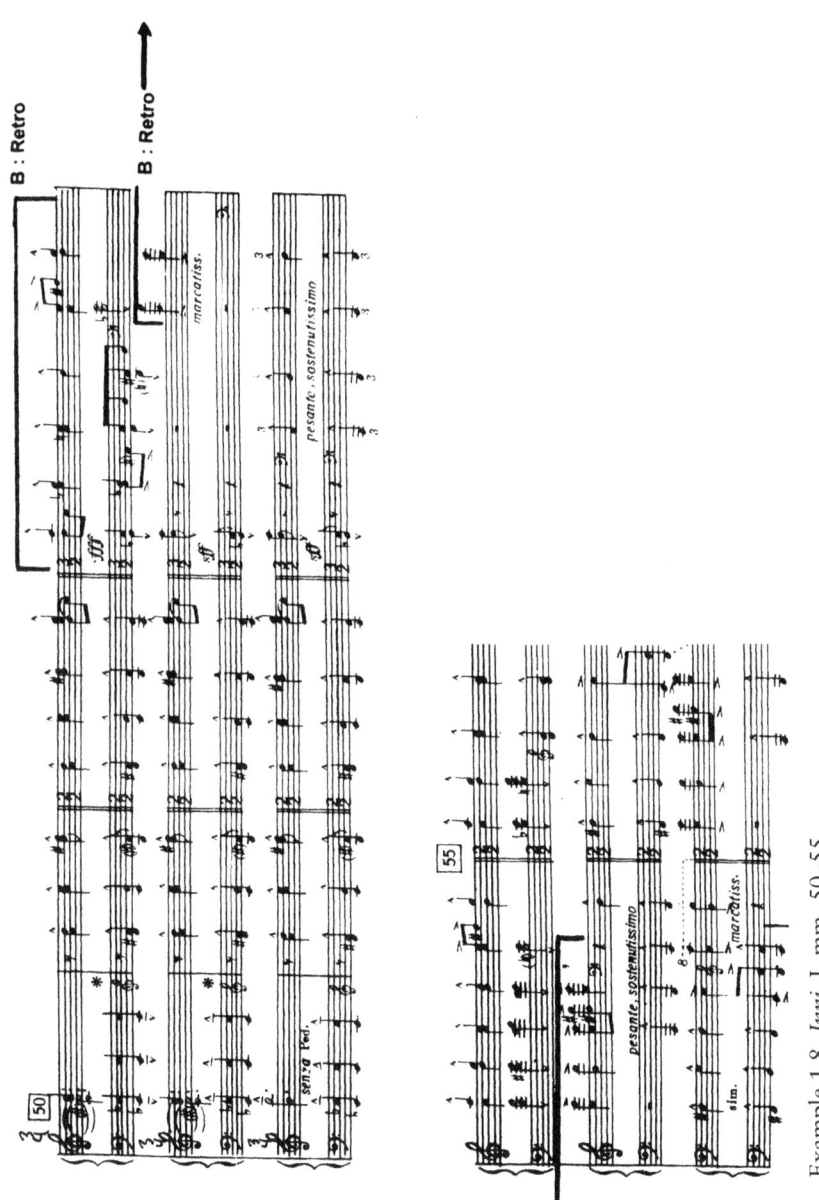

Example 1.8. *Inni.* I, mm. 50–55.

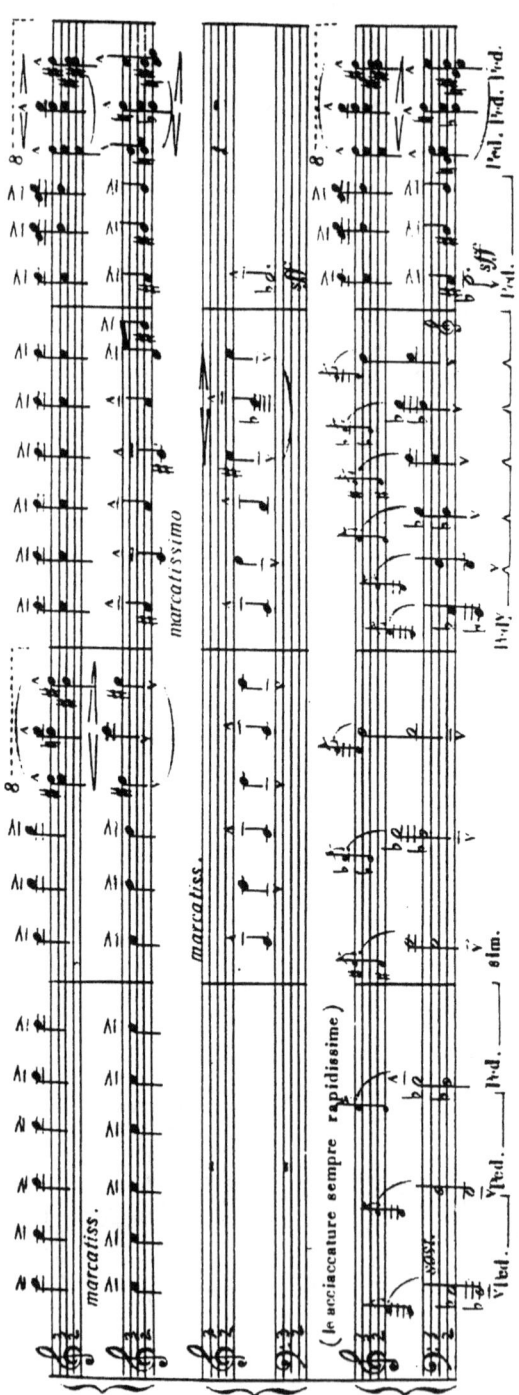

Example 1.9. *Inni*, II, mm. 61–64.

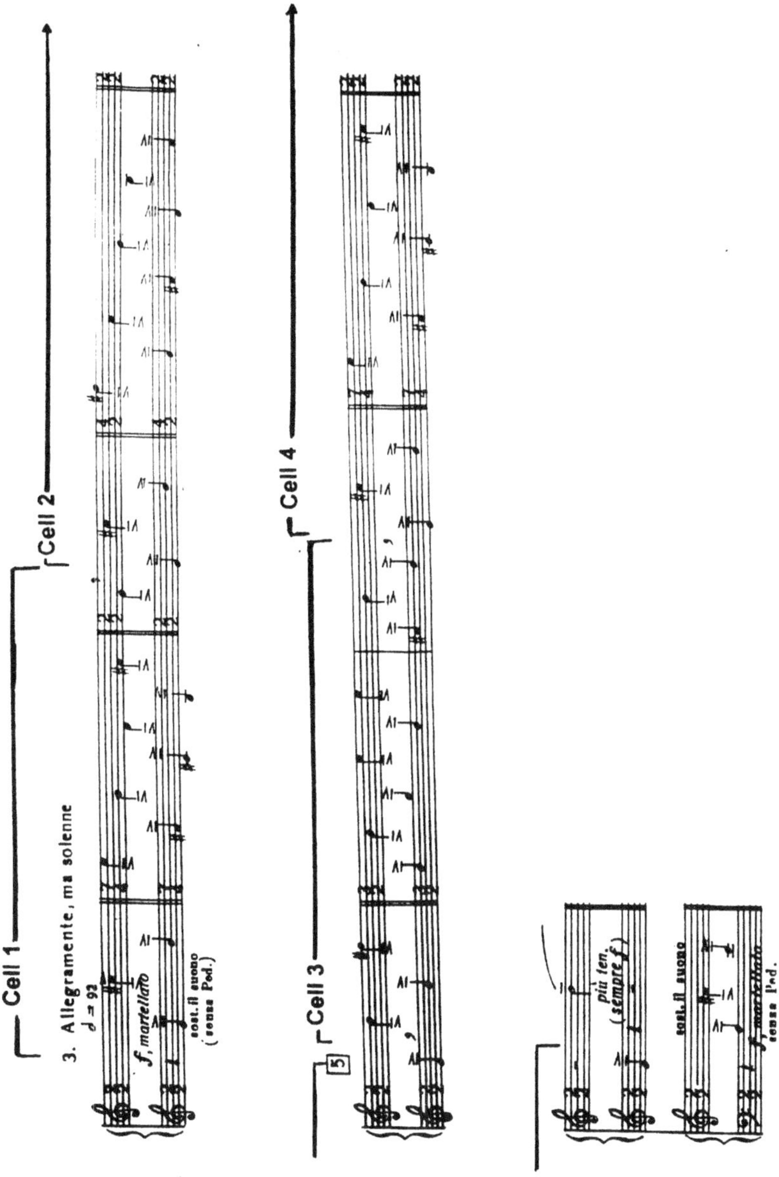

The Beginnings: 1904–1938

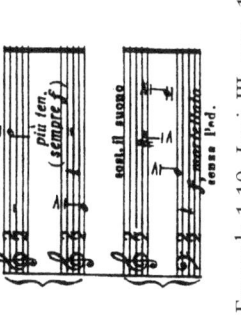

Example 1.10. *Inni*. III, mm. 1–9.

was to turn completely away from such a philosophy just a few years later, as we shall see shortly, but it is clear that at the time of the composition of *Inni* he shared with the majority of Italians an admiration for the regime.

Sei cori di Michelangelo Buonarroti il Giovane

From the latter part of 1935, Dallapiccola's artistic world was subjected to considerable upheaval brought about by external events. Mussolini's Ethiopian campaign caused the composer to "open his eyes," as he admitted, an experience he shared with many other Italians at that time. As a result, he was later to describe the *Sei cori di Michelangelo Buonarotti il Giovane* as his "last carefree work."[31] The composition of these choruses, the first pair for unaccompanied mixed chorus, the second for four solo singers or women's chorus and instrumental ensemble, and the third for mixed chorus and large orchestra, occupied the composer from 1933 to 1936 and represented the first major turning point in his creative life. The poetry of Michelangelo the Younger, nephew of the artist, had only recently become widely known, and the choice of such a Renaissance text is significant. In these choruses, Dallapiccola attempted to revive the passion and the vivid expressivity of the Renaissance Italian madrigal, in contrast to the cool, objective, and largely instrumental neoclassicism that characterized the followers of Casella. Some commentators have regarded these choruses as part of the "neomadrigalian" tendency which entered Italian music at that time, but Dallapiccola himself wished to stress other elements he regarded as much more important. He invited listeners to look beyond the madrigalian surface to see how they were enriched by what he called "more recent experiences":

> One might at first glance get the impression of hearing echoes of Italian music of the seventeenth century. But beyond this, one will also notice the "archaisms" that are by no means "reprises" (contrary to what was happening at that time, when everything seemed to be dominated by the neoclassical illusion). . . . These echoes are, on the contrary, filtered through quite different and more recent experiences.[32]

What Dallapiccola was referring to here was the revelation afforded by Malipiero's operas *Sette canzoni* and *Torneo notturno* of the possibilities for an expressive Italian vocal idiom enriched by study of earlier Italian vocal and dramatic music. Malipiero was an important figure in the earlier part of Dallapiccola's creative life, and Dallapiccola later referred to the way in which the older composer had "shown to our generation the true spirit of Italian music . . . [he] preserved me from neoclassicism—the worst period in the music of the twentieth century."[33] The influence of Malipiero's music on the Michelangelo settings of Dallapiccola represents one of only a remarkably few instances in which we find the impact of an Italian rather than a foreign composer on Dallapiccola's work. This is not to suggest that any Italian influence we might find in Dallapiccola's work is of little importance, and, as we shall see later, the composer later wrote with great eloquence of those elements of the work of Verdi that he felt had remained unnoticed or neglected by many scholars. However, despite his great admiration of the work of some of his immediate Italian predecessors, most notably, of course, the musical pioneers of the *generazione dell'ottanta*—Malipiero and Casella—his own musical outlook was far removed from that of those composers. In many ways he had more in common with the generation of composers who emerged after the Second World War in having a more inclusive and international perspective on contemporary music.

The First Series of Choruses consisted of settings of two linked texts, "Coro delle malmaritate" and "Coro dei malammogliati" (Chorus of Unhappily Married Women, and Chorus of Unhappily Married Men). The Renaissance madrigal composers' expressive stock-in-trade is here exhibited in abundance, especially in the way in which the complaints of the two groups of spouses are given an extra bitterness in their musical settings. An example can be seen in the constant return in the "Coro dei malammogliati" of the refrain "a devil from hell, a pumpkin without salt." The elegant wit of these remarkable poems is matched by some word painting in the music: in the "Coro delle malmaritate," for example, a reference to the cock-crow elicits a deliciously realistic imitation in the first soprano (Example 1.11).

Example 1.11. "Coro delle Malmaritate," mm. 57–60.

The significance of the madrigalian realisms in this First Series of Michelangelo choruses also touches upon a characteristic that was to reappear in the works of Dallapiccola's last years, what the composer himself would later call "ideograms." These are passages in which the visual aspect of the music, or some element of its musical shaping, is related to the meaning of the text at that particular point. Dallapiccola later wrote:

> Inheritances from the Baroque are many, in this First Series. I think one may truly and properly speak of ideograms in the passage "levarci a mattutini" [to bestir ourselves at matins], which, with its swinging motion, discreetly suggests that of a bell in the "Chorus of Unhappily Married Women"; moreover, certain word emphases designed to give power to the significance of the word, or one aspect of it, are of undoubted Baroque origin. As an example, I can cite the verse "Un buon uom mi disse Fa! [A just man said to me 'Do!'] in the "Chorus of Unhappily Married Men." The exclamation "Fa!" comes on the note Fa [F] in all the voices.[34]

Such symbolic elements had therefore already begun to play a part in the expressive language of Dallapiccola's music, and when visual symbols began to appear in later compositions such as *Cinque canti, Concerto per la notte di Natale dell'anno 1956* and *Sicut umbra*, this was in a sense simply a further extension of a technique that had been present in his music virtually from the start.

After the *a cappella* writing in the First Series of Michelangelo choruses, with its evocation of the Renaissance Italian madrigal, the remaining two sets began to explore instrumental forms. In the Second Series, for four solo singers or female chorus accompanied by a group of seventeen instruments, the two poems Dallapiccola set, "I balconi della rosa" (Balconies of the Rose) and "Il papavero" (The Poppy), are both based on the idea of a "flower puzzle." In the first, rose petals and the heart of the flower represent, respectively, brothers and sisters, while in the second the crown of the poppy symbolizes maturity and age, and the musical forms the composer employs are those of Invention and Capriccio.

The Third Series of Michelangelo settings is the largest of the three, and also the most extended work Dallapiccola had composed up to that point. It is for full chorus and large orchestra, and shares with the earlier sets the subtle treatment of poetic images, with the formal structures also mirroring the textual content. In "Coro degli Zitti" (Chorus of the Silent Ones), a Chaconne reflects the insistence upon silence of the ghostly "Silent Ones" as they wander around the streets of Florence at the start of Lent. This employment of the "persistent" form of the Chaconne to symbolize the obsessive character of the "Silent Ones" links this piece with Berg's characterization of the obsessive Doctor by means of a Passacaglia in *Wozzeck*. In complete contrast, in the second setting, "Coro dei lanzi briachi" (Chorus of Drunken Mercenaries), the choice of the Galliard, with its exaggerated, tipsy leaping, evokes the drunken soldiers' revels before they depart for war (Example 1.12). The refrain "Noi siam, noi siam gli Zitti, / Paggi, messaggi, ostaggio del Silenzio" (We are, we are the Silent Ones, pages, messengers, and hostages of Silence) recurs in each of its three verses, while in the central episode there is a fugue. In this Chorus, the composer also makes an allusion to passages from the two earlier sets, thus creating a degree of unity in the six choruses as a whole.

Example 1.12. "Coro dei lanzi briachi," opening.

Dallapiccola's musical language becomes more chromatic in these two choruses than in any of his earlier music.[35] The influence of Berg can be detected in the chromatic writing, as well as the inclusion in the orchestral ensemble of a saxophone, an instrument that would play an important part in Dallapiccola's first opera, *Volo di notte,* composed just over a year later. Furthermore, the choral writing incorporates a highly varied use of vocal gestures in a Bergian manner: *canto parlato,* murmured sounds (*mormorato*), slightly intoned (*poco intonato*), singing *a bocca chiusa,* and completely timbre-less whispering (*sussurrato e assolutamente senza timbro*), which carries only rhythmic indications for the choral voices. In the case of the *canto parlato* (*Sprechgesang*), this was not influenced by Schoenberg's use of the technique, since he used it in a choral rather than a solo context only in *Moses und Aron.* It is more likely that the roots of this technique lay in Wladimir Vogel's use of spoken choral enunciation in his *Wagadus Untergang durch die Eitelkeit* (1930). The close contact between Vogel and Dallapiccola, which we shall examine in detail later, almost certainly led to Dallapiccola's awareness of Vogel's use of the technique, which was to become of crucial importance in the latter's *Thyl Claes* (1938–45).

In "Coro degli Zitti," the theme of the Chaconne incorporates eleven different pitches in tritonal groupings, and its inversion, heard a little later, adds the twelfth tone, but its construction from a group of perfect and augmented fourths is indebted to Schoenberg's theory concerning chords of the fourth as enunciated in his *Harmonielehre,* as well as to its practical formulation in his Chamber Symphony, Opus 9 (Example 1.13).

Example 1.13. "Coro degli Zitti," principal themes.

The fugue forming the central section of this chorus, as the Silent Ones travel through Florence enforcing obedience to their demand for silence, employs a varied form of this Chaconne theme. In the final section the image of the spectral, nocturnal figures is portrayed by means of whispering choruses, finally resolving into a C-major chord, but with the transposed Chaconne theme placed above it (Example 1.14). This manner of presentation of the "row," with the major triad acting as an anchor point, was to reappear in the opening measures of *Tre laudi* (see Example 1.15).

The First Series of Michelangelo Choruses was first performed in Trieste in December 1937, conducted by Dallapiccola's former teacher Antonio Illersberg; the Second Series had been given in Rome in April 1935, and the

Example 1.14. "Coro degli Zitti," conclusion.

Third Series was performed in Florence in May 1937; the complete set of the six component parts of the work was given in Prague in April 1938. When the Third Series was given in Florence, conducted by Mario Rossi, the work appeared in the same program as the first Italian performance of Berg's violin concerto, a performance by the work's dedicatee, Louis Krasner, that was greeted with great enthusiasm by the audience as well as the critical community. Dallapiccola was also profoundly moved by the work, and wrote in his diary of its final pages as a revelation of "unknown firmaments." He said that in these pages "Alban Berg has found his *final verse* and has expressed it with a lightness that makes it impossible to think any longer of earthly matters."[36] There can be no doubt that the structuring of one of the scenes of his opera *Volo di notte* as a Chorale and Variations was influenced by the example of the final part of Berg's violin concerto.

The composer was to say of the *Sei Cori di Michelangelo*, "Here for the first time my musical physiognomy was clearly defined,"[37] and this work might be said to represent the end of his first period. During this period, Dallapiccola had vigorously pursued his "researches in sound," encompassing all elements of musical composition from pitch organization to aspects of form and timbre. From this point onwards, his music was to be profoundly affected by both internal and external disturbances, that is to say by his growing awareness of the possibilities inherent in more chromatic and twelve-tone compositional techniques, as well as by the historical events which became more threatening during those years. He was later to confess that after Mussolini's invasion of Ethiopia in October 1935, he "could neither feel nor compose as I had before."[38] The coincidence of Dallapiccola's growing discovery of the expressive language of the Viennese composers and the opening of his eyes to the true nature of the political situation in Italy was to prove explosive in his creative life. In the decade from 1935, a new musical language was to develop from a means of constructing simple musical "emblems" in *Tre laudi* in 1936–37, becoming an "alternative" language placed in relief against diatonic writing in *Canti di prigionia* in 1938–41, finally becoming the dominant, but not yet exclusive, language of *Liriche Greche* (1942–45) and *Il prigioniero* (1944–48).

Tre laudi

One result of Dallapiccola's crisis of conscience during the later 1930s is to be found in *Tre laudi* (1936–37), a work in which an expression of repentance for earlier sins, and a reaffirmation of religious faith, were also in a sense a reaction to the tide of historical events. Once again a medieval text formed the basis, this time taken from the thirteenth-century popular religious poetry that his future wife Laura Coen-Luzzato had found in the *Laudario dei Battuti* (Flagellants' Book of Laude), a collection of spiritual verses compiled in Modena in 1266.[39] The relevance of these medieval texts to the composer's mood at that time lay above all in their plea for a humble repentance of sins, combined with the powerful initial star-image that no doubt reminded him of his beloved Dante, and an expression of faith in the image of the Virgin:

> Altissima luce con gran splendore,
> In voi, dolze amore, aggia consolanza.
> Salve Regina pulzella amorosa
> Stella marina che non sta mai ascosa . . . (I)
>
> Da che Cristo venne al mondo e Adam mangiò del pomo
> Non fu mai sì gran bisogno a penitenzia retornare . . . (III)
>
> Supreme light of great splendor
> In Thou, sweet love, is consolation.
> Hail Thou Queen, loving Maiden,
> Never-fading star of the sea . . .
>
> Since Christ came to earth and Adam ate of the apple,
> Was there never such need to return to penitence . . .

The musical image Dallapiccola linked to the poetic image of "supreme light" in the first song of the set was to have a profound resonance for the remainder of his creative life. Against the fixed "firmament" of a sustained and brightly-instrumented B-major triad, the solo soprano's melody sets out prime and retrograde forms of a twelve-tone row as a symbol of the stars' radiance (this combination of a chromatic melodic line set against a held diatonic chord had earlier appeared in "Coro degli Zitti," shown in Example 1.14). It is highly significant that this first explicit appearance of the principle of row manipulation in Dallapiccola's music coincided with the powerful symbol of the brilliance of the stars, together with an associated metaphor of the Virgin, the "stella maris." This same musical image was to recur at significant points in the opera *Volo di notte* of the following year, and again in his opera *Ulisse* some thirty years later, in all instances allied with moments of powerful and all-embracing revelation (Example Ex. 1.15).

The use of a twelve-tone row and its immediate retrograde serves, at this stage in Dallapiccola's musical language, not as an element unifying a whole composition, or even a large section of music, but rather as a means of creating a musical symbol for the splendor of the stars in the firmament, with the row held against a fixed major triad. This linking together of stellar radiance, the religious symbol of the Virgin, and the first unequivocal appearance of a tone row in the composer's work also links this musical

Example 1.15. *Tre laudi*, mm. 1–9.

idea with the ideograms to which reference was earlier made in discussing the *Cori di Michelangelo*. The musical idea clearly has a symbolic significance here. The all-embracing "perfection" of the row, encompassing the whole chromatic space, is linked symbolically to the broader concept of perfection, and to the constant presence of the heavenly bodies, and in this way the row acts as a symbol of the spiritual comfort of the Virgin. Dallapiccola associated tone rows on many future occasions with other similarly powerful and universal images of perfection and beauty, as for example with the concepts of Hope, Liberty, and Prayer in *Il prigioniero*, and with the figure of beloved Suleika in his *Goethe-Lieder*. The importance of these opening measures of *Tre laudi* within the context of Dallapiccola's oeuvre as a whole can thus hardly be overestimated.

The rest of the work is, however, not based upon twelve-tone techniques; it is dominated by modal writing. While the jubilant, carillon-like music of the second *lauda* looks back to many similar passages in *Inni*, it also looks forward to *Volo di notte*, in which precisely the same music is used for the scene of the airfield workers running onto the tarmac to welcome an incoming flight (Example 1.16).

Example 1.16. *Tre laudi,* mm. 59–62.

The strongly diatonic character of this music, together with its incisive rhythmic outlines, could hardly contrast more with the limpid colorations of the opening of the work quoted above. However, in the course of the central part of this *lauda* (mm. 80–132), chromatic strands gradually invade the texture, reaching a climax in a twelve-tone chord as the Virgin's name is finally invoked in m. 97 (Example 1.17).

The third *lauda* (which Dallapiccola had composed first, apparently while sitting at a café table listening to a jazz band playing[40]) is dominated by the word *penitenza*, which occurs three times, as the Virgin is asked once more to receive the repentant sinner. The heartfelt prayer begins with a theme incorporating 14 pitches, which returns at its end to the initial tone E, and in which the penultimate tone marked "like a quarter tone" acts as a kind of "blue" tone within the haunting melodic line (Example 1.18).

In the central *tenebroso* section of this final *lauda*, we find the first occurrence of the B-A-C-H figure which was to assume great significance in several of Dallapiccola's later works, notably *Quaderno musicale di Annalibera, Canti di liberazione,* and *Concerto per la notte di Natale dell'anno 1956*. The composer's wry comment on this piece reveals his trenchant opposition to the prevailing trends in Italian music at that time: "My hatred of neoclassicism ('We must return to Bach') was such that I allowed myself this cynical attitude to a religious text."[41]

The overall shape of *Tre laudi*, with its three sections in a slow–fast–slow sequence, prefigures that of the *Canti di prigionia*, the composition of which was begun a little over a year later. In both cases, the fusion of

Example 1.17. *Tre laudi,* mm. 92–98.

Example 1.18. *Tre laudi,* mm. 156–60.

dodecaphonic and modal writing looks forward to the works Dallapiccola composed after the war. He was later to describe *Tre laudi* in a way that reveals its importance as one of his most expressive religious pieces, and at the same time perhaps expresses the precision and perfection of the work: he described it as "a painting on a golden background."[42]

During the period that followed Dallapiccola's visit to the I.S.C.M. Festival in Prague in September 1935, his gradual absorption of the influence of the Viennese composers' music—especially that of Alban Berg—only occasionally resulted in an identifiable point of direct influence, such as those twelve-tone "symbols" we have already observed. Nonetheless, he was reflecting upon the music that had so greatly affected him, and this is evidenced by a series of lectures he gave at the Florence Conservatory in March 1936.[43] The three lectures were entitled "Schoenberg and so-called atonality," "Schoenberg and his relationship with the audience," and "The theater of Berg," and they provoked a good deal of interest and discussion among those present. In the first, he dealt with the "emancipation of the dissonance" which he exemplified in some works of Busoni and Schoenberg (of the latter's work he drew upon examples taken from *Pelleas und Melisande,* the First Chamber Symphony, the Three Piano Pieces, Opus 11, *Pierrot Lunaire,* Orchestral Variations, and *Three Satires*). In the second, he confronted Schoenberg's so-called "inhumanity" by attempting to contrast *Pierrot Lunaire* and Richard Strauss's *Alpensinfonie*. Perhaps the most important for the future opera composer, however, was the third lecture, dealing with the theater of Alban Berg. Here, he examined the use of closed forms in various scenes in *Wozzeck,* in particular the Passacaglia in Act 1, Scene 4, and the Theme and Variations in Act 3, Scene 1. What interested Dallapiccola above all was Berg's achievement in creating concise musical forms within the space of a remarkably short scene, and how the music reflected the rapid change of mood between each of the many short scenes. This was to prove very influential on Dallapiccola's attempt in *Volo di notte* to create a number of almost free-standing musical structures within various scenes of the opera. Dallapiccola heard the broadcast of the first performance of Berg's *Lulu* from Switzerland during the period of composition of *Volo di notte* in June 1937, and as we shall now observe, the influence of Berg on many musical details of Dallapiccola's first operatic venture was enormous.

Volo di notte

As we noted earlier, even in the early 1930s Dallapiccola had begun to think about the composition of a work for the stage, but it was not until the latter part of the decade that his ideas began to take on a more definite form. The sketch for a libretto of *Rappresentazione di anima e di corpo* made at the end of 1932, despite its obvious immaturity, marked an important stage in the evolution of his theatrical ideas, and this will be discussed later in relation to *Ulisse* (see chapter 6). However, during the latter part of the 1930s, Dallapiccola came across a newly published book on the history of the theater by Joseph Gregor,[44] and his thoughts about an opera began to turn towards a subject with a distinctly realistic and present-day character. In Gregor's book he found the suggestion that a good subject for a drama might be the eruption of the volcano Mount Pelée on the island of Martinique in May 1902; or rather, not the eruption itself, but the series of telegrams sent to a Viennese press agency in the ensuing days, which recounted the gradual realization of the scale of the disaster.[45] The composer said that in these telegrams was to be found the origin of a dramatic idea that would eventually lead to his first opera *Volo di notte* (Night Flight), first staged in Florence in May 1940. What fascinated the composer in Gregor's account of the Martinique disaster was the gradual unfolding of a dramatic event by indirect means, through telegraphic communications, and we do find such a gradually emerging tragedy in the opera. In this case, it is an account of a plane lost in a storm in the Andean mountains during the pioneering days of aviation, news of which arrives at the airfield by means of the radiotelegraph.

The opera was composed in just one year, between 1937 and 1938, and after its first Florence staging in 1940 was seen once more in Rome two years later. The moment of its first appearance was hardly auspicious, and the reception of the work by the critical press was influenced by the historical moment and prevailing ideology, as we may judge from one review in a fascist newspaper, which the composer himself quoted:

> What a narrow concept of heroism, what a narrow vision from a human point of view! Should we send our pilots to see this opera as a tonic for their nerves and to freshen up their enthusiasm? . . . On the eve of the upheaval in Europe, whose mystical beginnings we are experiencing right now, and in which we Italians also want to take part. . . . The applause at the end was stronger than the quite feeble protestations, but it is a well known fact that Florence is the fortress of certain intellectual minorities, minorities who like to call themselves "European." . . . The only European thing they have is their attachment to the ideals of internationalism.[46]

These bizarre comments, made in an atmosphere of wild political intoxication, could hardly be expected to do justice to the work, but quite beyond this momentary judgment, the opera has always been something of a puzzle to commentators,[47] and the nature of the puzzle can perhaps best be seen if we look at the work's origins.

Dallapiccola had read the popular short novel *Vol de nuit* by the French writer and aviator Antoine de Saint-Exupéry in 1934, and had contemplated the opera project for three years before commencing its composition. The narrative in the novel is simply told. In the office of an air transportation company in Buenos Aires during the adventurous days of aviation in the 1920s, the Airline Director Rivière is anxiously awaiting the arrival of an incoming night flight from Patagonia, Chile, bringing mail bound for Europe. The flight is late, its pilot Fabien having encountered a violent storm in the mountains, as the radio telegrapher relates to Rivière, and the time is overdue for the departure of the Europe-bound mail flight with which it should connect. Fabien's wife arrives in the office to plead with Rivière not to continue with dangerous night flying, but he rejects her plea. Fabien reports that he has flown above the clouds in an attempt to evade the storm, and after describing seeing a brilliant starry night overhead, no more is heard from him. However, despite the tragedy, Rivière orders the night flight to Europe to take off.

Dallapiccola commented in a letter to Gian Francesco Malipiero in July 1938 on the reasons why he had chosen this particular contemporary novel as the basis for an opera:

> I would not have chosen Saint-Exupéry's book and would not have thought about it from 1934 to 1938 if I had not recognized a universal value in the figure of Rivière. The Americans made a film from *Vol de nuit* and the result was nonsense, given that they gave pride of place to the adventure of the pilot Fabien. The book, and also my opera, has at its centre the will of a man who looks towards the future, and therefore Rivière is you, is me, is all those of us who stand aside from the "mass," that mass to which nowadays one tries to attach a worrying degree of importance.[48]

This attitude of the composer to what he perceived as the heroic quality of Rivière was by no means the only factor in his approach to the drama. Indeed, one can detect a distinctly different tone between the comment quoted above, made at the time of completion of the opera, and that of a comment he made in the programme book of a 1965 performance of the work. In this latter he seems to suggest that Fabien and Rivière represented two distinct groups of human beings between whom one had to choose, and that he leaned very much more toward Fabien rather than Rivière: "Unbeknown to me, in *Volo di notte,* for the first time in my life, I made a choice: to prefer those who suffer to those who are victorious."[49]

The composer's initial motive for basing his first opera on Saint-Exupéry's "novel of action" was the novel's eulogy of the "heroic" decisions made by Rivière, whereas a rather greater emphasis is placed in the resulting opera upon the visionary, quasi-religious final moments of the pilot Fabien. This would seem to indicate that a significant change of emphasis took place during the period of composition itself, and the change can be accounted for in part by the composer's wish to emphasise the dramatic conflict between Rivière and Fabien, that is to say between the demands of technological progress and those of a visionary spirituality. There can, however, be little doubt that the historical moment of the opera's composition also played a part.

That historical moment was indeed enormously important, not only for the composer but for the very nature of the opera that eventually resulted. During the earlier part of the decade, Dallapiccola had been no less intoxicated by fascism than had many of his compatriots. A particularly telling testimony of this is to be found in an account given by his contemporary Goffredo Petrassi:

> Dallapiccola was at first a fervent fascist—so fervent that he sometimes annoyed us, his friends. At the time of the sanctions he took a firm stand in favor of the Italian Empire and against the British. . . . Then, with the coming of the special laws and above all the racial laws, things changed for him and he became a passionate anti-fascist.[50]

Dallapiccola had, as recounted earlier, experienced a complete disillusionment with the regime, in common with a great many other Italians, following Mussolini's Ethiopian campaign. He later admitted that the shock of this event had caused a hiatus in his creative activity for some time afterwards: "I could never again either feel or compose as I had before."[51] Subsequent events only increased the composer's antagonism to the regime, an antagonism he expressed in terms of a return to religious faith and idealisms in *Tre laudi* (1936–37). It was however, as Petrassi commented, only with the issuing of the antisemitic Racial Laws in Italy on 1 September 1938 that the composer's vehement opposition to the fascist regime burst out. With these laws, his own well-being was threatened: he had for some time had a relationship with a young Jewish woman, Laura Coen-Luzzato, and at the end of April 1938 she became his wife. As a direct result of the Racial Laws, she was removed from her post as a librarian at the National Library in Florence.

In this context, *Volo di notte* has considerable importance, composed as it was in the period between the two religious works *Tre laudi* of 1936–37 and *Canti di prigionia* of 1938–40: the latter work was later described by the composer as his first "protest music." With *Volo di notte,* he set out on a path that would lead him towards the powerful combination of lyrical expressivity and the symbolic use of serial techniques which would characterize his music from *Liriche Greche* and *Il prigioniero* on. Both the musical-stylistic and the ideological-dramatic aspects of *Volo di notte* are closely entwined, a feature that would remain a fingerprint of all his subsequent works for the stage.

Dallapiccola's comments about the centrality of the Airline Director Rivière within the drama of the opera are in tune with other interpretations of the drama's symbolism that had been made when the novel first appeared. In particular, the interpretation of Rivière as the dynamo of the novel's action, the figure around whom all the other players are placed centrifugally, was made in a preface to the novel penned by André Gide:

> More striking even than the aviator himself is, in my opinion, Rivière, his Chief. The latter does not act, himself: he impels to action, breathes into his pilots his own virtue and exacts the utmost from them, constraining them to greatly dare. His iron will admits no flinching and the least lapse is punished by him. At first sight his severity may seem inhuman and excessive. But its target is not the man himself, whom Rivière aspires to mould, but the man's blemishes. In his portrayal of this character we feel the author's profound admiration. I am especially grateful to him for bringing out a paradoxical truth which seems to me of great psychological import: that man's happiness lies not in freedom but in his acceptance of duty.[52]

Initially, Dallapiccola appears to have shared Gide's view that Rivière deliberately sacrifices ordinary human relationships in order to maintain his authority and to advance the progress of aviation. Rivière's authority is put in the service of a technological future: by means of night flying, humanity will be able to create more reliable, more effective and speedier means of communication. In this futuristic vision there is therefore, as Rivière sees it, no place for the doubts about safety expressed by Fabien's wife when she comes to plead with the Director.

There is, however, another aspect to the drama that the composer goes to great pains to stress, and which indeed provides the most memorably expressive musical image of the whole opera. This is the vision of the starry heavens that the pilot Fabien is granted as he tries to escape the storm by flying above the clouds, just before the tragic end of his journey. In the novel, Saint-Exupéry describes these moments with an expressivity that could only come from personal experience:

> In a flash, the very instant he had risen clear, the pilot found a peace that passed his understanding. Not a ripple tilted the plane, but, like a ship that has crossed the bar, it moved within a tranquil anchorage. In an unknown and secret corner of the sky it floated, as in a harbor of the Happy Isles. Below him still the storm was fashioning another world, thridded with squalls and cloudbursts and lightnings, but turning to the stars a face of crystal snow.
>
> Now all grew luminous, his hands, his clothes, the wings, and Fabien thought that he was in a limbo of strange magic; for the light did not come down from the stars but welled up from below, from all that snowy whiteness.[53]

The moment of clear and resplendent beauty described here is central in both novel and opera, and to characterize it in musical terms the composer took the memorable musical image he had earlier employed in *Tre laudi* to symbolize the starry heavens as a religious symbol of the Virgin Mary, the "stella maris" (see Example 1.15). The importance of this musical image is underlined by the fact that it appears at both the opening and closing moments of the opera. Here in this musical leitmotif, we see a symbolic embodiment in sound of the brilliance of the stars against the night sky, represented by the placement of a twelve-tone row in self-mirroring forms above a clear and unchanging major triad.

Such a moment of vision and revelation is indeed not confined to *Volo di notte*, but was to become a recurring element in Dallapiccola's stage works. In the final scene of *Il prigioniero*, the Prisoner emerges to see the night sky, not tentatively, as the prisoners emerge for a moment in the Act 1 Finale of Beethoven's *Fidelio*, but to the sound of a glorious chorus of a religious character. In the final scene of *Ulisse*, Ulysses, alone in a small boat on the ocean as he goes to meet his death, questions the meaning of his life's journey as he gazes with wonder upon the starry heavens. In each case, these moments of illumination follow a conflict: in *Volo di notte*, after the visit of Fabien's wife to plead with Rivière; in *Il prigioniero*, after the imprisonment and torture of an unnamed Prisoner; and in *Ulisse* after the visit of Ulysses to Hades, where he had encountered the spirits of his mother and of the seer Tiresias.

There is, however, one element that distinguishes *Volo di notte* from both *Il prigioniero* and *Ulisse*: the fact that in both latter works a substratum of autobiographical experience can be detected, which is not the case in Dallapiccola's first opera. The composer himself stated that events and experiences in his early childhood lay deeply embedded in his psyche, and had ultimately borne creative fruit in the operas. In *Il prigioniero*, his reaction to hearing during his childhood about the imprisonment of a woman who had killed her husband, and his own personal experience of virtual imprisonment during the family's enforced exile in Graz during the First World War, had in part prompted the theme of the opera. In *Ulisse* his memory of seeing a silent film on the Ulysses theme in his youth had provided the impetus for his lifelong fascination with the myth. No such early experience lay behind *Volo di notte*: its origins lay simply in his reading of Saint-Exupéry's novel, and its composition was prompted by a desire to make a concise modern opera from that topical and realistic novel.

The modernity of the novel's theme of aviation was without doubt a factor in the composer's decision to make an opera from it, but this subject matter of aviation was also a double-edged sword within the historical context. The aviation symbols and trappings had been a potent and engaging emblem of adventure, and of the revelation of higher spiritualities, in Italian art and graphic design around 1930. By the time Dallapiccola came to compose the opera, however, these same symbols, especially that of the pilot himself, had become a powerful weapon within fascist propaganda.

In September 1929, a group of Italian futurist painters (Mino Somenzi, Filippo Marinetti, Benedetta Marinetti, Giacomo Balla, Fortunato Depero, Enrico Prampolini, Fillìa [Luigi Colombo], Gerardo Dottori and Tato [Guglielmo Sansoni]) got together to sign a so-called *Manifesto dell'aeropittura futurista* (Manifesto of Futurist Aerial Painting). An exhibition of such paintings was held in the Gallerie Pesaro in Milan in October-November 1931, at which forty-one aerial painters were represented. The leading figure in this movement was Enrico Prampolini (1894–1956), based at that time in Paris, and in a catalogue statement he wrote for the Milan exhibition, he outlined the aims of the *aeropittori* (aerial painters) in visionary terms:

> I maintain that to reach the highest realm of a new extraterrestrial spirituality we need to transcend the transcription of visible reality, even in its formal properties, and launch ourselves towards the total equilibrium of the infinite, thereby giving life to images latent in a new world of cosmic reality.[54]

At first, the *aeropittori* wished to emphasise the "para-surreal" image, a vision of the vertiginous thrills of flight, and upon the representation of states of weightlessness and formlessness. This gradually changed as time went on, and in the work of Tato, Renato di Bosso, Alfredo Ambrosi, Tullio Crali and Sante Monachesi, we find literal renditions of planes in flight, aerial views of landscape, and the dizzying effects of soaring to great heights. The popularity of this form of painting is attested by Marinetti's claim that by 1934 there were more than five hundred *aeropittori* at work.[55] However, by the time of the Italian invasion of Ethiopia in 1936, the emphasis had shifted away from the spiritual dimension towards the simple glorification of the flying machines themselves and their heroic pilots as a means of supporting the military campaign. At the same time, Italian aviators, such as the prominent fascist leader Italo Balbo, were becoming the all-purpose heroes of the fascist regime. In 1933 twenty-four Italian-made airplanes, under Balbo's command, crossed the Atlantic, and the crews visited North American cities to enormous popular acclaim. It is clear, therefore, that the airplane and its operators represented a powerful symbol in Italy at that time, and that these symbols had come to represent modern life and modern heroism. At times, it was no more than a symbol of youthful heroic ambitions, but at other times of a somewhat more sinister nationalism. It is, however, equally clear that for Saint-Exupéry these ideological symbolisms of flying played no part in his novel, and that he was simply relying on his own experiences as a flyer as an impetus for his storytelling.

The musical style of *Volo di notte* is eclectic: pages that recall the operatic writing of Busoni, Debussy, or Puccini are placed alongside others that bear an imprint of Malipiero, and still others that of the contemporary Viennese composers. Without any doubt, however, the most important influence upon the opera was Alban Berg: by the time that he composed *Volo di notte*, Dallapiccola had studied the score of *Wozzeck,* and had also heard the broadcast of the première of *Lulu* from Switzerland in June 1937. The influence of Berg is seen most obviously in the incorporation of closed musical forms within the opera,[56] and we can see this in Table 1.1, in which the provenance of various musical sections of the opera from the earlier *Tre laudi* is also indicated.

Table 1.1. The incorporation of closed musical forms within *Volo di notte* and the provenance of various musical sections of the opera from the earlier *Tre laudi*.

Tre laudi	*Volo di notte*	Musical Forms
I:mm. 1–18	Prelude: mm. 1–18	
I: mm. 1–8	Scene 1: mm. 57–64	(Introduction)
II: mm. 60–133	Scene 2: mm. 96–168	(Ostinato)
	Scene 3	(Pezzo ritmico)
III: mm. 149–80	Scene 4: mm. 579–611	
mm. 181–215	mm. 660–94	
I: mm. 1–30	Scene 5: mm. 805–34	(*Chorale and Variations, Finale, Coda*)
I: mm. 1–8	Scene 6: mm. 988–96	(*Inno*)

The presence here of an "Ostinato," "Pezzo Ritmico," "Chorale and Variations," and "Inno" recalls the musical forms to be found in both of Berg's operas, in which dramatic action and musical form interpenetrate to a remarkable degree. In *Volo di notte*, similarly, Dallapiccola bases several scenes on a musical structuration. In the third scene for example, which is marked in the score as a "Pezzo Ritmico," the whole scene is based upon a rhythmic cell subjected to constant variation through augmentation, inversion, and the like. The growing intensity of the appearances of the cell leads gradually to a percussive climax of great power, a symbol of the growing storm as it is reported from the Andes. This is indebted to the Act 3, Scene 3 of *Wozzeck*, described by Berg as an "invention on a rhythm," as well as to the "Monoritmica" in *Lulu* (Act 1, Scene 2), leading to the Painter's suicide.

However, one important aspect of Dallapiccola's first opera distinguishes his work from the operas of Berg, and this is the symbolic use Dallapiccola makes of musical materials and passages from an earlier non-operatic composition, the *Tre laudi*. Here, the distance from Berg's practice is important, as in only one case had Berg taken over music from an earlier composition, music he had composed for a youthful symphonic sketch which, after a considerable transformation, became the final orchestral Interlude of *Wozzeck*. In this case, Berg had employed the music from an earlier period for expressive purposes, and had taken the passage from a piece he had never completed—not, therefore, because the original music formed any specific symbol. In contrast, the symbolic nature of some of the allusions to *Tre laudi* in *Volo di notte* is very clear. As one of the incoming flights touches ground in Scene 2, for example, the greetings of the airfield personnel are accompanied by the music of the *giubiloso* music taken from the second of the *Tre laudi,* as has already been noted (see Example 1.16). Dallapiccola wished to employ the already composed religious work as a resource from which to draw very specific symbolic elements for the musicodramatic workings of the opera.

In the vocal writing also, Berg's influence is profound. The register of vocal gestures in the opera is a broad one, and as in the third set of *Cori di Michelangelo,* Dallapiccola employs the whole gamut of vocal declamations. In the preface to the score of the opera, the composer distinguishes these various types in great detail, ranging from a rhythmic declamation almost without timbre, in which the pitches should be more felt by the performer than perceivable by the listener, to a rhythmic declamation with very little sound, which is nonetheless far from being sung. This large palette of vocal declamations is one of the most important parts of the sound world of *Volo di notte,* and shows the influence of Berg's operatic practice, as well as that of Wladimir Vogel's use of a speaking chorus that we discussed earlier. In both *Wozzeck* and *Lulu,* Berg had similarly employed the constantly varying vocal expressions as an integral part of the vocabulary of his dramatic articulation.

Berg's influence is also felt in the instrumental writing. The vibraphone and saxophone, which Berg had made such a fundamental element of the sound palette of *Lulu,* are similarly employed here in order to give a modern sound to the orchestral writing, and in the opening scene, Dallapiccola composes a somewhat Bergian "Movimento di Blues," played by an offstage band, as Rivière, opening the office window late at night, hears the sound of a singer from a nearby night club (Example 1.19).

In the final scene of the opera, Rivière enters the office to inform the airline employees of his decision to continue with night flying, and tells them that the mail plane bound for Europe must be made ready to depart. The work ends with an "Inno" (Hymn), in which a chorus of airfield workers invokes the name of Rivière, and this somewhat solemn conclusion of the opera was almost certainly influenced by the Hymn with which the Rondo movement of Berg's *Lulu Symphony* comes to an end. The airfield floods with light from enormous lamps, only gradually resuming its normal aspect, and the work ends *pianissimo* with the "Stars" image of a major triad and twelve-tone melody.

There is a certain ambivalence in the ideological stance exhibited by Dallapiccola in *Volo di notte.* It is clear from the examples we have seen that the composer's presentation of the moral dilemma of Rivière-versus-

The Beginnings: 1904–1938

Example 1.19. *Volo di notte*, mm. 71–74. (Reproduced by permission of Schott and Company Ltd., London.)

Fabien, in other words of progress-versus-spiritual-vision, led him to associate very specific kinds of music with each side of the dilemma. For the positive, optimistic, and technologically progressive elements of the drama, he employs strongly modal-diatonic music, as exemplified by the *giubiloso* music for the landing of an airplane shown in Example 1.16. In contrast, for the visionary, quasi-religious element of Fabien's final moments, he invokes chromatic-serial constellations, as shown in Example 1.15. But the chromatic-serial music extends beyond this motif, and encompasses a whole extended section of the opera. In Scene 5, as Rivière hears news of the impending tragedy of Fabien via the radio telegrapher, the mounting tension of the pilot's communications is conveyed through the "Chorale Variations," clearly modelled on the final part of Berg's violin concerto, and this is longest of the closed forms in the opera. Here, the Chorale melody is itself constructed from the row that had already appeared in the opening measures of the work, that same "Stars" motif from the *Tre laudi* in untransposed form that will finally, at the climax of the scene, herald the death of Fabien (Example 1.20).

Example 1.20. *Volo di notte,* mm. 695–98. (Reproduced by permission of Schott and Company Ltd., London.)

Volo di notte is a work of transition, written at a time when the composer was beginning to explore the possibilities of greater chromatic complexity and of dodecaphonic constructions. It does not make any clear-cut break with Dallapiccola's earlier manner, but it does show signs that he was in the process of creating a musical language that would encompass a much greater range of expressive possibilities. It is possible to see in the opera the counterpointing of music of an emphatic, positive, and largely modal character associated with technological progress, against the more profound, meditative, and largely chromatic music associated with the pilot Fabien and his struggles against superior forces. Perhaps, in this musical "conflict," if that is indeed what it is, there is a symbol for the change that Dallapiccola's music was undergoing at that time, when the balancing of modal-diatonic and chromatic-serial elements produced a very flexible, but by no means always consistent, musical language. This language, with all its inconsistencies, and with the precarious balancing of older and newer elements that it contained, would be essential in *Canti di prigionia,* without doubt the composer's masterpiece of those years.

II

Self Exile and Discovery: 1939–1945

The Discovery of Webern

During the Second World War, Dallapiccola decisively established the twelve-tone technique as the major dynamo of his music. In *Liriche greche* he combined the technique with the canonic structures that had long been a feature of his music, and the technique would also pervade the kaleidoscope of expressive devices in his second opera, *Il prigioniero*. In *Volo di notte,* the modal language Dallapiccola first adopted during his studies with Vito Frazzi in the 1920s had been set against the chromatic-serial language that had fascinated him since he had encountered Berg's and Webern's music. In the music he began to compose in the late 1930s, this dualism of modality-tonality on the one hand and twelve-tone techniques on the other, became an important factor, providing a major source of its expressivity. The motivation for Dallapiccola's adoption of twelve-tone techniques of composition was to be found above all in expressive necessities, and the composer himself gave an indication of this in an essay he wrote in 1950:

> To return to a question one hears very frequently: is the twelve-tone system a language or a technique? To my way of thinking, it is even a state of mind. In any case, it seems to me a natural development of music, and Schoenberg's recent definition *nuova logica* will perhaps one day be thought as satisfactory as the definition *seconda practica,* adopted by Monteverdi three centuries ago. . . . Personally, I have adopted this method because it allows me to express what I feel I must express.[1]

This shows that Dallapiccola could see the historical necessity for the twelve-tone method, but it makes it equally clear that he himself had adopted Schoenberg's method because of expressive necessity. He felt this necessity most keenly at precisely the moment when he had the greatest need of a language in which to protest against the tide of increasing totalitarianism then engulfing Italy. This is not a coincidence: the modal-diatonic language he had employed up to that point was inadequate to convey the vehemence and urgency of his mood of defiance and protest. In *Canti di prigionia,* and

Self Exile and Discovery: 1939–1945   51

even more in *Il prigioniero,* works in which oppression and liberty were the central themes, Dallapiccola employed significant elements of chromaticism and dodecaphony as an essential part of the expressive vocabulary, though by no means to the exclusion of other elements.

Dallapiccola made a journey to London in June 1938 in order to attend the Festival of the International Society for Contemporary Music being held there that year. He had taken a great interest in the I.S.C.M. from its founding in Venice in 1930, and we have already seen how his attendance at the Prague I.S.C.M. Festival in 1935 had proved decisive in pointing him towards the music of Berg and Webern. The Secretary of the Italian Section of the I.S.C.M. up to the Second World War was Alfredo Casella, and the older composer took a great interest in Dallapiccola's planned visit to London in 1938. After the end of the war, the pro-fascist stance Casella had adopted for many years led to his removal from his position in the I.S.C.M., to be replaced by Dallapiccola himself. In London in 1938, Dallapiccola attended a performance of Webern's cantata *Das Augenlicht* conducted by Hermann Scherchen, and this work made an impression upon him similar to what he had experienced a few years earlier with Webern's concerto, Opus 24, when he had heard it in Prague. Dallapiccola wrote in his diary about this London performance:

> To hear *Das Augenlicht* made the journey through France and the Channel crossing with all the clamor of the seagulls worthwhile. . . .
> What struck me forcibly in *Das Augenlicht,* at a first and—alas—single hearing, was the quality of the sound. . . . Webern shows us how, even when one is not working in a strictly contrapuntal way, two notes on a celesta, a light touch on glockenspiel, a scarcely audible mandolin tremolo, are able to encompass distances which at first sight seem to be divided by unfathomable spaces. Sound, color, articulation, instrumental distribution, it is all invention: just as important therefore as the overall construction. *Das Augenlicht,* when one hears it, shows itself full of poetic harmoniousness: voices and instruments, often at the greatest distances from each other, counterpoise each other's levels of sound. The score seems to be enriched by those mysterious vibrations that suggest a performance under a glass bell. The musical construction has its own internal rhythm, which has nothing in common with a mechanical rhythm. The refined writing would merit a discussion by itself; looking, for example, at how Webern avoids at all costs that brusque recall to reality represented by the strong beats, and which, in this case, would break the dream atmosphere that permeates the whole of this most poetic composition.[2]

This eloquent description of the sound qualities of *Das Augenlicht* might equally serve as a description of those same sound qualities that would make Dallapiccola's own *Liriche greche* such an engaging work. But it is also important to note that Dallapiccola, like many other musicians, was enthralled on his first encounters with Webern's music, not so much by the element of dodecaphonic intricacy, which would only be fully revealed after close scrutiny of the score, but more by the sound world Webern created with the simplest of means. Without an appreciation of this sound quality, it could be suggested, the serial aspects of Webern's music would not hold the fascination that they do for many musicians, whether composers or performers. In any case, these qualities of Webern's music had struck Dallapiccola in much the same way that those of Berg's music had enthralled him a few years earlier. In the three years that had passed between these two experiences, Dallapiccola had had no chance to hear any further live performances of Webern's music, but he took every opportunity to examine the music with great enthusiasm.[3] It is significant that, when he came to compose his first music in which twelve-tone writing plays a major role, the *Liriche greche* of 1942–45, it was not only in a work for voice and instrumental ensemble, but also one in which the sensuous, lapidary qualities of the text perhaps bore some similarities to those of the text by Hildegard Jone that Webern had set in *Das Augenlicht*. Both Webern and Dallapiccola shared a common concern for textural sensuousness and for a closely focused attention to poetic and musical details.

Dallapiccola married his companion Laura Coen-Luzzato on 30 April 1938, during a period of particular anxiety for the pair. During that year, rumors of Mussolini's impending Racial Laws began to circulate, and these Laws were eventually issued in September. From this point on, the precariousness of his wife's position became all too evident: she was removed from her post as librarian at the National Library in Florence, and the financial effect upon the young married couple was disastrous. Dallapiccola immediately began work on a composition that would have a much more specific "protest" character than the earlier *Tre laudi*. He wished to express unequivocally his opposition to the tide of historical events unfolding in Italy, and in Stefan Zweig's biography of Mary Stuart he found a text that perfectly expressed the turbulence of his emotions at that time, the prayer written by the Scottish Queen during her imprisonment:

O Domine Deus! Speravi in Te.
O care mi Jesu! nunc libera me.
In dura catena, in misera poena, desidero Te.
Languendo, gemendo et genu flectendo,
Adoro, imploro, ut liberes me.

O Lord my God, I have hoped in Thee,
O dear Lord Jesu set me free.
Though hard the chains that fasten me,

And sore my lot, yet I long for Thee.
I languish, and groaning bend my knee,
Adoring, and imploring Thee
To set me free.

The composer stated: "My intention was to transform the individual prayer of the queen into a collective song; I wanted the divine word *libera* to be shouted by everyone."[4] He thus made the protest character of the work quite explicit. He had broken off work on *Volo di notte* in order to complete the composition of this choral piece, but only for a few days. At this stage, the piece was to have been simply *Preghiera di Maria Stuarda* (Prayer of Mary Stuart), a short unaccompanied choral piece, not yet with the instrumental accompaniment and the companion movements which would together form the eventual *Canti di prigionia* (Songs of Imprisonment). *Preghiera di Maria Stuarda* was given its first performance as a single movement piece before the other two movements had been added. Significantly, this was in Brussels in April 1940, just a few weeks before Belgium was occupied.

Dallapiccola's financial position was made more secure by his appointment to a professorship in composition at the Florence Conservatory in 1940, a post he accepted despite his misgivings about his fitness to teach composition: the financial problems that had followed from his wife's dismissal would now be eased. Work on the composition of *Canti di prigionia* occupied him from 1938 until the first performance of the work in Rome in December 1941, since he had decided a few months after completing the *Preghiera di Maria Stuarda* that it should be placed at the center of a larger triptych of movements.

Piccolo concerto per Muriel Couvreux

The only other composition dating from this period was *Piccolo concerto per Muriel Couvreux*, a lightweight but attractive concertino for piano and chamber orchestra in a style which, at first glance, seems to bring it close to Ravel, but which on closer inspection reveals some of the composer's more characteristic traits. Muriel Couvreux was the young daughter of Lucienne Couvreux, whose father had been of great assistance to the composer in his attempt to contact Antoine de Saint-Exupéry about plans for *Volo di notte*. The dedication of the concerto to the seven-year-old girl influenced the simplicity and directness of its style: the composer spoke of his intention to write music of a "childlike" character in the piece.

In the opening Pastorale, the engaging simplicity of the musical texture, with the solo piano outlining a pentatonic theme in bare octaves (almost certainly a reference to the young pianist's manner of playing simple tunes), hides a strictly canonic imitation between the piano and the two flutes accompanying it (Example 2.1).

Example 2.1. *Piccolo concerto per Muriel Couvreux*. I, opening measures.

This theme is formed from the pentatonic group E–G–A–B–D, and its inversion appears towards the end of the introductory Andantino (Figure 6 in the score); in the Ripresa at the end of this movement, the two melodic forms are combined. The asymmetrical rhythmic units between the pianist's hands, together with the setting for harp, clarinet, and piccolo clarinet, all contribute to the clarity of the canonic exposition. The two forms of the basic theme are further elaborated in the piano part during the central section of the first movement, to which the composer gives the title "Girotondo" (Ring-around-a-rosy), the playful simplicity of the child's circular singing game being mirrored in the canonic interplay.

The cadenza of this little concerto is displaced from its normal position at the end of the first movement to the opening of the second, and thus functions in the reverse of its normal manner, as a free extemporization upon the three themes that will form the main material of the movement that follows. As the cadenza comes to its conclusion, the solo piano outlines a clear twelve-tone idea (the descending exposition of tones 2–11 follows the "missing" B flat, which can be heard as part of the chord held over from the previous passage) (Example 2.2).

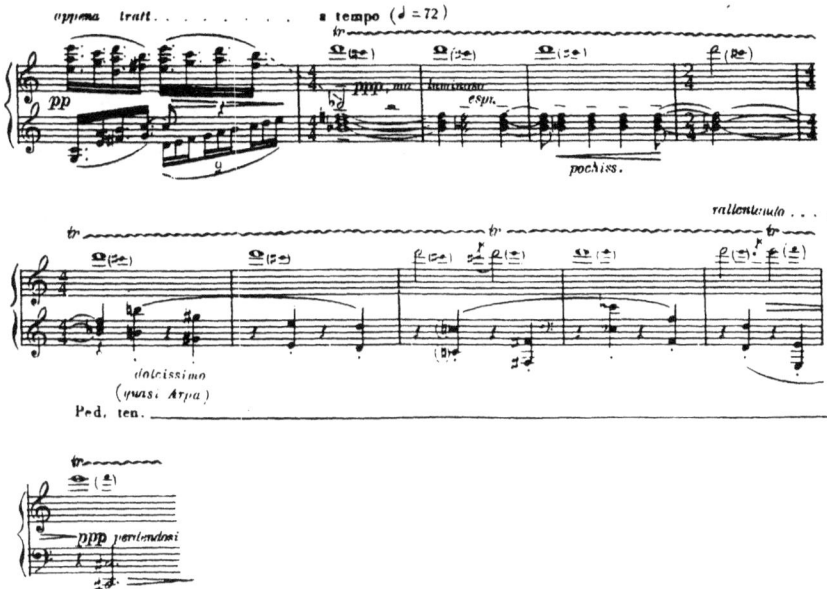

Example 2.2. *Piccolo concerto per Muriel Couvreux*. II, cadenza: conclusion.

This appearance of a twelve-tone idea in the midst of what is otherwise a strongly diatonic composition might at first glance suggest a certain lack of stylistic cohesion in the work. However, the manner in which this idea is presented makes it clear that Dallapiccola by no means envisaged a "serial" construction, with a unifying function within the work as a whole, but simply a coloristic idea, a means of introducing the most atmospheric and engaging passage of the whole concerto. The pianist is, indeed, here asked to play *quasi arpa,* as if to underline the orchestral suggestions implicit in this short passage. It is true that in the passage that follows, dominated in its opening measures by diaphanous string harmonics, all four basic row forms do appear (between figures 34 and 37 in the score), just as mirror forms of the row had appeared in the "Stars" motif of *Tre laudi* and *Volo di notte* (Example 1.15). The present passage, however, is somewhat isolated from the surrounding sections of the work, a moment of poetic suggestion. The Finale, based upon the three ideas which had already made an appearance in the cadenza, reverts once more to the very simple, diatonic style of the opening of the concerto, and is dominated by the virtuosities of the piano writing.

Canti di prigionia

The composer's attempt to find texts for the companion movements to *Preghiera di Maria Stuarda* proved troublesome. He wished to find texts that would not only be religious in character, but would also suggest a clear and decisive protest against the tide of events then engulfing his country. His wife's researches directed him towards two texts which, like that of Mary Stuart, were not only in Latin, but were also composed by "heretics" who later died as a result of their defiance. The text he finally chose for the "apocalyptic scherzo" which would form the second part of *Canti di prigionia* was a passage from "The Consolation of Philosophy" of Boethius, who had been imprisoned by Theodoric the Ostrogoth on a charge of treason in A.D. 523–24:

> Felix qui potuit boni
> fontem visere lucidum,
> felix qui potuit gravis
> terrae solvere vincula.

> Happy the man whose eyes once could
> Perceive the shining fount of good;
> Happy he whose unchecked mind
> Could leave the chains of earth behind.

The music was composed by August 1940, but he once again encountered difficulties in finding an appropriate text for the final movement. He considered and then rejected a text from a madrigal of Tommaso Campanella and others from Socrates and Sébastien Castellion (from whose writings he was to select a letter for the text of part of *Canti di liberazione* in 1951–55). Fate came to his aid in this matter. When Hitler threatened to bomb Britain in August 1940, the British Minister of Aviation Samuel Hoare asked the people in a famous broadcast to pray for release from their enemies, and when Dallapiccola heard this he immediately turned to Savonarola's meditation on the Psalm "In Thee, O Lord, have I put my trust":

> Premat mundus, insurgant hostes, nihil timeo
> Quoniam in Te Domine speravi,
> Quoniam Tu es spes mea,
> QuoniamTu altissimum posuisti refugium tuum.

> The world crowds in, the enemy is at hand, but
> naught do I fear, since in Thee o God do I trust,
> since Thou art my hope,
> in Thee have I found my greatest refuge.

Self Exile and Discovery: 1939–1945   57

The Boethius movement was completed by July 1941, the movement on Savonarola by October, and on 11 December of the same year the whole work was given its first performance in Rome. Little attention was paid to the work on this occasion however, since this was the very same day that Musssolini declared Italy to be at war!

Canti di prigionia could by no means be called a twelve-tone composition, in the sense of the techniques of row manipulation providing the basis of the whole musical mechanism of the piece. It was, nonetheless, the first work of Dallapiccola in which a row is present in all three movements, acting as one of the binding threads of the composition as a whole. It is important to make this distinction,because, as we have already seen, Dallapiccola's assimilation of the techniques of serial composition had been gradual and rather haphazard during the preceding period. By the time that he composed *Canti di prigionia,* he had had very few opportunities to study scores, let alone hear performances, of the Viennese composers' music, and he himself confessed to the problems he had encountered in his attempts to find out more about such music. There was, however, one person to whom he could turn to receive some guidance in the possibilities offered by the twelve-tone approach: the Russo-German composer Wladimir Vogel, who had already had some contact with the Viennese composers some years earlier. Dallapiccola and Vogel had met in Venice, at the Festival of Contemporary Music in 1934, and on that occasion they had begun to talk about serial technique and about the music of the Viennese composers. This is evident from a letter Vogel wrote to Dallapiccola in 1939: "If you recall, we had just begun to chat, in the Piazza San Marco in Venice, about the employment and development of the twelve-tone principle of composition."[5] Dallapiccola then wrote to Vogel about his more general aims in wishing to understand the principles of twelve-tone composition:

> In my researches on the twelve-tone row I had noted that my music sounds diatonic, in general, even when it is based upon a twelve-tone series. You take your researches much further, which means that you very often arrive at consonance. From all this we can deduce several interesting things, perhaps the most remarkable being that there is a new melodic domain to exploit, isn't there? Because traditional "melody" is inconceivable nowadays.[6]

Vogel had progressed much farther along the "twelve-tone road" than Dallapiccola at that point, and Vogel replied to these comments by trying to explain the twelve-tone elements present in his *Madrigaux* (1938–39):

> The music above all had to free me from what had been troubling me, showing me one of the possible uses of the twelve-tone system, and thus showing that it does not have to lead "to Schoenberg", and that compo-

sition can keep or else acquire its own physiognomy without following slavishly in the footsteps of the Viennese school. In this way I could demonstrate how the system can be used in a consonant manner, or in the closest form to consonance properly understood, and therefore with representational systems which are still valid for a large number of people. . . . You say quite correctly that the utilization of the melodic domain is one of the things the system offers us, at the same time also giving us the means to balance up a melody which is conceived with this system. The unfolding of the row, its retrograde, and all the combinations open up for us a form, whether small or large, that can lead to a perfection of proportions and of unity which could rarely be attained in the expressionist, impressionist, naturalist, or even romantic periods.[7]

Dallapiccola wrote again to Vogel just a few weeks later, this time asking for some assistance in his own attempt to unravel the mysteries of dodecaphonic composition:

The little that I have researched in the area of the new musical technique has, up till now, been mainly in the matter of melody. For the moment it will not be possible for me to do anything comparable for example to Schoenberg's Opus 28 (*Three Satires*), which otherwise I so much admire. . . . Do you know any treatises on twelve-tone composition? For myself, I have only been able to read Krenek's *Über neue Musik* and something by Hába, and that is all.[8]

Vogel replied:

As for publications about the composition in the twelve-tone system you will find some remarks in back numbers of *Anbruch*. Dr Schlee will let you have them. If you want to get to know the various procedures you have to stick to the works of Schoenberg and Berg: the Suite, Opus 25, and Third and Fourth Quartets of the former, this last-named played by Kolisch showed me that even Schoenberg is reverting to simplicity, a simplicity which with him, clearly, is relative but evident; even the face of a romantic, of German origin, reappears sometimes very clearly.[9]

At the time of his plea to Vogel, Dallapiccola had already been busy analyzing some scores of the Viennese composers, as the account given in the previous chapter demonstrated. Just a short time before he wrote to Vogel, he had published in the Italian music journal *Rassegna Musicale* an analysis of three of Webern's works, the Piano Variations, Opus 27; the String Quartet, Opus 28; and *Das Augenlicht*. The comments on *Das Augenlicht* are the most extensive in the essay, and here Dallapiccola stressed aspects of the work that would become a cornerstone of his own serial writing within a few years. These were, firstly, the *sound* of Webern's music, which had struck him right at the first hearing of the work in London; secondly, the perfect equilibrium in the overall structure of the composition; thirdly, the employment of the four forms of the original row in canon within the space of just a few measures (mm. 8–19); and, fourthly, the intimate fusion of text and music, which is revealed especially at the climax of the work in mm. 64–69.[10] What is important about Dallapiccola's essay, therefore, is not so much the analytical insights and discoveries he makes, which in any case could only be fully revealed after a much longer period of consideration, but the glimpse it gives us of the directions his own music would take within the next few years. In Dallapiccola's own twelve-tone compositions, all the aspects of *Das Augenlicht* that he had observed, the equilibrium, polyphonic-serial conciseness, and the intimate relationship to the text, can be seen in equal measure.

The friendship of Dallapiccola and Vogel was such that they regularly exchanged scores for each other's study during the later 1930s. During the period of composition of *Canti di prigionia,* Vogel sent Dallapiccola a copy of his cantata *Thyl Claes*; Vogel in his turn received the score of the *Preghiera di Maria Stuarda* in December 1939, about which Vogel commented:

> Clearly the text is thrilling, but for a musician it is the music that carries it along, and for me it is the composition itself which is particularly exciting. Despite the difference between our music I am happy to detect an affinity of spirit and a unity with you as a consequence, something which touches me deeply.[11]

Canti di prigionia is an example of "protest music," as the composer himself defined it,[12] and is without doubt one of the works by which such a category can be defined, along with Darius Milhaud's *Mort d'un tyran* (1933), Michael Tippett's *A Child of Our Time* (1939–41), Wladimir Vogel's *Thyl Claes* (1938–45), and Schoenberg's *Ode to Napoleon Bonaparte* (1942) and *A Survivor from Warsaw* (1947). In each of these works, the composers had felt the necessity of forging for themselves a musical language through which the most urgent and heartfelt emotion might be expressed. In the two examples most closely contemporaneous with *Canti di prigionia,* Tippett's oratorio and Schoenberg's *Ode to Napoleon Bonaparte,* the composers had similarly created a language in which chromatic and diatonic writing were combined. In each piece also, allusions to music from the past or from a wholly different musical world create quite extraordinarily powerful expressive tensions, at the same time universalizing the work's message. This is one of the most powerful expressive aspects of each work, whether Tippett's use of spirituals, Schoenberg's of Beethoven's "Eroica" Symphony, or Dallapiccola's reference to the *Dies Irae,* the thirteenth-century plainchant melody speaking of the coming Day of Judgment.

What perhaps distinguishes Dallapiccola's *Canti di prigionia* from many other works of protest, however, is the degree to which the intense emotion that lies behind it is set within a musical form of a remarkable degree of organization and rationality. The texts used in the work determined the dual nature of the musical setting, combining the highly impassioned, almost desperate pleading of the prayers of Mary Stuart and Girolamo Savonarola which frame the work, with the central, more reflective and philosophical prayer of Boethius. The musical dualism of the work, similarly, combines the timeless lines of the modal plainsong taken from the opening of the *Dies Irae* with the greater tensions and modernity of the twelve-tone row (shown earlier in Example 1.5 (b)), and these therefore mirror the nature of the work's text and philosophy (Example 2.3).

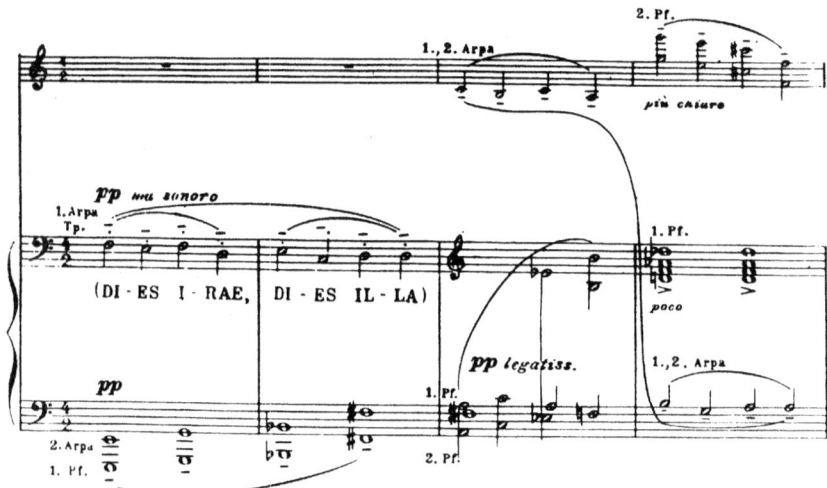

Example 2.3. *Canti di prigionia*. I, mm. 1–4.

Dallapiccola commented on this opening of the work in a letter to Vogel, in which he emphasised the atmospheric rather than constructive employment of the row:

> In this very free composition, it was not my intention to construct it strictly: the twelve-tone row is such, it seems to me, only in appearance. The first four tones of measures 1 and 2 are transposed in the third measure. And I think this would not be allowed in the strictest form of twelve-tone composition. And again: I have used the 12 tones of the row as a general color, as an atmosphere in the whole piece, not as a principle of construction.[13]

The basic row had already been prefigured in the *Preghiera di Maria Stuarda* from which the whole work had grown, and even here in the germinal work the combination of modality and twelve-tone elements in the musical language creates an expressive tension. In the opening measures of the *Preghiera di Maria Stuarda* the polyphony on the text "O Lord my God, I have hoped in Thee" is based upon reiterations of the four-tone cell that forms the opening of the row, combined with descending chromatic lines (mm. 26–37), while the setting of the subsequent part of the text "O dear Lord Jesu set me free" is set in a modal counterpoint (mm. 37–43). This leads to the powerful climax of pleading humanity (mm. 44–50) which reintroduces the four-tone cell only momentarily within the accompanying instrumental *ostinati*. In this way, the interweaving of modality and serialism no longer functions by simply contrasting the expressive "symbolisms," as had been the case in *Volo di notte,* but is now taken a stage further, fusing the two languages into a complex entity that is not always easy to untangle. Without doubt, this was one of the lessons that Dallapiccola had learned from his study of the later music of Berg, in which this creation of a musical vocabulary by integrating both diatonic and dodecaphonic elements had enabled Berg to pen some of his most expressive pages.

The congruence between the pitches of the row and those of the *Dies Irae* in the introductory measures of the work produces a harmonic tension which will remain unresolved even at the end of the final "Congedo di Savonarola," when the whispered retrograde of the row is set against bare fifths in the choral voices. The row itself is symmetrical, with two four-tone groups combining intervals of minor third and sixth, and a third segment in which the final interval is modified to a perfect fourth, avoiding a return to the initial pitch of the row. This restriction of the intervallic content of the row to minor thirds and sixths and a perfect fourth produces melodic and harmonic material characterized by a high degree of mellifluousness. The three melodic cells of which the plainchant is comprised (1: "Dies irae, dies illa"—2: "solvet saeclum in favilla"'—3: "teste David cum sybilla") each receives varied treatment in the three movements of the work. In the first movement, only the first fragment appears, while in the second all three cells dominate the opening section (but even here with the fragments gradually dissolving as the movement progresses). In the final movement, only the first fragment appears regularly after the first eleven measures in which all three segments are set out.

In the formal structure of *Canti di prigionia,* Dallapiccola exhibits his characteristic concern with clarity of musical design. This is evident both in the large-scale forms, with all three movements constructed in the arch form that was almost a constant in Dallapiccola's work, and also in smaller-scale canonic procedures. Canons abound in all sections of the piece, but the composer himself was particularly proud of one point in the work. This is a passage at the center of the final "Congedo di Savonarola," to which the composer attached a note in the score pointing out the canons. They begin with a canon at the fifth between contralto and soprano voices (m. 33), becoming a canon at the fourth a little farther on (m. 46), and a canon at the diminished fifth in contrary motion between basses and tenors (m. 48). Canons in direct and retrograde form in the instrumental parts, meanwhile, support the whole passage. He wishes these canonic forms to be clearly audible to the listener, and asks that they be given some prominence in the performance of the work. Such rationality of design contributes greatly to the expressivity of *Canti di prigionia,* and in this way the work provides a vital link between the earlier and later periods of Dallapiccola's creative life. The canonic and polyphonic textures are by no means simply a matter of formal design, nor simply a demonstration of contrapuntal bravura, but they act, like the employment of the familiar plainchant *Dies Irae,* as a means of universalizing the heartfelt prayers embedded in the work. This canonic aspect of the work had been present from the start of composition, in the *Preghiera di Maria Stuarda* from which the whole work had grown.

In *Canti di prigionia* we find a truly remarkable degree of unity within diversity. The musical language hovers between modality and twelve-tone writing, and between structures of the utmost rigor and a free, rhapsodic lyricism, and these diversities in the musical language create an intense drama within each movements of the work. This can be observed in the final movement, the "Congedo di Savonarola," in which the progression from fear, through hope, to the concluding faith expressed in the short prayer, is reflected in the changing character of the musical expression. In this sense, the movement can be seen to parallel in its emotional "narrative" what we shall see in the opera *Il prigioniero,* which, however, ends not with faith but with despair. At the opening of the movement, the author presents a picture of resistance to his enemies, couched in the most dramatic terms ("Premat mundus, surgant hostes, nihil timeo . . ."); here, the unison cries of the chorus are set against the *Dies Irae,* which appears in the two piano parts like a tolling of bells (Example 2.4). In the central section of the movement (mm. 15–32), the fear of the enemy is gradually replaced by the steadfastness of the oppressed, and this ends in quiet repetitions of the phrase "nihil timeo," modal in character in the choral parts and supported less emphatically by the *Dies Irae.* Towards the end of the section the row that had appeared in both previous movements is reintroduced. The final part of the movement, expressing a faith in God as our only hope, is built from the tightly controlled canons mentioned earlier. The expressivity here comes in equal measure from the chromaticisms of the melodic lines and from the canonic shaping, a recourse to a "Bachian" language free of any neoclassical restraint, and one which works as a direct conveyor of urgent emotion (Example 2.5).

Self Exile and Discovery: 1939–1945   63

Example 2.4. *Canti di prigionia*. III, mm. 1–7.

Canti di prigionia is a work whose powerful expression is based upon an almost timeless mixture of the universal and the particular. We hear a mingling of the choral counterpoint that had reached its apogee in the works of the Leipzig *magister ludi,* and the piano-and-percussion instrumental colors so many modern composers since Stravinsky have made their own. We hear the ancient inflections of modality mingling with the chro-

Example 2.5. *Canti di prigionia*. III, mm. 32–41.

matic and serial language the composer had begun to absorb from the Viennese composers. And we hear the ancient gravity of the Latin texts taken from historical figures whose death had acquired a universal symbolism, placed at the service of the desperately crucial historical moment in which the work was penned. The triptych of *Canti di prigionia, Il prigioniero,* and *Canti di liberazione* frames a period of the composer's life in which the themes of imprisonment and liberation were symbols of universal and not simply personal significance. This was also the period in which the twelve-tone techniques that had begun to seep into Dallapiccola's music from the late 1930s began to assume a more definite form, gradually becoming the most important aspect of the composer's musical language.

It would, however, be a mistake to consider the development of Dallapiccola's musical language during the preceding period in teleological terms, as though there had been some ultimate "goal" of the composer's adoption of Viennese serialism. It was not the case that Dallapiccola had seen the path that lay ahead of him and, in each successive composition, had taken careful steps towards this inevitable future. As we have seen, the opposite would be nearer to the truth: that the composer had worked from moment to moment in the very gradual assimilation of new elements into his musical language. Viennese serialism came into his orbit only quite late in this period, remaining at first somewhat peripheral to his musical thinking, but assuming greater significance as expressive demands made its inclusion more and more necessary.

Dallapiccola's art, having begun from what might be termed "neomodalism" at the beginning of the decade under consideration, might not be thought to have progressed very far to reach the language of *Canti di prigionia*. After all, modalism here is still present as a vital force, and the composer has not yet broached the organization of large-scale areas of music by serial means. But this would miss the point entirely. In the first place, this development was undertaken in a decade when an Italian composer's path towards serial techniques was blocked at least as much by practical as by ideological considerations. And in the second place, the motivation for Dallapiccola's gradual refinement and clarification of his language came from inner compulsion and not from external influences. It had, above all, been the need to find a musical language capable of the most impassioned expression, yet at the same time one imbued with rational and perceptible order, which had driven the composer along the path he had taken between the *Partita* of 1930–32 and *Canti di prigionia* of 1938–41. Those two elements of expressivity and rational order were constants in Dallapiccola's artistic vision, and both demanded the most rigorous exploration in order to be fully realized. The following decade was to see both these elements in Dallapiccola's art pursued with even greater energy, producing as a result a musical language that was increasingly focused and controlled in character.

During a visit the composer and his wife made to Paris in 1939, Laura Dallapiccola had picked up a copy of Villiers de L'Isle-Adam's *Contes Cruels* from a second-hand bookstall on the banks of the Seine, and she was immediately struck by one tale in particular, "La torture par l'espérance" (Torture through Hope). This story of the imprisonment of a rabbi by the Spanish Inquisition during the reign of Philip II, and the false hope raised in him by a jailer who appears to offer him the possibility of escape, was to become the basis of the composer's second opera, *Il prigioniero*. The composer had already been struck by the haunting image of the tyrant Philip II and the terrors of the Oficial in Saragoza many years earlier, when a school friend had pointed him to the episode called "La Rose de l'Infante" (The Rose of the Infanta) in Victor Hugo's *Légende des siècles*. Dallapiccola wrote later of how the idea of Philip II as a threat hovering over mankind had been fixed in his mind ever since, and he was later to identify the Spanish king with "other, much more terrible figures."[14] Dallapiccola also related an incident during his childhood that had left a decisive impression, and which undoubtedly also played a part in the gradual formation of the idea that would eventually lead to *Il prigioniero*. When he was six years old, a woman in the district had murdered her husband, and had been condemned to six years' imprisonment. To the six-year-old child, this sentence had seemed almost infinite, and he was unable to grasp the horror of incarceration for such a length of time.

In a newspaper article written in 1941, not long after *Volo di notte* was first seen on the Florentine stage, the composer had written, "I am always thinking of the theater, which remains the thing that interests me most. Perhaps I have spotted something that I shall be able to realize later on."[15] However, the composition of *Il prigioniero*, indeed even the assembly of a libretto for the opera, was not to begin immediately, in part because it would be extremely unlikely that the opera would be put on stage at that time. The unfavorable criticisms made by the press after the Rome performance of *Volo di notte* of the work's lack of any "heroic" emphasis played a part here, but in any case Dallapiccola wished to spend a good deal of time contemplating the new project. It is important to note, however, that the formulation of the dramatic idea of *Il prigioniero* overlapped with the composition of *Volo di notte*: the contrast between the two operas could, in many respects, hardly be greater, despite the common threads which, as we shall see later, link together all Dallapiccola's works for the stage.

Marsia

Dallapiccola devoted the whole summer of 1942 to the composition of a theatrical work of a quite different kind from the opera he was then planning. This was the ballet *Marsia* (Marsyas), a collaboration with the choreographer Aurel Milloss, which would be seen on stage only in September 1948. The composer had got to know the Hungarian-born Milloss (Aurél Milloss de Miholyi) in December 1941, at the first performance of *Canti di prigionia* in Rome, and the two had immediately begun to discuss plans for a ballet project. Milloss was an important figure in Italian cultural life at that time: he produced the first Italian performance of Berg's *Wozzeck* in Rome in 1942, and after working with Dallapiccola on *Marsia*, he also collaborated with Goffredo Petrassi in the creation of two important ballets, *La follia di Orlando* and *Ritratto di Don Chisciotte*.

The narrative of *Marsia* is taken from Greek mythology. Marsyas, who has gained a complete mastery of flute playing, challenges Apollo to a musical contest, but is unable to match the artistic power of the God, eventually paying for his overweening pride with his own cruel death. The work ends with the funeral procession of Marsyas, and with Apollo bemoaning the bitter tragedy. Milloss set out the idea of the ballet in succinct terms in a Preface to the score:

> The gift of art was given to the primitive being in order that he might arrive at human dignity; but he abused the gift and, through the sin of presumption, regarded himself as so great that he could challenge the god. He was sure of himself, and therefore forgot the limits to human enterprise, and lost himself in drunken ecstasy. Too late, he realized that miracles are the work of God alone. His challenge had to be punished by a terrible death. In this way heaven gave a generous warning about the equilibrium of human life.[16]

Dallapiccola and Milloss devised a scenario for the ballet in which clear opportunities for dramatic presentation appear in each of the three scenes.

Scene 1. "The Presentation of Marsyas": Marsyas discovers the flute, and through improvising creates the art of music; in the climax at the end of the scene, he dances in ecstasy.

Scene 2. "The Drama of Marsyas": Marsyas challenges Apollo to a musical duel, and Apollo calls on the aid of the Muses and Scythian warriors to act as judges of the contest. As Marsyas plays, his magical sound brings nymphs from the woods, and everyone is astounded at the power of his art. Apollo then begins, dancing to the sound of his lyre, but the music continues even after the instrument is broken, to the amazement of all the onlookers. He then breaks Marsyas's flute, and asks him to demonstrate his equal skill; Marsyas tries in vain to summon up his powers through dance, but is unable to do so. The Muses pass judgment, and Marsyas is flayed alive.

Scene 3. "The Death of Marsyas": Marsyas dies in the arms of the nymphs, whose bodies are transformed into tears; these, combining with Marsyas's blood, go to form the river Marsyas.

Dallapiccola and Milloss enjoyed a close and happy creative partnership in preparing this work, but whereas Milloss had originally planned a conclusion with Apollo's triumph in the musical contest, Dallapiccola wished to place the emphasis upon the victim rather than upon the victor. He would later say, "A triumph on Mount Olympus, after Apollo has killed Marsyas, was repellent to me. I found it unbearable, and I wanted to end with the tears of the nymphs. The victim was more important to me than the triumph of a god."[17]

This comment makes it clear that, for Dallapiccola, the ballet project was not simply a fortuitous opportunity to compose a larger-scale work, but one in which we can trace once more the theme of an individual's struggles against inexorable forces, a theme that had already been present in *Volo di notte*. When viewed as a whole, all of Dallapiccola's dramatic works are centred upon this theme, and its presence in so many compositions spanning over thirty years prompts the question of its broader meaning in his work. For the composer, this was the central and most powerful image in his creative life, and its significance may well lie in the symbolism it contained. All the struggles represented on stage are in one way or another symbols of a human being wrestling with God and with the meaning of existence. The struggle in which the drama's protagonist is involved, whether Rivière, Marsyas, the Prisoner, Job, or Ulysses, is in some sense a struggle to come to terms with inexorable and inscrutable forces. These therefore also symbolize a human being's attempts to understand his fate, and beyond this they also symbolize the composer's own spiritual questioning. Dallapiccola was by no means a conventional Christian, and on many occasions his personal views differed from the orthodox Catholic view. Nonetheless, he retained a fundamental Christian belief, an element that became more assured in his later years, and to which the religious nature of several of his later compositions bears witness.

The musical means through which Dallapiccola expresses the drama of Marsyas and Apollo involves the same duality of diatonic and dodecaphonic elements as in *Canti di prigionia*. Here in the ballet, however, the two modes are not fused or interrelated as in the choral piece, but remain as distinct entities. This makes *Marsia* a work of a rather bewildering diversity of language, one in which we do not find the stylistic unity that most often characterizes a work of Dallapiccola. The predominant language of the work is a broad-based modalism, but despite this, the composer's growing mastery of the techniques of row manipulation does make the twelve-tone portions of the score among the most successful in the ballet.

Marsia begins with "The Presentation of Marsyas," as he lies stretched out on the ground amusing himself with his pipe playing. This is expressed in the manner to which Debussy's *Prélude à l'après-midi d'un faune* had accustomed us, here with a solo wind instrument, this time the oboe, outlining a haunting pentatonic melody. A similar opening appeared a few years later in *Job*, on that occasion suggesting the pastoral nature of the biblical narrative. At the opening of *Marsia*, the composer is once again unable to resist the charms of canonic exposition (Example 2.6).

Example 2.6. *Marsia,* opening measures.

An *ostinato* passage follows, in which Marsyas, having discovered the power and beauty of sound, begins to improvise in the wildest manner, becoming more and more ecstatic. At this point, there appears a sudden pianissimo passage in which the composer sets out an eleven-tone row (Example 2.7).

"Row"

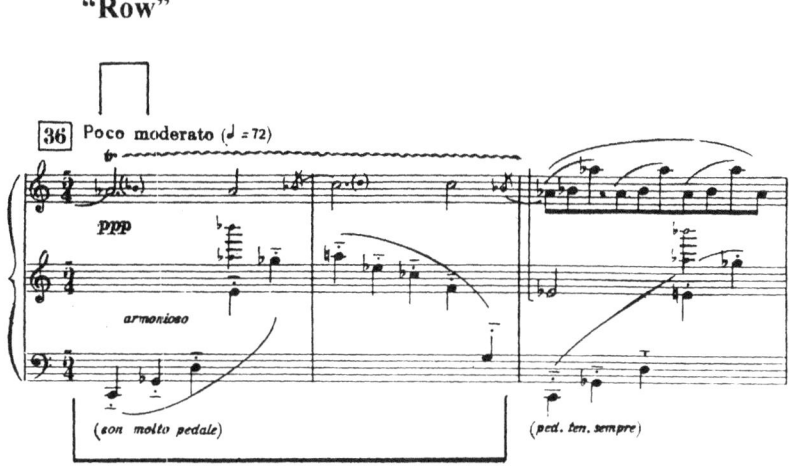

Example 2.7. *Marsia,* fig. 36.

Only at the end of the work, in the scene called "The Death of Marsyas," will the twelfth tone be added to complete the chromatic aggregate. As in a somewhat similar passage in the *Piccolo concerto per Muriel Couvreux* (see Example 2.2), the employment of the row here is coloristic rather than structural, but it is also significant that this row once again has a clear symbolism. At the opening of Scene 2 ("The Drama of Marsyas"), the row reappears in a very decisive form, as Apollo calls his followers to assist him as he competes in artistry against Marsyas (Example 2.8).

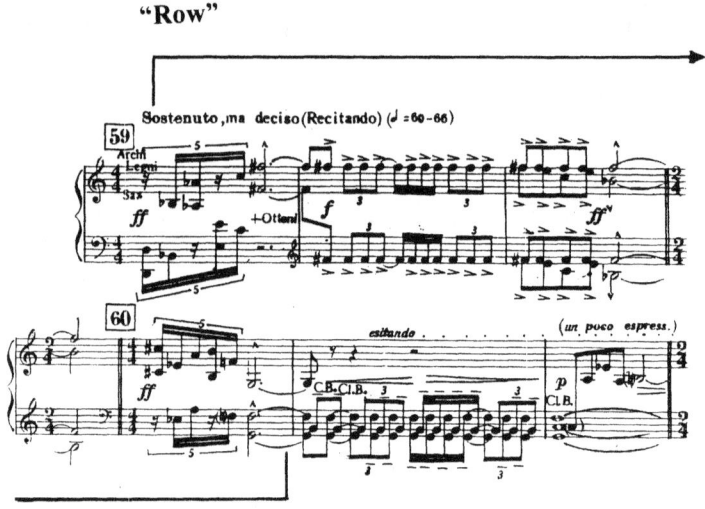

Example 2.8. *Marsia*, fig. 59.

Here, the relationship of the row to that earlier set out at the end of the *ostinato* passage is explained by Dietrich Kämper[18] as one of hexachordal combination: tones 1–6 at figure 59 are a transposition (and slight reordering) of tones 1–6 of the "original" form of the row (which has not yet appeared in full but which is already outlined), thus forming a new variety of row (Example 2.9).

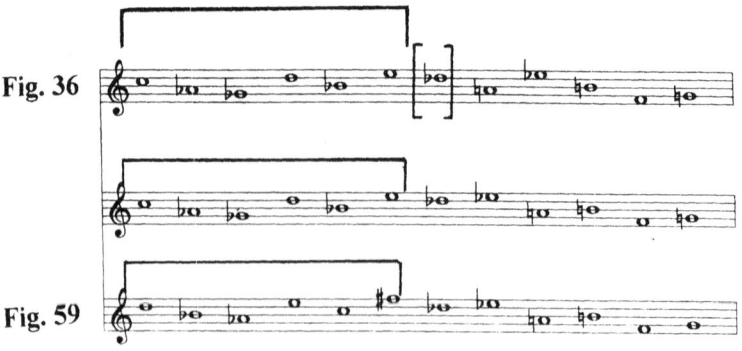

Example 2.9. *Marsia*, rows.

Self Exile and Discovery: 1939–1945

It is significant that Dallapiccola was here setting out on a path of serial manipulation, a path that would be of the greatest importance in his later work. As we have already noted earlier in discussing the first appearances of tone rows in Dallapiccola's music, he had not previously gone further than the simple exposition of an unchanging row in its basic forms. Here, on the other hand, we find the first example of the derivation of a new row from one already presented, showing that he had already, even at this stage, begun to learn from the example of Schoenberg. After Marsyas has attracted the nymphs to listen to his flute playing, they dance a Dionysian dance, but the music of Apollo is by contrast truly Apollonian: bright, luminous, and modal (Example 2.10).

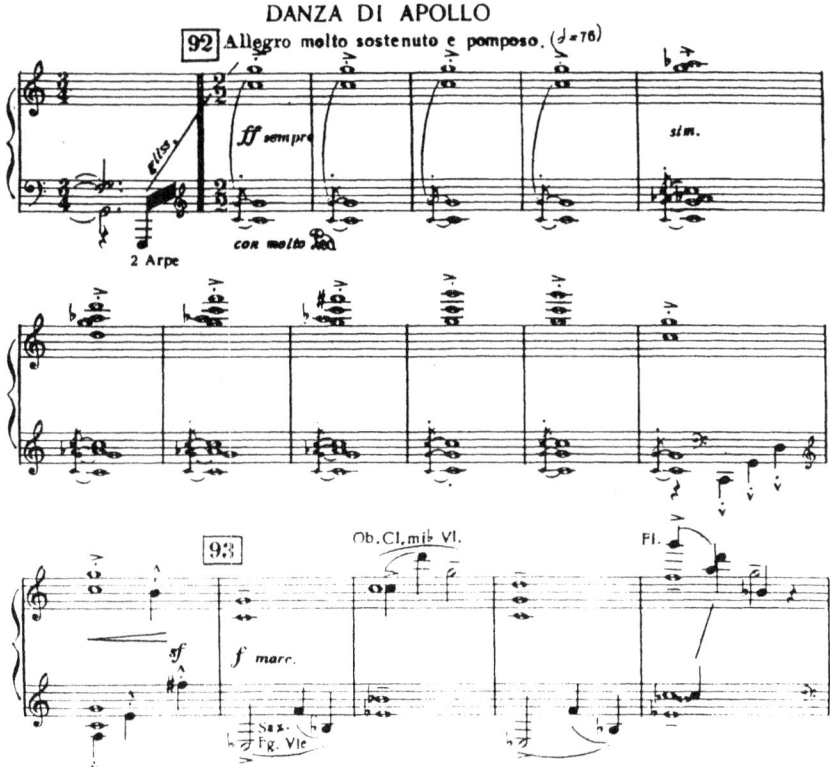

Example 2.10. *Marsia*, fig. 92.

It is clear that within Dallapiccola's oeuvre as a whole, *Marsia*, like the opera *Volo di notte*, is a work of transition. The ballet, however, lacks the unified musical style that *Canti di prigionia* exhibits; although both works combine modal writing with some twelve-tone elements, the two approaches are not brought into a close interrelationship as they are in the choral work. Furthermore, *Marsia* is straightforwardly episodic in formal terms, lacking the overall unity of design that is so apparent in *Canti di prigionia*. Nonetheless, the ballet does point towards the employment of a tone row as a symbolic musical entity, and this was to become a crucial component of Dallapiccola's approach to serialism in the years that followed.

Editing Monteverdi's *Ulisse*

The years of the Second World War represented without doubt the crucial period in Dallapiccola's creative life, but during those years he became involved in a variety of musical activities alongside composition. He helped Guido Gatti in the translation of a group of Busoni's writings on music, he made an edition of Mussorgsky's *Pictures at an Exhibition,* and in 1941–42 he edited Monteverdi's *Il ritorno d'Ulisse in patria* for a performance in Florence. Mario Labroca, then Director of the Maggio Musicale Fiorentino, had asked Dallapiccola to prepare a performing edition of Monteverdi's opera for the Festival in 1942, as part of the celebrations of the three hundredth anniversary of the composer's death. Dallapiccola readily agreed, but he was unfortunately unable to view the manuscript of the work held in the National Library in Vienna, as this had been sent away for safekeeping during the war years. Nonetheless, in preparing what he called a "transcription and reduction for the modern stage" of Monteverdi's opera, Dallapiccola went about the task in a characteristically thorough manner. He was already familiar with the editions of the opera made by Robert Haas (1922), Vincent d'Indy (1925), and Gian Francesco Malipiero (1930), and he was also aware that doubts had begun to surface in musicological circles at that time about the authorship of the work. Dallapiccola had no doubt whatsoever about the work's inherent quality, and he regarded the question of its precise authorship as purely secondary.[19]

Dallapiccola did not attempt to apply the rigors of musicological scholarship in his work on the opera. For him, the primary task was to give the work a form that would be practical within the constraints of the modern opera house and that would make it accessible to the modern opera audience. To achieve these ends, he made drastic cuts to the score in order to tighten its dramatic outlines, reducing the opera from its original length to one closer to a normal modern opera. He made many cuts to the recitative passages, as well as to some scenes he regarded as less essential to the drama (such as the fourth scene of Act 2, between Melanto and Eurimachus), and he also omitted some scenes altogether, such as the Prologue between Human Frailty, Time, Fortune, and Love.[20] All the additional instrumental music he placed at various points in the opera was based upon Monteverdi's original music, but he employed a full modern orchestra.

More modern scholars might frown upon the methods Dallapiccola employed in undertaking this task, and indeed might question his fundamental aim of "modernizing" the opera. The fact remains, however, that the importance of his transcription within the modern performance history of Monteverdi's opera was considerable, and it was heard in Geneva, Brussels, and Milan within a short time after its Florence performances. Between the time of Dallapiccola's edition of the opera and our own day there is, of course, an almost unbridgeable gulf. Since Paul Hindemith produced his edition of Monteverdi's *Orfeo* in 1943 (envisaging a performance on original instruments that Hindemith finally brought to fruition in Vienna in 1954[21]), the modern ear has become increasingly sensitive to the demands of authenticity in performance of earlier music. By the present day, we have become attuned to a quite different sound in performances of Monteverdi's work from that heard by previous generations. Dallapiccola was frank about the constraints he had to work with in making his edition, saying that whereas the musicologist is free of the necessity of adapting the ancient work to modern conditions, the practical musician must of necessity always work within these constraints. This means that the kind of edition he was making was, like the free modern translation of a literary text, inevitably going to last only a short time, to be replaced by other editions expressing the needs and tastes of a later time.[22] What is clear, however, is that Dallapiccola was sensitive to the demands of the drama expressed in Monteverdi's opera, and that this had some effect upon his own treatment of the Ulysses theme some decades later.

The task of preparing a transcription of such an important Baroque opera was a labor of love for Dallapiccola. While he did not go so far as to share all of Malipiero's enthusiasm for unearthing the many buried treasures of earlier Italian music through his editing of Monteverdi and Vivaldi, Dallapiccola nonetheless regarded the music of Monteverdi as a major monument of the Italian musical heritage. The repertory of the opera and madrigal composers of the late sixteenth and early seventeenth centuries was to be a major field of exploration and delight for many musicians in the ensuing decades, inspired above all by Nadia Boulanger's ground-breaking recordings of Monteverdi madrigals issued in 1937. Indeed, the whole modern perception of early Baroque music was to be radically transformed by the editions, studies, and performances that appeared after the end of the war. The "archaeological" rediscovery of Monteverdi's music during the earlier part of the twentieth century, in which Malipiero had played a major role, had an enormous impact upon musicians at that time, and this was felt not least in Italy. The effect can be seen not only in the music of Malipiero himself, but in that of younger composers who came within Malipiero's sphere of influence, such as Dallapiccola, Maderna, Nono, and Berio. For Dallapiccola, the immersion in the world of Baroque opera, with its formal and dramatic conventions and clear relationships between poetic and musical languages, was also something of an antidote to the Romantic and Verismo opera that had earlier dominated the Italian operatic stage.

Sonatina canonica

One important byproduct of editing the Monteverdi opera was that through this work Dallapiccola made contact with the Milan music publisher Suvini Zerboni. At that time, the director of the firm, Paulo Giordani, wished to publish an album of piano music by contemporary Italian composers that would fill the gap left by the foreign publications unavailable in wartime. Dallapiccola therefore began work on a piano piece to be entitled *Studio sul Capriccio no. 14 di Niccolò Paganini* (Study on the Fourteenth Caprice of Paganini), his express wish being to investigate the contrapuntal possibilities that he felt had been somewhat neglected by the Romantic composers who had treated Paganini's Caprices for solo violin to pianistic transformation. He clarified his aim in composing the piece somewhat later:

> It is a little series of trifles on various Paganini Caprices. Just as Liszt created a pianistic equivalent to the technique of Paganini, so within due proportions I wanted to use a contrapuntal equivalent of the same technique, and the whole thing with only the slightest changes to the original harmony. By good fortune, the piece is very difficult (it is dedicated to Scarpini) and there is no danger that it will be played by the girls in the Conservatory.[23]

The reason for the extension the one-movement Study into a full-scale work called *Sonatina canonica in E-flat Major on Caprices by Niccolò Paganini* was revealed by the composer himself. He said that he had seen the single-movement Study in the Anthology Suvini Zerboni had published in 1942, and he made this characteristically wry comment:

> I was shown the published Anthology and I remember my disappointment that the composers, rather than 12 or 24, had become 89! And among these there were music critics who had taken from their bottom drawer pieces written—probably many years earlier—during their student years, musicians whom it would be too much to describe as modest, friends of the editor of the Anthology. I remember that I was indignant, and I wrote to my wife to look in a certain drawer to see if there were still the Caprices that I had worked on in Borgunto. These still existed. And as soon as I got back to Florence I sent the three Caprices which, along with the one I had already worked on, make up the *Sonatina canonica in E-Flat Major*.[24]

This comment, made somewhat later than the events referred to, does not appear to tally with the sequence of events as revealed in the correspondence between the composer and Paolo Giordani of Suvini Zerboni. On 22 July 1942, the composer asked Giordani how many composers were actually contributing to the Album of piano pieces Giordani was attempting to produce, and expressed his great interest in the publication. By 31 October 1943, he had apparently still not received a copy of the one-movement Study, and asked in any case that publication should be held back, as he had by then written a further Study based on Paganini's Caprice No. 20 (that is to say, the piece that eventually formed the first movement of the *Sonatina canonica*). He said this one was "more interesting than the first." By 17 November 1943, he said he had completed the whole of the *Sonatina canonica*, and gives some details of the work, revealing that it was indeed the work eventually published under that name. Finally, on 10 August 1945, some two years after the completion of the *Sonatina canonica*, he asked Giordani whatever became of the original plan for an Anthology of pieces for piano by various composers.[25] Perhaps the development of the one-movement Study into the eventual *Sonatina canonica* might with some justification be likened to that of Beethoven's contribution to Diabelli's publication into the full flowering of the Diabelli Variations!

The Caprices of Paganini on which the four movements of the *Sonatina canonica* are based are:

1: *Allegro comodo—Allegro misurato* from Caprices 13 and 20.
2: *Largo* from Caprice 19.
3: *Andante sostenuto* from Caprice 11.
4: *Alla marcia; moderato* from Caprices 14, 9, and 17.

In the *Sonatina canonica*, Dallapiccola created a work which, despite its thematic basis in music from an earlier musical age, is far removed from the neoclassical aesthetic so beloved of many Italian composers at that time. The work is, rather, imbued with the spirit of Busoni's attempts, in his colorful pianistic reworkings of earlier music, to undertake "research" into the compositional possibilities of the original material, to explore the material rather than simply evoke some of its more obvious characteristics.

Dallapiccola also demonstrates in this piece an awareness of the possibilities of the modern piano for the creation of new sounds, such as Mussorgsky, Debussy, Ravel, and Bartók had explored, and this element combines with the canonic and polyphonic writing Dallapiccola had inherited from Busoni. By this time, such polyphonic writing had become a characteristic feature of Dallapiccola's music, as we have already observed in *Inni* for three pianos, composed some eight years earlier. Dallapiccola composed only three works for solo piano, despite his own gifts as a pianist: apart from *Sonatina canonica*, only *Quaderno musicale di Annalibera* in 1952, and a piano version of parts of the music of the ballet Marsia in *Tre episodi dal balletto "Marsia"* that he made in 1949.[26] His awareness of the timbral possibilities of the piano is clearly shown in all these works, and is also evident in the comments he made in the preface to his edition of the *Pictures at an Exhibition* of Mussorgsky:

The "musical" value of this work has never been denied . . . but its pianistic value has often been denied, and it is this above all, which is still misunderstood in part, that I hope will be brought to the fore in the edition I have made. I am convinced that it is precisely the sound qualities, the daring, and the novelty of the work that represent elements of such importance as to make it worthy of its own chapter in the history of the piano. When before now had one heard sounds produced like those in Gnomus or Bydlo? A scene like Catacombs opened up many new roads, and however impenetrable it might seem at first sight, precisely because of the extreme novelty of its "appearance", nowadays it is an unrivalled model of "pianistic sonority."[27]

Sonatina canonica undoubtedly exhibits in many of its pages Dallapiccola's acute sensitivity to the sound of the piano, but on the other hand it gives little indication that he had by this point begun to immerse himself in the music of the Viennese twelve-tone composers. The element of contrapuntal exploration we referred to is certainly present right from the start of the first movement, as Dallapiccola expands in relaxed manner upon the rather monochrome original theme from Paganini (Example 2.11 (a) and (b)).

Example 2.11 (a). *Sonatina canonica*. I, mm. 1–16.

Example 2.11 (b). Paganini. Capriccio No. 20, mm. 1–9.

This opening movement is in ternary form, with the outer and inner sections based upon corresponding sections in Paganini's twentieth Caprice, here transposed from D to E-flat major. This transposition was doubtless made in order to provide a tonal balance to the fourth movement of the *Sonatina canonica* that he had already composed, while in the inner movements he is able to show contrasting tonal centers, in keeping with the "Sonatina" component in the title of the piece. In the opening section, he retains Paganini's 6/8 meter in the upper part, while the lower part is set out in 3/4, and, most significantly, he adds a middle voice to the melody-and-drone form in which Paganini's original had been cast. This is in 6/4 meter, and consists of a canon by augmentation of the upper melody, but without its attendant octave displacements. In this way, Dallapiccola creates a contrapuntal texture in three layers, of the greatest melodic and rhythmic contradistinction.

The octave displacements in the upper part, besides adding a constantly changing coloration to the melody, also suggest a more angular contour of leaping sevenths, and again this element is not present in Paganini's original. From measure 9 the superimposition of the first and the second phrases of the given original adds a further layer to the contrapuntal texture of the passage. At the same time, the parallel sixths Paganini had introduced in the second statement of the theme are echoed in the organum-like fourths *quasi suoni armonici* of the upper melody. This later changes to sixths (m. 17) and ninths (m. 21), as though to enrich the harmonic resonance of the latter part of this passage. A pedal tone sustained throughout by gentle reiterations gently underpins the whole contrapuntal texture, but whereas Paganini had moved from the pedal-tone at cadential points, Dallapiccola retains the pedal on E flat throughout. The middle section of the movement also introduces a left-hand pattern that takes some elements from the figurations of the thirteenth Caprice. The composer asks that in this central section of the work, the pianist should play roughly (*ruvido*), in contrast to the outer sections of the movement, but even here he cannot resist the temptations of canonic writing. From measure 9, the two hands exchange materials for the second eight-measure phrase, treated as invertible counterpoint together with the necessary minor adjustments to the harmony. When the opening section of the movement returns, it is further enriched in its colorations by the enlargement of the middle part to parallel thirds.

The second movement of the work, acting as a kind of scherzo within the Sonatina structure, is built around Paganini's nineteenth Caprice, omitting the middle section of the original. This opens and closes with a largo passage in which Dallapiccola has considerably widened the tonal implications of Paganini's theme. In its original form it had been no more than a simple arpeggio gesture, but by shifting the arpeggio up a half step, and by adding a scintillating array of trills and *acciaccature*, Dallapiccola arrives at the dominant of the principal key of E-flat major only at the very last moment (Example 2.12 (a) and (b)).

Example 2.12 (a). *Sonatina canonica*. II, mm. 1–6.

Example 2.12 (b). Paganini. Capriccio No. 19, mm. 1–4.

The main section of the movement, marked *vivacissimo*, once again develops Paganini's original by canonic expansion, with imitations between the two hands maintained throughout the passage. Here, the delicacy of Paganini's virtuoso violin writing is reflected in Dallapiccola's enlargement of the texture to cover the whole upper range of the piano keyboard (Example 2.13).

Example 2.13. *Sonatina canonica.* II, mm. 7–12.

The third movement is the heart of the work in terms of contrapuntal elaboration of the original material. Dallapiccola himself described it as a "crab canon in which even the trills and ornaments are crabbed."[28] The entire movement is based upon the first eight measures of Paganini's eleventh Caprice, repeated three times in the course of the piece and gradually ascending through the various registers of the piano. The three sections of the movement are distinguished by the contrapuntal treatment of the material within them: in the first, a simple canonic imitation between two bass voices of the first four measures of the theme (mm. 1–4); in the second, a fuller statement of Paganini's original theme (mm. 5–12), followed by the crab canon to which the composer referred (mm. 13–20); and finally another simple canon of the opening measures of the theme, suggesting a modulation to F major and coming to rest on its dominant (mm. 21–26) (Example 2.14).

Example 2.14. *Sonatina canonica.* III, entire movement.

Example 2.14. *Continued.*

Dallapiccola's desire to explore to the full the contrapuntal possibilities of the thematic material in the central portion of this movement gives rise to a passage in which canonic intricacies take precedence over harmonic considerations. This creates harmonic and textural complexities that greatly tax the pianist's skill in the articulation of the contrapuntal strands.

As noted earlier, the final movement of the *Sonatina canonica* was the first to be composed, originally planned as a single-movement "Paganini Study" with, at least in part, a didactic intention for pianists. We certainly do not find here any great density of contrapunal elaboration, and there is indeed something of a carnival gaiety and wit that come from the straightforward rhythmic impulse of the movement. Indeed, its rhythmic insistency and pianistic verve perhaps bring Schumann to mind. The movement is built around Paganini's fourteenth Caprice, onto which Dallapiccola superimposes a canon at the octave, varying it only in rhythmic spacing of the two canonic voices (beginning at 2/4, but becoming at 1/4 in some later passages). In two sections of the movement, Dallapiccola briefly introduces "foreign" material into the texture: in mm. 50–54, a tiny phrase, whose origins lie in Paganini's ninth Caprice ("La caccia"), a snatch of hunting horn call which briefly contributes to the overall simple rhythmic flow; and in the last four measures a similar snatch from the seventeenth Caprice. There would appear to be no particular reason why these two very brief moments from other Caprices are introduced here, beyond the possibility of a kind of residual memory of the other Caprices that was in Dallapiccola's mind while he was composing the work, and no doubt also to enhance the playful character of the movement.

Should we view the *Sonatina canonica* as another example of Dallapiccola's activities as an editor or transcriber of older music, that is to say as a further extension of the kind of work he had just undertaken on Monteverdi's *Il ritorno d'Ulisse in patria*? Or should we view it as an essential part of his fully creative activity, as an important final stepping stone on the path to the *Liriche greche,* which he had just at that moment begun to compose? The truth must surely lie in both; with Dallapiccola, as with so many Italian composers of the twentieth century (Gian Francesco Malipiero, Bruno Maderna, and Luciano Berio come most readily come to mind), editing and transcribing older, and especially Italian, music was an essential element in their creative activities. Certainly no study of Dallapiccola's music could ignore these "re-creative" activities, which were an essential part of his musical personality. The *Sonatina canonica* may be said to occupy a position in Dallapiccola's music rather similar to that occupied in Stravinsky's work by the reworking of Bach's Organ Variations on the Chorale *Vom Himmel hoch da komm'ich her.* Both are works that reveal each composer's musical "researching" of canonic and contrapuntal techniques, and both also acted as a springboard from which the composers could launch themselves towards more fully original composition. When, in a later part of this study, we come to examine the two works in which Dallapiccola made use of the music of his Istrian predecessor Giuseppe Tartini, other facets of the composer's "re-creative creativity" will equally be revealed.

Encounter with Webern

On 9 March 1942, during a train journey Dallapiccola made from Hungary to Italy when returning from a concert tour, he had to spend some hours in Vienna, where he was able to meet Anton Webern at the house of Alfred Schlee, Director of Universal Edition. This was the only occasion on which the two composers met; Dallapiccola recorded his impressions in his diary:

A mystic, a short man, who talks with some inflection of Austrian dialect: kind, but capable of a burst of anger, cordial to the point of treating me like an equal. . . .

As Webern had not witnessed the immense success of *Das Augenlicht* in London, I tell him about the great impression it made upon me. And Webern immediately asks "Were you impressed by the sound also?" (The sound. I understood it correctly.) While discussing problems of orchestral sonorities, the refined researcher (history won't ignore his enormous contribution to the formation of the new language) states, "A chord of three trumpets or four horns is by now unimaginable to me."

Incidentally, the name of Kurt Weill is mentioned. And Webern suddenly explodes. He points his finger towards me (but I had not been the one who pronounced the name of a composer he dislikes!) "What do you find of our great Middle European tradition in such a composer? . . . that tradition which includes the names (and here he starts to enumerate them on his fingers) of Schubert, Brahms, Wolf, Mahler, Schoenberg, Berg, and myself?"

I was embarrassed. I do not say that an answer would not be possible; but what confounds me most is that Webern used the term "tradition," a term which, knowing the Variations, Opus 21, the cantata *Das Augenlicht,* and, even through a single hearing, the concerto, Opus 24, I supposed had been eliminated from Webern's vocabulary. Not only that. But that he should consider himself as an heir to that tradition; that he should believe in the continuity of language. . . . And finally that what separated him from Kurt Weill should not be a question of aesthetics and of taste, but rather the fact that Kurt Weill had refused the Middle European tradition.[29]

Dallapiccola's meeting with Webern was of necessity brief, and fate prevented the two composers from furthering the friendship they forged on this occasion. This can only be regretted, since it was evident that they shared some common ground in their approach to music. Dallapiccola had first become acquainted with Webern's music just seven years earlier, and the very gradual and painstaking study of the few available scores that he had undertaken has been discussed earlier. But despite the brevity of this encounter, made under strange circumstances during wartime, it is clear that the real influence of the elder composer upon the music of his younger colleague can be dated from precisely this moment. This influence began to appear in the *Liriche greche,* which Dallapiccola was just then beginning to pen, and indeed, from this point on, the figure of Webern was to remain an almost constant presence in Dallapiccola's music. The two would remain briefly in contact by letter: Dallapiccola sent Webern some of his own scores, and received a reply in which Webern remarked upon a certain affinity of the two composers despite differences in their musical style. It is perhaps curious to speculate how much more apposite this reply of Webern might have been had he written it just a few years later, by the time that Dallapiccola had composed the *Liriche greche*:

> I was most delighted to receive your friendly letter! I would have liked to reply by return post, but I had to await the arrival of your scores. They have now arrived, and I set to studying them without delay. Now I must tell you: be assured that from the moment when we first met, it was very clear to me what world was opening up. Even if your style is very different from mine, our thinking moves in areas that I think are close to one another. And it is certain that in this sense we are both travelling on the same path.[30]

The period now under consideration, the years between the completion of *Volo di notte* in 1938 and that of the *Liriche greche* in 1945, represents a turning point in Dallapiccola's creative life. It is therefore essential to retain a clear grasp of the different strands of his activity at that time, since only in this way will the overall unity of the directions he was then taking become clear. Some of his works from the earlier part of this period, such as *Sonatina canonica* and the *Piccolo concerto per Muriel Couvreux*, might at first glance be viewed as representing a stylistic retrenchment on the part of the composer, as a distinct move away from the chromatic and proto-serial writing that had begun to appear in *Tre laudi,* in *Volo di notte,* and, above all, in *Canti di prigionia*. If this were the case, the directions in which Dallapiccola was going at that time might appear puzzling. However, it is important to consider the works he wrote during the earlier war years as a whole, and in relation to the context, both musically and historically, in which they appeared.

The composition of *Canti di prigionia* overlapped that of both the more lightweight *Piccolo concerto per Muriel Couvreux* and the *Sonatina canonica,* with its thematic basis in earlier music. However, this latter work immediately preceded the creation of the much more adventurous *Liriche greche,* and here Dallapiccola began to absorb the influence of Webern. In this way, the decisive step forward into wholly new and unexplored territory that Dallapiccola would take in the postwar period was preceded by a moment of creative reflection, by the exploration of contrapuntal territory within a modal language in the *Sonatina canonica*. In any case, quite beyond this creative reflection, it was inevitable that the composer, faced with the harsh realities of musical life during wartime, should find himself occupying more than one musical world at the same time—one more public and the other more personal, one responding to commissions, the other to inner compulsion. What is more remarkable is the extent to which the varying languages of expression found in Dallapiccola's music from this period do overlap, most notably in the overriding concern with canonic and contrapuntal flair and exuberance which every single work exhibits.

On only two occasions in his life, in the *Piccolo concerto per Muriel Couvreux* and the *Sonatina canonica,* both created during the war years, did the composer create works which, at least to judge from their titles, would appear to be cast as traditional sonatas, but in neither case does the piece fit comfortably into such a form. For Dallapiccola, composition based upon the thematic and harmonic principles underlying the developmental sonata structures of Classical and Romantic music held no attraction. Instead, it was the polyphonic principle, with its imitative, contrapuntal forms and symmetrical structures, which was always the basis of his musical thinking. In other words, Dallapiccola was drawn from the start towards the musical forms of the Renaissance and Baroque, and in this he differed from any of the Viennese serialists whose music had otherwise had such an influence upon him. Nowhere in Dallapiccola's music do we find a single work that approaches the principles of a developmental sonata structure, and at no point did he contemplate the composition of a symphony. Such avoidance of the classical forms is only partially explained by his aversion to the neoclassicism that so dominated Italian music between the two world wars. Dallapiccola had an affinity of temperament with composers of the Renaissance and Baroque periods that he did not have with composers of the Classical or Romantic periods. In the light of this, the *Sonatina canonica* would appear to be a work only accidentally given the title "Sonatina," and indeed we might even be tempted to ask why the composer did not call the work a Suite. The reason must lie in his awareness of the example provided by his revered predecessor Ferruccio Busoni, whose six Sonatinas, composed between 1910 and 1920, equally avoid the sonata idea, returning to the original sense of the term Sonatina as a small piece of purely instrumental music of an exploratory kind.

Liriche greche

The contrapuntal exuberance of *Sonatina canonica* is also evident in the *Liriche greche* (Greek Poems), a set of thirteen short pieces in three groups based upon poems originally by Sappho, Alcaeus, and Anacreon: *Cinque frammenti di Saffo* (Five Sappho Fragments), 1942–43; *Sex carmina Alcaei* (Six Songs of Alcaeus), 1943; and *Due liriche di Anacreonte* (Two Poems of Anacreon), 1945. In these compositions, all of an engaging personality and attractiveness, the most important developments of Dallapiccola's art during the war years are to be found. Here for the first time he employed the techniques of twelve-tone composition in a consistent manner, though not yet basing a whole composition on a single row, and combined these techniques with the contrapuntal procedures that had earlier become a hallmark of his style.

It is not coincidental that Dallapiccola took the texts for these three compositions from Salvatore Quasimodo's collection of poetic reworkings of ancient Greek poetry published in 1940 under the title *Lirici greci* (Greek Lyrics). These reworkings (Quasimodo adapted the original Greek texts with too much licence for us to call them simply "translations") marked a decisive turning point in Quasimodo's poetry, just as their musical setting was to mark a decisive turning point in Dallapiccola's music. Quasimodo was to remark some years later in his "Discourse on Poetry"[31] that poetry is often subject to profound change during and immediately after a period of war, and the directness of expression that we find in these Greek lyrics represented a change from the quintessentially "hermetic" voice to be found in much of his earlier poetry. The hermetic movement in Italian poetry had been of particular importance in Florence during the 1920s and 1930s, and one of the most important media through which the movement began to be heard was the magazine *Solaria*, the journal which, as we noted earlier, had introduced Dallapiccola and others to many contemporary trends in literature. The movement was far from being programmatic, with clearly defined aims and characteristics, as futurism had been somewhat earlier.[32] The poetry of Salvatore Quasimodo, Eugenio Montale, and Giuseppe Ungaretti was certainly often difficult, and at times it could be enclosed within a complex self-absorption, but by the late 1930s the poets associated with hermeticism were strongly anti-fascist, and the interior expression in their poetry acted as an antidote to the vociferous slogan chanting with which they were surrounded at that time.

Dallapiccola had never previously engaged with contemporary Italian poetry. During his student years, he had made some settings of dialect poetry, and on one occasion he had set a text of Gabriele D'Annunzio (in *La canzone del Quarnaro* of 1930), but the work of the most important Italian poets had not previously appeared in his work. Many composers from the earlier part of the twentieth century had found inspiration, even a model for change, in the poetry of their contemporaries and immediate forebears: Debussy in the poetry of Paul Verlaine, Charles Baudelaire, and Stéphane Mallarmé; Schoenberg in Albert Giraud and Marie Pappenheim; Berg in Peter Altenberg; and Webern in Hildegard Jone. The case of Dallapiccola's poetic inspiration is one in which a particular relationship of contemporary poetry and music is to be found. With his *Lirici greci*, Quasimodo had initiated a new phase in his poetry, creating what is generally regarded as one of his masterpieces. This employs at times the elements to be found in his earlier poetry, but expressed now in a language of the greatest possible clarity and simplicity, with every word carrying the maximum expressive content. These poetic qualities are paralleled to a remarkable extent in Dallapiccola's settings, with an emphasis upon the utmost clarity of melody, harmony, and formal structure. The canonic forms we see employed here, rather than overwhelming the poetic expression, give it a great incisiveness. The tone painting of the musical setting is subtle and gentle, often a mere suggestion, but the composer goes to great pains to avoid the musical impressionism to which he might so easily have been led by the poetic allure of Quasimodo's texts.

Quasimodo's espousal of a strongly anti-fascist stance (for a time he was a member of the Communist Party) no doubt contributed to the attraction Dallapiccola felt towards this poetic model, and in this sense, if in no other, the *Liriche greche* might almost be regarded as another example of Dallapiccola's "protest music." The work's limpid, highly personal, occasionally erotic poetic expressions are in all senses far removed from the prevailing fervors of the Italian fascist state. Without a doubt, there is also a certain element of escapism in Dallapiccola's choice of this poetic model during that period, but it is important to stress that the work was composed between Dallapiccola's most heartfelt protest works, *Canti di prigionia* and *Il prigioniero*. It therefore provided a necessary withdrawal into a more interior world during that turbulent and, for the composer and his Jewish wife, particularly dangerous period.

Therefore, far from simply taking a convenient poetic text that had recently been published in Italy, Dallapiccola deliberately embodied an artistic philosophy in his selection of poetry. He always chose the texts he set to music with great care, and was always fully aware of the implications of his selection: he spoke on one occasion of how "it is not always we who choose our texts; but at times it is the texts themselves which, coming to meet us, choose *us*."[33] The composer returned on several occasions to the poetic world of classical literature, and *Liriche greche* and the opera *Ulisse* represent the most important of these occasions. In these two works, one a setting of some of the greatest lyric poetry of ancient Greece, the other a version of its most powerful myth, are to be found some of the most expressive and profound pages Dallapiccola wrote. The fact that Dallapiccola's father, for whom he had the greatest admiration, had been a teacher of classical languages and literature is an important influence here, but beyond this, Dallapiccola himself conceived his ideals as essentially part of the humanist tradition, ideals that were firmly rooted in the most ancient expressions of the human spirit.

Despite its division into three sets, *Liriche greche* forms a unified whole with an overall structure leading from simplicity towards complexity: from an interior to an exterior landscape, from the delicate and highly personal poetry of Sappho, through Anacreon's adoration of Eros, to the idyllic pastoral scenes and nature imagery of Alcaeus. The composer expressly suggested that the whole cycle should be performed in this sequence: Sappho–Anacreon–Alcaeus, and not in the order of composition. The song cycle represents one of the most important steps in the gradual evolution of Dallapiccola's musical language: he spoke of taking a "rational decision" in favor of twelve-tone technique in the work. No longer do we find twelve-tone elements employed simply as musical "emblems," nor is the twelve-tone writing any longer a means of providing a certain tension when set against diatonic-modal writing. Now, it is a thoroughgoing technique through which the composer is able to manipulate melodic and harmonic entities in order to give free rein to his imagination in the realization of the poetic texts.

In *Cinque frammenti di Saffo,* twelve-tone techniques are used consistently for the first time in the composer's work, but with different rows, sometimes more than one, in each lyric. It is possible to trace an increasing sophistication and rationality of musical design through the constituent parts of *Liriche greche,* in terms of both the canonic and the twelve-tone techniques employed. In *Cinque frammenti di Saffo,* the first and fifth songs of the set contain many canons, the second and fourth none, while the central third lyric is a constructed as a palindrome. *Due liriche di Anacreonte* is subtitled "canons and variations." *Sex carmina Alcaei* is formed completely of varieties of canon in each of its movements. The confidence and sophistication of Dallapiccola's employment of the techniques of twelve-tone composition is evident in all three pieces, culminating in the *Sex carmina Alcaei,* the only part of the *Liriche greche* that is unified through the use of a single row for the whole piece.

The individuality of Dallapiccola's way of adopting the twelve-tone principle and the distance of his approach from the Viennese models, are immediately clear in *Cinque frammenti di Saffo.* In the first song, the composer's portrayal of the sunset glow of Sappho's poem, with its image of the evening star reuniting what the dawn had scattered, and with beasts and humans returning home as night falls, is made with the simplest of elements. In the opening measures, an instrumental ritornello (which will reappear unchanged in mm. 8–9 and again at the conclusion in mm. 17–21) incorporates a row in which open fifths predominate. The vocal line introduces a further row, dominated by minor thirds and incorporating simple repetitions. This prime row is immediately followed here by its retrograde inversion: such a symmetrical exposition had appeared in the opening measures of *Tre laudi* (in that case, as P and R forms of the row), and the symmetrical exposition of row-forms was to become a feature of several later compositions of Dallapiccola (Example 2.15).

Example 2.15. *Cinque frammenti di Saffo*. I, mm. 1–7.

The instrumental accompaniment of this first Sappho fragment is formed almost exclusively from canonic imitations of the vocal line in the upper wind instruments (voice and flute in mm. 3–7, voice and oboe in mm. 9–13, voice and clarinets in mm. 13–15). The voice, with its clear-cut enunciation of the text, is the central focus of the expression of this very simple poem. At the same time, the identity of vocal and instrumental parts by means of canonic imitations also suggests a musical metaphor for the identification of the human and natural worlds that the poem itself encapsulates: "Evening star, you bring back all that the bright dawn had scattered. You bring back the sheep, you bring back the goats, you bring back the child to his mother."

Dallapiccola has made the canonic aspect of this song, in which the instrumental echoing of melodic phrases between the vocal line and the instrumental parts are identifiable to even the least practiced ear, into an essential aspect of its expressivity. Already in this, his first twelve-tone composition, the composer has a remarkably clear conception of the possibilities of serialism as a means of heightening both the melodic expressivity of the piece and the fusion of poem and musical setting. The dodecaphonic and canonic aspects of the piece are inextricably mingled, seeming to arise from the same impulse to create an intimate unity in the polyphonic web that parallels the poetic text. Such a clarity of vision is indeed truly remarkable: it might seem to have come from the pen of a composer long versed in the dodecaphonic technique, rather than one who is here essaying it for the first time. On a broader level, the whole of *Cinque frammenti di Saffo* is held together by a simple device. In the final song, a setting of a single poetic phrase (". . . long have I spoken in dreams with Aphrodite"), the row that had been presented in vertical form in the instrumental ritornello at the opening of the first song, appears now in melodic guise, and with pedal harmonies on open fifths dominating the piece.

This predominance of horizontal and contrapuntal expressions of the row material in the first Sappho fragment is not always maintained in the subsequent songs of the set. In the fourth song, for example, Dallapiccola employs two rows, one of which is divided into three-tone segments in order to provide a recurring sequence of quasi-tonal triads, while the second row is treated in more linear fashion (Example 2.16).[34]

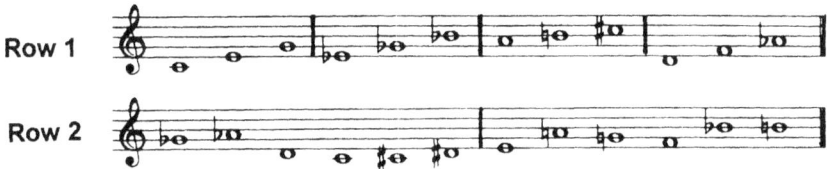

Example 2.16. *Cinque frammenti di Saffo*. IV, rows.

The vocal line of the piece is derived entirely from the first "triadic" row, creating a correspondence between the vocal line and its instrumental accompaniment. In this way, Dallapiccola finds a perfect expression of Quasimodo's tender and atmospheric text, with its evocation of graceful nocturnal dancing:

The full moon had risen
when they halted beside the altar:
and the Cretan women danced
gracefully, with lightest tread,
carefree around the altar,
on the soft and fresh-grown grass.

As the poet describes the graceful dancing of the Cretan women, the music gently suggests the dance steps, with the lightest eighth-note figurations beginning to appear in the instrumental accompaniment, in which both rows are now clearly discernible (Example 2.17).

Example 2.17. *Cinque frammenti di Saffo.* IV, mm. 68–74.

These figurations gradually intensify, only to fade away once more in the final measures, and the music comes to rest on a chord ambiguously suggesting both a major and a minor harmony by means of a clarinet trill.

Due liriche di Anacreonte, the last of the *Liriche greche* to be composed, but the work which Dallapiccola suggested should be placed centrally in a complete performance of the work, was the subject of an important note by the composer himself:

> It is possible to see how, in this first adoption of "serialism," I had by no means excluded certain tonal reminiscences (and this was the case even in the formation of the series), nor had I yet eliminated octave relationships or false relations of octaves: that would come later. And at the same time one can see how I had by no means abandoned what for centuries has been called "singability" [*cantabilità*], a quality which, however important might be the transformations it has undergone over the years, I still do not abandon nowadays. . . .

The *Due liriche di Anacreonte* follow one other without a break and carry the subtitles "Canons" for the first and "Variations" for the second. In the first, after a nine-measure introduction, there follow three canons, separated by short intermezzi, the canons in two, three, and four parts respectively. The overall character of the piece maintains a languid and nostalgic atmosphere. The Variations, of a biting and dramatic character, exhibit sudden contrasts of dynamics and accentuation.[35]

In *Due liriche di Anacreonte*, the serial and thematic aspects of the work are brought into the closest possible relationship. The canonic construction is explicitly indicated in the score, with the voice and accompanying instrumental group (clarinets in A and E flat, viola, and piano) constantly exchanging points of imitation, and the row is set out in almost emblematic manner in the nine-measure introduction (Example 2.18).

Example 2.18. *Due liriche di Anacreonte*, mm. 1–7.

The languid character of this first part of the piece, as the composer himself described it, is achieved in the same manner as in the first Sappho fragment, by a close identification of voice and instruments. Three distinct canons (mm. 9–16, 17–24, and 28–34) are separated by brief interludes, and the reliance of the instrumental lines on the row is evident. In contrast, the decisive character of the Variations that form the second Anacreon setting is emphasized right from the start in the instrumental chords. The vocal line here makes use of a "foreign" row, that which had made its appearance in the last of the *Cinque frammenti di Saffo* (Example 2.19).

Example 2.19. *Due liriche di Anacreonte*, mm. 37–44.

Dallapiccola makes this connecting thread between the two sets of songs explicit at a later point in the work, indicating in the score that the piano part is here quoting from the final Sappho setting in its clearest and most audible form as open fifths (mm. 66–67).

The function of the various tone rows that appear in the *Liriche Greche* is most often thematic, and this can be seen in *Sex carmina Alcaei* that concludes the cycle. Dallapiccola dedicated the piece to Webern on his sixtieth birthday (3 December 1943), and the piece was composed in the months immediately following Dallapiccola's meeting with Webern in March 1942. Despite this, many of the most important characteristics of the piece reveal the distance still separating Dallapiccola's approach from that of Webern. It is true that each of its component movements is quite brief, and equally true that both the contrapuntal intricacies and the clarity of instrumental writing might suggest the influence of Webern. But these had already been characteristics of Dallapiccola's work for many years, and in any case the melodic outlines are those of a very Italian *cantabilità*. The theme set out at the start in the solo soprano's melodic line is based on prime and retrograde forms of the row, the latter raised a half step. This is not only precisely the same manner in which the composer had set out the mirroring serial forms in the "Stars" theme of the *Tre laudi* a few years earlier, but is also the form in which the greatest degree of melodic symmetry may be both seen and indeed heard (Example 2.20).

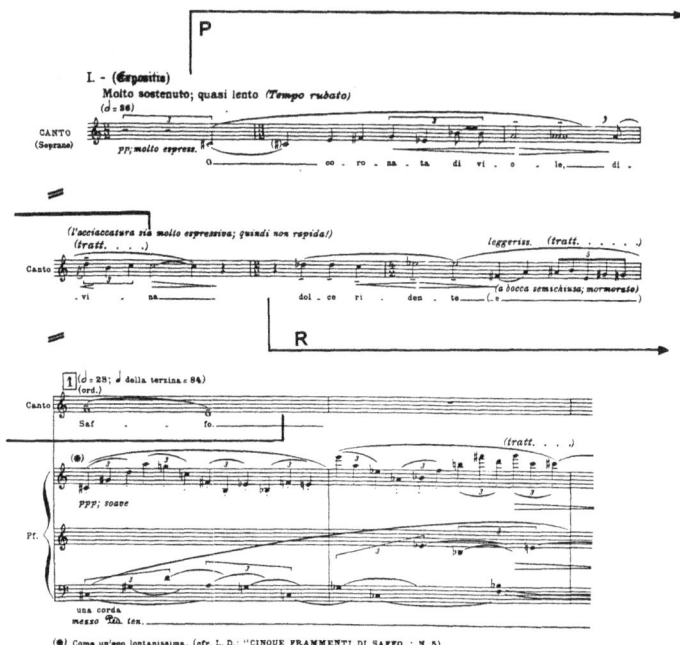

Example 2.20. *Sex carmina Alcaei*. I, opening measures.

The initial row immediately invokes a further echo in the piano part of the row with which *Cinque frammenti di Saffo* had begun, and this clearly audible reminiscence, as Alcaeus speaks of the "sweet, smiling, divine Sappho," serves to underline the essential unity of the *Liriche greche* cycle as a whole.

Canonic treatment of the musical material in *Sex carmina Alcaei* makes this by far the most complex group of the work from the contrapuntal point of view, but on the other hand, this also represents the simplest part of the *Liriche greche* with regard to its serial constructions. It employs a single row, given right at the start in its basic forms and running as a constant thread throughout all the various sections of the piece. The contrapuntal forms employed in the piece are set out in the titles of each section:

1: Expositio
2: Canon perpetuus
3: Canones diversi
4: Canon contrario motu
5: Canon duplex contrario motu
6: Conclusio

The composer's extraordinary insistence upon the greatest contrapuntal elaboration in this eight-minute piece, whose Latin titles serve to emphasize its connection with Bach's *Musical Offering,* reaches a climax in the fourth song of the group. The text here is a simple, direct expression of a sensual image: "But our necks are encircled with intertwined rings of dill, and sweetly perfumed oils are poured on our breasts." Dallapiccola has, in a sense, created here a musical parallel to the hermetic ideal of *poesia pura,* to which Quasimodo had aspired in these free translations. The voice begins with an exposition of the principal theme, followed immediately by an instrumental elaboration of this theme as a canon in contrary motion between flute and oboe. Thus the expression of the text here is allowed, as it were, to flow over into the canonic instrumental lines (marked to be played *quasi parlando*), while the bassoon and horn—and later the upper strings—sustain a pedal B flat throughout the song. The voice grasps hold of the pedal B flat ("murmured") from the central line of the text, and reverts to the principal theme in its original form (prime and retrograde) only for the final decaying phrases. In this way, the contrapuntal writing becomes not merely a means through which the composer has set the text, but indeed an expressive extension of the text: the instrumental parts do not simply accompany, but are themselves a part of the music's interpretation of the poetic images (Example 2.21).

Example 2.21. *Sex carmina Alcaei*. IV, opening measures.

The *Sonatina canonica* and *Liriche greche* both present a summation of Dallapiccola's formidable powers as a contrapuntist, and in this respect few other composers of the twentieth century can be compared with him. But at the same time it should not be forgotten that, in common with his great Leipzig mentor in an earlier age, he found in the farthest reaches of contrapuntal complexity not only an arena for virtuosity, but also an arena for the joyful, *spiritoso* employment of canonic devices. This manner of presenting the contrapuntal labyrinth almost playfully to the attentive listener is a characteristic that Dallapiccola shares with Joseph Haydn, that most genial of contrapuntists. But beyond this formal aspect, which gives to his work an almost timeless resonance, the two compositions also represent the contemporary moment. Dallapiccola's gradual approach to the serialism of the Viennese composers, a lonely voyage of exploration of strange territory that he had been undertaking by absorbing elements of the Viennese composers' musical language into his own more Mediterranean melodic idiom, here reaches a decisive point.

Both Webern and Dallapiccola, of course, shared this intense and all-pervading love of contrapuntal writing, and it could be said that in the *Sonatina canonica* Dallapiccola had tested the ground in preparation for the more personal, more intimate expression he would make in the *Liriche greche*. No composer could successfully attempt to imitate the very personal style shown in these Greek lyrics, but in the years immediately following the end of the war, they became a primary source of study for the younger generation of composers, particularly, but by no means exclusively, in Italy. None felt the influence of this work more than Luigi Nono, whose first contact with Dallapiccola was prompted by his enormous admiration for the *Liriche greche*. Nono's earliest works, particularly the settings of Federico Garcìa Lorca that he composed in the *Epitaffio* of 1952–53, would have been unimaginable without the example and the inspiration of the *Liriche greche* that he had studied assiduously. Dallapiccola's form of serialism was, however, largely sidestepped by the younger generation of Italian composers as they approached the formal rigors of the "Darmstadt generation." Bruno Maderna's description of Dallapiccola's form of serialism as a "rock-crystal"[36] was both an expression of admiration for the older composer and a way of distancing himself from it. Nonetheless, Dallapiccola himself, in the years that followed the composition of the *Liriche greche*, was to pursue his path with remarkable consistency. In his second opera, *Il prigioniero*, he was to create the most important Italian operatic masterpiece of the postwar period.

III

Towards the Light of Freedom: 1945–1948

The composition of *Liriche greche* continued during the later war years, and by October 1943, when the almost year-long occupation of Florence by German forces began, Dallapiccola had already set the translations of Sappho and Alcaeus. At that crucial moment in the war, when the people of Florence had to endure the misery and degradation of foreign occupation, the composer was faced with a double threat, from the dangers of the war, and from the anti-semitism then sweeping Italy and threatening the security of his Jewish wife. For a time, Dallapiccola considered emigrating to Switzerland, where he had many friends and had frequently given concerts, but he decided instead that he and his wife Laura would take refuge in various places in Florence and Fiesole. It was while he was there, hiding from the authorities and in constant threat of betrayal, that he began work on the libretto of his second opera *Il prigioniero* (The Prisoner): he read the complete libretto through to a group of close friends in Fiesole at Christmas 1943. The opera was eventually completed in 1948 and given its first performance at the end of 1949, and together with the *Liriche greche,* the work represented Dallapiccola's most important creative activity during the later war years.

As the hostilities in Europe came to their conclusion, however, new creative projects began to appear. The immediate postwar period in Italy was a difficult one for musicians. Although Italy had not suffered the large-scale destruction of infrastructure experienced in Germany during the same period, there were nonetheless serious problems to be overcome, and in an article Dallapiccola wrote for a music journal during this period, he vividly described some of the difficulties he had encountered:

> Italian musicians lack everything: composers lack manuscript paper, violinists and cellists lack strings, and it is no wonder that for years harpists have had to set up their instruments with any old bits and pieces. Pianists and composers have to go to absurd lengths to hire an upright piano, first-class young instrumentalists have to get experience "in the abstract," or else by grasping any heaven-sent opportunity to make use

of a Steinway. If I am not mistaken, there are just two (and I mean two!) hammer xylophones in Italy, one in La Scala and the other in the Maggio Musicale Fiorentino, while other orchestras carry on using the hopeless keyboard xylophone, the only one in the country. I have never yet heard the sound of a glockenspiel in Italy, since this is usually replaced by that dreadful so-called sistrum. Few, if indeed any, of our clarinettists have all the three types of instrument that are needed, and because of this it is well-nigh impossible to hear a clarinet in E flat. . . .[1]

The situation Dallapiccola describes so poignantly was to change rather quickly. The major musical festivals began to resume their activities in the first few years after the end of hostilities (the Venice Festival of Contemporary Music in 1946; the Maggio Musicale Fiorentino in Florence, Sagra Musicale Umbra in Perugia, and Accademia Musicale Chigiana in Siena in 1947), and the opera houses began to reopen their doors. The concert repertory was inevitably influenced by the need to provide popular musical fare that would appeal to the members of the Allied forces who were often going to concerts for the first time. In Florence, the Teatro Comunale had been damaged but was soon repaired, and meanwhile, performances were given in the Teatro Verdi. The broadcasting organization EIAR, which had been active in the prewar period, and whose large-scale political corruption had led some to interpret its acronym as "È indispensabile avere raccomandazioni" (Recommendations are indispensable), was re-formed as RAI (Radiotelevisione Italiana), promoting a considerable musical activity.[2] Television did not develop in Italy until the 1950s; until then, one of the most important aspects of Italian culture was to be found in the cinema, the principal form of entertainment for the majority of Italians. The work of various Italian film directors during that period, in particular the neorealist films pioneered in such masterpieces as *Ladri di biciclette* (Bicycle Thieves) and *Paisà,* were powerful and important vehicles of expression for social and political issues, and some composers, among them Goffredo Petrassi, were drawn into the composition of film scores. Dallapiccola was not substantially involved in this, although he did prepare, or adapt, music for a few films, among them *Incontri con Roma* and *L'esperienza del cubismo* (see the Appendix). He did, however, undertake some work at this time that was designed to help meet the demands of daily life. He became involved in musical journalism and he took on a larger teaching commitment than he would ideally have wished. He also composed a number of pieces on commission, most importantly the *Ciaccona, intermezzo e adagio* (Chaconne, Intermezzo, and Adagio) for solo cello, which was commissioned by Gaspar Cassadó, and *Due studi* (Two Studies) for violin and piano. The nature of these two works was to some extent influenced by the need for music that would be assured of performance, in the one case by his Spanish cellist friend Cassadó and in the other by the Materassi-Dallapiccola duo. These two works, created at a time when Dallapiccola was beginning to absorb the principles of twelve-tone composition much more rigorously than he had before the war, represent the composer's creative imagination at one of its most expressive points.

Ciaccona, Intermezzo e Adagio

Ciaccona, intermezzo e adagio quickly established the composer's reputation abroad through the frequent performances given by Gaspar Cassadó, the cellist, who was living in Florence in 1946. He advised the composer in technical matters of the piece, as he was later to do for *Dialoghi*. The work is without doubt one of the most important contributions made by any twentieth-century composer to the cello repertoire, and among the works written for unaccompanied cello, it can be compared with the Suites Benjamin Britten composed for Mstislav Rostropovich. *Ciaccona, intermezzo e adagio* was the first twelve-tone composition of Dallapiccola to be performed, being given its premiere in Milan in February 1946 by Cassadó, and alongside *Due studi, Rencesvals,* and *Liriche greche,* it was one of the works that brought the composer recognition before the appearance of *Il prigioniero* late in 1949.

Dallapiccola's adoption of twelve-tone techniques in the work shows the individuality of his approach to those techniques. At the same time, it is important to recognize that, as in the case of several of the earliest twelve-tone compositions of Schoenberg, these serial techniques are employed in conjunction with traditional musical forms, in this case chaconne and ternary forms. In the opening movement, the chaconne form acts, as in the Baroque examples, as an invitation to a musical fantasy whose freedoms are at the same time tightly controlled. As Dietrich Kämper pointed out, there is a clear suggestion in the opening Chaconne of C as a tonal center of the movement,[3] but this by no means implies that the work is in any sense "tonal." It is worth noting what the composer himself had to say about the tonal component in his twelve-tone music:

> I came to the conclusion that if, in the twelve-tone system, the tonic had disappeared, taking with it the tonic-dominant relationship, and if, in consequence, sonata form had completely disintegrated, there still existed, nevertheless, a power of attraction, which I will call *polarity* (I do not know whether such a definition has been used before, or whether there is another): I mean by this term the extremely subtle relationships that exist between certain notes. These relationships are not always easily perceptible today, being much less obvious than that of tonic to dominant, but they are there, all the same.[4]

What Dallapiccola meant by these "extremely subtle relationships" can clearly be heard at work in the cello piece. He does not use a single unifying row in the work, but each movement is based upon a new row, and this in itself is of some significance. He has clearly now moved beyond the simple presentation of twelve-tone constructions as momentary "symbols," as at the opening of *Tre laudi,* and beyond the employment of twelve-tone writing as a contrast to diatonic and modal writing, as in *Volo di notte* and *Canti di prigionia*. Here in the *Ciaccona, intermezzo e adagio,* as in *Liriche greche,* there is a consistency in the twelve-tone writing, as well as a clear vision of the ways in which such serialism can act as a focus of the work's expressivity.

The intervals of the row are used to generate melodic and harmonic relationships within each movement. In the Ciaccona, the basic row is set out in the opening measures in the form of a harmonic progression, in keeping with Baroque chaconne practice (Example 3.1 (a) and (b)).

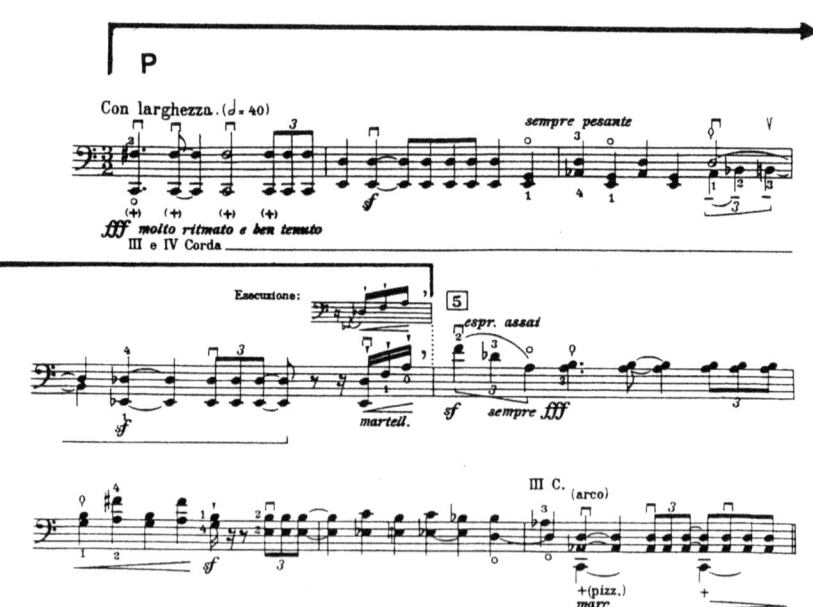

Example 3.1 (a). *Ciaccona,* mm. 1–8. (Reproduced by permission of Schott and Company Ltd., London.)

Example 3.1 (b). *Ciaccona,* row.

An eight-measure phrase is articulated 4 + 4, with prime followed by transposed retrograde, in such a way that a natural bridge is formed at the midpoint (mm. 4–5) by the pitches F–D flat–A shared by both serial forms. However, there is also some suggestion of a tonal resonance to be heard towards the end of this theme. In mm. 6–8, the reiterated alternation of E flat and E natural, combined as it is with B–C in the upper part, seems to suggest that the Ciaccona theme is coming to a cadence in a C tonality, and the introduction of a pedal tone C in the final measure, quite redundant from a purely serial point of view, seems to confirm this. In any case, this addition of the pizzicato C in the final measure also signals the end of the chaconne theme and a point of return to the opening, as many Baroque examples of the form had similarly done.

This theme is then subjected to thirteen free variations, shaped largely in terms of contrasting dynamic characterizations. The first variation, beginning in measure 9 and marked *misterioso, pianissimo*, is almost an echo of the theme, but now in a more "interior" form, and the contrasting dynamic levels, *pianissimo* and *fortissimo*, alternate regularly throughout the movement. One might parallel the articulation of Dallapiccola's chaconne in terms of dynamic characterization with Bach's practice in his famous D-Minor Chaconne for solo violin (in the Partita, BWV 2001), in which the sixty-four variations on the four-measure theme are articulated in terms of varying densities of melodic and contrapuntal writing. Camillo Togni has suggested that the frequent occurrence of passages of a whole-tone character in the movement, a feature that can already be observed in the construction of the row itself, produces a degree of "harmonic neutrality."[5] In addition, the frequent introduction of open strings and natural harmonics, particularly at points in which the melodic and harmonic material becomes static (as in mm. 27–32, and again in mm. 59–65) serves to emphasize the "string" character of the piece. Within this context, the row becomes not so much a simple melodic resource or a means of creating unity over a unit of time, but a generator of a host of associations and echoes within the movement. When the final variation is reached at measure 84, the pedal tone C assumes a particular importance, once again returning the focus of the movement to its basic pitch center: a final point of repose, but in no sense a straightforward "tonic" (Example 3.2).

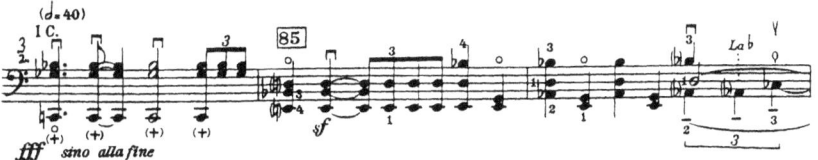

Example 3.2. *Ciaccona*, mm. 84–92. (Reproduced by permission of Schott and Company Ltd., London.)

Example 3.2. *Continued.*

The Intermezzo is based upon a new row, and once again the movement opens with a clear presentation of two serial forms, this time a basic set and its transposed inversion. In this movement, the writing for cello contrasts with that of the first movement: no longer do we hear the kind of rhapsodic melodic utterance that had run through the Chaconne, but instead we find strongly rhythmic writing, adhering strictly to an unchanging 5/4 + 5/8 unit (which the composer asks to have treated as essentially a single unit of 3 x 5/8) (Example 3.3).

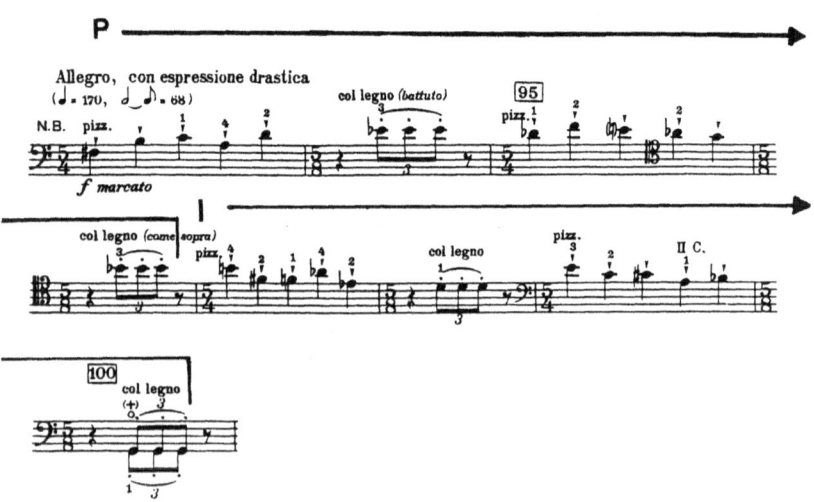

Example 3.3. *Intermezzo*, mm. 93–100. (Reproduced by permission of Schott and Company Ltd., London.)

It is not too far-fetched to suggest that this theme, with its emphatic antecedent and more rapid and insistent three-tone consequent, might contain at least an echo of the rhythmic cell Berg had devised for the "Invention on a Rhythm," the basis of one of the scenes in *Wozzeck* (Act III, Scene 3) (Example 3.4).

Example 3.4 (a). *Intermezzo,* rhythmic cell.

Example 3.4 (b). Berg. *Wozzeck,* rhythmic cell.

The Intermezzo has a strongly scherzo-like character, and at regular intervals Dallapiccola once again inserts momentary figures on isolated open strings, quite independent of the serial framework (mm. 101, 105, 109–10, 126, 130, 134–35, etc.). The Trio (mm. 137–52), marked *visionario,* forms a distinct contrast to the outer sections of the movement. Dallapiccola here reorders the sequence of intervals in the row by displacing the third pitch to fifth, and the emphasis placed in this episode upon the interval of perfect fourth anticipates the perfect fifths that will form the basis of the row in the final Adagio. Dietrich Kämper suggests that the Intermezzo as a whole seems to be constructed around a scheme of tonic-dominant and dominant-tonic progressions in the outer sections,[6] emphasized by the held harmonics on bare fifths at the end of each of these sections. This recourse to a traditional harmonic framework further suggests that the interpretation of C as a pitch center for this movement would seem to be valid.

The fifths, which have been such an important recurring feature in each of the first two movements, now become crucial in the row construction for the final Adagio. The first hexachord is formed solely from this interval, and the second hexachord seems to imply the primacy of the fifth. The similarity to the row Berg had used in his violin concerto is here unmistakable, both sharing the "string" fifths (Example 3.5 (a) and (b)).

Example 3.5 (a). *Adagio,* mm. 201–13. (Reproduced by permission of Schott and Company Ltd., London.)

Example 3.5 (a). *Continued.*

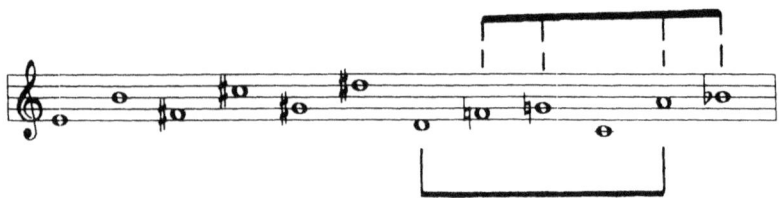

Example 3.5 (b). *Adagio,* row.

The Adagio contains some of the most expressive and eloquent pages Dallapiccola had written up to this point. The naturalness with which "quasi-tonal" elements are brought into play in the serial writing, already prefigured in both previous movements, makes the final measures, with their emphasis on the pedal tone C once again, an eloquent finale to this remarkable piece. The open and ethereal quality of these final measures perhaps contains a hint of the open ending of Berg's *Wozzeck* in their static, but at the same time tense, harmonies (Example 3.6).

Example 3.6. *Adagio,* mm. 262–75. (Reproduced by permission of Schott and Company Ltd., London.)

Towards the Light of Freedom: 1945–1948 105

Example 3.6. *Continued.*

Due Studi

The origins of the *Due studi* for violin and piano are found in a request Dallapiccola received from Luigi Magnani in October 1946 for music for a short documentary film on the life of the artist Piero della Francesca (1416?–1492). Knowing in particular Piero's great cycle of frescoes in the church of San Francesco in Arezzo, and remembering red and white as the dominant colors of two of the frescoes (*The Procession of the Queen of Sheba* and *The Battle of Heraclius*), Dallapiccola immediately began to compose music to accompany these two visual images. It is clear that the composer had these two striking paintings and their vivid colorations in mind while he composed the music, but a few weeks later the film project was abandoned. He immediately decided to transform the music he had already composed into two pieces for violin and piano, in order to fulfil another commission he had received from the Swiss section of the International Society for Contemporary Music. The *Due studi* were performed by the violinist Sandro Materassi and the composer in a concert in Basel in February 1947, and Dallapiccola also made a purely orchestral version, without violin solo, to which he gave the name *Due pezzi*.

The degree to which *Due studi*, while highly organized from a formal point of view, still retains a degree of atmosphere and coloration from its film music origins, is attested by a fascinating note the composer wrote to Alfred Frankenstein in 1962:

> In this work, in which the dodecaphonic system is used very freely, there are two series A and B [Example 3.7]. Series A with which the Sarabande begins (I had wanted to call it "Sarabanda bianca," but I cut out the adjective at the last moment in order to avoid falling into the literary), becomes in contrary form the countersubject of the Fugue, and the second theme of the Sarabande, based on series B, is transformed into the principal subject of the Fugue.
>
> Even the short Fanfare, placed midway and serving as an introduction to the Fugue, uses the series B. In the Sarabande, the dynamic indi-

cation is predominantly *pianissimo* (a single passage of three tones is written *mezzo forte* and also *diminuendo*), while in the Fanfare and Fugue it goes from *forte* to *fortissimo*, never *mezzo forte*.[7]

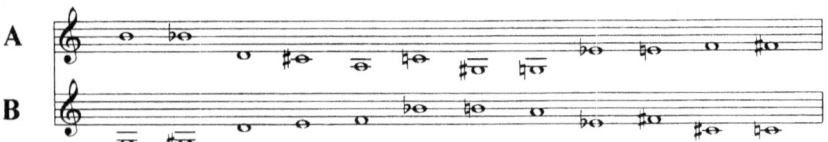

Example 3.7. *Due studi*, rows A and B.

It would appear from this note that Dallapiccola wished to some extent to cover up the traces of the original illustrative nature of the music in this work, as his decision to avoid the description of the opening section as a "white sarabande" would seem to imply. However, the speed with which the composer completed its composition, and the abruptness of its transformation from incidental music into an apparently "abstract" two-movement chamber piece undoubtedly left a residue of musical illustration in the work. Even if the work does adhere to the traditional Baroque *lento-allegro* form, we can surely hear, in the stately dance steps of the opening Sarabande, a hint of the formality of Solomon's meeting with Sheba, as illustrated in Piero's fresco in Arezzo. Equally, we can hear echoes of the riotous confusion of color and action in Piero's depiction of the flag-waving armies at the Battle of Heraclius in the Fanfare and Fugue.

As the composer wrote, the piece makes use of two tone rows, one introduced by the violin right at the start of the Sarabande, the second in the middle of the movement, both interwoven contrapuntally as the movement progresses. The Fanfare takes up the second row, and in the Fugue, subject and countersubject are formed from the two rows of the piece, set out in almost diagrammatic fashion (Example 3.8).

Example 3.8. *Due studi*. Fuga, mm. 108–16.

Example 3.8. *Continued.*

The first row, shown in Example 3.7, is one whose first hexachord can be combined with the first hexachord of its transposed I (or alternatively the second hexachord of P with the second hexachord of the transposed I) to produce a further row. This technique of hexachordal complementarity had already been experimented by Schoenberg in such works as the violin concerto (1934–36), and Dallapiccola uses the technique not simply as a means of filling out the chromatic space: his attention is focused on the possibilities for echoing between melodic phrases, and for doublings of pitches between the various forms and transpositions of the row.[8]

The opening of the Sarabande sets out row A in a characteristically dual presentation, as prime and transposed retrograde, and with the last two pitches of the R form (C–C sharp) given over to the piano. The typical rhythmic pattern associated with the Baroque sarabande, with a dotted second beat, is also clearly evident right from the start (Example 3.9).

Example 3.9. *Due studi*. Sarabanda, mm. 1–9.

The ensuing piano passage (mm. 9–12) is predominantly harmonic, in contrast to the melodic exposition of the row given to the violin. The most important characteristic of row A is its intervallic content: two intervals predominate, half step and major third, with a single minor third between pitches 5 and 6, and in the opening sixteen measures of the piece, this row appears in all four basic forms. Row B emerges in a passage beginning at measure 36, which the composer marks *sognante* (dreaming), as a kind of *cantabile* theme contrasting in character to the opening of the movement. Above an accompaniment of bare fifths in the piano, the violin reveals the new row in a manner recalling the entry of the solo violin in Berg's violin concerto, but in the subsequent passage there is a constant exchange of this material between the two instruments. The metrical shift in mm. 47–51, where the entry of the sarabande rhythm is delayed by a quarter note in the violin part, is repeated in mm. 60–65 with the role of the two instruments reversed. This metrical shift not only creates a momentary feeling of canon between the instrumental parts, but it also gently eases the rhythmic motion of the movement towards the concluding section. There is a clear reprise of the opening of the movement in the final measures: beginning in measure 74, material from mm. 1–8 is repeated constantly, ending with the chord with which the piano had first entered.

Row B reemerges at the start of the Fanfare, but now forming a theme that could hardly be in greater contrast to the *sognante* guise in which it had been presented in the Sarabande. It now forms an energetic unit incorporating the emphatic repeated triplets and dotted figurations that are a feature of many of Dallapiccola's themes; row B dominates the whole of the Fanfare section of the movement. As we have already noted, the fugal exposition employs row B as subject and row A as countersubject, and Dallapiccola avoids the suggestion of a tonic-dominant relationship of the entries of the subject by placing them at the interval of diminished, not perfect, fifth. In the Fugue, which extends for ninety-one measures, the composer indulges his passion for contrapuntal flair and virtuosity, incorporating an array of intricacies and subtleties, including rhythmic augmentation and diminution of the subject. The point of greatest contrapuntal intensity is reached on mm. 150–57, in which a close two-voice canon on the fugue subject is immediately followed by a mirror version of the same (Example 3.10).

Example 3.10. *Due studi*. Fuga, mm. 150–57.

Example 3.10. *Continued.*

The traditional characteristics of a fugue are exhibited throughout the movement: towards the end, we hear a *stretto* (from measure 182), and in the final measures Dallapiccola writes a reprise of the Fanfare (from measure 193). The work concludes with the opening gesture of the Sarabande played *fortissimo* by the violin, rushing headlong towards the final chord of the work, a C-sharp Major triad, a conclusion that Camillo Togni aptly refers to as a "defiant gesture of challenge."[9]

Dallapiccola here combines dodecaphony and fugue in masterly fashion. The question of contrapuntal forms within a twelve-tone musical language was one the composer himself touched upon in an essay he wrote just after the completion of the composition of *Due studi,* in which he evokes the authority of Busoni:

> It was at Weimar in 1923 that Busoni, in his crystal-clear way, spoke, on the subject of form, words that seemed to me definitive:
> "Even today it is still possible to write fugues, using traditional or even modern and atonal methods, yet to every such fugue there will always cling an antiquated character, for fugue is a "form," and as such, timebound, mortal." On the other hand, polyphony is not a form, but a principle; as such it is timeless and, just as long as music continues to be created, 'immortal.'"
> Is it necessary to emphasize that *canon,* which occupies such an important place in the twelve-tone dialectic, is not a *form,* but part of the *principle* of polyphony?[10]

Dallapiccola suggests here that twelve-tone fugues, including by implication the present example, will always retain a certain "antiquated" character even when placed within a modern context. He is also making an important distinction between the "form" of fugue and the "principle" of polyphony (of which canon is a part), and this distinction has great relevance to his own music, in which, as we have frequently observed, the canonic principle is often involved. Such a distinction between canon and fugue only serves to emphasize the exceptional nature of the Fugue that we find in *Due studi,* since on no other occasion in his music is this form explicit. Its use here would therefore appear to demand some justification, and this is surely to be found in the origins of the work as a whole. In assessing the degree to which he was successful in attempting to fuse traditional fugal form with a modern musical language in *Due studi,* we must bear in mind the expressive purpose to which this form is put, since whether Dallapiccola wished it to be so or not, its origins in a visual representation—in the fresco of Piero which had initially inspired its composition—does remain potent. The common thread between painter and composer that we suggested at the beginning of this study, that interpenetration of poetic expression and rational ordering, lies behind the formal subtleties of the latter part of the work. It is possible, of course, to hear the work without any acquaintance with the pictorial model, but perhaps the visual recollection increases rather than undermines an understanding of the piece. The intense and confusing activity of the battlefield that Piero depicts in his fresco must surely be reflected in the constant thematic activity found in the Fugue that Dallapiccola had originally planned to accompany this visual image. Despite the music having later assumed, as it were, an independent existence, the fugal form remained as an essential facet of this remarkable piece.

Rencesvals

Another commission to which Dallapiccola responded just after the war came from the baritone Pierre Bernac, who wished to include a work of Dallapiccola in the program of his concerts with Francis Poulenc. The friendship of Dallapiccola and Poulenc had begun during the 1930s, and the warm admiration felt by Poulenc towards his slightly younger Italian colleague can be sensed in a letter he wrote to Dallapiccola in October 1938, in which he encourages him to believe that the dark days through which they were then living would eventually come to an end.[11] Bernac had originally suggested to Dallapiccola that he might might base the work on texts by Michelangelo, but the composer decided instead to set parts of the medieval *Chanson de Roland,* the most famous of the jongleurs' *chansons de geste,* and he also wished to retain the original archaic language, as he was to do in several later vocal compositions. The work that eventually appeared as *Rencesvals,* heard in December 1946, took its place alongside the earlier works in which Dallapiccola had set antique texts in a modern musical language. It represented also the second occasion on which he had taken a subject from the myth of Roland, the first being the *Rapsodia sulla morte del Conte Orlando,* composed in 1932–33. The title *Rencesvals* refers to the valley of Rencevaux in the Pyrenees, where the army of Charlemagne, commanded by Roland, suffered a crushing defeat at the hands of the Saracens in 778 C.E. The composer made it clear that his choice of this theme was made in order to render homage to France, and arose from his

> undying love for the land of France, for the "dulce France" of Roland. Those who know me know how much I suffered on account of the very sad events that led my country to be an adversary of France during the war years.[12]

The text is taken from Cantos 55, 56, and 66 of the *Chanson de Roland*, and describes in vivid manner the preparations for the great battle in Rencesvals:

> Towards Douce France that Emperour has hasted.
> Upon a lance Rollant his ensign raisèd,
> High on a cliff against the sky 'twas placèd;
> The Franks in camp through all that country baited.
> Cantered pagans, through those wide valleys racèd,
> Hauberks they wore and sarks with iron plated,
> Swords to their sides were girt, their helms were lacèd,
> Lances made sharp, escutcheons newly painted:
> There in the mists beyond the peaks remainèd,
> The day of doom four hundred thousand waited.
> God! what a grief. Franks know not what is fated.
> . . . .
> Passes the day, the darkness is grown deep.
> That Emperour, rich Charlès, lies asleep;
> Dreams that he stands in the great pass of Size,
> In his two hands his ashen spear he sees;
> Guenès the count that spear from him doth seize,
> Brandishes it and twists it with such ease,
> That flown into the sky the flinders seem.
> Charlès sleeps on nor wakens from his dream.
> . . . .
> High are the peaks, the valleys shadowful,
> Swarthy the rocks, the narrows wonderful.
> Franks passed that day all very sorrowful.[13]

The choice of these particular passages from the medieval epic evidently brought to the composer's mind the battles that had only recently been raging in his own homeland, and which had caused such dramatic upheavals in his personal as well as his creative life. It might also have brought to his mind the *Battle of Heraclius* so vividly depicted in Piero's fresco in Arezzo, one of the paintings that had recently prompted the composition of part of the *Due studi*.

Hans Nathan, writing about the conversations he had with the composer about his working methods, pointed out how Dallapiccola had begun the composition of *Rencesvals* with the opening chords, from which he then extracted the two hexachords of the row. The composer asks that these chords be played in a loud and rough manner, and Nathan notes that this seems to have been "the only case where a row was gained from chords" (Example 3.11 (a), (b), (c)).[14]

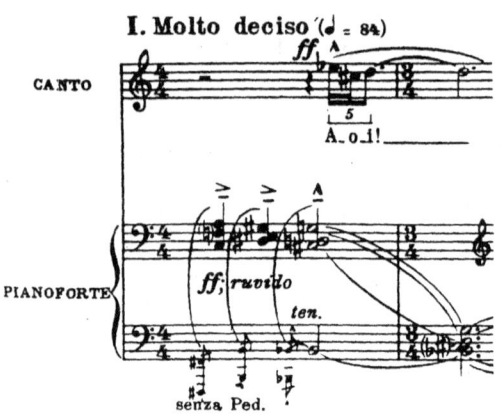

Example 3.11 (a). *Rencesvals*, mm. 1–2.

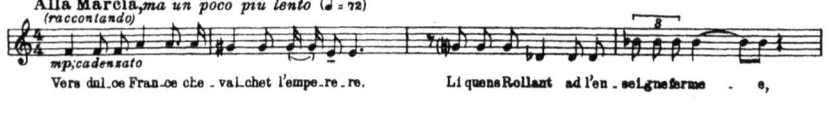

Example 3.11 (b). *Rencesvals*, mm. 6–12.

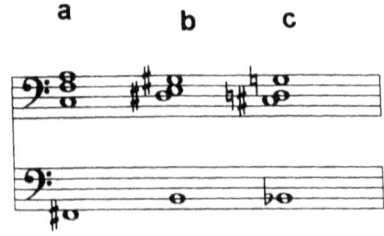

Example 3.11 (c). *Rencesvals,* serial derivation.

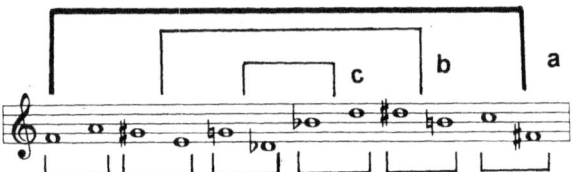

Example 3.11 (c). *Continued.*

Dietrich Kämper, however, points out that this derivation of a row from a chord progression was to recur in several of Dallapiccola's subsequent works, including the *Quattro liriche di Antonio Machado* and the *Parole di San Paolo*.[15] It would seem that for Dallapiccola, the first presentation of a row could be made in either vertical-harmonic or in horizontal-melodic form. The row as a musical entity, as a character in the musical narrative as it were, retained its fundamental symbolism whatever the form of its initial presentation.

In this context, it is worth quoting a very revealing comment the composer himself made, in which he drew a striking analogy with the manner in which Marcel Proust presented the characters in his novel. First of all, Dallapiccola related how Proust presented the character Albertine at various points in such a way that the character is rounded out only gradually; she is presented elliptically, as it were, through her reflection in other characters' conversations. He contrasts this with the manner of presenting a character in the classical novel, giving as an example Padre Cristoforo in Alessandro Manzoni's *I promessi sposi* (The Betrothed), a very full description of whom is given on his first appearance. Dallapiccola then parallels these two approaches with the presentation of themes in the traditional sonata form, and in music based on a series, which he calls a "difference of dialectic":

> We see . . . that the difference between the presentation of characters in the classical novel and that in the novel of Proust corresponds with the difference in the exposition of a classical sonata and serial music. . . . We can find a twelve-tone row condensed into a single chord comprising the twelve tones of the tempered chromatic scale, or else in two six-tone chords, or four three-tone chords . . . or finally in six bichords.[16]

Kämper likens this gradual revelation of the row's characteristics to the slow, almost hesitant unfolding of the row to be found in Schoenberg's *Variations for Orchestra,* Opus 31.[17]

Rencesvals as a whole is not only a rare example of Dallapiccola composing a work that is textual, narrative, and descriptive at the same time, but it is also one that does not exhibit a clear relationship to any fundamental row. Dallapiccola himself referred to the piece, in reply to a question from a Canadian musicologist, as "studies in the total chromatic."[18] This is in line with Dallapiccola's reaction to an analysis of the work made by Camillo Togni in 1960 for publication in an Italian music encyclopedia, an analysis that eventually appeared in print in 1964.[19] Togni had written that the piece returned in some sense to the Lied form Dallapiccola had inherited from Alban Berg: he saw the three sections into which the work falls (mm. 1–45, 46–69, 70–110) as in A-B-A form, with the outer panels based upon the row discussed earlier, while the central section was much more loosely based upon this row. Kämper seems to accept the composer's own judgment of *Rencesvals* as largely free of any overall dodecaphonic structuring,[20] citing as evidence the appearance of an eight-tone theme in the third section of the work (mm. 75–82), and with the remaining pitches appearing solely in the piano accompaniment. Togni's analysis of the serial elements in *Rencesvals* surprised the composer when the two discussed it in December 1960; Dallapiccola had "always had the impression that [*Rencesvals*] was a work that was serially very free and irregular." Togni also reported that Dallapiccola was unable to offer any clarification of the way that the central section of the work related to the fundamental row set out in the opening measures of the work.[21]

Whatever might be its "serial" nature, it is clear that at several points in the work there are "quasi-tonal" suggestions. This is true not only in the opening measures, where the first gestures in voice and piano are "resolved" into a G-Minor triad in mm. 4–5, but also at other points in the piece. In the final measures, the work comes to rest on a G-Major triad, but this is undermined by the unresolved A-flat appoggiatura in the bass. This unresolved tone is a remnant of the three-tone figure in mm. 105–7, which seems to echo the initial cry of "Aoi!"—but from a distance, as it were, with the figure's earlier chromaticism opened out slightly.

In terms of overall structure, however, it is neither through a tone row nor through an implied tonal center that Dallapiccola creates a structural unity. It is in large measure through the narrative itself that the work is held together, and the music mirrors as closely as possible the contours of the text. In the first section, the description of the scene of the coming battle is interspersed with the repeated cry "Aoi!" with its attendant three-tone motif. In the second, *calmissimo* episode, the dream of Charlemagne is recounted. In the third episode the brooding mountain landscape is evoked in the *metallico* chords and the wide chromatic leaps in the vocal line from measure 75, seeming to reflect the fears of the Franks as they await their fate. Other elements in the music are directly illustrative: the marching figure that first appears in the piano part in mm. 7–8 is suggestive of the horse's tread as the Emperor goes forth into "la dulce France," while the fanfare figure in mm. 34–37 clearly symbolizes the assembly of the armed forces. Perhaps an analogy might be made here with another Italian composition from an earlier age in which narrative considerations seem to have taken precedence over matters of musical cohesion, namely Monteverdi's *Il combattimento di Tancredi e Clorinda*. The colorful musical illustrations that had been a feature of Monteverdi's remarkable work are also present here. Monteverdi, it should be remembered, composed *Il combattimento di Tancredi e Clorinda* not as a miniature opera or intermezzo, but as a dramatic madrigal, to be included in his eighth book of madrigals published in 1638. Both this work and *Rencesvals* are settings of fragments of text taken from a much larger poem (in Monteverdi's case, from Torquato Tasso's *Gerusalemme liberata*); both were intended as purely musical representations, without the necessity of any stage trappings; both have a battle as their major theme; and both incorporate realistic sound (fanfares, the tread of horses, and the like). It is, perhaps, not stretching the term too far to describe Dallapiccola's *Rencesvals* as, in a sense, a modern version of what Monteverdi termed the *stile concitato*.

Il prigioniero

Dallapiccola's comment that the central idea of all his stage works was always the same, namely "the struggle of man against some force much stronger than he,"[22] reveals one of the fundamental facets of his dramatic oeuvre. This links together works otherwise as disparate as the "modern-realistic" *Volo di notte,* the "classical" *Marsia,* the "historical-symbolic" *Il prigioniero,* the "spiritual" *Job,* and the "universal" *Ulisse,* and might seem to be merely a convenient device by which the composer brought his dramatic works together under a single heading. This would be misleading. Dallapiccola's works for the stage do present a continuous, constantly varying commentary on universal problems, and it is in this light that they can best be understood as a whole. The struggle between Rivière and the pilot's wife on the subject of night flying, the struggle between the satyr Marsyas and the god Apollo for artistic supremacy, the Prisoner's struggle against the power of the Inquisition, the struggle of Job against divine inexorability, and finally the struggle of Ulysses to uncover the hidden layers of his own soul—from these historical, mythological, and existential conflicts Dallapiccola created the dramas. His comment reveals that the conflicts each dramatic work dealt with were linked, despite their obvious differences, and each of the conflicts presents a metaphor, the full meaning of which would be unraveled only in his last opera, *Ulisse,* indeed only in its very last pages.

With the exception of the ballet *Marsia,* in none of these dramatic conflicts do we witness a complete and unequivocal victory, and the limits of human power are in each case clearly set out. Indeed, in *Il prigioniero,* the illusory freedom granted to the Prisoner in the final scene becomes the most poignant moment in the opera through the musical allusion to the *Canti di prigionia*. The Prisoner's despair at the end of the opera, with his realization that his faith in the Jailer has been misguided, might seem to fit oddly with Dallapiccola's abounding personal optimism and faith in human destiny. If the opera is viewed as a document of the historical moment in which it was created, then the despair that we find in its final scene will be seen as a profoundly pessimistic one. On the other hand, if we bring together the particular nature of the opera and the more general symbols found in Dallapiccola's stage works, then we can see that the ending is in keeping with the composer's constant expression of an inner struggle towards the light, a metaphor which had already appeared in *Volo di notte*.

In any case, *Il prigioniero*, like many operas before it, was as much a document of the time in which it was written as it was an eternal artistic symbol. The Prisoner's final question—"Freedom?"—was penned at a time of enormous danger for Dallapiccola and his wife as they went into hiding from the authorities, but it was also one of the darkest moments of the history of Dallapiccola's adopted city, a moment at which there would seem to be no hope of release. Dietrich Kämper has provided an eloquent account of the way in which the opera had deep roots not only in the events that were occurring in the period of its composition, but also in events and experiences in the composer's childhood.[23]

In any case, the philosophical basis of the opera was largely determined by the literary sources from which the text was drawn. The two principal sources were the short story "La torture par l'espérance" (Torture by Hope) by Villiers de L'Isle-Adam, from which the fundamental framework of the narrative was taken, and the Flemish epic *La légende d'Ulenspiegel et de Lamme Goedzak* (The Legend of Ulenspiegel and Lamme Goedzak) as recounted by Charles de Coster.[24] The first of these was discovered by Laura Dallapiccola in a collection of Villiers de L'Isle-Adam's stories she picked up when browsing in the bookstalls on the banks of the Seine in Paris a few years earlier. From this, Dallapiccola drew the major part of the narrative of the opera, but he by no means adhered slavishly to either literary source. By making the protagonist "The Prisoner" rather than L'Isle-Adam's more specific "Rabbi Aser Abarbanel," he universalized the action, while at the same time retaining the historical roots of the story within the Wars of Religion. During the composition of the opera, the libretto of which underwent several major revisions, the composer also made a thorough study of many historical and literary aspects of the period in which it was set.[25]

The creation of the opera began from the center of the work. Having written the first draft of the libretto, Dallapiccola read it to a group of close friends in the Villa Le Pozzarelle in Fiesole where he and Laura were in hiding in December 1943. He then immediately composed the three-verse aria in which the Jailer sings of the hopes for freedom embodied in the Beggars' Revolt then breaking out in Flanders. There is therefore a parallel to the way that he had broached the composition of *Canti di prigionia,* when he had first composed the setting of the prayer of Mary Stuart before beginning to write the rest of the work, and in both cases the smaller piece became of crucial importance within the larger context. The optimism expressed in the aria would eventually be dashed, but the aria undoubtedly served as an "Anthem to Liberty," and it was for this reason that the composer allowed its publication in a Paris music journal even before the opera as a whole was completed.[26] The remainder of the opera was composed between the beginning of 1944 and April 1947 and orchestrated in the months that followed.

The three-verse aria, a passionate and heartfelt hymn to freedom, was to prove the germ from which an important element in the opera would grow, since it incorporated one of the three tone rows on which much of the opera would be built. This row, identified by the composer as the "Liberty" row,[27] is presented in all four basic forms within the aria's melodic line (Example 3.12 (a) and (b)).

Example 3.12 (a). *Il prigioniero,* mm. 360–70.

Example 3.12 (a). *Continued.*

"Liberty" Row

Example 3.12 (b). *Il prigioniero,* "Liberty" row.

The optimistic tone of the text here is paralleled in the confident progression of the intervals of the row: the natural division is as two five-tone cells linked to a final triadic shape, with each unit having a clear "diatonic" character, and this character is maintained throughout the aria.

The opera begins with a Prologue, in which the Prisoner's mother sings passionately of her hopes and fears for her son, and the musical figure that appears in the opening measures is not only of arresting power, but also of considerable irony in the context of the opera as a whole. It consists of three chords, repeated three times in rhythmically contracting form, a leitmotif that will appear three further times in the course of the opera, stridently orchestrated. At its first appearance, it is immediately followed by the Mother singing "I shall see you again, my son," an optimism which is belied by the nature of the leitmotif itself. It reappears at the end of the Prologue, at the climax of her description of Philip II as a figure of death (mm. 117–19); briefly in the third scene as the Prisoner speaks of his attempt to escape (mm. 645–46); and finally as the Prisoner rushes out of the prison, believing for one ecstatic moment that his sufferings have come to an end (mm. 794–96). At the opening of the opera, this leitmotif is immediately followed by a similar figure which complements it rhythmically, producing a startling effect of terror right at the opening of the opera, and in the course of the work it becomes evident that this leitmotif symbolizes the tyranny of Philip II and of the power of the Inquisition. The terror of this leitmotif comes in part from its chromaticism, which encompasses all twelve tones rapidly within the three chords, but equally significant is the manner in which Dallapiccola has ordered them. The joyful diatonicism of the upper parts in woodwinds and strings may seem to grant some hope through their fanfare-like character, but the lower parts, in muted trumpets and trombones and each vehemently displaying a tritone, work counter to such optimism. This ambivalent character of hope and despair was to produce the brutal irony of the final appearance of the leitmotif in the opera, a symbol of misplaced hope (Example 3.13).

Example 3.13. *Il prigioniero*, mm. 1–4.

From the first four tones of this leitmotif, Dallapiccola derives the "Prayer" row, whose first appearance comes as the Prisoner pleads for God's help in his desperate desire for freedom, employing words the composer had found in a prayer-book for children.[28] It is not accidental that the first part of this "Prayer" row is identical with the final tetrachord of the row used in *Canti di prigionia* (see Example 1.5 (b)) (Example 3.14 (a) and (b)).

Example 3.14 (a). *Il prigioniero*, mm. 240–44.

"Prayer" Row

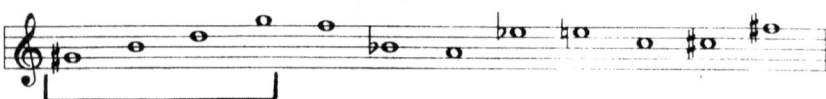

Example 3.14 (b). *Il prigioniero*, "Prayer" row.

The third row on which the opera is based, identified by Dallapiccola as the "Hope" row, first appears as the Prisoner tells his Mother how the Jailer had offered him hope by calling him "fratello" (brother). In musical terms the relationship of Prisoner and Jailer, of the one who is incarcerated and the one who appears to offer hope and encouragement, is symbolized by an identity of melodic shape. The Jailer's "fratello" is formed from the comforting figure of a descending half step and minor third, but as the Prisoner recounts this, wondering at the beauty of the word "brother," it is followed by a three-tone chromatic figure that prefigures the opening of the "Hope" row. In the course of the opera, the Jailer's utterance of "fratello" occurs in this melodic form on all but two occasions; in these two instances, when a version in ascending half steps is employed, the other version is placed immediately before it in the orchestral accompaniment (mm. 282 and 305). The "fratello" motif, in fact, acts as a complement to the three-chord "Terror" leitmotif with which the opera opens; it is a constant symbol of hope in the opera, and its most important appearance will be in the excited orchestral passage after the Prisoner has been left alone in his cell, when the rays of light penetrating the darkness reveal to him that escape might be possible (mm. 505–13). In the "Hope" row itself, which arises from the Prisoner's recounting of the jailer's "fratello," the very shape of the row is a symbol of hope itself, gradually expanding from its first hesitant, close intervals, to the full confidence of the octave (Example 3.15 (a) and (b)).

Example 3.15 (a). *Il prigioniero*, mm. 198–203.

Example 3.15 (a). *Continued.*

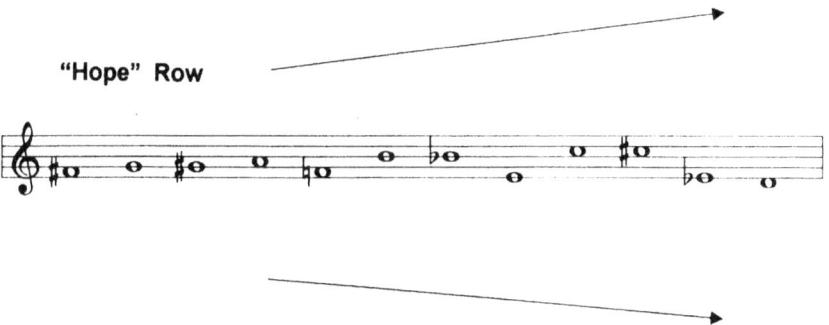

Example 3.15 (b). *Il prigioniero*, "Hope" row.

The three-tone "*fratello*" motif is indeed one of the major leitmotifs in the opera, and its first appearance is of great significance, but in an ironic sense. In the Prologue, the Mother of the Prisoner recounts the recurring dream she has had, in which the figure of Philip II gradually transforms itself into a "Death's Head," and her first tentative utterances (mm. 39–42) are expressed through the "fratello" leitmotif, apparently casual here, and seemingly no more than a melodic expression of her sadness. However, within the context of the whole opera, it clearly presages the identification of the Jailer's "fratello" with Philip II–Grand Inquisitor–Death which will represent her son's final destiny.

In the third scene, as the Prisoner creeps fearfully along the corridor, hoping that this will lead him to freedom, the mounting tension is created in a group of three Ricercari: the first is on "Signore, aiutami a camminare" ("Prayer" row: Example 3.13 (b)), the second on "fratello," the third on a leitmotif associated with "Roelandt," the great bell in Ghent whose silencing by Charles V had come to symbolize the oppression of the Flemish people. For this latter, the composer once more derives from the initial chords of the opera a "Roelandt" leitmotif, whose diminished fifths are a vivid sound picture of the cracked bell. The Jailer speaks to the Prisoner about the silencing of Roelandt in his account of the revolt in Flanders (mm. 316–24), as the accompaniment suggests the leitmotif that will be associated with it. When the Prisoner finally emerges into the open air, the opening chords of the opera announce that the stake is now awaiting him, but in his ecstasy he imagines that Roelandt is giving news not only of the end of his own sufferings, but the end of the degradation of the Flemish people (Example 3.16).

Example 3.16. *Il prigioniero,* mm. 806–15.

The fundamental tone rows of the opera, and the leitmotifs derived from them, together form an implicit interpretation of the drama, and this is evident in countless pages of the score of *Il prigioniero*. On occasion, however, this goes further than the rows themselves and extends to the versions of the row employed. For example, the optimism the Mother of the Prisoner encourages in him in his wretched state is characterized in her first utterance by a determined and positive row on the words "I shall see you once more, my son" (mm. 9–12). However, during the dialogue between the two in Scene 1, immediately following the Prisoner's first enunciation of the "Hope" row, his Mother's question ". . . which gave you more hope in life?" appears as an inversion of the row, a doubting reaction to her son's optimism.

This intimate identification of row and cell material, that is to say the three principal rows of "Prayer," "Hope," and "Freedom," as well as the two motifs of "fratello" and "Roelandt," with the dramatic meaning of the work, is clearly indebted to the example of Alban Berg. *Lulu* can be seen as the most obvious source of inspiration for Dallapiccola in his attempt to forge the closest links between drama and music. Although Berg's influence had already been present in the incorporation of closed musical forms in *Volo di notte,* in *Il prigioniero* the influence of Berg goes much deeper, penetrating to the level of intricate serial devices and symbolisms. Dallapiccola certainly does not go so far as to integrate the whole of the opera around a single fundamental tone row and its derivatives, as Berg had attempted to do in *Lulu,* but nonetheless the small number of rows in the opera, and the repetition of their associated leitmotifs, makes a similarly unified impression within this one-act opera.

There is, however, a clear distinction to be made between Berg's *Lulu* and *Il prigioniero*. Berg had been faced with a particular problem, that of an extraordinarily large number of principal characters, many of them making frequent appearances on stage, and the device of deriving their rows from the row associated with Lulu herself was a means of ensuring unity over the opera as a whole. In Dallapiccola's case, no such device was necessary: the one-act opera has only three principal characters, and the nature of the drama meant that there was no need to create rows or leitmotifs associated with each character. The rows and leitmotifs of *Il prigioniero* are linked with concepts or objects, not characters: hope; prayer; liberty; terror; fraternal protection; Roelandt, the "Liberty Bell." The strongest connecting thread between *Lulu* and *Il prigioniero,* however, is more general but no less significant. This is the insight with which each composer entered into the psychological and expressive world inhabited by each opera's main protagonist, whether the woman whose captivating presence ensnares men and brings both them and her to their doom, or the prisoner whose life is held by a thread, under the power of forces completely beyond his control and his will.

Dallapiccola had long pondered what he saw as the "opera problem," and had attempted to formulate the problem faced by the composer of a modern opera in an essay written at the time of the first performance of *Volo di notte* in 1940.[29] Here he spoke of the "dramatic crescendo," the drive towards the final scene and the dramatic convergence on the conclusion, which in opera can be brought about only through the music. He had been struck in particular by three examples that had solved the problem of opera in individual ways:

> While studying several modern operas, I observed how individual composers had solved, time after time, the problem that for me represented the core of the drama. Debussy achieves a vast crescendo during Acts I to IV of *Pelléas et Mélisande* and resolves it in the concluding Act V. In the turbid *Wozzeck,* Alban Berg keeps tightening the screws throughout fourteen scenes, and only in the final scene does he admit a pale shaft of sunlight. Darius Milhaud, in the first part of *Christophe Colomb,* arrays five large and extremely diverse musical frescoes: Queen Isabella praying to St James of Compostela; the boisterous southern port of Cadiz; the mysterious council of the Mexican gods; the sailors' mutiny; and, as a final resolution, the Te Deum for the discovery of America.
>
> The first impressionist opera, the first big expressionist opera, and the first modern opera of "the masses" all have in common the fact that the composer's utmost effort is a drive towards the final scene, a convergence on the conclusion. Otherwise, for the listener, Debussy's opera would end *musically* in Act IV with the death of Pelléas—that is, with its *dramatic* close—Berg's opera with the drowning of Wozzeck, and the first part of *Christophe Colomb* with the appearance of the dove, the messenger of peace.[30]

Dallapiccola had already offered a particular solution to the problem of the "dramatic crescendo" in *Volo di notte,* where a clear musical and dramatic distinction is made between the disappearance of the pilot Fabien from the radio telegraph reports and the final exultant hymn of praise to the Airline Director Rivière. In *Il prigioniero,* similarly, we find a distinction between the sudden emergence of the Prisoner into the cool air of freedom, with the overwhelming choral interjection accompanying it, and the final despair of the Prisoner as he falls into the arms of the Grand Inquisitor. In this case, even more than in the previous opera, the ground has been carefully prepared for the musical conclusion of the opera, with the reiteration of the "Roelandt" motif in the final Ricercare as the Prisoner attempts to escape, and with the tremendous choral intermezzo immediately preceding the final moments of the opera.

Il prigioniero is an opera in which all the elements of solo singers, chorus, and orchestra contribute to the expressive power of the whole. In the solo parts, Dallapiccola made full use of the range of vocal possibilities that had been explored by both Schoenberg and Berg, from *parlato* through *Sprechgesang* to the full singing voice, and in the orchestral passages of the work, most notably the three Ricercari in Scene 3, his mastery of orchestral writing is complete. The third Ricercare, that on the "Roelandt" motif, exhibits the mastery of orchestral writing that Dallapiccola possessed: Dietrich Kämper speaks of the combination of enormous contrapuntal intricacy and the delicacy and atmosphere of the instrumentation in this passage as reminiscent of the "Mondfleck" movement in Schoenberg's *Pierrot Lunaire,* or the double fugue in Act II, Scene 2 of Berg's *Wozzeck*.[31] The three Ricercari constitute an essential point in the musical workings of the whole opera, as Massimo Mila pointed out in an article written immediately after the opera's première.[32] Dallapiccola here wished to suggest in purely musical terms the Prisoner's attempt to escape, and as far as the stage presentation was concerned, he envisaged a revolving stage to suggest the seemingly endless corridors of the prison. Without such stage resources (or, indeed, the more flexible possibilities that might be offered by a film presentation of the opera), the whole tension of the dramatic moment is conveyed by the music alone, and, as Massimio Mila suggested, the stage action can be limited only in normal circumstances. In the Ricercari that accompany his attempted escape, Dallapiccola composes both the actions and the emotions of the Prisoner: firstly the Ricercare on "Signore, aiutami a camminare," based upon the "Prayer" row, in which he sees a torturer pass by with his deadly instruments, freezing the Prisoner with fear; secondly the Ricercare on "fratello" ("Hope" row), as he hears an inner voice encouraging him in his attempt to escape; and finally the Ricercare on "Roelandt," as he feels the first breath of the open air on his fingers, and the great bell of Roelandt seems to ring out for him. The Prisoner's progression towards the light is paralleled in the three Ricercari in musical symbolisms, through the three musical motifs established in the earlier part of the opera. It ends, however, not with a Ricercare on the "Liberty"' row, as we might logically expect, but with a merely illusory liberty, musically symbolized in the cracked bell of Roelandt.

A very special place in the opera is taken by the off-stage chorus. It might be thought that the employment of a large chorus in such an opera is not essential, and that, quite apart from the purely practical considerations involved, the drama itself does not warrant the use of a chorus. The justification for the choral episodes comes from their position in the work as a whole: the two choral intermezzi placed between the Prologue and Scene 1, and between Scenes 3 and 4, are crucial in transforming the personal drama of the Prisoner into a larger and more universal symbol. This is aided both by the use of the Latin texts they sing and also by their sudden and overwhelming appearance, which the composer is at pains to emphasize (in the second instance, including the suggested use of amplification through loudspeaker). The two choral intermezzi, clearly ecclesiastical in tone, are essential elements in the drama as a whole, almost, as it were, an addition to the *dramatis personae*. The first, after the Mother's Prologue and immediately before the drama proper begins, has a somewhat stark, severe character, with its block harmonies and strict contrapuntal imitations: in the light of the eventual crushing of the Prisoner by the Inquisition, its religious expression of the powerful majesty of God is certainly ironic. The second is in complete contrast: placed between Scenes 3 and 4, it begins quietly with just female voices in a gentle imitative counterpoint (mm. 869–76) accompanying the Prisoner's ecstatic declarations. An important point is reached at measure 877: here, the Prisoner's gasp on seeing the stars in the night-sky ("... le stelle!") is accompanied by a C-major chord, a clear allusion to the "Stars" motif which had appeared in *Tre laudi* and *Volo di notte*. After the intervention of the Grand Inquisitor, the second half of this choral intermezzo quotes from *Canti di prigionia* (mm. 920–40), and the irony of this has already been noted.

When *Il prigioniero* was first seen on stage in Florence in May 1950, discussion was provoked which extended beyond the nature of its musical language, involving a supposed "ideology" that some people saw in the work. On one side, the Italian Communist Party, then in its most fervently Stalinist phase, feared that the public might see in the oppressions of the opera a symbol of Stalin's work camps, while the Catholic Church resented the portrayal of the Spanish Inquisition during the Holy Year of 1950. The composer wisely spent no energy attempting to counter such criticisms, and in any case, the acclaim the opera received from the more discerning made any such discussions worthless. He was, however, anxious that his own position vis-à-vis the portrayal of the religious dimension of the opera should not be misunderstood, as he wrote in a letter to his publisher in 1957: "As a believer, I would like to stress that there is nothing in my *Il prigioniero* which is against the Catholic Church, but only a protest against tyranny and oppression."[33] His reaction to the polemics which followed the first performance of the opera was documented in the article which he wrote for an American newspaper in 1962:

> This performance was followed by heated polemics (in which, it goes without saying, there were political elements) and by endless philosophical discussions particularly of the question which the principal character of *The Prisoner* poses at the end: "Freedom?" Some saw a complete negation of life and its values in this question. Their attitude was not astronomically distant from the question of Pilate: "What is truth?" They had forgotten that Busoni had ended his masterpiece *Doktor Faust* (1924) on a point of interrogation put by Mephistopheles, guardian of the night: "Shall this man be damned?" This marked the birth of a new dramatic form, the open opera. I have always refused to explain the question

posed by *The Prisoner*. I have always confined myself to saying that some day I should give an answer. . . .[34]

In an essay Dallapiccola wrote in 1960, in which he contemplated the problems faced by both composer and listener in contemporary opera, he was intrigued in particular by those operas which were, in one way or another, concluded only with doubt or questioning. Busoni's *Doktor Faust* has already been mentioned, and the second act of Schoenberg's *Moses und Aron* concludes with Moses' desperate inability to find the word through which he might express his innermost, solitary thoughts. Dallapiccola commented about these:

> By the same token, the question at the end of my own opera *Il prigionero* ("Freedom?") implies that the action is not yet finished.
>
> Why do I love opera? Because it seems the most suitable medium for the expression of my thought (not that I consider opera a philosophical treatise, of course . . .). Some day, after all the question-marks—mine and others—I should like to succeed in expressing a "certainty." The difficulty of this personal problem is what fascinates me.[35]

By the time Dallapiccola penned these words in 1960, he had embarked upon his final, full-scale operatic project, the composition of *Ulisse*. Only in the final moments of that work do we find the resolution of the problem which he had described here, a final "answer" to the philosophical problem which had already been posed in *Il prigioniero*.

IV

The Serial Idea: 1948–1953

The Principles of Serialism

Dallapiccola had been the first Italian composer to engage with the serialism of the Viennese composers,[1] and by the time that he completed *Il prigioniero* in 1948 he had composed a number of works in which the twelve-tone idea had played a central role. Nonetheless, he had not up to that point composed a work in which a single tone row was used to unify a whole composition. In the majority of his compositions before 1948, the dodecaphonic procedures and ideas had appeared alongside other musical elements of equal importance. This is an essential matter in understanding the development of Dallapiccola's music. His adoption of the serial idea was a conscious choice, as he was constantly to stress in later years; the choice had been made not simply because of his inherent tendency to employ highly rational musical devices, but also for reasons of expressivity. Serialism was a means to create a musical language capable of generating the large-scale tensions and resolutions that he exploited in building whole works. The serial principle provided a focus for the essentially lyrical and polyphonic nature of Dallapiccola's musical expression, and through this he was able to forge a language capable of an extraordinarily wide expressive range, moving from the tortured anguish of many pages of *Il prigioniero* to the limpid beauty of *Liriche greche*.

It should not be thought, however, that the establishment of the serial idea as a guiding light in Dallapiccola's music after 1945 was in any sense "pre-ordained," that his move in this direction somehow obeyed some historical law of inevitability. It has already been observed that Dallapiccola's path towards serial composition had been a slow and in some ways tortuous one, given the lack of guidance available in Italy that might have assisted him on this path. The necessity of finding an individual musical voice had played a part, as had his natural inclination towards polyphonic writing. Also, the meeting with Anton Webern in the spring of 1942 in Vienna provided the composer with a "moral example" of the possibilities of serialism, but, nonetheless, after 1945 several paths were open to him.

Dallapiccola's adoption of serialism contrasts in some ways with its adoption by other composers. The fact that he had never studied with any of the members of the so-called Viennese School was important, of course, as the slow and careful study of their scores he began from the mid-1930s was the only way he was able to absorb the essence of this approach. The emigration of a significant number of musicians from Germany and Austria during the 1930s, as a consequence of the political situation in their native lands, was of great importance. They established a sense of the significance of serialism among some musicians, predominantly in Britain and the United States, wherever the emigrés found a new home. Italy did not, of course, benefit from this migration, and as a consequence it was only through individual initiative by composers there that they could be enlightened about the techniques of serialism. Dallapiccola, like Stravinsky some years later, approached serial composition simply through a fascination with the compositional possibilities it offered him. However, if we compare Dallapiccola's "twelve-tone road" with that of Stravinsky, whose adoption of serialism in the early 1950s has been exhaustively studied,[2] we find significant differences. In the first place, Stravinsky never undertook the kind of slow and gradual approach to serialism that Dallapiccola had made in the period after his first acquaintance with Berg's and Webern's music in 1935, gradually importing more and more significant serial elements into his music. For Stravinsky, the "conversion" to serialism occurred quickly, beginning in effect a short time after the death of Schoenberg in 1951, and was also characterized by an exalting of Webern at the expense of Schoenberg. For Dallapiccola, on the other hand, despite the significantly greater influence of Berg and Webern that we can detect in his music, Schoenberg also remained a figure of great importance. In essence, Stravinsky's choice of the "twelve-tone road" was simply that, a choice made from among many possibilities. It cannot be claimed that Stravinsky in his later serial period was pursuing an "inevitable" path in the way that Dallapiccola's serial scores would seem to have grown logically from the ever-present concern with clarity, polyphony, and rational structuring in his music. In Stravinsky's case, the reason for his adoption of serial procedures from the early 1950s was very specific, a means by which he could expand the harmonic vocabulary of his music, as he explained to Robert Craft:

> The rules and restrictions of serial writing differ little from the rigidity of the great contrapuntal schools of old. At the same time they widen and enrich harmonic scope; one starts to hear more things and differently than before. The serial technique I use impels me to greater discipline than ever before.[3]

After the war, when the music Dallapiccola had composed in relative isolation during the previous decade came finally to be judged in wider circles, it was inevitably viewed in relation to his Viennese serialist predecessors; the earliest commentator to do this was René Leibowitz. He had met Dallapiccola at the first postwar I.S.C.M. Festival in London in 1946, and conducted the *Sex carmina Alcaei* in Paris the following year. Dallapiccola and Leibowitz were in correspondence right from their first meeting, and Leibowitz wrote at that time of the composer's tendency towards a certain "hedonism" in the creation of euphonous musical textures, and of what he regarded as his only half-hearted acceptance of the influence of Anton Webern.[4] It was to be these comments of Leibowitz that would set the seal upon Dallapiccola's entry into the mainstream of European post-war music as the representative of what was immediately labelled a "sensuous Italianate lyricism" strain in serial composition. This position aided his acceptance among the more conservative circles, but it hardly endeared his music to the tougher, more structuralist young composers who would follow Webern's lead in the next decade or so. In any case, this description of Dallapiccola's music was almost laughably partial, inevitably so, given that Leibowitz was by no means aware of all the paths the composer had taken in the preceding decade. In particular, this view did not take into account that element of canonic and contrapuntal exuberance that had been present in his music from the very start.

In the years that followed, particularly in the works he composed immediately after *Job* in 1950, Dallapiccola was to undertake the most rigorous researches into the structural aspects of dodecaphony, and these researches were to reach their apogee in *Canti di liberazione,* composed in 1951–55. However, alongside the establishment of serialism as the predominant element in Dallapiccola's musical language, there was a further change, equally significant, in the immediate postwar period: a very distinct broadening of the composer's literary horizons. In the earlier years of his creative life, Dallapiccola had made initial contact with varieties of text to which he was to return on later occasions: firstly, the medieval poetry found in *Due laudi di Iacopone da Todi* (1929), the final movement of the orchestral *Partita* (1930–32), *Divertimento in quattro esercizi* (1934), and *Tre laudi* (1936–37); and secondly, the poetry of classical antiquity which he had set in *Estate* (1932) and in *Liriche greche* (1942–45). He had been fully aware of more modern literature for a long time (it was noted in an earlier chapter that he had encountered many contemporary literary movements through his Florentine intellectual contacts, among whom was the poet Eugenio Montale), but it was only after 1945 that he became seriously involved, in a creative sense, with literature drawn from a wider variety of sources. These came both from both past and present, and by no means exclusively from an Italian environment: Antonio Machado, James Joyce, Michelangelo, Goethe, Heine, Oscar Wilde, Juan Ramon Jiménez, and Murilo Mendes were to figure in his work after this point. The fact that this broadening of the literary component in the composer's work should coincide with the establishment and refinement of serial techniques in his music is perhaps not simply fortuitous. Dallapiccola's was after all quintessentially a vocal rather than an instrumental musical art, one whose communication depended upon very specific verbal images and expressions, as well as upon a very precise and carefully measured employment of language. The qualities of a literary text were therefore crucial in stimulating the composer's musical image-making, as can readily be seen in two vocal pieces composed in the immediate postwar period, *Quattro liriche di Antonio Machado* (1948) and *Tre poemi* (1949).

Quattro liriche di Antonio Machado

As is the case in so many of Dallapiccola's poetic settings, the composer arranged the sequence of the four poems in the *Quattro liriche di Antonio Machado* in such a way that a symmetrical shape is evident. The brief texts of the first and fourth poems both celebrate the arrival of spring, the second speaks of a dream in which the poet spoke with God, realizing later that it was no more than a dream, and in the third he cries to God that He has taken away what was dearest to him. The form of the poetic text is therefore such that an expressive climax is reached at the end of the third poem in the line "Señor, ya estamos solos mi corazon y el mar" (Lord, we are now alone, my heart and the sea)—a line which struck the composer so forcibly that he had constructed from it a line in *Il prigioniero*. Twenty years later, the line would also be adapted to become the very last utterance of Ulysses alone on his boat during his final voyage in the opera *Ulisse*.

In the music of *Quattro liriche di Antonio Machado*, there are symmetries and echoes that closely parallel those of the poetic texts. The opening gesture of the work, a fanfare-like figure in the piano, imitating the sound of two trumpets and seeming to herald the arrival of spring, encapsulates the basic row in two-part form (mm. 1–4), while the ensuing transposed statement of the row in single voice (mm. 5–8) conveys the impatient scurrying of the renewal of life in spring (Example 4.1 (a) and (b)).

Example 4.1 (a). *Quattro liriche di Antonio Machado*. I, mm. 1–8.

Example 4.1 (a). *Continued.*

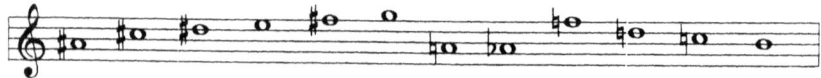

Example 4.1 (b). *Quattro liriche di Antonio Machado.* I, row.

Both the fanfare figure and the melodic version of the row appear again in easily recognizable form in the fourth song, and in this way the beginning and end of the work are linked. If the vocal version is taken to be the basic set, then the initial two-voice version presents the pitch classes of the row in the following sequence:

3	4	5	9	11	10
1	2	6	7	12	8

The row, as it is presented in the single-voice *scorrevole* version beginning in measure 5, is of considerable interest. Not only are its component intervals limited in number (half and whole steps, and minor thirds), but it also comes remarkably close to a "mode of limited transposition" similar to what Olivier Messiaen had been experimenting with in the previous decade.[5] The melodic row resonates with the freshness of burgeoning life through the immediacy of its easily recognizable melodic shape, ascending and descending by different routes as if it were a melodic minor scale. This melodic rise and fall recurs almost continually throughout the song, in both the vocal line and accompaniment, adding a joyous flavor to the setting of Machado's brief lyric. The climax is found in canonic reiterations of prime and inverted forms of the row in the last measures, and the song finally comes to rest on a tritone/minor-third harmony that had earlier formed the basis of the opening fanfare figure. This harmony provides a link between the first two songs through its clear similarity to the chord that opens the second song.

The second song is based upon a row which is immediately stated in prime and inverted forms in the vocal line (Example 4.2 (a) and (b)).

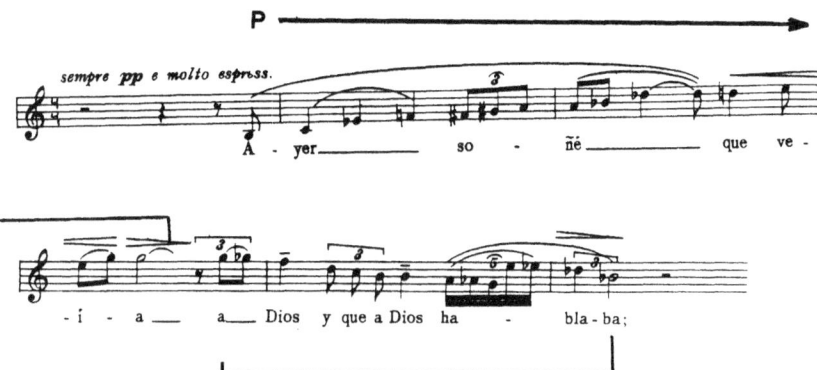

Example 4.2 (a). *Quattro liriche di Antonio Machado*. II, mm. 46–51.

Example 4.2 (b). *Quattro liriche di Antonio Machado*. II, row.

Here, the dream of the poet is recounted, and the music reaches an expressive climax of considerable power through the gradually ascending tessitura of the vocal line, but without however any recourse to the melodramatic.

The third song, the final line of which was to bear such significance for the composer, is based upon yet another row (Example 4.3).

Example 4.3. *Quattro liriche di Antonio Machado*. III, row.

The violent cascade in the piano part, which reappears in mm. 7–12 and is transformed into the final despairing "Ay!" in the voice at mm. 80–81, provides a degree of unity over the song as a whole.

The fourth song of the piece returns once more to the original row which had been enunciated so clearly in the cascades of the first song, a row whose fresh, tumbling form has by now a clear association with spring. Here, at the end of the work, this melodic form of the row is heard as a reminiscence of the first song (Example 4.4).

Example 4.4. *Quattro liriche di Antonio Machado*. IV, mm. 91–96.

The Machado settings were completed on 13 September 1948, a date of considerable symbolic significance for Dallapiccola—the seventy-fourth birthday of Arnold Schoenberg. In an essay headed with this date, Dallapiccola linked this with the same date in 1492 when:

> [A]fter sailing for forty days, Christopher Columbus made the surprising discovery that the compass was pointing to another North. . . . Schoenberg also discovered that North might not always, in all circumstances and in all latitudes, be that tonic which had been spoken of in school. And the Master, like Columbus, swore to silence, a long silence lasting eight years (1915–1923). In those years he elaborated the fundamentals and the complex laws of dodecaphony. His instinct and his faith led him to discover new lands, lands that are still in part unexplored even today.[6]

Tre poemi

The very first work in which Dallapiccola employed a single row as a thread running through an entire composition was *Tre poemi* (Three Poems), composed in 1949. The fact that Dallapiccola referred to the work, in a letter to his publishers, as "three poems for mezzo-soprano and chamber orchestra (variations on a twelve-tone row)" is highly significant in this context. The texts were taken from a variety of sources, but are all sung in Italian. They are James Joyce's "A Flower Given to my Daughter" (in the translation by Eugenio Montale), part of a *ballata* by Michelangelo Buonarroti, "Chiunque nasce a morte arriva," and the composer's own translation of part of the poem "Ars moriendi" by Manuel Machado; the three poems all share the common themes of human mortality and the fragility of earthly joy.[7] The thematic unity of the three poems is therefore supported and paralleled by the musical unity provided by the single tone row appearing in the work's opening measures (Example 4.5 (a) and (b)).

Example 4.5 (a). *Tre poemi*. I, mm. 1–3. (Reproduced by permission of Schott and Company Ltd., London.)

Example 4.5 (b). *Tre poemi*. I, row.

Dietrich Kämper refers to the "quasi-tonal" characteristics of this row, pointing out that its first hexachord can be interpreted in terms of an F minor tonality, the second as E major.[8] This is, perhaps, rather misleading: while it is certainly true that the hexachordal components of the row can be seen in this way, the melodic line constructed from it seems to work against such implied tonal centering, both by the angularity of its melodic shape and its natural division into two phrases that do not coincide with the hexachordal division. What is certain, however, is that the row had considerable personal significance for the composer. In sketches for the work made in July 1949, alongside the original poem of Joyce and its translation by Montale, he places the four row forms above the short-score sketch of this song, the row forms bearing the title "Quadrinità di Annalibera" (Quadrinity of Annalibera). He sent a copy of this to his four-year-old daughter, who was then staying in Switzerland, with the dedication "To my dearest daughter Annalibera on Saint Anne's Day 1949. . . ."[9] It is clear that this first song, with its loving text written by Joyce for his daughter, was composed as a gift for Dallapiccola's own daughter, and the sketch carries the signature "Il babbo di Annalibera" (Annalibera's father).

This first song exhibits two of the most important characteristics of Dallapiccola's serialism, indeed of his musical thinking as a whole, in its combination of formal rigor and an intensely expressive melodic lyricism. There can be little doubt that the composer set the text of Joyce precisely because it combines similar poetic qualities, its internal rhyming, repetitions and alliterations being at the same time both structural and expressive, both a means of ordering thought and a quasi-musical element in the lovely poem:

A Flower given to my Daughter
From *Pomes Penyeach*

Frail the white rose and frail are
Her hands that gave
Whose soul is sere and paler
Than time's wan wave.

Rosefrail and fair—yet frailest
A wonder wild
in gentle eyes thou veilest,
My blueveined child.[10]

The echoing and alliterations of words and phrases (frail . . . frail are . . . rosefrail . . . fair . . . frailest . . . veilest; wan wave . . . wonder wild) that are such a feature of this poem are suggestive, even in themselves, of music, and Dallapiccola has here found a means of creating a musical parallel to this poetic characteristic. Thus, a parallel "internal rhyming" can be seen in the musical setting of the poem, and this is made explicit in the sketches of the work.[11] In the first verse, the composer employs the four serial forms in parallel between voice and instruments, in a geometrical matrix that produces echoes and correspondences between elements of the row-structure (see Figure 4.1).

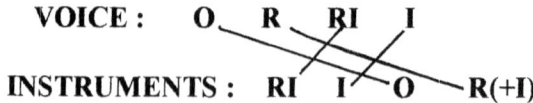

Figure 4.1. *Tre poemi*: correspondence of the elements of the row-structure in the first song.

The final F sharp to which the instruments come to rest at the end of this first verse becomes a pedal tone for the second verse, where it accompanies the four row forms in the voice, following the pattern set by the instruments in the first. In this way, the whole setting is based not only upon a complete exploration of the melodic possibilities of the row, but upon a musical "rhyming" on a structural-melodic level, in which echoes of row forms create an important component, bringing poem and song into the closest possible relationship.

Similar formal-expressive devices can be observed in the two other songs in *Tre poemi*. In the second song, a dark setting of Michelangelo's famous poem on mortality, the row is transposed a full step lower and divided between the various instruments, and the whole movement is constructed canonically. But perhaps of greatest significance from the point of view of the composer's absorption of serial techniques is that in this song we find him for the first time employing row forms in vertical shape. In mm. 4–8, he combines a horizontal prime with a vertical retrograde inversion (Example 4.6).]

Example 4.6. *Tre poemi*. II, mm. 1–9. (Reproduced by permission of Schott and Company Ltd., London.)

In the final song, the Machado setting, Dallapiccola once again creates the strange, unearthly atmosphere that had already appeared in the second of the *Quattro liriche di Antonio Machado*. Here the row returns to its original pitch levels but is modified in its rhythmic shape, and the music once again incorporates canonic forms in its various sections. The opening vocal line in this song is clearly a variation upon the melodic line that had appeared in the first song (Example 4.7).

Example 4.7. *Tre poemi*. III, mm. 1–3. (Reproduced by permission of Schott and Company Ltd., London.)

Tre poemi was written in homage to Schoenberg; the manuscript bears the completion date of 13 September 1949, Schoenberg's birthday, exactly one year after the completion of *Quattro liriche di Antonio Machado*. It was at precisely this moment that Dallapiccola first made contact with Schoenberg, and the exchange of letters between the two was to continue right up to Schoenberg's death in 1951. Dallapiccola had seen Schoenberg on just one occasion, when he was present at the performance of *Pierrot Lunaire* given under the composer's direction in Florence in 1924, but on that occasion he had not had the courage to speak to Schoenberg. When Dallapiccola wrote to him, Schoenberg replied by gently reproving him for this, but saying that he had heard of Dallapiccola's work through Erwin Stein and René Leibowitz. He had somehow formed the impression that Dallapiccola had studied with Webern in Vienna, and he asked for any information Dallapiccola might have regarding Webern's death, a matter which at that time still remained shrouded in mystery.

Dallapiccola asked Schoenberg to accept the dedication of the *Tre poemi* that he had just completed;[12] at that time the work was simply called *Variations for Voice and 14 Instruments*. In accepting this dedication, Schoenberg commented upon Dallapiccola's idea of writing variations for voice, calling it "extremely original" and saying that it had never occurred to him to attempt this. This prompted Dallapiccola to reply:

> When I asked you to accept the dedication of my recent work, it was simply from brevity that I spoke to you about *Variations*. . . . The original title is *Three Poems for Voice and Chamber Orchestra* and the subtitle is *Variations on a Twelve-Tone Series*. They are three pieces that from the formal point of view are closer to the concept of variation that Webern adopted in his Opus 27 than to the classical variation form. It is for this reason that, when I read your phrase "I envy you that you have done this. It is a pity that it never occurred to me," I said to myself that a true variation for voice and instruments still has to be written, and I would be happy to learn that you have achieved it.[13]

Dallapiccola corrected the mistaken impression Schoenberg had formed regarding his studying with Webern, and went on to relate some of the problems he had encountered in approaching twelve-tone composition:

> The little that I have been able to learn about the twelve-tone system I had to learn without treatises, without articles, trying to understand something by analyzing those of your works which I was able to obtain from Vienna in wartime. Anyway, I do not know whether my effort is precisely to overcome "the unnecessary difficulties." . . . [U]p to the present time I have worked more in the melodic domain than in the domain of harmony. And I still feel that I am a beginner. The only thing that sustains me is a great faith and certitude that your path, Maestro, is the only one that might guarantee the continuity of music.[14]

That Dallapiccola should invoke the name of Webern in attempting to explain to Schoenberg the nature of the *Tre poemi* is significant, since it was to Webern above all that he owed the economy and the clarity of the writing. The influence of Webern might seem to link Dallapiccola with the younger generation of European composers who, at that moment, were beginning to mine some of the rich resources of Webern's serialism. However, his equally strong leaning upon the traditional Italian vocal lyricism set him very much apart, distinguishing his approach from that of those composers who were then beginning to view Darmstadt as their spiritual home. Whereas the younger avant-garde at that time pursued compositional rigor as an end in itself, and held the creation of "pure music" as one of their highest goals, for Dallapiccola it was rationality rather than rigor, and the closest identification of musical with poetic and human ideals, that drove him towards Webern. This is an important point to grasp, since despite Dallapiccola's music moving in the direction of Webernian serialism during the postwar period, both the motivation and the process of this movement differed from that of the Darmstadt composers.

Allied with his first contact by letter with Schoenberg, there was another event that had an impact upon Dallapiccola at that time. This was the appearance in 1947 of Thomas Mann's novel *Doktor Faustus* and the subsequent polemics which were initiated by Schoenberg, who saw in Mann's use of the twelve-tone idea as a *leitmotif* in the novel a completely inappropriate use of his own intellectual property.[15] Dallapiccola's knowledge of twentieth-century literature was extremely wide, increasingly so after the war had come to an end, and he admired three writers above all, writers whose work acted as a constant emblem in his own creativity: James Joyce, Marcel Proust and Thomas Mann. He set texts only by Joyce, but he referred to Proust and Joyce as "the two great poets of memory,"[16] and in *Ulisse* he was to create a decidedly Joycean labyrinth of musical and poetic references to his own creative life. The significance of Thomas Mann in Dallapiccola's work was, however, quite different from that of Joyce or

Proust, and indeed, in the decade between the end of the war and Mann's death, this writer provided an almost constant motif running through a whole group of Dallapiccola's compositions.

Dallapiccola had become acquainted with the work of Thomas Mann some years earlier, and the publication of the constituent parts of Mann's tetralogy *Joseph and His Brothers* between 1933 and 1943 was clearly important for him. By happy coincidence, Mann's daughter Monika studied piano with the composer in 1935, although Mann's residence in the United States from 1938 onwards precluded the meeting of author and composer until after the end of the war. The composer's wish that a part of his *Canti di priginia* (1938–41) might be dedicated to Mann proved impossible, but nonetheless, Mann himself did place a dedication of the Italian translation of *The Tales of Jacob* to Dallapiccola in 1935. Once hostilities came to an end, the figure of Thomas Mann began to assume greater significance for Dallapiccola than ever before. The publication of *Doktor Faustus* in 1947, and the severely hostile polemic from Arnold Schoenberg, elicited a supportive and balanced response of Dallapiccola towards Mann, as the author himself acknowledged in a letter to his Italian translator.[17] The period during which the figure of Thomas Mann acted as an important symbol in the creative life of Dallapiccola coincided not only with the gradual establishment of the serial idea as the major structural force in his music (in the works from *Il prigioniero* of 1944–48 to *Canti di liberazione* of 1951–55), but also with the years in which his creative work was dominated by the themes of imprisonment and liberation. The figure of Thomas Mann may indeed be seen, in one guise or another, behind three very important works of this period: *Job, Goethe-Lieder,* and *Canti di liberazione.*

Job

In an article entitled "What is the answer to *The Prisoner*?" published in an American newspaper in 1962, the composer said that *Job,* composed in 1950 and performed that same year (the year that also saw the first staged performance of *Il prigioniero*) represented "a kind of reply, a first step that will lead to *the* reply." He intimated that the opera which he was by then completely absorbed in composing would contain the fuller reply to the question with which *Il prigioniero* had ended:

> I have always refused to explain the question posed by *The Prisoner.* I have always confined myself to saying that some day I should give an answer, perhaps THE answer, in my own way, in the only manner possible to me. But, just as one must move from the intuition of a new work to its realization (and it is superfluous to observe that the road from the one to the other is not precisely a straight line), I still await my reply. I

know now what it is: it will be found in the final line of my Opera in Progress, Ulysses.[18]

The precise nature of the question and of the answer were to be clarified by the composer in a radio talk he gave on the occasion of the first performance of *Ulisse* in Berlin in 1968:

> Ulysses, having travelled so much, thought so much, loved so much, . . . at the end he discovers God. . . . [T]his is the reply to the question on liberty which is placed at the end of *Il prigioniero*.[19]

For Dallapiccola, the question—"Freedom?"—had not simply been a cry of despair, a response of the opera's protagonist to the frustration of his attempt to escape the powers of the Inquisition, but a cry that seemed to bring into question the meaning of all human action. Dallapiccola, perhaps in response to the criticisms made after the work's early performances that the Prisoner's final words were pessimistic in tone, therefore wanted to compose a work in which this questioning might be taken a stage further.[20]

As noted earlier with reference to *Il prigioniero,* all the dramatic works of Dallapiccola are closely bound together in philosophical terms, despite the obvious differences between them. Most importantly, each successive dramatic work adds further layers of significance to the philosophical questioning, to the exploration of a human being's relationship to the divine. In the progression from one dramatic work to another, Dallapiccola uncovers more layers of his personality, each work being more personal, more interiorized, and at the same time more universal in significance. The succession *Volo di notte—Il prigioniero—Job—Ulisse* is one we can describe as steps on a path of discovery. In *Ulisse,* the composer's vision encompasses a glance back over his entire creative life, ending with a momentary epiphany, a vision of the divine to which all the composer's previous stage works had been leading. In terms of this progression, *Job* is the work in which the composer's attention turns most clearly towards the religious dimension, and this contrasts sharply with the realisms of both *Volo di notte* and *Il prigioniero,* despite the presence of a quasi-religious vision in each of the two earlier operas.

The composer's approach to the biblical story was explained in an essay he wrote to coincide with the first performance of the work:

> [A]nd thus I confronted the "poem of pessimism": because this is how some commentators have defined the Book of Job. But perhaps it would be more accurate to define it as a "poem of revolt," making it quite clear that Job is disposed to bear the evils since they are sent to him by God. But his rebellion is unleashed when he becomes aware that he receives no pity from his neighbors. The attitude of Job's friends, who are only

able to condemn him, and who are unable to admit that he has been punished without having sinned, is as far as one could imagine from a Christian mentality.[21]

Job is thus not simply a religious work, it is also a biblical one. Dallapiccola, as we have already noted, had the greatest admiration for Thomas Mann's religious-literary epic *Joseph and His Brothers,* and although there is no reason to suppose that the novel had a direct effect upon the composer's decision to set a biblical narrative in *Job,* both Thomas Mann and Dallapiccola presented a historical-moral symbol through the re-creation of the ancient narratives cast in modern form.

Job is also the work in which Dallapiccola moved farthest from a traditional conception of the theatrical stage towards a somewhat greater degree of experimentation. This is by no means to suggest that Dallapiccola was drawn towards any kind of experimental theatre; the radical dramatic ideas of Bertolt Brecht, which were to have an enormous influence in Italy during the latter part of the 1950s, reached the musical drama only in the work of Luigi Nono, Giacomo Manzoni, and Luciano Berio. Nonetheless, the nature of *Job* as a dramatic work was undoubtedly influenced by the circumstances surrounding its conception. It had been commissioned by "L'anfiparnaso," a group of musicians, painters, and poets in Rome, named after Orazio Vecchi's madrigal comedy *L'anfiparnaso* (1597), revived by the group in 1950. The leaders of the group, Guido Gatti and Alberto Savinio, wished to bring to life forgotten dramatic works from earlier historical periods, and placing alongside them performances of chamber operas by contemporary composers. The enterprise, begun with such lofty aims, was bedeviled by financial problems and survived for only one season. Despite this, Rome audiences in 1950 were able to see, along with *L'anfiparnaso* itself, a revival of Rossini's *Il Turco in Italia* and four new operas including Petrassi's *Morte dell'aria* and Dallapiccola's *Job*. All these works were given in productions in the most modern style, very much influenced by the new manner of production that had been initiated by Giorgio Strehler in the Teatro Piccolo in Milan.

The request from the Rome group for a *sacra rappresentazione* (mystery play) accorded well with the composer's idea of a work that would focus upon Job's struggles with God, an idea that had arisen from a number of seemingly unconnected experiences in the composer's life. It is worth noting these, all of which had an influence on the work Dallapiccola eventually composed. The subject of Job had first been prompted in his imagination when he saw a dance performance on the Job theme given by the German dancer and choreographer Harald Kreutzberg in Florence in June 1949; included in Kreutzberg's performances that evening was a short dance entitled "Job struggles with God." The impression this performance made on the composer was considerable, and he began to ponder how Job, despite his proverbial patience, was the person who directed the most insistent questions at God. In forming his approach to the Job figure, he also had in mind another theatrical performance he had seen during his youth, by the German actor Alexander Moissi as Oedipus in Sophocles' tragedy, and here the impression left was both visual and aural. He remembered in particular how Moissi, dressed in a white tunic, intoned the text around a central tone of A, and how he had spread his arms wide as he first came on the stage, as if he were fixed to a cross.[22] In addition to these two dramatic experiences, the composer also received some stimulus from another source, this time of a visual kind. During the later stages of the work's composition, he visited the sculptor Jacob Epstein in his London studio, and there saw his most recent sculpture *Ecce Homo* (Behold the Man). Dallapiccola, whose work desk always subsequently carried a photograph of Epstein's masterpiece, commented on the striking nature of the work, and its similarity with the Job figure with which he was himself then wrestling:

> This *Ecce Homo,* who had on his lips a bitterness such as I had perhaps never seen in effigies of Christ, with the exception, or partial exception, of that of Piero della Francesca in Borgo San Sepolcro, who seemed to look around and almost, if I may be permitted such a powerful phrase, to despair of the fate of human kind. . . .[23]

The composer adhered very closely to the biblical narrative, and he shaped the work as a series of seven distinct tableaux. The narrative is related by the speaking figure of an *historicus*; God and Satan would be represented by speaking choruses; the other parts, consisting of Job, four messengers, and three friends of Job, are sung. Although the employment of a speaking chorus within a dramatic context might at first sight seem to have been influenced by Schoenberg's practice in *Moses und Aron,* this opera had not been heard at that time (its first performance in concert form took place only in 1954), and the model for such choruses was in Wladimir Vogel's *Thyl Claes* and Darius Milhaud's *La mort d'un tyran,* with both of which Dallapiccola was familiar at that time. Dallapiccola had a very precise idea of the function this speaking chorus would perform in his drama: he wished not only that the two dialogues between God and Satan should inform the listener about the "antecedents of the drama," but also that there should be a clear distinction between the enunciation of these two spoken choruses and the sung chorus through which God replies to Job's question.

In terms of its musical language, *Job* is more fully permeated with serial techniques than *Il prigioniero*. In the dramatic presentation of the narrative, however, Dallapiccola makes use of traditional, often indeed "antique" procedures. These include not only the tableau form in which the work is cast, but also the manner in which the singing chorus representing the Voice of God in Tableau 6 is made distinct by being accompanied by an onstage *obbligato* ensemble of two horns, two trumpets, and trombone, with the addition of an organ. The words of God sung by the chorus are emblematically expressed through the fundamental row of the work, underpinned by the Ambrosian *Te Deum laudamus* in the onstage group (Example 4.8 (a) and (b)).

Example 4.8 (a). *Job*, row.

Example 4.8 (b). *Job*. VI, mm. 1–10.

Example 4.8 (b). *Continued.*

This combination of a row with an ancient melody recalls the integration of the *Dies Irae* plainchant into the texture of *Canti di prigionia*, which had been composed almost a decade earlier (see Example 2.3). But whereas in the earlier work the plainchant melody had been extraneous to the row, here in *Job* the two layers are brought close together, the major and minor seconds of the plainchant being successively transposed and reversed in order to encompass the chromatic space. The quotation of the plainchant melody is, therefore, not simply an allusion to an ancient and distinct musical world, but an integral element of the melodic expression of the tableau, and it is further integrated into the texture by the canonic treatment. These opening measures of Tableau 6 of *Job* bear a certain resemblance to the opening of the final movement of *Canti di prigionia,* the "Congedo di Girolamo Savonarola." Both share the initial percussion chords, followed by a unison choral passage encompassing all twelve tones of the chromatic scale, and the accompaniment in each case incorporates a plainchant melody. This entry of the chorus in Tableau 6 of *Job*, in combination with the onstage plainchant group, forms the dramatic climax of the work.

The fundamental row had made its first appearance in a quite different guise at the very opening of the work: here, as the *historicus* relates the story of Job, a solo oboe seems almost to improvise the melodic steps of the tone row, each step emphasized by repetitions (Example 4.9).

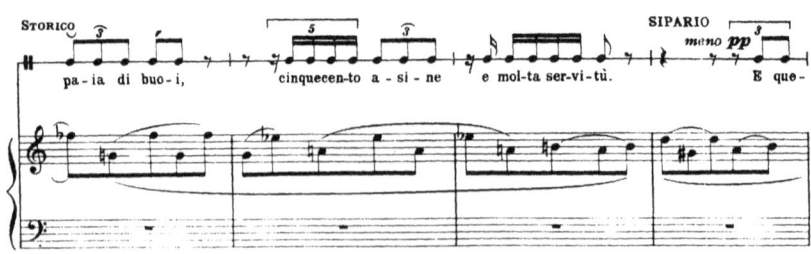

Example 4.9. *Job.* I, mm. 8–22.

Example 4.9. *Continued.*

The row is thus presented in melodic manner, in a pastoral evocation of the desert landscape in which the narrative is set. At the end of this tableau, the flute retraces the row in retrograde form as Job enters the scene (mm. 63–71), thus placing the tableau as a whole within a musical frame (Example 4.10).

Example 4.10. *Job.* VII, mm. 4–13.

Example 4.10. *Continued.*

The other major constituent of the musical fabric, the *Te Deum* chant melody, is also introduced in this first tableau, in the orchestral accompaniment at the words "Thou hast blessed the work of his hands" from measure 43.

In the second tableau, the good fortune of Job is dramatically destroyed, as a group of three Messengers bring him the dreadful news. This announcement uses the basic forms of the row in imitative manner. The First Messenger (soprano) begins by calling Job's name in the dramatically telling interval of minor ninth, followed by P (mm. 3–5), R (mm. 8–11), and I (mm. 12–14); the Second Messenger (contralto) similarly in mm. 17–31; the Fourth Messenger (bass) in mm. 33–43; and finally the Third Messenger (tenor) in truncated form in mm. 50–52. Ute Schomerus has provided a full analysis of the use of the row in this tableau, as indeed in the whole work,[24] but Camillo Togni, in his discussion of the tableau, strangely identifies only the inverted form of the row as forming the basis of the whole tableau.[25] Job's reaction to the dreadful announcement, "I came forth naked from my mother's womb . . . ," is also expressed in terms of the row (mm. 70–74), but here a suggestion of the *Te Deum* chant is also incorporated: the division of the row between voice and accompaniment highlights its three initial tones (E flat–D–C).

In the third tableau, God and Satan, represented by the two speaking choruses, again discuss the fate of Job: the dialogue begins quietly and gradually increases in intensity, reaching a climax as Satan asks God to put Job to the ultimate trial (mm. 25–31). As he asks God to spare nothing but Job's life, the fateful words, which had been accompanied by only a suspended cymbal, are followed by a statement of the row in its fundamental form. This is expressed as a set of chords played *fortissimo* by the full forces of orchestra and organ (mm. 36–40).

Job's lament over the reversal of his fortune is expressed in the fourth tableau, and here the fragmentation of the row acts as a symbol for the disordering of his earlier life. The vocal line in which Job expresses his despair (mm. 2–24) is constructed from four three-tone fragments into which the row is divided, while at the same time the instrumental accompaniment contains subtle suggestions of the *Te Deum* chant that seems to symbolize the persistence of Job's faith in God. Togni pointed out that the only non-biblical text Dallapiccola uses in the whole work occurs in this fourth tableau at mm. 48–55, a quotation from the Church Fathers: "Blessed is he whom God corrects: there is no death without sin, no suffering without blame." Here Dallapiccola introduces a new form of the fundamental row, in which the pitches are re-ordered in the sequence 1–8–3–10–5–12–7–2–9–4–11–6, thus employing a permutational principle that Alban Berg had practiced in *Lulu*, the new row being constructed from every eighth tone of a revolving sequence (Example 4.11).[26]

Example 4.11. *Job*. IV, mm. 47–50.

Dallapiccola explained this permutational row formation in a letter to Hans Nathan, not simply in terms of the structural principle involved, but more broadly in terms of its relationship to the underlying meaning of the drama being enacted on stage:

There is a serial derivation in the fourth episode just where Job's friends, instead of offering him some human consolation, talk theology to him ("Blessed is he whom God corrects: there is no death without sin, no suffering without blame").[27]

In this fourth tableau, the composer's contrapuntal inclination is effortlessly combined with the techniques of row manipulation. The visit of the three friends Elifaz, Baldad, and Zofar to the despairing and terrified Job is introduced by a "Canon Dupex a 6," in which a three-part canon on the inverted row is placed against another three-part canon on a row derived from the first (mm. 32–39). At the end of the tableau, as the three friends depart, another three-part canon is added on another derived row, thus forming a "Canon Triplex a 9" (mm. 114–22).

The fifth tableau consists of Job's highly impassioned monologue, in which he complains of his fate, finally calling upon Jehovah to respond to his grief, and this is again based upon the fundamental row in its basic forms. At the same time, the remembrance of better times in the past that Job expresses here brings a certain quasi-tonal suggestion into the melodic line and the harmony of this passage. For Ute Schomerus, this seemed to be another example of the symbolic use of musical language to suggest elements in the text.[28]

A rather curious, and uncharacteristically bad-tempered, element appears in the course of the fifth tableau. At two points, in mm. 32 and 34, the composer adds to particular musical figurations the remark "N.B.: sottolineando; come una citazione!" ("N.B.: to be underlined: like a quotation!"), and these have a somewhat strange history. The quotation at measure 32, repeated in measure 46, is taken from the fourth movement of Giorgio Federico Ghedini's *Concerto dell'albatro* ("Albatross" Concerto) for piano trio, speaker, and small orchestra composed in 1945, in which the reciter relates Ishmael's meeting with the albatross in Hermann Melville's *Moby Dick*. At measure 34, repeated from measure 40, the quotation is taken from the opening of Goffredo Petrassi's *Salmo IX* (Psalm IX) dating from 1938. Both of these compositions had been crowned with considerable success, and performances of them had made the names of their respective composers more widely known. The motive for including these quotations in *Job* has been unravelled by Rosemary Brown in her study of the composer's work;[29] when he had submitted his *Liriche greche* for a composition prize in 1948, whose jury included Petrassi, he was informed that the work was not valid for consideration, since it was in effect three separate shorter compositions. When the prize was announced, it was won by . . . Ghedini, for a collection of compositions he had written over a number of years! Dallapiccola's reaction to the slight given to his work is reflected therefore in the *furioso* indication which lies above the quotation from Ghedini's work in *Job*, and it explains also the inclusion of a quotation from Petrassi's psalm setting. The appearance of these quotations within the texture of *Job* is of little consequence within the overall flow of the work's music, but does nonetheless place the opera within a historical context, as a witness to an event which had hurt Dallapiccola more than a little.

On a macroscopic level, *Job* exhibits the self-mirroring form that can be seen in many of Dallapiccola's compositions, and indeed the composer himself wished the listener to be fully aware of this aspect of the work's construction, so that he should know "how the work begins and ends." The first and the last tableaux correspond one with another, both related by the *historicus,* and both sharing common melodic material; the second tableau, in which the four Messengers appear, corresponds to the sixth, in which the chorus interprets God's voice; the third, in which God hands Job over to Satan, parallels the fifth, that of Job's solitude. At the center of this structure lies the fourth tableau, depicting the visit of Job's friends. The listener who is aware of the "palindromic" shape of this thirty-five-minute work will thus be greatly aided in understanding it, and the musical parallels aid this.

Dallapiccola was not to compose another work for the stage for a further decade, when he began work on *Ulisse*. However, there are some hints that theatrical ideas began to form in his mind, even in an incomplete form, not long after the completion of *Job*. The evidence for this is the existence of a preliminary sketch for the scenario of a one-act drama based upon Villiers de L'Isle-Adam's *L'enjeu* (The Stakes) made in 1954. In all probability, this would have formed a one-act opera that might be performed together with either *Il prigioniero* or *Job*; nothing came of this idea, however, and it remained in a purely preliminary state.[30]

Dallapiccola's first visit to the United States was made during 1951. He taught at the Tanglewood Summer School during July and August at the invitation of Serge Koussevitzky, following in the footsteps of Olivier Messiaen and Jacques Ibert, who had been there in previous years. Dallapiccola's impressions of Tanglewood were recorded in rapturous mode in a letter to his wife:

> Tanglewood is neither a city nor a village. It is nothing. There is an enormous barn for the big symphonic concerts, one for the theater, one for chamber music. There are offices. One hundred meters in this direction, I could hear a horn practicing Strauss's *Don Juan*; in a space in the middle of the fields, a conductor was taking the brass players through their parts for Brahms's Third. Musical activity at all hours. And an enchanting greenness everywhere about. Even I noticed the *countryside* this time! And the smell of the new-mown hay reminded me of Pisino.[31]

Dallapiccola was invited to return to Tanglewood in the summer of 1952, and it was during this visit that Luciano Berio, who had recently graduated from the Milan Conservatory, spent a period of eight weeks studying with him. Also during this second visit, Dallapiccola fulfilled a number of other invitations to attend performances of his works and to give lectures, resulting in an extensive tour of North America, from Canada to Mexico. In the course of this journey, Dallapiccola sketched out the first movement of *Canti di liberazione* and later began work on a group of piano pieces that would become *Quaderno musicale di Annalibera*. This latter would prove to be the composer's best-known work, one which has drawn many musicians towards Dallapiccola's music. Not least among the reasons for this is that in the work two of the fundamentals of Dallapiccola's art, his individual approach to serialism and his admiration for the contrapuntal art whose greatest master is J. S. Bach, are brought together in particularly expressive and satisfying fusion. During the composer's second visit to America, Dallapiccola met Thomas Mann for the first time, and this acquaintance with the writer Dallapiccola admired above all other living writers had an important bearing upon *Canti di liberazione,* the second movement of which was to be dedicated to Mann. The two artists met for the first time in New York in June 1952, although they had been acquainted since the 1930s, and they met on one further occasion, when Mann visited the Dallapiccola house in Florence during the writer's stay there in 1954. The encounter in New York was clearly one which was to hold great significance for Dallapiccola; afterwards, he wrote to his wife:

> We spoke about music, and he wanted to know my attitude towards Wagner, an attitude I had no difficulty in defining. He told me, with gentle irony, that he had spent many hours with Hanns Eisler, who had told him how certain parts of Wagner's *Die Meistersinger* had been well written, while others were written badly. I replied that some professor of Italian had found more than five thousand linguistic infelicities in *I promessi sposi*. This amused Mann greatly, while Mrs. Mann spoke of that book as something colossal, and he stressed how even Goethe had had an unconditional admiration for Manzoni. He then spoke about the enormous influence exercised by James Joyce, in which writer he saw the possibility of transforming "mythologically" each and every event in life. Just as I had already read previously, so also in what he said, he took pains to stress a link between *Ulysses and Joseph and His Brothers,* even if his book is easier to read.[32]

Tartiniana

Dallapiccola returned to the language of tonality on a couple occasions, and he viewed such returns as fully legitimized by the tonal compositions Schoenberg had written in his later years. When Dallapiccola had just begun to enter the serial arena in *Tre laudi* and *Canti di prigionia,* work on his first full-fledged serial composition *Liriche greche* had been prefaced by the composition of *Sonatina canonica* based upon themes from Paganini. Once again in 1951, before penning *Canti di liberazione* and *Quaderno musicale di Annalibera,* he immersed himself in the composition of a work on a strongly tonal basis, *Tartiniana,* which he described as a "divertimento for violin and chamber orchestra on themes by Tartini." It would appear that each time Dallapiccola made an important new step forward in the direction of a more rigorous serial organization of his music, a preliminary step backwards was necessary, and on each occasion he reworked specific models from earlier Italian music. The composer admitted to the necessity he felt to return to tonal writing at regular intervals: "After each tonal episode, my dodecaphonic procedures have gained in severity."[33]

His preliminary work on the Tartini material is contained in a number of sketch pages that contain ideas for ways he might work on the original material, in which he jotted down possibilities for contrapuntal elaboration in quite specific manner, such as :

First Movement (I) Vl. Solo.
Ritornello: some slight modification to the Vl. in order to obtain the Crab Canon for 8 measures—followed immediately by one of 16 measures.[34]

It is evident from these notes that Dallapiccola's main concern was finding the most appropriate way in which the music of Tartini could be subjected to a greater contrapuntal rigor. His aim was not simply to compose a "Tartini Fantasy" on given themes, nor indeed to envelop the Tartini originals in any kind of neoclassical aura, but a process that has much more in common with the way that Busoni had undertaken a thoroughgoing "research" of material taken from Bach chorales and fugues in his *Fantasia contrappuntistica.* .

Dallapiccola was to approach the work of Tartini on one further occasion, when he composed *Tartiniana seconda* in 1956, again a piece written for his violinist friend Sandro Materassi, but the composer's collaboration with Materassi, with whom he had frequently played Tartini sonatas in concerts, is not the complete explanation of the genesis of these two compositions. The significance of Dallapiccola's choice of music by Giuseppe Tartini (1692-1770) on which to frame his musical elaborations was certainly in part geographical, in the fact that Tartini had been born in the Istrian peninsula some two hundred years before Dallapiccola was born there. However, the personality and preoccupations of Tartini also played a part in this choice. The fertile mind of Tartini, whose improvements in the violin bow and discovery of "resultant tones" had been documented by Charles Burney as early as 1789,[35] no doubt appealed to Dallapiccola's sense of the rational basis of musical expression as much as the fact that the two composers were born in the same area.

Tartiniana, written while Dallapiccola was teaching in the Tanglewood Summer School, had been commissioned by the Koussevitzky Foundation, and the score bears a dedication to Serge and Natalie Koussevitzky. Once again here, as in the *Sonatina canonica* on themes of Paganini, Dallapiccola elaborates the given themes in a predominantly contrapuntal manner. The provenance of the thematic material of *Tartiniana* is to be found in the sonatas of Tartini that Dallapiccola and Materassi had performed in their duo recitals:

1. Tartini, Opus 1, no. 6 in D Minor. Larghetto (transposed to G Minor).
2. Tartini, Opus 2, no. 7 in G Minor. Allegro assai.
3. Tartini, Opus 2, no. 7 in G Minor. Andante affettuoso (transposed and modified).
4. Tartini, Opus 2, no. 12 in G Major. Presto assai.

The edition of the sonatas that Dallapiccola used as the basis for his work was that of Vincent d'Indy and Hubert Léonard, and in the work he is as far removed from any archaeological desire to re-create authentic Baroque performance practice as he is from any tendency towards the neoclassicism he disliked so much. He is, however, concerned to present a sound image with very distinctive qualities, and to this end he employs a small string group of medium-to-low register (no violins, but with divided violas), placing against this a wind group that includes piccolo, E-flat and bass clarinets, contrabassoon, harp, and xylophone.

The theme of the first movement in the original sonata is one in which contrapuntal imitations both within the solo part and between solo and accompaniment are an important feature. Dallapiccola simply translates the two contrapuntal voices implicit in the opening violin part to two flutes, later imitated by other instruments. In this movement, he does not employ the kind of complex canonic artifices that had appeared some eight years earlier in *Sonatina canonica*; the emphasis here is placed upon the instrumental color and articulation, and the kind of *Klangfarbenmelodie* that can be seen in the orchestral version of the work is clearly influenced by the example of Webern's instrumentation of Bach's Ricercare from the *Musical Offering*.

The second movement (*Allegro misurato, ma con fuoco*) takes its thematic cue from a Tartini movement in which the dactylic rhythm so characteristic of later Baroque instrumental practice is all-pervasive. In this movement, one commentator has detected a manner that comes remarkably close to that of Stravinsky's "Dumbarton Oaks" Concerto,[36] a somewhat curious coincidence if one takes into account the composer's stated attitudes to the neoclassicism of Stravinsky. Nonetheless, the motor rhythms that run through the movement seem to evoke some characteristics of neoclassical practice (Example 4.12).

Example 4.12. *Tartiniana*. II, mm. 1–7.

It is in the third movement (*Molto sostenuto*) that we find Dallapiccola undertaking the most rigorous reformulation of the original material in contrapuntal terms. The formal organization of the movement rests upon the re-articulation of thematic cells to be found in Tartini's original (Example 4.13 (a) and (b)).

Example 4.13 (a). Tartini. *Sonata 2/7*, mm. 1–2.

Example 4.13 (b). Tartini. *Sonata 2/7*, mm. 7–8.

The structure of the movement is built from an alternation of episodes based upon each of the two thematic nuclei indicated as A and B in Example 4.13: one fragment in the first, third, and fifth sections, the other in the second and fourth, the latter sections being considerably shorter than the former. Dallapiccola has once again created a symmetrical arch form, and he has also pointed the greatest emphasis in this structure towards the central episode (score figures 33–40), at the heart of which he places a crab canon, the passage of greatest contrapuntal elaboration in the whole work. Above this point in the score, he puts a quotation from the Gospel of St John: "Qui post me venturus est, ante me factus est" ("He is come after me, but he was made before me," John I:15) (Example 4.14).

Example 4.14. *Tartiniana*. III, fig. 33.

A passage at the end of this movement, in which the main theme is transformed once more, is marked *funebre,* a gesture in memory of Serge Koussevitzky, who had died in 1951.

In the final movement (*Allegro assai, ma non precipitato*), Dallapiccola places the thematic material from Tartini within the context of a very simple, repetitive formal structure, and the movement is largely free of the contrapuntal devices that had been such a feature of the preceding movements. At one point (score figure 55), Dallapiccola introduces Tartini's famous "visiting card," the "Devil's Trill," which appears in the violas of the accompanying ensemble.

Quaderno musicale di Annalibera

With *Quaderno musicale di Annalibera* (Annalibera's Musical Notebook), Dallapiccola would at first glance appear to have come the closest he ever came to the composition of an abstract work, one that bears no reference to any poetic or textual component. Of his other works, it is really only *Inni* and the solo cello piece *Ciaccona, intermezzo e adagio* that can be similarly described. At the same time, this set of eleven short piano pieces represents one of the composer's most intimate and personal works, and we should not be deceived into thinking of it as in any sense Dallapiccola's Musical Offering or Art of Fugue. The work occupies an important place in Dallapiccola's output, one to which he devoted a good deal of care; he prepared a fully worked first version before returning to it to prepare the version that would eventually be published. Anne Basart has investigated the changes made between the two versions, as well as looking in detail at the relationship of the work to *Canti di liberazione.*[37] This relationship between the two versions of the piano work is of some importance, since not only was the work used as the basis of incidental music for the film *Il cenacolo,* dealing with the restoration of Leonardo da Vinci's *The Last Supper* in Santa Maria delle Grazie in Milan,[38] but also, more importantly, it served as a sort of preliminary study on the tone row he would explore in a different context in *Canti di liberazione.*

Quaderno musicale di Annalibera is a work that owes a significant debt to J. S. Bach: not only does it incorporate an emblematic, symbolic use of the B-A-C-H motif which had been used by many earlier composers as an homage to Bach, but its very title recalls Bach's *Notebook for Anna Magdalena.* Furthermore, the titles given to the contrapuntal movements (Contrapunctus primus, secundus . . .) are indebted to those in the *Art of Fugue.* It is important to stress, however, that Bach had prepared the *Notebook for Anna Magdalena* as a work that his wife might play for her musical instruction and delight, whereas in Dallapiccola's case it was composed simply as a musical gift for his eight-year-old daughter, not as material for her performance. In terms of its musical content, the piece seems to share some common ground with Schumann's *Kinderszenen*: some of the individual movements bear titles that are clearly pictorial ("Accents," "Lines," "Decorations"), in contrast to the strict contrapuntal forms that are employed elsewhere in the work.[39]

Quaderno musicale di Annalibera represented "preliminary studies'" for *Canti di liberazione*; the two works share a common "all-interval" row, and in the former, Dallapiccola unified the series of eleven short piano pieces by using this row in all of them. The macro-structure, framed by the outer "illustrative" movements ("Symbol" at the beginning, "Shadows" and "Quatrain" at the conclusion), incorporates a succession of movements employing strict contrapuntal procedures and movements largely free of such devices. This alternation of freer and stricter movements recalls the Prelude and Fugue pattern of Bach's *Well-Tempered Clavier,* or the pattern of the *Goldberg Variations,* in which canonic movements recur at regular intervals. The freer movements explore the coloristic possibilities of the material, and overall the piece can be seen as a set of variations upon a single row (in fact, when in 1954 the composer arranged the pieces for orchestra, he gave it the title *Variazioni per Orchestra*).

The "Symbol" of the first piece, around which a large part of the piece is constructed, is the well-known musical symbol representing the name of Bach, and this makes its first appearance immediately in the upper melodic line as the fundamental row is unfolded. In the course of the movement, this motif is presented seven times in clearly audible fashion, with brief interludes between each appearance. The composer highlights the most important transformations of the B-A-C-H motif at each presentation by means of a slight dynamic emphasis—a note says that these appearances should be set "in relief" against the rest of the texture. Although these transformations of the motif are the most clearly discernible part of the contrapuntal texture, they are by no means the only transformation of the motif in "Simbolo," and David Lewin has shown that there are many more, often very subtle, manifestations of this B-A-C-H motif discernible in the inner parts of the piece as well.[40] At those points at which the motif is the most important melodic component of the texture, the composer places it in such a way that certain quasi-tonal suggestions can be heard, with the B-A-C-H motif as the upper or lower part of "diatonic" chords, and with a two-tone ostinato in the other hand underpinning each entry, as in its opening appearance (Example 4.15 (a) and (b)).

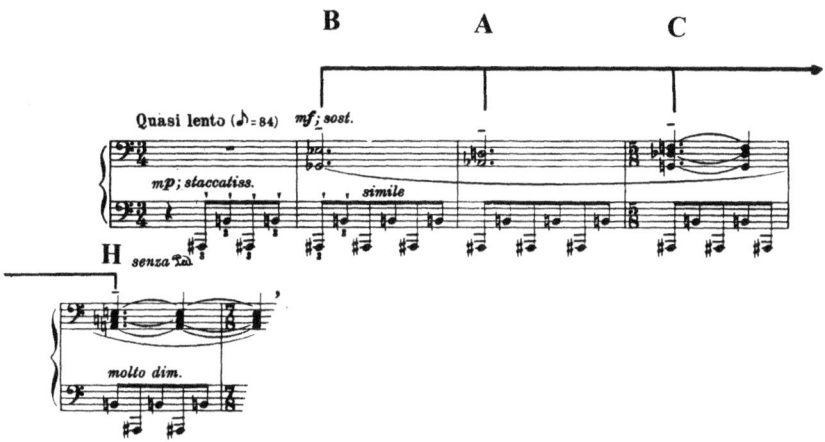

Example 4.15 (a). *Quaderno musicale di Annalibera*, I, mm. 1–6.

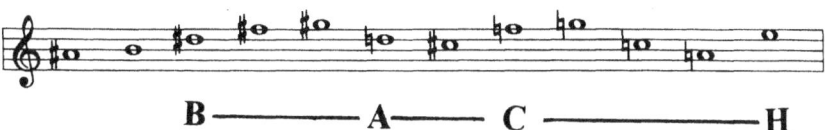

Example 4.15 (b). *Quaderno musicale di Annalibera*, row.

These opening measures reappear at the end of the movement, creating a circular form for the piece as a whole, and there is also a suggestion of a ternary structure in the tempo changes, with the central episode (mm. 17–28) at a slightly faster tempo. The eighth-note ostinato runs almost constantly throughout the piece, particularly supporting the major appearances of the B-A-C-H motif, and these moments seem almost to recall the typical Bachian texture of two melodic solo instruments or voices supported by a faster-moving continuo line. The piece ends with a fading A-minor triad, without any retardation, and with an exact measuring of the length of the final chord. The fact that this triad is simply the conclusion of the serial presentation, together with the A-sharp–B ending of the ostinato, tend to preclude any hint of a "quasi-tonal" conclusion to the piece.

With the second piece, "Accenti" (Accents), there begins the sequence of alternating freer and stricter movements that will be maintained throughout the rest of the work. The titles of the first of each pair seem to hint at their character ("Accents"—"Contrapunctus primus"; "Lines"—"Contrapunctus secundus"; "Friezes"—"Contrapunctus tertius"), whereas the contrapuntal forms employed in the second of the pairs explore the canonic possibilities of the material. In "Accenti," we see the serial and dynamic components of its construction brought closely together: the *sf* indications occur without exception in conjunction with the half-step fragment that recurs frequently (Example 4.16).

Example 4.16. *Quaderno musicale di Annalibera*. II, mm. 1–6.

The serial structure of the piece is very simple, with each two-measure phrase based upon a new presentation of the row, alternating prime and inverted forms in symmetrically sequenced transpositions.

In the "Contrapunctus primus," Dallapiccola begins to present the contrapuntal devices to which he was constantly drawn. Here, he writes a canon at the unison, in two voices for the first eight measures, a third voice added thereafter, but it is the rhythmic parameter of the canon that provides the greatest interest. Dallapiccola reverses the durations of the tones within each phrase, at the same time increasing each duration by the addition of a dot, and in this way the melodic interplay of the voices becomes one of a constant echoing of one voice by another within a seemingly irregular rhythmic framework. This becomes particularly dense in the second part of the piece, in which three voices are present, but even in the first measures the melodic and rhythmic texture is of great subtlety, with contrasting articulations of one voice against another, and involving a very delicate use of the pedal (Example 4.17).

Example 4.17. *Quaderno musicale di Annalibera*. III, mm. 1–8.

There is a clear indication here that Dallapiccola had absorbed a certain influence from the rhythmic thinking of Olivier Messiaen, who, in the third chapter of his *Technique de mon langage musical,* published in 1944, had set out the possibilities for such "rhythms with added values."[41] It is known that Dallapiccola always held Messiaen in the highest regard as a composer, and the feeling was mutual. In April 1947, Messiaen wrote to Dallapiccola thanking him for arranging some Italian concerts for him, and requesting more scores of his works than he had been able to obtain, so that he could study them in detail.[42] This is not to suggest that Messiaen's ideas on music were to exercise a profound and lasting influence upon Dallapiccola—the two composers, after all, came from very different musical cultures, and absorbed different influences. Nonetheless, at various points, notably in *Quaderno musicale di Annalibera* and in *Canti di liberazione,* one can detect a certain influence at work. Dallapiccola and Messiaen shared a fascination with the rhythmic parameter, and while Dallapiccola never described himself as a "rhythmician" in the way that Messiaen did, nonetheless the "rhythmic researches" he undertook in certain works were an important part of his musical explorations. Here in the *Quaderno musicale di Annalibera,* these researches were not an end in themselves, but one of the means through which the composer explored the poetic and colorful sonorities of the piano. It must be admitted, however, that Messiaen had already created a far more adventurous and original pianistic language, in such works as *Quatre études de rhythme* and *Cantéodjayâ,* than Dallapiccola would ever achieve. The astonishing pianistic exuberance not only of Messiaen's solo piano music but of the piano parts of such works as the "Turangalila" Symphony and of *Oiseaux exotiques*—created for the most part for the composer's wife, Yvonne Loriod—never formed a part of Dallapiccola's sound world.

The fourth movement, "Linee" (Lines), is built from simple elements: a counterpoint of melodic lines in contrasting rhythms, employing only two serial forms, prime and inversion. The two-part counterpoint of this movement, with its gentle evocation of Bach's *Two-Part Inventions,* outlines a simple harmony that, while having no obvious tonal center, nonetheless seems to float between chord groupings that suggest a sequence of dominant seventh harmonies (Example 4.18).

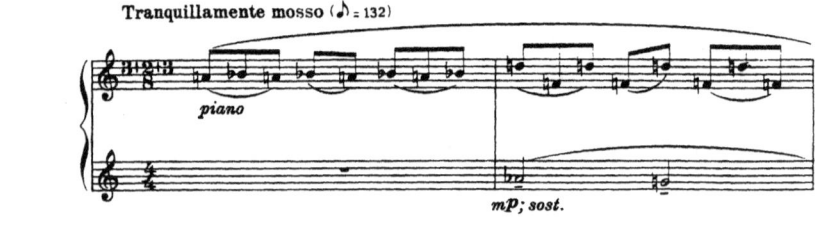

Example 4.18. *Quaderno musicale di Annalibera.* IV, mm. 1–5.

The "Contrapunctus secundus (canon contrario motu)" forms what would at first sight seem to be simply a further link in the chain of strictly composed movements, but it also introduces a further element. Here, in a piece whose expressionistic brevity recalls Schoenberg's *Six Little Piano Pieces,* Opus 19, eight serial forms are distributed between the two hands, and the whole movement has a perfectly symmetrical shape. This is made up of canons in contrary motion over the eight measures of the piece, reversing the roles of *dux* and *comes* at the midpoint (mm. 4–5), with the right hand employing P and R forms while the left uses I and IR. Dallapiccola has here clearly been influenced by Webern: in the second movement of his Piano Variations, Opus 27, Webern had similarly created a piece from rows in symmetrically canonic form around a central axis (Milton Babbitt discussed the influence of Webern here in an essay on "contextual counterpoint"[43]). What distinguishes the writing of the two composers is very clear.

Whereas in the row structure of the piece Dallapiccola has clearly adopted a Webernian model, he has also incorporated some important quasi-tonal reference points that were entirely foreign to Webern's way of writing, with the seventh-chord figurations that conclude each row statement (mm. 4 and 8) acting as a kind of cadence to each half of the piece (Example 4.19).

Example 4.19. *Quaderno musicale di Annalibera.* V, mm. 1–4.

Over and above this purely constructional aspect, what is brought into play for the first time in the work is a reference to a particular musical manner, that of the instrumental Serenata, in the performance indication placed at the head of the piece. Dallapiccola has thus moved away from the rather general indications of textures ("Symbol"—"Accents"—"Lines") that had appeared in the earlier movements of the work, and has brought to the work a suggestion of a particular musical characterization. The characterization even extends to adding an indication in measure 2 that a detail of the musical figuration should sound as if the "players" of the serenade are tuning up (*quasi accordando*). Furthermore, the movement contains many more indications of dynamics and expression than are present in some other movements of the work: *più espressivo, affettuoso, quasi pizzicato, fuggevole,* all of which would suggest that the evocation of a serenade in the little piece is significant. It is surely not too far-fetched to suggest that the little Serenade, with its delicate lightness of touch and its dance-like character, might have been composed specifically to charm the composer's young daughter Annalibera.

The sixth movement, "Fregi" ("Friezes"), is, like the fifth movement, also cast in strictly symmetrical form. Again, there is a central axis at the exact midpoint of the piece (mm. 6–7), where the melodic line is transferred from right to left hand and at the same time inverted, while the accompanying harmony from mm. 3–6 in the left hand is similarly inverted in the right hand in mm. 8–12, producing a double counterpoint of great simplicity. This contrapuntal symmetry is matched by a symmetry of row statements: after the row exposition in mm. 1–4, the melodic line then simply goes into reverse, P followed by R in mm. 4–6, and I in the left hand in mm. 3–6. This is answered by its symmetrical opposite, with I and RI in the left hand and P (from measure 8) in the right hand. Once again, it is perhaps possible to see a musical "characterization" here, as in the serenade that precedes it, this time a kind of recitative, with the upper melodic line marked to be played not only *dolcissimo, ma intenso,* but also *con espressione parlante* (Example 4.20).

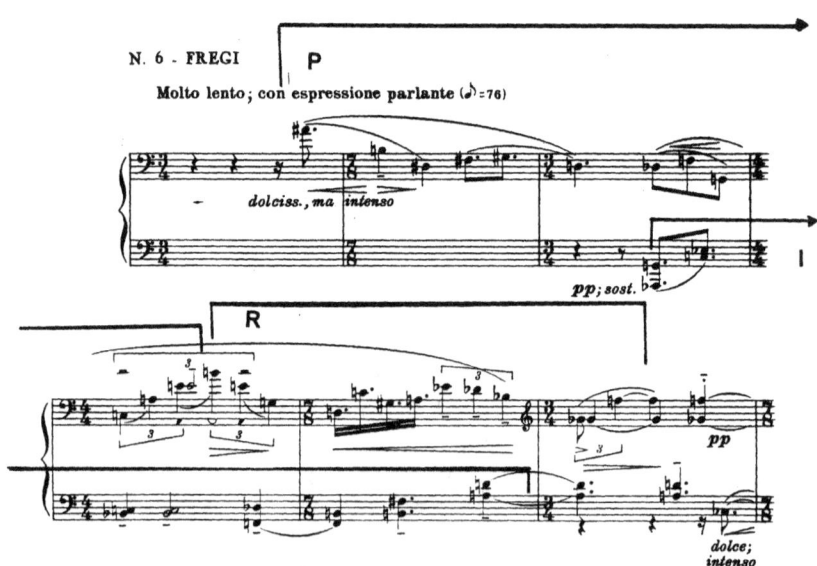

Example 4.20. *Quaderno musicale di Annalibera.* VI, mm. 1–6.

The "Andantino amoroso e contrapunctus tertius (canon cancrizans)" which follows is a remarkable tour de force of Dallapiccola's canonic bravura. Here, as in the fifth movement, he approaches the lapidary serial canons of Webern, with the crab canons laid out in enigmatic form in red at the head of the page in the manner of the Flemish contrapuntists. Eight measures of the *dux* are followed by a further eight measures of *dux* and *comes* together (the *comes* a retrograde form of the *dux*). The scheme of serial forms simply supports the crab canon, and again the atmosphere of the movement is highly important, a gentle whisper hardly rising above *pianissimo* throughout, as though in the gentlest evocation of a lovers' duet (Example 4.21).

Example 4.21. *Quaderno musicale di Annalibera*. VII, mm. 1–9.

```
1–8:   Dux:    P–R–I–IR      9–16:   P–R–I–IR
       Comes:                         I–IR–P–R
```

"Ritmi" ("Rhythms"), in contrast to the preceding movements, concentrates upon the rhythmic parameter. Dallapiccola links segments of the row to fixed rhythmic figurations: this can be seen in mm. 1–5, in which each half of the row is presented through a highly differentiated rhythmic figure (**a** and **b**). In the measures that follow, the initial rhythmic figuration **a** is repeated twice, linked first to a fragment of the I-form of the row, then to the initial fragment of P. The final tone F sharp of the row is extended to provide a pedal underpinning the second row exposition in mm. 5–9. The first three tones of the row are repeatedly presented in a 3:2:1 rhythmic form (bracketed in the score), and in this way the movement is clearly a study for the second movement of *Canti di liberazione* (Example 4.22).

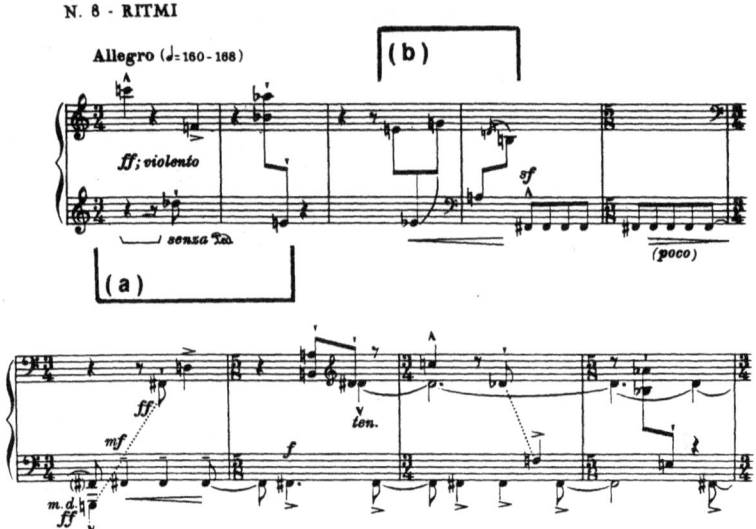

Example 4.22. *Quaderno musicale di Annalibera*. VIII, mm. 1–9.

The rhythmic features of the theme that appears at the start of this movement dominate the whole piece, and are especially apparent in the chord figuration that interrupts the flow of canons in the central section from measure 29 onwards. The canonic intensity can be seen most clearly in mm. 24–28, in which two rows are presented canonically (based on P and I and beginning on F sharp and C respectively in measure 24, concluding on the repeated tones C and G flat (= F sharp), all to be played *marcatissimo* (Example 4.23).

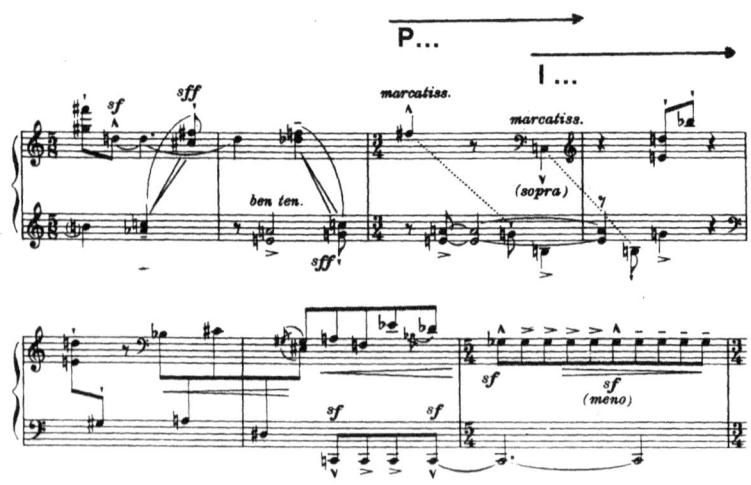

Example 4.23. *Quaderno musicale di Annalibera*. VIII, mm. 24–30.

In contrast to "Ritmi," the ninth movement, "Colore" ("Color"), presents contrapuntal and serial procedures of great simplicity. In a movement of only nineteen measures, with very clear reversals between the two hands (at mm. 5 and 9), five serial forms are employed (P: mm. 1–4; R: mm. 5–8; I: mm. 9–10; I: mm. 11–12; IR: mm. 13–19). In measure 8, with a repeated chord *ppp*, Dallapiccola emphasizes the harmony that then propels the serial forms into reverse. The character of this movement is that of a lullaby, marked to be played in an "affectionate, cradling" manner. In the final measures Dallapiccola extends the durations of each pitch of the row, and in this way its last statement occupies considerably longer than its predecessors. This lingering upon a static harmony might well suggest a child's descent into sleep, but it might also bring to mind the famous example of Schoenberg's color movement "Colors: Summer Morning on a Lake" in his *Five Orchestral Pieces*, Opus 16. In each case, the largely static harmony diverts the listener's attention towards aspects of timbre, but in Dallapiccola's case without the element of *Klangfarbenmelodie* that had made Schoenberg's orchestral piece so remarkable (Example 4.24).

Example 4.24. *Quaderno musicale di Annalibera.* IX, mm. 8–19.

The tenth movement, "Ombre" ("Shadows"), is constructed entirely from harmonies formed from the P and I row forms. The movement as a whole is in a ternary form (mm. 1–7; mm. 8–17; mm. 18–23), with the central episode at a different dynamic level, marked to be played *misterioso*. In each serial exposition, the composer emphasizes each half of the row by a reiteration of the chords through which it is invariably presented. It would seem that the title of this movement reflects the contrasting loud and soft utterances of the outer and inner episodes (Example 4.25).

Example 4.25. *Quaderno musicale di Annalibera*. X, mm. 1–7.

The final movement, "Quartina" ("Quatrain"), had borne the title "Sogni" ("Dreams") in an earlier draft, and here a highly expressive and wide-ranging melody runs right through the whole piece. The four phrases of this melody are each constructed from one of the four serial forms, and each is accompanied by a chord sequence. The change of title from "Dreams" to "Quatrain" is significant: whereas the earlier title had suggested no more than a simple, rhapsodic form, the later title suggests the poetic "quatrain form" in which the movement is cast. Dallapiccola had analyzed this form in an essay on nineteenth-century Italian operatic practice, in which he had noted that the emotional heart of such a melodic form, which he demonstrated in arias from Verdi's operas, was to be found in the third of its four lines; in more extended examples it nonetheless remained in this penultimate position, and always maintained a similar expressive outline:

> In 1939 the great English musicologist Edward J. Dent asked me whether I knew an Italian treatise, or chapter of a treatise, that described the structural principles of the aria in *melodramma*. My answer was negative, although I couldn't help wondering why so formidable a scholar as Dent should have asked me, a layman, for such information.

Today I believe I can say that there was a tradition, transmitted verbally or by example. I should now like to consider what the poetic quatrain has given composers of *melodramma*. . . . [T]he emotional crescendo is always found in the third verse of a quatrain, or on the third couplet of a quatrain-pair. It can be effected by means of rhythmic excitation, harmonic surprise, or an upward thrust of the vocal line. More often than not the end result is achieved through the collaboration of two, or even all three, of these elements; rarely will a fourth element contribute to the crescendo, namely an absolutely novel twist of instrumentation.[44]

This description of the melodic phenomenon would seem to fit remarkably well with the form in which this final movement of the *Quaderno musicale di Annalibera* is cast. In this brief, almost epigrammatic piece, we find four distinct phrases, each constructed from a duality of rows in melody and accompaniment (see Table 4.1).

Table 4.1. *Quaderno musicale di Annalibera*: the four distinct phrases, each constructed from a duality of rows in melody and accompaniment.

	Melody	Accompaniment	
mm. 1–4	I	R	
mm. 5–8	R	RI	
mm. 9–12	RI	P	
mm. 13–16	P	I	

The third of the four little phrases, with its almost Monteverdian repeated-note palpitations, is not only more breathless and rhythmically agitated than any of the other phrases, but indeed bears the indication *con la massima espressione* (Example 4.26).

Example 4.26. *Quaderno musicale di Annalibera*. XI, mm. 10–18.

Example 4.26. *Continued.*

Perhaps Dallapiccola was creating a subtle homage to one of his great Italian predecessors in the finale of the set of piano pieces. On many occasions he acknowledged the importance of Verdi, and of the *melodramma* in general, and in the same essay he described the words and music of nineteenth-century Italian opera as "filling a lacuna in Italian literature. It compensates for a true Romanticism."[45] "Quartina" ends without the finality that would be provided by the normal double bar, but with the sound of the final chord and its ambiguous quasi-tonal implications (B Minor–B-flat Major), left to float freely *a niente*. It is not far-fetched to suggest that the tonal ambiguities and delicately breathed sigh of these final measures recall the ending of the last of Schoenberg's *Six Litle Piano Pieces,* Opus 19 (Example 4.27).

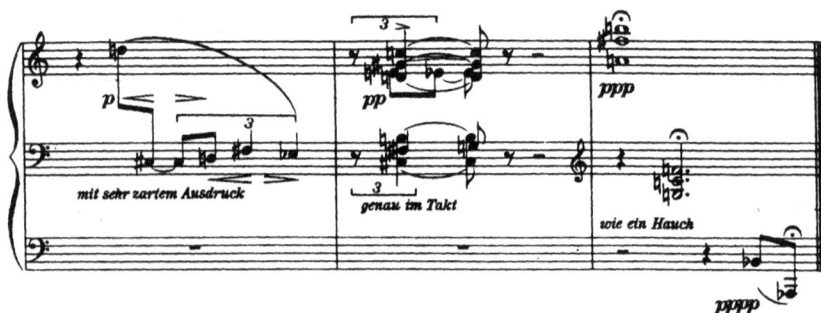

Example 4.27. Schoenberg. *Six Little Piano Pieces,* Op. 19, no. 6, conclusion. (Reproduced by permission of Schott and Company Ltd., London.)

Dallapiccola continued to work at the score of *Quaderno muscale di Annalibera* even after it had received its first performance by Vincent Persichetti in Pittsburgh in November 1952, and he welcomed the appearance of a disc of the first performance, as he regarded this as an important document of the work's original version. The material from which the piano pieces had been formed remained in his mind for some time to come, and eventually appeared in quite different guise in *Canti di liberazione,* which was completed in 1955. It has already been stressed that the conception of *Canti di liberazione* owed something to Dallapiccola's acquaintance with Thomas Mann, the composer's most important "spiritual mentor" during these postwar years, and indeed the connections of the German author with the Italian composer's work were to come somewhat closer in his next work, the *Goethe-Lieder.*[46]

Goethe-Lieder

Dallapiccola completed *Goethe-Lieder* for mezzo-soprano and three clarinets within the period of only a few weeks between January and March 1953, after the first performance of *Quaderno musicale di Annalibera* as a piano piece and before its orchestral version was completed, and it received its first performance in Boston in April 1953. The significance of Thomas Mann as a figure whose presence can be felt in the background to the *Goethe-Lieder* is considerable. Dallapiccola had frequently read Goethe's poems in the *West-Östlicher Divan* in his youth, but despite knowing the several songs of Schubert bearing the title *Lied der Suleika,* he had never been tempted to delve further into the character of Suleika who is portrayed there, until prompted to do so by reading Thomas Mann's *Joseph and His Brothers*:

> Being a passionate reader of Thomas Mann's work, and especially of his tetralogy *Joseph and His Brothers,* I owe to Mann, alongside other debts of gratitude, that of having clarified for me the figures of Suleika and Yussuf. Mann recounts the "trial" of the unhappy wife of Potiphar (while admitting to being partial to Mut-Em-Enet), and thereby succeeds in throwing new light on the figure of this woman ("After the passing of much time, the lady fixed her eyes on Joseph, saying 'Sleep with me'": Genesis 29:7), so that she emerges in quite a different light from that shed by the very brief biblical account and by her depiction in countless paintings and tapestries. Mann is inclined to forgive Mut-Em-Enet a great deal, and in the final reckoning deplores only one thing, the "noted harangue" that she directed in demagogic tone to the Egyptians, inciting them against Joseph. At this point Mann comes very close to Dante in the evaluation of facts. And Dante ("L'una è falsa ch'accusò Giuseppo": Inferno XXX, 97) places the woman among the falsifiers of words. In "Joseph the Provider" (cf. the chapter called "The Sunken Treasure"), Mann narrates how and with what modifications the legend of Mut-Em-Enet passed into Persia: Suleika is the name which Persian legend

gave to the wife of Petepre; Yussuf is the name given to the son of Jacob and Rachel. It is only after such a clarification that the figure of Suleika appeared defined to me, at least insofar as was needed to set my fantasy in vibration.[47]

There is no doubt that in composing a work for a combination of mezzo-soprano and three clarinets, Dallapiccola was influenced by Webern's *Canons,* Opus 16 for soprano, clarinet, and bass clarinet, not least in the symmetrical form in which *Goethe-Lieder* is cast, with the voice accompanied successively by 3–1–2–3–2–1–3 clarinets. This symmetry focuses the work around the outer and central movements, to which all the forces contribute, with the tempi of the movements moving progressively towards and then away from the fast central movement. Furthermore, the composer stressed the importance of the sequence of the poems from Goethe's collection: "One recognizes its spiritual stature as soon as one has understood from the score what this succession of verses has predisposed for the music."[48]

The degree to which Dallapiccola creates a unified symbolic world encompassing the text and music of *Goethe-Lieder* is indeed truly remarkable, and Michael Eckert has demonstrated that this is a central element in the work's expressivity.[49] The row itself is the most important object in this symbolism—appearing and disappearing, being transformed, fragmented, hidden, or restated—always in relation to the meaning of the text; this may be observed in every section of this remarkable composition. The fundamental row of the work begins with the three-tone cell that becomes the "Question" motif, which will assume great significance in the final song of the work (Example 4.28).

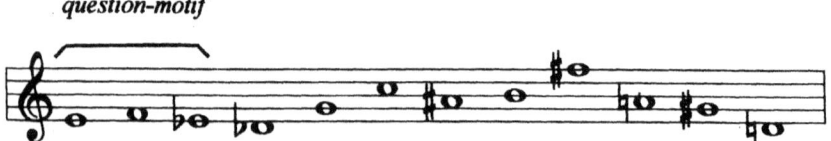

Example 4.28. *Goethe-Lieder,* row.

In the first song, the poet speaks of the thousand different forms of the natural world in which his beloved attempts to hide herself ("In tausend Formen magst du dich verstecken"), a parallel to the "Thousand names of Allah." The row, in analogous manner, can at first be discerned only through the intricate weaving of the clarinet parts, while the voice part sets out the row in its P and IR forms (Example 4.29).

Example 4.29. *Goethe-Lieder*. I, mm. 1–10.

In the third verse, as the poet speaks of the "magic veils" with which his beloved hides herself ("Du magst mit Zauberschleiern dich bedecken"), Dallapiccola restricts the material to the initial three-tone "questioning" group of the row, a unit that will take on a fuller significance later in the work. This unit would also appear much later in the composer's work, in the opera *Ulisse* and in *Three Questions with Two Answers* (Example 4.30).

174   The Music of Luigi Dallapiccola

Example 4.30. *Goethe-Lieder.* I, mm. 11–13.

At the end of the song, as the poet speaks of his recognition of his "ever-present" beloved ("Allgegenwärt'ge, gleich erkenn'ich dich") the complete row appears once more in its clearest melodic form, at the climax of a canonic passage (Example 4.31).

Example 4.31. *Goethe-Lieder.* I, mm. 14–20.

In this way, the identification of the object of the poet's desire with the constantly changing appearance of the row (the "allgegenwärt'ge"—the "ever-present one"—of Goethe's text) is made explicit within the space of a very short song. The complete row acts as a symbol of recognition of the beloved, hidden from view at the opening of the song, while the fragmentary three-tone cell is a symbol of disguise and of the lover's guile. In the complete poem as Goethe originally wrote it, the invocation of the thousand names of Allah is finally revealed to be itself a symbol for the poet's naming of his beloved, and we can therefore see how Dallapiccola, similarly, sets out the row not simply as a musical device but as a symbol of the poetic image.

In the second song, the twin poetic symbols of sun and moon are symbolized respectively by P and I forms of the row. The composer himself remarked upon the fact that Goethe's reference in the text to a "puzzle" (*Rätsel*) had prompted him to set this text in the form of a puzzle canon. The sickle moon appears to embrace the sun in all its splendor, and the two row forms similarly embrace and reflect each other. P is immediately followed by I in the solo vocal opening of the song, as the poet sings "Die Sonne kommt! Ein Prachterscheinen! / Der Sichelmond umklammert sie" ("The son comes! A glorious vision! The sickle-moon embraces her"). Even the question placed by Goethe in the middle of the little poem ("Who could bring together such a pair? How can this puzzle be explained?") signaling the entry of the E-flat clarinet, with its contrasting symmetries, also elicits an open, questioning ending to the tiny song. The layout of the row dispositions in the song, with the "sun" and "moon" forms creating a rounded shape, is remarkable in its symmetry (Example 4.32).

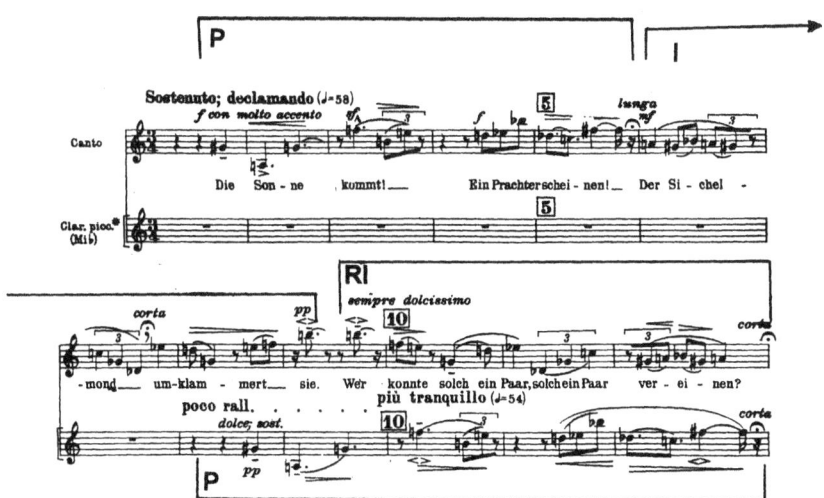

Example 4.32. *Goethe-Lieder*. II, entire movement.

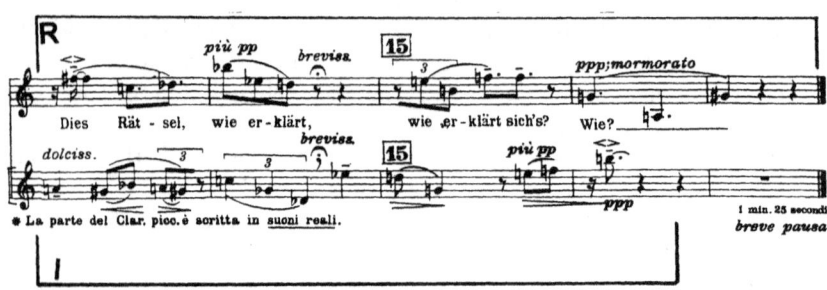

Example 4.32. *Continued.*

In the third song, canonic forms are employed to symbolize the ardent lover's importuning of his beloved: the vocal part is imitated, in a foreshortened form, by the B-flat clarinet in double augmentation, while the E-flat clarinet, beginning last, sets out an inverted form of the vocal melody. Just as close imitations and echoing have long been a stock-in-trade of the operatic composer when suggesting the closeness of a pair of lovers, so here the identity of melodic line between voice and instrumental accompaniment is employed by Dallapiccola to suggest the lovers' desire for fulfilment of their love.

The whole of *Goethe-Lieder* is focused towards the central fourth song, at whose heart lies the only utterance of the name of Suleika, in the phrase "Von Suleika zu Suleika ist mein Kommen und mein Gehen" ("From Suleika to Suleika is my coming and my going"). This is not only the emotional heart, but also the constructional axis of the whole work. Once again, in a song marked to be played *impetuoso, appassionato*, the composer makes great use of the initial three-tone group of the row, but he also makes a slight re-ordering of the final pitches of the row. He had done this, by his own admission, simply because the original form did not satisfy him in this case, and he justified the change by saying that it is made only at the end of a phrase, and some way into the composition.[50] The passionate outburst in the final moments of the song, based upon the three-tone group in all four parts, is followed by a long pause before the next song begins.

In the fifth song, the text itself seems to suggest the structure of the musical setting: "Der Spiegel sagt mir, ich bin schön" ("The mirror tells me that I am beautiful"), giving rise to a whole group of mirror canons (Example 4.33).

Example 4.33. *Goethe-Lieder.* V, mm. 1–10.

The sixth song, similarly, takes its cue from Goethe's text : "Bist du still in dich gekehret" ("When you are silently self-possessed . . .") Here, the composer builds the whole song exclusively upon the three-tone group at the start of the row, but in the seventh and final song, this motif has become enigmatic, a symbol of the poet's questioning ("Ist's möglich?"—"Is it possible?") (Example 4.34).

Example 4.34. *Goethe-Lieder.* VII, mm. 1–5.

178 *The Music of Luigi Dallapiccola*

Example 4.34. *Continued.*

The dodecaphonic symbolism Dallapiccola presents in *Goethe-Lieder* had already, of course, been present on several occasions in the composer's work, beginning right at the first appearance of a row in his work, in the opening measures of *Tre laudi*. But in *Goethe-Lieder,* more than in any previous composition, it becomes a key which can unlock some of the work's secrets. This symbolism was to remain as an essential component in his expressive language in all his later compositions, and Dallapiccola himself warned of the dangers of any analysis of the serial aspects of his music that might not take fully into account this vital link between technique and expression. Simply to reveal the structural and unifying aspects of row manipulation in any work is not enough in the case of Dallapiccola's music, and indeed would greatly distort the importance of the serial techniques themselves. One must go further and reveal the expressive purposes of the row as a symbol, with a much broader significance in the all-embracing expressivity of the work.

There is surely nothing accidental in the fact that the completion of *Quaderno musicale di Annalibera* overlapped the initial composition of *Goethe-Lieder*. These two compositions, among the most frequently performed of all Dallapiccola's works, are at first glance highly contrasted in character: one without a text, the other crucially dependent upon Goethe's poetry, one apparently abstract in its musical designs, the other referential to a quite remarkable degree, and so on. However, as the examination of the two works has shown, they seem to reach out towards each other in a highly significant way. The miniature poetic dramas of *Quaderno musicale di Annalibera* seem at times almost to touch hands with the highly expressive musical symbols we find embedded in *Goethe-Lieder*. In this way, the "pure" instrumental music of Dallapiccola (of which *Quaderno musicale di Annalibera*fhan *through* a text. This element in Dallapiccola's music was to reach its point of greatest significance in the relationship of a nontextual to a textual composition, that is to say in the orchestral *Three Questions with Two Answers* and the opera *Ulisse* some fifteen years later.

V

Text and Symbol: 1954–1964

By the early 1950s, Dallapiccola's name had become better known throughout Europe, and his music began to be played more frequently, especially in Germany, England, and France, rather less so in his native Italy. At the same time, some of the younger generation of European composers, those born in the early 1920s whose first mature music had begun to emerge after1945, were beginning to move in the direction of a radical experimentation, on occasion almost to an *ab ovo* reexamination of fundamental principles. This experimental spirit was represented above all by those composers who attended the Darmstadt Summer School during its earliest years,[1] and the Italian presence at Darmstadt was spearheaded by the enormously active and influential figure of Bruno Maderna, closely followed by his pupil Luigi Nono. Dallapiccola, on the other hand, never visited Darmstadt. For him, the radicalisms that soon began to be linked with the name of Darmstadt were far removed from his own artistic concerns. These concerns were not centered upon a root-and-branch realignment of music, nor upon the rather one-sided view of Webern's music espoused for a while by many of the Darmstadt composers. Dallapiccola based his aesthetic view on all three Viennese serialists—Schoenberg, Berg, and Webern—readily encompassing the highly emotional and expressive music of those composers, and he wished to integrate such expression with his innate Italian lyricism. Dallapiccola, therefore, in some sense ploughed a rather lonely furrow during the period, but at the same time his ground-breaking and highly rational approach to serialism had an enormous influence on his younger colleagues, most particularly on Luigi Nono. Although Luciano Berio had briefly been a pupil of Dallapiccola in Tanglewood and had retained a warm relationship with him, it was Nono with whom Dallapiccola had the closest artistic rapport, above all through their shared humanitarian and libertarian concerns.

Piccola musica notturna

Piccola musica notturna reflects the element of poetic and highly colorful expression that we have already identified as one of the most important components of Dallapiccola's art. It was written in response to a request from Hermann Scherchen for a short orchestral piece for the "Jeunesses Musicales" Festival in Hanover in June 1954, and, like *Goethe-Lieder,* its composition occupied Dallapiccola for only a few weeks. He prefaces the score with a poem of Antonio Machado, "Noche de verano" ("Summer Night"), depicting a nocturnal walk in a village square in the moonlight, and it seems clear that the music reflects in some way the atmosphere evoked in the poem. Dietrich Kämper has suggested that the relationship of the poetic text to the music might be likened to that Beethoven suggested for the poetic idea in his Pastoral Symphony—"an expression of feeling rather than description"—and this would seem to be the most accurate definition of the relationship.[2] Certainly, one cannot ignore the poem in attempting to understand the music, if only because Dallapiccola on no other occasion placed a poem at the head of a score. This was not the first occasion on which he had incorporated pictorial elements into a purely instrumental composition, since, as we noted earlier, *Due studi* had begun life as music to accompany images on film of two scenes in Piero della Francesca's frescos. Pictorialisms had, of course, entered into Italian music on several occasions in the past, from the frequent allusions to the phenomena of nature found in many of Vivaldi's concertos, to the highly coloristic and vivid evocations in Respighi's orchestral music, but the idea of "descriptive music" never found a home in Dallapiccola's music. Despite this, the nocturnal atmosphere of Machado's poem is reflected in the calm melodic lines of the piece, with frequent melodic flow of one instrumental line into another in the manner of *Klangfarbenmelodie*. If there are any pictorial elements in the piece, they are symbolic rather than descriptive, and the clearest example of this might be found in the final section of the work, where from measure 45 a number of mirror canons begin to appear, leading at measure 58 to a double canon that makes use of all four serial forms. Kämper has suggested that that this might reflect the poem's description of the complex play of light and shade in the village square through interweaving the basic serial forms as tightly as possible (Example 5.1).[3]

Example 5.1. *Piccola musica notturna*, mm. 57–63. (Reproduced by permission of Schott and Company, Ltd., London.)

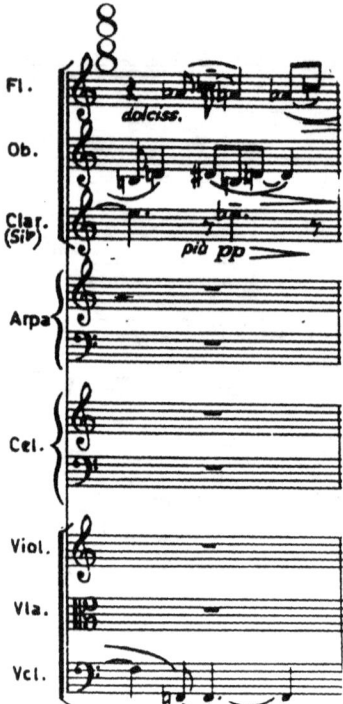

Example 5.1. *Continued.*

Piccola musica notturna has entered the standard repertory of modern music, not least because of its attractiveness as an example of evocative instrumental writing. It has done so, not so much in its original orchestral version, but rather in the version for chamber ensemble that Dallapiccola made for Queen's College in New York in 1961. This is set for just eight instruments: flute, oboe, clarinet, harp, celesta, violin, viola, and cello. A comparison of the two versions of the work reveals the complete mastery of instrumental technique that Dallapiccola exhibited; despite the reduction in the forces, he manages to make the piece even more atmospheric and subtle.

Piccola musica notturna, in common with both *Quaderno musicale di Annalibera* and *Canti di liberazione,* is based upon an all-interval row (A) and also (as had already happened in *Il prigioniero* and *Goethe-Lieder*) upon a further row derived from it by the transposition and mirroring of its initial three-tone segment (B), appearing in mm. 39–41. The important point here is that, whereas Dallapiccola had already experimented with a duality of rows within a single composition in the *Due studi,* the two rows in *Piccola musca notturna* are now closely related, with an instantly recog-

Text and Symbol: 1954–1964   183

nizable resemblance in their patterning of major and minor thirds. It is interesting to note also that, in a double page of preliminary sketches for the primary row of the work, three versions dated 23–27–31 October 1953, the composer took great joy in finally "discovering" the version of the "all-interval" row on the latter date—All Saints' Day! (Example 5.2)

Example 5.2. *Piccola musica notturna,* rows A and B.

Sandro Perotti has pointed out that that *Piccola musica notturna* shares some common features with Bartók's *Music for Strings, Percussion, and Celesta,* suggesting that the latter work acted as an influence.[4] Not only does the instrumentation—with its string group, celesta, and large array of coloristic percussion—bear some resemblance to the Bartók model, but indeed the opening melodies of the two works also contain several points of contact (Example 5.3 (a) and (b)).

Example 5.3 (a). Bartók. *Music for Strings, Percussion, and Celesta,* opening measures. (Reproduced by permission of Universal Edition [London] Ltd.)

Example 5.3 (b). *Piccola Music Notturna,* opening measures. (Reproduced by permission of Schott and Company, Ltd., London.)

In both cases, the choice of the medium range of violas, the common employment of the pitches B flat–C sharp–B, and the limitation to a melodic line contained within the interval of a perfect fifth, would certainly seem to indicate a possible influence of one upon the other. Furthermore, the fact that Bartók sets out the melodic cell simply in terms of the five-pitch group presented at the very opening, and that Dallapiccola similarly employs simply the initial five pitches of the row (B flat–G–B–C sharp–D) for the main theme, seems to support such an influence. Dallapiccola admired Bartók's music, and was perhaps drawn to the Bartók model on this occasion by the association of the nocturnal aspects of his own piece with the well-known nocturnal music of Bartók, of which the opening of the *Music for Strings, Percussion, and Celesta* is an example. There is, however, another intriguing possibility that the nocturnal setting of the work might have prompted. The three-tone figure with which the row, and indeed the work itself, opens is an inverted form of the highly important three-tone figure to be found at the head of the passacaglia bass in "Nacht" ("Night"), one of the most striking movements of Schoenberg's *Pierrot Lunaire*. Whether the composer consciously or unconsciously drew out this figuration because of the nocturnal connection between the two pieces is of course a matter that cannot be finally resolved, but it is certainly a possibility.

The structure of the work, which is constructed in a ternary pattern, revolves around the use of the two rows A and B (see Table 5.1).

Table 5.1. *Piccola musica notturna*: the ternary pattern revolving around the use of the two rows A and B.

A:	mm. 1–21:	based upon row A: P (mm. 1–5), I (mm. 6–13), P (mm. 14–21).
B:	mm. 22–44:	based upon rows A and B (mm. 22–32), on a free total chromatic (mm. 33–38), on B (mm. 39–44).
A':	mm. 45–57:	based on A (mm. 45–57, as a reprise of mm. 1–12).
	mm. 58–68:	a double canon on all four row forms.

Beyond the light "pictorialisms" to which reference has already been made, *Piccola musica notturna* is a highly colorful and atmospheric evocation of the poem with which the score is prefaced. With its nocturnal *chiaroscuro*, the work is one of Dallapiccola's most attractive instrumental compositions, and one whose delicate and refined instrumental textures neatly counterbalance the remarkably simple symmetries of its melodic and harmonic language.

Canti di liberazione

The most important composition on which Dallapiccola worked during this period was *Canti di liberazione* (Songs of Liberation), completed in 1955. *Quaderno musicale di Annalibera*, which immediately preceded it, acted as a rich fund of material into which the composer delved for the choral work; he said that the relationship of the two works was a logical one, the titles of both containing "... *libera* ... ," a root of both the name of his daughter Annalibera and of "liberation."[5] In *Canti di liberazione,* the composer takes up once more the themes of oppression and liberation that had appeared over a decade earlier in *Canti di prigionia,* both works encompassing a reflection of contemporary events. The year 1955, when *Canti di liberazione* was completed, was, after all, the year of the bus boycott in Montgomery, Alabama, which led directly to the Civil Rights Movement led by Martin Luther King. The work combines Schoenbergian serialism with the polyphonic writing that had long been an essential component of Dallapiccola's musical language. The composer clearly intended that *Canti di liberazione* should be understood as a companion work to *Canti di prigionia,* and it is known that he had envisaged such a companion piece at the time of writing the earlier work.[6] On many occasions between the two compositions, Dallapiccola had let it be known that he was working on this project, and his obvious hesitation about commencing work on *Canti di liberazione* points to the work's significance, especially as his first large-scale piece employing serial techniques. The points of similarity between *Canti di prigionia* and *Canti di liberazione,* both in three movements arranged slow-fast-slow and in exact durational proportions, both for choral and instrumental forces, and both on historic texts in Latin taken from separate authors, all suggest that the two works form a kind of "dyptich." However, between the two stands another significant composition, the opera *Il prigioniero,* and it may therefore be more accurate to speak of a "tryptich" of compositions all having the theme of liberty. The "fratello" motif of *Il prigioniero* is frequently quoted in the third movement of *Canti di liberazione,* a movement that also contains an allusion to the *Preghiera di Maria Stuarda,* and this allusion was, according to the composer's own account, the only part of *Canti di liberazione* that was free of the "serial disciplines." If we bear in mind this close intermeshing of the three major compositions, it would not be inappropriate to describe the period 1938–55 as one dominated by the themes of imprisonment and liberation.

The choice of appropriate texts for the work caused the composer considerable difficulties, but as on so many earlier occasions since *Tre laudi* in 1936, his wife's literary researches came to his aid. For the first movement, he chose part of a letter written by the Reformation theologian Sébastien Castellion counseling firmness of faith:

> O my brother, my brother . . . if our faith is firm, the divine will be with us. . . . Those who deny that it is possible to expel the Canaanites will disappear; they will die in solitude, and those who believe will enter into the land of Canaan.

For the second, he chose part of the Book of Exodus (Chapter 15, verses 3–5), in which Moses sings God's praises for the drowning of the Egyptians in the Red Sea:

The Lord is a man of war: the Lord is His name. Pharoah's chariots and his host hath he cast into the sea: his chosen captains also are drowned in the Red Sea. The depths have covered them: they sank into the bottom as a stone.

For the third, he picked an ecstatic song of devotion taken from the *Confessions* of Saint Augustine:

You called and cried out loud and shattered my deafness. You were radiant and resplendent, you put to flight my blindness. You were fragrant, and I drew in my breath and now pant after you. I tasted you, and I feel but hunger and thirst for you. You touched me, and I am set on fire to attain the peace which is yours.

In contrast to the texts Dallapiccola had set in *Canti di prigionia,* all of which were supplications to God from those who were to have their faith brought to the ultimate trial, here in *Canti di liberazione* the texts express a firm religious faith. The first movement, dedicated to the composer's father, stresses the need for a firmness of faith; the second, dedicated to Thomas Mann, expresses pride in God's deliverance of his people from oppression; but the third, bearing no dedication, is altogether different, an inward confession of faith that is given a distinctly devotional character by the composer. The *Canti di liberazione,* it is important to stress, are not "songs of liberty" but "songs of liberation," that is to say not a rallying cry but an expression of faith and hope, as well as gratitude to God for His gift of freedom.

Although sharing common musical materials with *Quaderno musicale di Annalibera, Canti di liberazione* is in a quite different emotional climate. The few passages that appear in both works are transformed almost beyond recognition, such as the change from a gentle *pianissimo* to a violent *fortissimo* when part of the seventh piano piece is placed in the crab canon of the new work's first movement (mm. 85–91). In the work, the composer makes use of the whole gamut of serial constructions that he had learned from the Viennese models, in particular the technique developed by Schoenberg of constructing a new row by transposition and rearrangement of hexachords of the original row in its P and I forms. Dallapiccola was very proud of the mastery of the techniques of serialism that he was thus able to display.[7]

Canti di liberazione contains many allusions to the B-A-C-H motif that had been of central importance in *Quaderno musicale di Annalibera*; the composer no doubt used this particular row for both works because it contained a reference to the motif, which can be constructed from the row by simply combining its first two pitches with their transposition. The very first appearance of the motif in *Canti di liberazione* is to be found at the culmination of a passage in which the most rigorous serial procedures are employed. This is in mm. 10–14 for orchestra (based upon mm. 8–12 of "Ombre," the penultimate piece in *Quaderno musicale di Annalibera*), followed by a choral elaboration of fragments of the row, pitches 7–9 in mm. 14–18, and pitches 1–3 in mm. 18–26. The vertical appearance of the B-A-C-H motif is finally reached at measure 26, and in this way Dallapiccola seems to call upon Bach's name at the climax of this passage (Example 5.4 (a) and (b)).

Example 5.4 (a). *Canti di liberazione*, row.

Example 5.4 (b). *Canti di liberazione*, mm. 20–26.

The "rhythmic researches" which were referred to in the discussion of *Quaderno musicale di Annalibera* are taken a stage further in *Canti di liberazione,* and this aspect of the work has been thoroughly explored by both Dietrich Kämper and Rosemary Brown.[8] In the central movement, a rhythmic cell based upon the proportions 3:1:2 appears right at the start in the orchestral parts, a rhythmic proportion that had already appeared in "Ritmi," the eighth movement of *Quaderno musicale di Annalibera*. Here in the choral work, however, it is not simply an abstract element of the composition, but is linked with the word "Dominus" (Lord) sung by all the choral voices (Example 5.5).

Example 5.5. *Canti di liberazione*. II, mm. 1–6.

A passage of great constructional refinement begins at measure 39: here, the rhythmic-melodic cell from earlier continues to dominate the orchestral parts, but now Dallapiccola combines a *melodic* canon by contrary motion with a *rhythmic* canon by augmentation (Example 5.6).

Example 5.6. *Canti di liberazione*. II, mm. 39–47.

As the movement progresses, the "rhythmic researches" become more clearly linked to the meaning of the text. In mm.101–4, for example, as the text speaks of the abyss opening up in the Red Sea to swallow up the Egyptians, rhythmic units lengthen progressively, while in mm. 106–9, the downfall of the Egyptian forces is portrayed musically by the opposite, a rhythmic intensification by gradual diminution. At measure 113, the rhythmically proportioned cells are laid out graphically in a rhythmic canon for percussion instruments in six "voices," surely one of the most telling examples of Dallapiccola's tendency to musical depiction in simple terms. This rhythmic canon is placed at the most dramatic moment of the whole movement (Example 5.7).

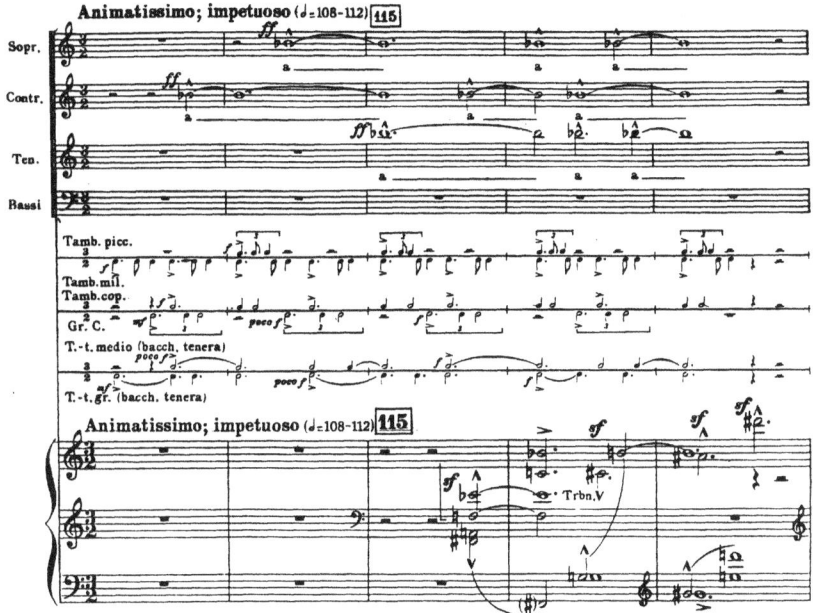

Example 5.7. *Canti di liberazione*. II, mm. 113–17.

The "depiction" contained in these measures is a subtle reference to Thomas Mann's tale "The Tables of the Law." In this tale, Mann, the dedicatee of this central movement, had written a passage describing the virtuosity of Miriam, Aaron's sister, in playing the timpani, and Dallapiccola stated that this prompted him to invoke the percussion instruments at this point in the piece. Indeed, Dallapiccola described the whole movement in a letter to his publisher as ". . . brick-red, the color of the desert . . . also derived in part from reading 'The Tables of The Law.'"[9] The final part of the movement contains many parallels with the opening, and the density of the canonic elaboration here becomes even greater. Allusions to the B-A-C-H motif appear when the name of God is invoked once more ("... *nomen eius* ... ," mm. 164–688), and the movement comes to rest on a twelve-tone chord in chorus and orchestra (Example 5.8).

Example 5.8. *Canti di liberazione.* II, conclusion.

We noted earlier how *Canti di liberazione* is in some sense a companion work to *Canti di prigionia,* but the two choral works differ radically in style and language, as our examination has demonstrated. *Canti di prigionia,* it should be remembered, had been composed at a very early stage in Dallapiccola's gradual absorption of serial techniques, whereas *Canti di liberazione* was composed with a clear desire to demonstrate the composer's full mastery of the technique. During the period of composition of *Canti di liberazione,* Dallapiccola had heard the news of Schoenberg's death in America, and there can be little doubt that he also intended the work as a kind of homage to the great Viennese composer, just as *Quaderno musicale dii Annalibera* had paid homage to J. S. Bach.

Canti di liberazione is one of Dallapiccola's most important compositions, and it represents a milestone in the development of the composer's approach to twelve-tone techniques. Any examination of the serial intricacies of the work reveals that Dallapiccola had, by the mid-1950s, not only completely absorbed these techniques, but integrated them with the polyphonic way of thinking that had always been present in his work. He had also moved beyond the implicit "quasi-tonal" references in the harmonic and melodic language of his earlier twelve-tone works such as *Liriche greche, Ciaccona, intermezzo e adagio,* and *Quattro liriche di Antonio Machado,* towards a richer and more all-embracing serial vocabulary. This richer vocabulary would become an essential part of the expression in all his later compositions.

An Mathilde

Dallapiccola composed the cantata for soprano and orchestra, *An Mathilde,* in 1955, on a commission from Southwest German Radio in Baden-Baden, with whose Music Director Heinrich Strobel he had been in contact since 1945. The choice of a group of poems by Heinrich Heine as the text for the work grew not only from his love of German Romantic Lieder (he frequently took part in performances of Schumann's *Dichterliebe*), but also from his great love of the poetry of its greatest representative, Heine. Laura Dallapiccola, to whom the work is dedicated, helped the composer to choose the three texts, taken from collections of poetry Heine had written during his last illness: *Den Strauss, den mir Mathilde band, Keine Messe wird man singen,* and *Das ist der böse Thanatos*. The first poem, addressed to the poet's wife, to whom he gave the name Mathilde, was found among Heine's papers after his death; the second and third had appeared in *Romancero,* a collection of Heine's poems published in 1851. In the first poem, the poet's wife brings him a bunch of flowers, which makes him deeply melancholy because the fragrance reminds him of happier and healthier days. In particular, it brings to his mind the memories of a ballet troupe with its bright and sparkling splendor, but the poem ends in despair, with a foreboding of death. In the second poem, he imagines his death, and counsels his wife not to stand too long by his graveside, and to take a carriage home afterwards. The third poem imagines the figure of Death coming to take him away, and he implores the angels in heaven to protect and guard his wife after he has gone.

As in so many of Dallapiccola's works, the initial poetic image—here, that of the bunch of flowers the poet gives to his wife Mathilde—is symbolized in musical terms through fundamental forms of the row. The full tone row appears only in the opening of the vocal part, while the four four-tone groups in the flute, oboe, horn, and viola are built from fragments of all four row forms, creating harmony of the most delicate timbre (Example 5.9 (a), (b), and (c)).

Example 5.9 (a). *An Mathilde*, mm. 1–3.

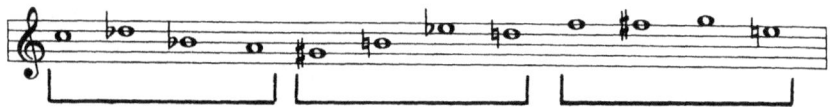

Example 5.9 (b). *An Mathhilde*, row.

Example 5.9 (c). *An Mathilde*, row fragments.

As in *Goethe-Lieder*, the first appearance of the complete row occurs only as the voice enters, and this slight delaying of the full basic row was to recur in several later compositions. The third part of the cantata—"An die Engel" ("To the Angels")—introduces a new version of the row, this time formed from the initial three-tone segment of the first, just as the latter part of *Goethe-Lieder* had concentrated upon the three-tone "questioning" motif.[10] In *An Mathilde*, the row outlined by the saxophone and bassoon is built from this three-tone segment and transposition, together with their inversions. Dallapiccola places these four constituents together in such a way that the first and second hexachords also demonstrate a relationship of original and inversion: Roman Vlad pointed to this, emphasising how the composer had employed to expressive ends a technique that he had learned from his study of Webern (Example 5.10).[11]

Example 5.10. *An Mathilde*. III, mm. 1–2.

In this way, Dallapiccola emphasizes the clearly audible three-tone motif around which the piece revolves, and thus seems to link together the concept of questioning, associated with a similarly close-knit three-tone motif in *Goethe-Lieder,* with that of death, the theme that runs through the final poem of *An Mathilde.* This connecting thread of textual theme and musical motif would, in due course, become of crucial importance in the final scene of his opera *Ulisse.*

The opening of the third part of *An Mathilde* quoted in Example 5.10 also demonstrates another aspect of this part of the work, one to which Dietrich Kämper attached great importance.[12] Dallapiccola here indulged what he called an "intellectual pleasure" by incorporating allusions to two monuments of German musical culture, from composers whose influence upon his own musical thinking had, in their different ways, been considerable. These are the opening of Bach's *Three-Part Invention* in F minor, and the "Destiny motif" from Wagner's *Die Walküre.* The allusion to Bach is of particular importance; it can immediately be seen that the basic cell from which the row of the movement is built is related to the melodic cell from which Bach constructs his Invention (Example 5.11).

Example 5.11. Bach. Three-Part Invention (Sinfonia) in F Minor, mm. 1–3.

Goethe-Lieder and *An Mathilde* were clearly conceived as a pair of related works. This relationship comes not only from the proximity of their dates of composition, but also from the way in which they represent Dallapiccola's homage to the German poetic spirit that had permeated the work of Lieder composers right up to the Second Viennese School. Hans Nathan has investigated this whole matter, pointing to the ways in which the Austro-German tradition of Lied composition seems to find melodic "echoes" in these works of Dallapiccola.[13] However, a further connecting thread links *An Mathilde* with *Ulisse.* The final scene of the opera, as the examination in the next chapter will show, was to be full of allusions to earlier compositions of Dallapiccola, and one of these allusions is to the opening and closing parts of the final song, "An die Engel," in *An Mathilde.* The opening measures, with the text "Das ist der böse Thanatos..." ("This is dread Thanatos . . . "), with its closely interwoven eighth-note ostinato figurations, was to become a part of Melanto's "Dance of Death" (*Ulisse*, Act II, mm. 727ff.), while the final measures of the same song ("Beim Wort, das nur der Priester kennt . . ." ("by the awesome Word that's known / And said aloud by priests alone . . .") returns in the Epilogue of the opera, linked to Ulysses' attempt to find the word with which he might express his conception of divine reality.

Dallapiccola would later state that the year 1956 represented a decisive turning point in his development.[14] The completion of *Canti di liberazione* in the previous year had been a significant achievement in the composer's work, rounding off as it were the period that was earlier described as dominated by the themes of imprisonment and liberty. During the year that followed, he composed *Tartiniana seconda, Cinque canti* (Five Songs) for baritone and eight instruments, and *Concerto per la notte di Natale dell'anno 1956* (Concerto for Christmas Eve in the year 1956) for solo soprano and chamber orchestra. The two latter-named compositions undoubtedly set the basis for the style of Dallapiccola's later composition, while the first represented another return to the music of his Istrian predecessor Giuseppe Tartini.

Tartiniana Seconda

Dallapiccola's violinist duo partner Sandro Materassi, for whom he had written *Tartiniana* in 1951, had requested a further work along the same lines in 1956. He had returned from a visit to Padua in 1955 armed with a bundle of photocopies of manuscripts of music by Tartini,[15] and he asked Dallapiccola whether he could do something with them. On this occasion, however, the work that resulted was rather different from the earlier *Tartiniana*. Dallapiccola composed two versions of *Tartiniana seconda,* one for violin and piano, first performed in Vienna in March 1956, the other for violin and chamber orchestra, given in Turin early in 1957, and there is a marked contrast of atmosphere between the two versions. The spare textures from which the piece is built appear somewhat ascetic in the piano version, whereas the sense of fantasy and imaginative elaboration of the original models is greatly enhanced in the version with orchestral accompaniment. This is largely due to the sharply defined instrumental colors, with English horn, celesta, glockenspiel, vibraphone, side drum, and cymbals contributing to the bright, almost playful sonority.

In *Tartiniana seconda,*[16] the canonic bravura that had long been a feature of Dallapiccola's music is once again in evidence, and the composer was clearly proud of this aspect of the composition, unraveling it in an article he wrote in connection with the first performance of the chamber orchestra version.[17] The four movements of the work ("Pastorale," "Tempo

198   *The Music of Luigi Dallapiccola*

di Bourrée," "Presto," and "Variazioni") do not fundamentally alter the Tartini originals in nature, but simply draw from them the contrapuntal possibilities that, at an earlier point, Dallapiccola had similarly drawn from themes of Paganini in *Sonatina canonica,* and this process of contrapuntal elaboration is at its most intricate in the outer movements of the work. In the opening "Pastorale," the violin and accompaniment between them set out a crab canon, with the two principal melodic lines delicately harmonized (Example 5.12).

Example 5.12. *Tartiniana seconda.* I, fig. 1.

This opening canon is set out in two halves (mm. 1–8 and mm. 9–16), followed by a further exposition in mm. 17–30, but there is a constant one-measure displacement of the two voices throughout the movement. It is worth noting that at the point where the two canonic expositions converge (measure 17), the two voices meet with the identical opening measure of each melody, one *recto* and the other *inverso*.

The second and third movements of the work—"Tempo di Bourrée" and "Presto leggerissimo"—do not involve the intricate canonic procedures that are a feature of the outer movements. In fact, Dallapiccola's contribution is here more or less limited to realizing the bass for keyboard, in much the same way that, a year earlier, he had contributed a realization of the bass of six cello sonatas of Vivaldi for an edition made by Leonard Rose. At a certain point in the third movement, as the violin remains silent, the theme from Tartini's Sonata No. 25 in A Minor, which will form the basis of the final movement, makes an early appearance.

The fourth movement, "Variazioni," is articulated in distinct episodes, its various sections bearing titles that allude to the canonic forms employed ("Alla Sarabanda: Canon cancrizans," "Doloroso: Canon per augmentationem, contrario motu"), but the entire movement is full of canons. Even in passages such as the "Maestoso," in which the principal feature is the emphatic *coup d'archet* of the solo violin, Dallapiccola cannot resist constructing an accompaniment tracing each measure of the violin's part in reverse (Example 5.13).

Example 5.13. *Tartiniana seconda*. IV: Maestoso, mm. 1–8.

The movement as a whole is constructed as a chaconne and twelve variations, and the climax of the canonic bravura is reached in the section marked "Doloroso," in which the composer concentrates on the accompaniment alone, creating a canon by augmentation in contrary motion in four contrapuntal parts (Example 5.14).

Example 5.14. *Tartiniana seconda*. IV: Doloroso, mm. 1–4.

Cinque canti

In addition to revisiting the arena of tonal composition on occasion, Dallapiccola also at several points returned to areas of literature he had made very much his own in earlier compositions. One example is the translations of ancient Greek literature made by Salvatore Quasimodo that he had first explored in the *Liriche greche* and to which he was to return in *Cinque canti* in 1956. Another is the medieval *lauda* which he had first visited in his settings of Iacopone da Todi in 1929, and later with *Tre laudi* in 1936–37, *Concerto per la notte di Natale dell'anno 1956*, and finally his last completed work, *Commiato*, in 1972. *Cinque canti* is important within

Dallapiccola's work as a whole: it demonstrates not only that he had by this point gained complete mastery of twelve-tone composition, but also that the remarkable fusion of text and musical expression we have frequently mentioned had by then taken on great importance. The sequence of poetic texts in the work arises from expressive as well as structural necessity, as always in Dallapiccola's multi-movement vocal compositions, and indeed here it is crucial to the work as a whole. As Jacques Wildberger pointed out in his study of the piece, *Cinque canti* is symmetrical, with man and his sufferings placed in the central movement, framed by two morning songs and two night songs.[18] The subject matter is man and time, and it thus bears a symbolism of birth and death. The first and fifth poems describe respectively the morning star and the night sky, the second describes a dawn chorus of birdsong, and the fourth the sleeping of all earthly creatures. This thematic form of the text is also reflected in the symmetries of the work's tone row, with clear parallels between its constituent parts at both the hexachordal and trichordal level. This symmetry of the row is similar to that exhibited in the rows of Webern's String Quartet, Opus 28, and his Cantata No. 1, Opus 29 (Example 5.15).

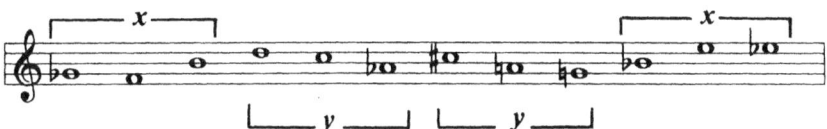

Example 5.15. *Cinque canti,* row.

Dallapiccola commented upon this row:

> It is probably the case that I had chosen a series of this kind because of the need which I felt to draw the Cross on the score in musical notes, and at the same time to be able to show graphically the idea of the arms attached to the Cross by means of two other lines.[19]

What he refers to here are those pages of the central movement in which he has placed a cross image in the musical score. The central chord, played by the whole instrumental ensemble, is isolated graphically from the rest of the page—as the trunk of the cross, as it were—while the vocal line is constructed symmetrically in terms of its component intervals, as if to represent arms suspended from the branches of the cross. This the composer called an "ideogram" (Example 5.16).

Example 5.16. *Cinque canti.* III, mm. 55–59.

Such "eye music" has a long history, and many examples are to be found in the music of the Middle Ages and Renaissance. What is of great interest here, however, is that Dallapiccola, to judge from the comment quoted above, seems to have constructed the row itself with the possibility of such a use already in mind. It would appear that the close identification of musical constructions and textual reference was not a fortuitous, even incidental, by-product of the process of composition. It was inherent in the very formation of the *materia musica,* and this suggests that the matter of musical symbols lay at the heart of Dallapiccola's musical thinking. We have already observed how twelve-tone rows had frequently carried a symbolic content in Dallapiccola's music—the rows of *Il prigioniero* as symbols of Hope, Prayer, and Liberty; the appearances and disguises of the row of *Goethe-Lieder* as representations of the poet's beloved Suleika—and this recourse to a visual as well as a musical symbolization takes this one stage further.

The reference to the central Christian symbol of the Cross here is remarkable in more than one sense. In the first place, Dallapiccola has displaced the poetic expression of human suffering, in the text of Licimnios that he sets in this movement, from its original location in ancient Greece to the Christian world by employing this cross image. In the second place, the image occurs in the central third movement of the work, the axis of the work's symmetry, and the placement of this powerful image at the core of the work, surrounded by images taken from the natural world in the other movements, makes it even more significant in the work as a whole. The text of this movement expresses in lacerating manner the sufferings of humanity:

> Acheronte
> che tormenti reca agli uomini,
> d'infinite fonti di lacrime e dolori ribolle.

> Acheron
> Who brings torments to men
> Boiling up from infinite springs of tears and sorrow.

Dallapiccola's employment of the Cross symbol in the score occurs five times in the course of this movement, perhaps as a reflection of the number of movements within the work as a whole. As we shall see, a similar visual symbol will occur also in the *Concerto per la notte di Natale dell'anno 1956.* The composer admitted that in the case of the *Cinque canti,* the idea for the crucifix symbol had occurred to him when he remembered the crucifix placed above the high altar in the Church of San Felice in Florence.[20]

This "eye music" is, however, neither an antique nor an idiosyncratic feature of the compositions in which Dallapiccola employs such images. Stravinsky does not seem to have understood the significance or function of this "eye music": he commented, "[I]ts Cross shapes in the manner of George Herbert are for the eye and present no aural problems; one does not hear musically-shaped Crosses."[21] However, what is most significant about the presence of this symbol in the score is not its audibility but simply the fact that the composer connected this *visual* symbol with the central *musical* image of the work, the principal tone row. In equal measure, one cannot really *hear* the palindromic form of Guillaume de Machaut's *Ma fin est mon commencement* (My end is my beginning), but the musical form acts in a similarly cryptic manner to the cross symbol in *Cinque canti*. The composer's sense of the importance of this symbol within *Cinque canti* as a whole is clear from his insistence to his publisher that the passages in which it occurs should appear in this precise form on the page. At the same time, he refused to allow any explanatory note to be added, saying, "[W]hoever has eyes and ears will understand, without the need for any explanations."[22]

Concerto per la notte di Natale dell'anno 1956

The *Concerto per la notte di Natale dell'anno 1956*, for soprano and small chamber orchestra, was composed to fulfil a commission from the Rameau Chamber Music Society of Tokyo, and received its first performance in Tokyo in October 1957. The period of composition of the work, during which the Dallapiccola family was living in New York while the composer was resident at Queen's College, was one of great international tension, with both the Suez crisis and the uprising in Hungary. The very title of the work, *Concerto for Christmas Eve in the Year 1956*, seems to encapsulate both the sense of outer tension that fateful year had brought into being, and at the same time the inner peace of the Christmas season that his family so much enjoyed in the United States.[23] In setting medieval religious poetry once again at such a point in history, as he had done in 1936–37 with *Tre laudi*, and by placing such settings within the "optimistic" framework of a "Corellian" Christmas concerto, he was obviously conscious of the wider significance of the gesture. He said, "Iacopone speaks of *peace on earth,* he repeatedly invokes *love*. In contrast, I was compelled to cry out, and with almost unbearable stridency."[24] In this five-movement work, Dallapiccola frames two settings of *laude* by Iacopone da Todi in the second and fourth movements with an instrumental Prologue, Intermezzo, and Epilogue, thus creating the kind of symmetrical form that was present in virtually all his later music. The whole work, in fact, describes a circular form, beginning and ending with a verticalization of the B-A-C-H motif that had already been a potent symbol in *Quaderno musicale di Annalibera* and *Canti di liberazione*. As in these earlier works, Dallapiccola went to great pains to explore the contrapuntal and canonic possibilities that the row material afforded him, and the uniquely comprehensive collection of sketch material for the work has been closely examined by Hans Nathan.[25]

One of the most noticeable features of the work is the sharp contrast in expression between the purely instrumental movements—Prologue, Intermezzo, and Epilogue—and the two "Hymnus" vocal movements, the former predominantly quiet and peaceful in character and the latter dominated by almost expressionistic vocal writing. When Dallapiccola spoke of the "almost unbearable stridency" with which he had been compelled to cry out in the work, he no doubt had in mind the vocal movements, the first a song of praise to God and a prayer for earthly peace, the second a joyful hymn to Divine Love. In both, he employs vocal writing recalling that of Webern in his *Five Canons,* Opus16, on similar religious texts. The central instrumental Intermezzo of the Concerto is itself in "mirror" form, with opening and closing measures a retrograde one of the other, enclosing a short passage of great intensity of expression.

"Eye music" appears in the *Concerto per la notte di Natale dell'anno 1956,* as it had in *Cinque canti.* The poet's image of the circle as a symbol of divine love in the *lauda* Dallapiccola sets in the fourth movement, "Amor, amor, tu se' cerchio rotondo" (Love, love, you are a circle), elicits instrumental phrases in which prime and inverted forms of the row together describe circles on the printed page accompanying the setting of the text. As Dietrich Kämper points out, the image of the circle had its origins in Dante as a symbol of perfection, and Dallapiccola could not fail to be aware of this.[26] This symbolic association also makes it clear that the various forms of the row are to be conceived as mirroring one another not simply in musical terms, but in forming a significant musical symbol, as a kind of picture in sound of the image of divine love which lies at the heart of the entire work (Example 5.17).

Example 5.17. *Concerto per la notte di Natale dell'anno 1956.* IV, mm. 23–26.

Requiescant

During his stay in the USA at the end of 1957, Dallapiccola began work on a composition provisionally entitled *Dirge Music*. However, when he had completed a part of the composition, based upon the poem "Requiescat" that Oscar Wilde had written in memory of his sister, he then received a commission from Rolf Liebermann for a cantata to be performed in Hamburg during 1959–60. He therefore decided to frame the Wilde setting with movements also having texts in English, from the Gospel According to St. Matthew ("Come unto me all ye that are heavy laden . . .") and from James Joyce ("Ding dong! The castle bell! / Farewell my mother!"), giving the work the plural title *Requiescant*. As in *Cinque canti* and *Concerto per la notte di Natale dell'anno 1956*, the five movements of *Requiescant* are arranged symmetrically, but this time with the reverse scheme to that adopted in the *Concerto per la notte di Natale dell'anno 1956*, with the two loosely palindromic instrumental intermezzi now placed between the movements for chorus and orchestra. Despite the misgivings of those charged with preparing the first performance, Dallapiccola insisted on the inclusion of a children's chorus alongside the female voices in the final movement. His choice of the three texts set in the work points to an overall theme of death and memorial, but the work is in no sense to be understood as a Requiem—Dallapiccola spoke of the final setting of Joyce's poem "Dingdong! The castle bell!" as providing a "serene conclusion," and with an "almost a childish tone."[27] The presence of a Gospel text alongside the other two texts taken from some of the most expressive pages of Irish poetry is also significant in suggesting a religious inspiration for the work as a whole, and this accords with the increasing religiosity of Dallapiccola's compositions during his later years. His predilection for an arrangement of literary texts in which the listener is led naturally from one movement to the next had been a characteristic of earlier works such as *Liriche greche, Tre poemi*, and *Cinque canti*, and this is also evident here. The work begins with the stoical acceptance of death in the Biblical first movement, passing on to the sad memorial of Wilde's poem, and finally arriving at the serenity and childlike simplicity of the Joyce setting. The composer himself commented that in *Requiescant*, the theme of Death, which had figured on several earlier occasions in his work, had here for the first time achieved "a relatively happy tone."[28] However, his first poetic choice, that of Wilde's poem, might not have suggested this. The composer had been led to Wilde's "Requiescat" through a suggestion from a composition student at Queen's College, and the setting of this poem lies at the emotional as well as the structural heart of the composition.

Dallapiccola stressed the novelty of certain rhythmic procedures in the purely instrumental second and fourth movements: "[I]f one day someone has the patience to look at *Requiescant*, that is, to study it note for note, he will see that its two instrumental movements represent something quite novel."[29] Without a doubt, the manipulation of rhythmic and metrical units that Dallapiccola undertakes in these movements, an element to which Dietrich Kämper and Rosemary Brown have devoted a good deal of attention,[30] is an important aspect of these movements. However, as we have already seen, this element had already begun to appear some time earlier, in *Canti di liberazione*. Perhaps it is inevitable that Dallapiccola's manipulation of rhythmic units based upon fixed numerical proportions, the closest that he ever came to the "total serialism" developed by younger European composers, should excite a great deal of interest. However, as was always the case with Dallapiccola, this structural aspect of the music remained very much secondary to the expressivity of the work as a whole.[31] On no occasion in his creative life did Dallapiccola show any interest in exploring such structural principles purely as an end in themselves; as we have constantly stressed, it was the composer's nature to bring such structural ideas under the control of expressive needs, and the "rhythmic researches" in *Requiescant* are no exception.

The alternation of vocal and purely instrumental movements in *Requiescant* would also appear in some later works, notably *Commiato*, composed in 1972, and it is intriguing to speculate on the possible origins of such an alternation in *Requiescant*. The intermingling of vocal and instrumental movements is, after all, a feature of several of the symphonies of Gustav Mahler. It was noted earlier that Mahler's music, whose expressive world was far removed from anything favored in Italy during Dallapiccola's youth, had made a powerful impact on the young composer when he first encountered it in Berlin in 1930. The often heartfelt nature of *Requiescant* is perhaps not so far removed from the music of his Austrian predecessor, but beyond this general feature, we can perhaps detect some specific points of contact. The orchestration of the third movement of *Requiescant* is closely related to that in the fifth movement of Mahler's third symphony (in which the women's chorus sings "Es sungen drei Engel," and the children's chorus has the "Bimm, Bamm" bell refrain). And not only this: perhaps there is in Dallapiccola's setting of Wilde's poem a parallel with the texts of Friedrich Rückert that Mahler had set in *Kindertotenlieder*. Of course, whereas Rückert's poems are despairing in tone, that of Wilde sets out the resigned expression of the poet's feelings on the death of his sister:

Peace, peace, she cannot hear
Lyre or sonnet,
All my life's buried here,
Heap earth upon it.

At the opening of the setting of this poem, there are gentle canonic imitations in the choral voices, with the gradually dissolving musical lines providing an eloquent musical symbol of the Death motif at the heart of this expressive poem, alternating with delicately instrumented orchestral passages. The poet's whispered lines are set in similarly subdued melodic interweaving (Example 5.18).

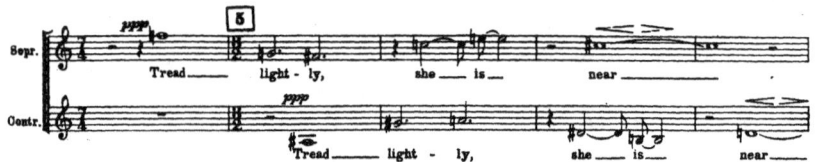

Example 5.18. *Requiescant.* III, mm. 4–10.

Only when the poet's anger suddenly erupts in the second stanza ("She that was young and fair / Fallen to dust") does the composer lift the dynamics to a dramatic *fortissimo,* but lets it subside quickly once more to a whispered *pianissimo parlato* (mm. 41–45), producing a moment of exquisite poignancy (Example 5.19).

Example 5.19. *Requiescant.* III, mm. 41–45.

Example 5.19. *Continued.*

The virginal purity of the dead girl ("Lilylike, white as snow, / She hardly knew / She was a woman . . .") invokes once again the gently intersecting canonic lines that had appeared at the opening of the movement. As the poet's anger returns in the fourth stanza ("Coffin-board, heavy stone, / Lie on her breast"), an impassioned and bitter response is once again elicited from the choral voices (mm. 68–85), and the movement ends with a return to the chant-like gentleness of the opening. This is one of the most evocative examples of twentieth-century choral writing, the expressivity of which is inextricably linked to the serial language in which it is cast. It is another example, alongside *Canti di prigionia, Job,* and *Canti di liberazione,* of Dallapiccola's enormous powers as a choral composer, an element in his work that would find its ultimate expression in the choral passages of his opera *Ulisse* and in the *a cappella* choral work *Tempus destruendi—Tempus aedificandi.*

In the last movement of *Requiescant,* the setting of James Joyce's "Dingdong! the castle bell!" the composer has similarly created an intimate expression of the poetic text. Here, a musical evocation of the poet's "castle bell" image seems to sound almost continually, present in both the women's and children's voices and in the instruments through the staccato alternation of rising and falling intervals in imitation from one line to another (Example 5.20).

Example 5.20. *Requiescant*. V, mm. 1–7.

Only in the central episode, as the poet bids farewell to his mother, do the swaying intervals of this bell image give way for a moment to more emphatic outlines (mm. 22–25), but the image returns once more in the final moments of the work, when voices and instruments gradually dissolve the fragments, as if the bells themselves are now falling silent (Example 5.21).

Text and Symbol: 1954–1964

Example 5.21. *Requiescant.* V, conclusion.

It is interesting to note that, in a single page of the sketches for *Requiescant*,[32] Dallapiccola set out the row on which the work was based, in its prime version marked "Pisa Station, 26 July 1957 (St. Anna's Day)," and the inversion of the row marked "on the way to Rapallo"; he dedicated the row to his daughter Annalibera with the words:

> To Annalibera
> This "first idea" for *Requiescant*,
> Or, HOW LIFE BEGINS [in English]
> Her loving father
> 7 October 1960, Florence.

The reference in English to a phrase taken from James Joyce, together with the dedication to his daughter, is clear evidence of the personal as well as the musical importance of this note row. Having already composed the *Quaderno musicale di Annalibera* for his young daughter, he evidently felt the need, not for a further work to be dedicated to her, but rather, to present to her a small image of the musical beginnings of this important composition. *Requiescant* was given its first performance in Hamburg in November 1959, conducted by Hermann Scherchen. The composer had originally hoped that the performance would be directed by Lorin Maazel; his fear that Scherchen would place the work in one of his notoriously mammoth programs of modern music was not unfounded, since it was put together with works by Nono, Fortner, Xenakis, and Berg.[33] Dallapiccola had already decided that the ideal conductor for the opera he was beginning to prepare would be Lorin Maazel, and in the course of the next few years, the composition of the opera was to absorb a major part of his energies.

Although his earlier stage works had all been single-act compositions, on this occasion he had in mind a full-length opera. It was not the case, however, that the idea of an opera based upon the Ulysses myth only occurred to the composer at this time: indeed, the idea had already begun to form in his mind during the late 1930s. By the autumn of 1958, the composer was able to communicate to his publisher that he had drafted the libretto of the opera but the music was not yet begun; as he commented, "God only knows how many years of work the music will take."[34] In fact, another decade was to pass before the opera was finally staged, since not only did it consume an enormous amount of his energy, but its composition was also frequently interrupted in order to complete other works.

Dialoghi

One of the interruptions Dallapiccola made in the composition of *Ulisse* came from a further collaboration with the Spanish cellist Gaspar Cassadó, for whom he had already composed *Ciaccona, intermezzo e adagio* in 1946. Cassadó was a guest at Dallapiccola's summer home on the Tuscan coast for a couple days in August 1959, when the two were able to discuss technical matters of cello playing, before Dallapiccola left for a stay in America in September. The composition entitled *Dialoghi per violoncello e orchestra* was completed in short score by December that year, and by the time

Dallapiccola met Cassadó in August, three sections of the work had already been sketched out. The composer explained his involvement in this, one of the few purely instrumental compositions he wrote, simply in terms of its contrast with the composition of the opera with which he was beginning to be preoccupied: "Before dedicating myself for many years to this work, I felt that I would like to immerse myself for some time in a purely instrumental problem."[35]

Dallapiccola knew that the title *Dialoghi* (Dialogues) had been given to a series of instrumental pieces Gian Francesco Malipiero had composed a few years earlier, and he commented on this:

> I like the word *dialoghi,* a word G. Francesco Malipiero chose for eight of his compositions in recent years: *Dialoghi* in 1956–57. Not that we can consider the various concertos for instrumental soloist and orchestra as "monologues." However, the very fact of having called this work *Dialoghi* demonstrates that the soloist, while being the protagonist, converses at every moment with the instrumental ensemble, even in the cadenzas.[36]

Once again in *Dialoghi,* we find the same symmetry of overall shape that we observed in several of the other works Dallapiccola composed during this period. The odd-numbered movements of the five-movement work are in a contemplative mood, the other two more dynamic in character, an alternating pattern that would be taken a stage further in the orchestral *Three Questions with Two Answers* three years later. The row on which the work is based also displays a certain symmetry, the second hexachord being a transposed RI of the first, and the compositional possibilities offered by this kind of row are fully exploited by Dallapiccola (Example 5.22).

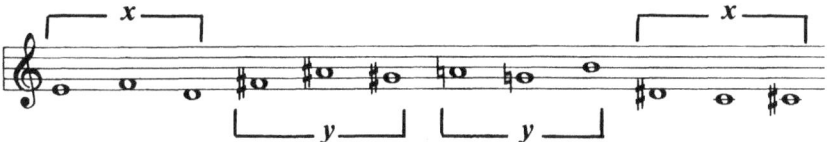

Example 5.22. *Dialoghi,* row.

Another aspect enters into play in *Dialoghi,* however, one which had never before appeared in Dallapiccola's work, and indeed one that made its only appearance on this occasion. This is a symmetry in the metronome indications given at the head of each movement, replacing the verbal tempo markings that the composer had always previously employed. These tempo indications outline a formal scheme of alternating slow and fast movements, played without a break, and a numerical ratio between the metronome indications is clearly discernible (Table 5.2).

Table 5.2. *Dialoghi*: the numerical ratio between the metronome indications.

1	1–56:	♩ = 40:	[1]
2	57–134:	♩ = 80:	[2]
3	135–80:	♩ = 40:	[1]
4	181–264:	♩ = 120:	[3]
5	265–315:	♩ = 40:	[1]

This highly rational organization of the tempo markings in the piece has occasionally prompted the observation that Dallapiccola was approaching, albeit in small measure, the kind of thoroughgoing serial organization that some of the younger composers such as Boulez and Stockhausen had attempted during the 1950s.[37] Indeed, in some pages of the work, pages we shall examine below, Dallapiccola has adopted elements of the "total serial" approach. However, there is absolutely no reason to infer from this isolated, and extremely limited, application of numerical proportioning to the work's tempo parameter that the composer was drawn more generally towards "total serialism." This case, like so many others in Dallapiccola's work, is surely no more than a further example of his desire for symmetry in a musical form, such as we have observed on many occasions in his work. Given his desire for rationality, it is hardly surprising that the composer should set out in this way these two aspects of the work, the design of the row and that of the tempo relationships in the constituent sections of the work.

At the opening of the first movement, a characteristic verticalization of the serial material appears, six chords within which the composer has embedded three inverted forms of the row. The solo cello responds with the prime row, and continues with versions of prime and inverted forms, but omitting some pitches (Example 5.23).

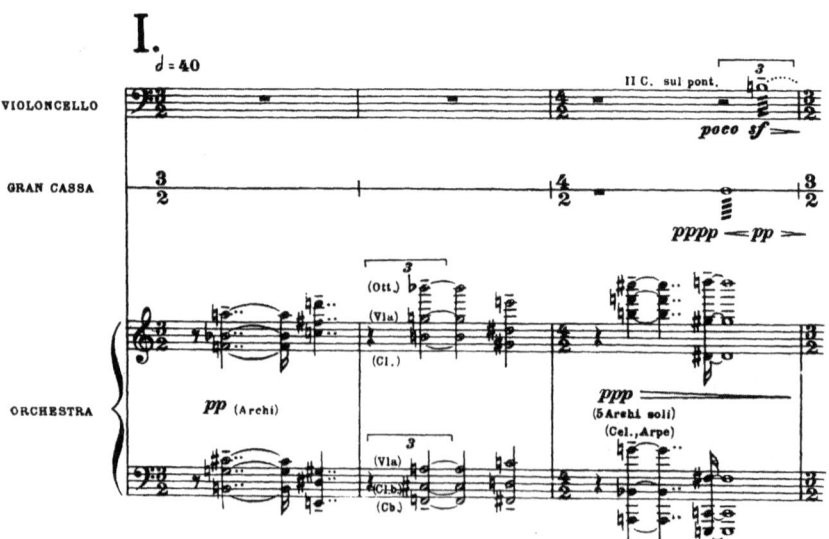

Example 5.23. *Dialoghi*, mm. 1–13.

Example 5.23. *Continued.*

These six initial orchestral chords reappear in mm. 31–33, followed by an extended solo passage for the cello (mm. 34–44), once more based around P and I, but with only pitches 2–12 given to the soloist, the first (E flat) appearing as a kind of single-tone *Klangfarbenmelodie* dispersed among strings and winds. Dietrich Kämper pointed to the remarkable degree of serialization of rhythms in this passage: the E flat appears always as a duration of 9 quarter notes in the winds, whereas in its appearances in pitched percussion instruments it gradually grows from 3 quarter notes to 10.[38] This whole passage reappears towards the end of the final movement of the work (mm. 302–12). Again at the opening of the second movement, to which the composer adds the adjective *furioso* in parenthesis after the tempo indication, chord forms once again serve as an introduction, based upon fragments of the basic row and strictly serialized in durations (woodwinds in terms of sixteenth notes, brass in terms of eighths, strings in thirty-seconds), and again the whole passage is repeated at the end of the movement (mm. 127–34).

It is clear that Dallapiccola was experimenting with the serialization of parameters other than pitch in some passages of the work, and, as we have observed, this experimentation was undertaken in a characteristically thorough manner. Nonetheless, the clear rationalities in the structuring of tempo and rhythm cannot engage the listener, and at its first performance, the work proved more than a little puzzling to its audience. Some were disappointed that, in his second work written for Gaspar Cassadó, Dallapiccola had not presented a work of the haunting beauty and poetry of *Ciaccona, intermezzo e adagio,* which had been composed more than a decade earlier, while others had perhaps hoped for a major realignment of the composer's approach to serial composition. Both remained unfulfilled in the work that was heard at that time.

Preghiere

Dallapiccola had become more and more involved in the composition of the opera *Ulisse* during the 1960s, and he cut back drastically on his other activities in order to devote as much time as possible to the task. Nonetheless, his music was being performed with increasing regularity in Europe and the United States at this time, and so, inevitably, he continued to receive commissions for new compositions. One which seems to have greatly interested him, to judge from the warm reply he made in declining it, came from David Lepine, organist of the newly rebuilt Coventry Cathedral in England, for a setting of the Mass.[39] There were, however, two occasions on which he felt able to accept: these resulted in *Preghiere* (Prayers) in 1962 and *Parole di San Paolo* in 1963–64, and it is significant that both works were religious in character. The commission for *Preghiere* came from the University of California at Berkeley. Dallapiccola composed it during his summer vacation in August 1962 in the villa he rented each year on the Tuscan coast, and completed it by October. It consists of settings of poems by the Brazilian poet Murilo Mendes in an Italian translation by Ruggero Jacobi;[40] Mendes had gotten to know Dallapiccola while the poet was living in Rome, and this personal acquaintance, combined with the concern with social and political matters that were shared by poet and composer, helps to explain the choice of texts for the work. But there was also the fact that the poems express fundamental religious thoughts in a heartfelt and powerful manner, and this accorded with Dallapiccola's deeply felt religious beliefs. Dietrich Kämper places the work firmly within the group of compositions that Dallapiccola himself called his "religious vein,"[41] as well as within the historical moment in which the work was penned. As *Preghiere* was being completed, the Cuban crisis was bringing the world face-to-face with the possibility of war between the United States and the Soviet Union. This was, of course, not the first occasion on which Dallapiccola had composed a work based upon prayers at a moment of great political tension: we saw earlier how *Canti di prigionia,* with its settings of Latin prayers by three authors condemned to death, had acted as a focus for the composer's emotional reaction to the tide of events. The imminent danger felt in 1962, and the possibility that the world would once again be drawn into the kind of conflict that had severely affected the composer's life a couple decades earlier, influenced his decision to interrupt work on the opera in order to fulfill this commission. Dallapiccola saw the world events reflected in Mendes's texts, but it was also important that the texts had an overall shape, and of particular significance here was how the texts gradually led towards the image of the cross that dominates the final poem.

In comparison with *Canti di prigionia,* the group of prayers Dallapiccola sets in *Preghiere,* a short work for baritone and eighteen solo instruments, are on a much more intimate and personal scale. The row on which the piece is based is one that allows the composer to use segments of it for the creation of chords, similar to his earlier experiments in *Requiescant* (Example 5.24).

Example 5.24. *Preghiere,* row.

This chordal use of row segments appears right in the first measures of the work, in which pitches 3–6 of the row are used to form a chord that will recur frequently in the course of the work (Example 5.25).

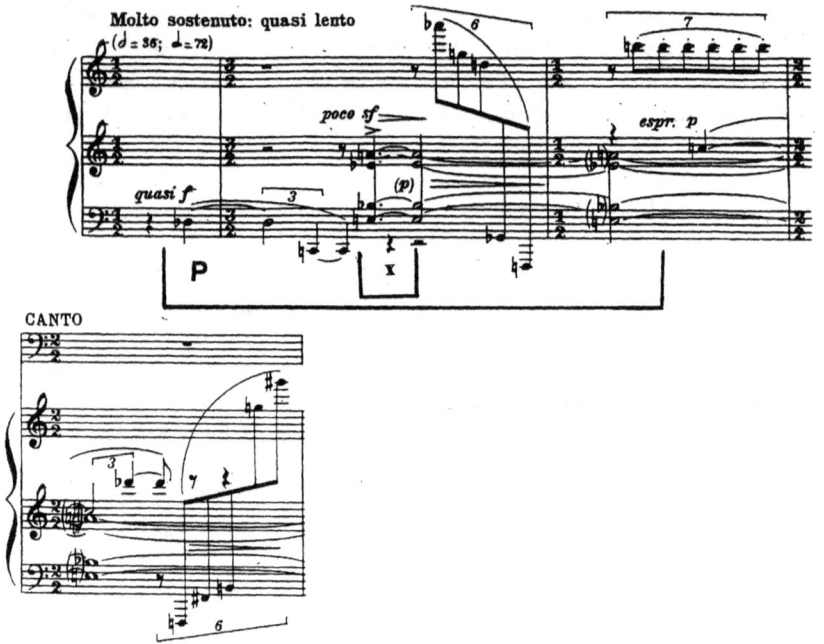

Example 5.25. *Preghiere*. I, mm. 1–4.

According to Kämper, this chord, with its clashing interlocked sevenths, is linked in some way with the key symbol of the Cross, which appears in the third and last song of the work,[42] but Michael Eckert disputes this interpretation.[43] The symbolic interpretation that Kämper gives to this chord, which is undoubtedly an important part of the musical fabric of the work, seems to accord with the use of serial symbolisms to which many of Dallapiccola's works bear witness. However, in virtually all the cases in which such symbolisms are apparent, Dallapiccola makes the connection of text and music apparent right from the start, not with such a symbol detached from its textual reference, as would appear to be the case here. Whether or not this chord can be understood as a "cross symbol" however, there are in any case further musical symbolisms embedded in *Preghiere*. In several passages the composer has provided a symbol or "ideogram" that expresses an idea, even a single word, of the poetic text, such as the interpretation of the word "disegni" (designs) in an almost graphic sense in the interweaving clarinet lines in mm. 10–13. It would seem that by this stage, Dallapiccola's expressive vocabulary turned quite naturally towards such interpretations of the text in his music, without any need for overemphasis and without any artificiality.

In the setting of Mendes's second poem, it is powerful, large-scale poetic metaphors, in particular in the metaphor of the "immense wheel" grinding down the aspirations of humanity, that dominate:

L'immane ruota
Che trita anime e corpi
Degni della rugiada del mattino,
Della presenza d'amore
Della musica d'uccelli

The immense wheel
Which grinds souls and bodies
Worthy of the morning-dew,
Of the presence of love
Of the music of the birds

This metaphor of the wheel stands at the center of an extended passage in crab canon form that runs from measure 52 to measure 83, and the phrase "l'immane ruota" seems to invoke an instrumental gesture in which a three-tone figure is treated in close imitation, almost as if crushed under the weight of the wheel itself (Example 5.26).

Example 5.26. *Preghiere*. II, mm. 65–70.

[The images found in Mendes's poems, whether the "designs" which, in the first poem, the poet asks life to reveal to him in all their fullness, or the giant wheel evoked in the second, crushing the aspirations and spirit of mankind, seem to converge at the end of the final song in the most powerful image, that of the Cross. Here, in a powerful reinterpretation of the crucifixion image, the poet asks the Son of God to remove humanity from the cross to which it has been nailed, and the musical expression of this image is impassioned, even angry (Example 5.27).

Example 5.27. *Preghiere*. III, mm. 126–33.

Dallapiccola appears not to have been content with the version of the work that was performed in Berkeley in November 1962, and he made a number of changes to the score before the work was given its first performances in Europe: these changes are reflected in the published score. When he returned home to Italy from his stay in California, he had to wait some time for a copy of the score to arrive from Berkeley, and in the meantime he began to reconstruct the score, adding both E-flat clarinet and English horn to the accompanying chamber orchestra "for reasons of sound," as he later explained; this entailed a rather larger revision of the score, obliging him to "change it all."[44] The opportunity to revisit the score after the first performance of the work evidently provided the composer with an opportunity to think again about the piece as a whole, and he went beyond a simple reorchestration. He added thirteen measures of new music, rewrote the vocal melody at the beginning of the second song, made transposition changes in several passages, and changed some of the metrical notation. These changes were incorporated in the version performed in the BBC in London in November 1963. This was one of the rare occasions on which Dallapiccola undertook fairly major revisions to one of his scores after its first performance. He had, of course, made a second version of a number of compositions for different forces (notably *Due studi,* which became *Due pezzi* for orchestra, *Quaderno musicale di Annalibera* became *Variazioni* for orchestra, and *Piccola musica notturna* was recast for chamber ensemble). But only in the case of *Quaderno musicale di Annalibera* for piano, a revision of which was made after Vincent Persichetti had performed the work's original version in Pittsburgh in 1952, do we find such revisiting.

Parole di San Paolo

Parole di San Paolo was composed in 1963–64, and resulted from a commission from the Library of Congress in Washington for a work which would form part of a concert to celebrate the work of the American arts patroness Elizabeth Sprague Coolidge. The circumstances that led Dallapiccola to accept this commission, in the midst of working on his opera, have been elucidated by Dietrich Kämper: despite the composer's reluctance, when he remembered that Webern's string quartet, Opus 28, had been dedicated to Mrs. Coolidge, and that this commission had come as a shaft of light into the darkness of Webern's artistic isolation in 1938, he decided to accept.[45] The increasingly religious nature of Dallapiccola's works during this period made it quite natural that once again, as in *Preghiere,* he should turn to a religious text. This time, the text was taken from the thirteenth chapter of Saint Paul's Epistle to the Corinthians: "When I spoke the language of men and of angels . . . ", in the Vulgate Latin version. This was, apart from *Job,* the only occasion on which Dallapiccola set a text taken from the Bible. He had, of course, set many religious texts, and would do so later as well. The work that resulted on this occasion was one of Dallapiccola's most engaging compositions, one whose small-scale and intimate character creates a unique sound world.

The ensemble chosen by Dallapiccola to accompany the voice in the work comprises eleven players: flute, flute in G, clarinet, bass clarinet, piano, celesta, harp, vibraphone, xylorimba, viola, and cello. The constitution of this ensemble forms an essential element in the work's expression: Dallapiccola creates with this group of instruments, involving a significant number of keyboard instruments, a sound world of great clarity, encompassing sounds of richness and variety. He envisaged that the vocal part ideally be taken by a boy, and although this is not easy to realize, it gives a particular directness to the expression of the vocal line, and combines with the transparent qualities of the accompanying instrumental ensemble to great effect. One characteristic of the vocal part that contrasts with that of *Preghiere,* which was composed immediately before it, is the frequent mingling of normal singing articulations with *parlato,* not for whole phrases, but for individual words of the text. This is not frequently employed, but does add to the flexibility of expression in the vocal line.

The writing for the accompanying ensemble is one of the finest examples of Dallapiccola's instrumental composition, every page displaying the greatest sensitivity to the possibilities of the instrumental group. Details of the instrumental writing reveal the care with which Dallapiccola wrote the work: in the opening measures, for example, the four initial chords in flute, flute in G, and viola—an important recurring motif in the work as a whole—are marked to be played with only the briefest possible breaks between the chords, perhaps as an equivalent of the legato effect of piano pedalling (See Example 5.28 (b)). The contrast between the sustaining instruments, winds and strings, and those with a decaying sound, piano, celesta, harp, vibraphone, and xylorimba, is an important part of the sound palette of the work. The latter group is frequently used together in the work, in effect maintaining a separate identity from the rest of the ensemble (this can be seen in mm. 4–6, 16–18, 22–24, etc.). Also, as Pierre Michel has pointed out, there are many examples of instruments used briefly at the beginning of a sound in another instrument, in order to modify the attack characteristics (as, for example, the vibraphone is used on the same pitch as the flute in measure 8).[46]

Parole di San Paolo is, apart from *Piccola musica notturna,* the only single-movement composition Dallapiccola wrote. (Some works, such as *Dialoghi,* are continuous but clearly marked in distinct episodes or movements.) As such, it is important that the work's formal shape should be evident to the listener, and Dallapiccola does this by means of recurrences, of both motif and instrumentation, that articulate the eight minutes of the work's duration. One of the motifs that recurs at several points appears in the opening measures; once again here, as in *Preghiere,* the composer has verticalized the row to create an easily memorable set of four three-tone cords (Example 5.28 (a) and (b)).

Text and Symbol: 1954–1964   223

Example 5.28 (a). *Parole di San Paolo*, row.

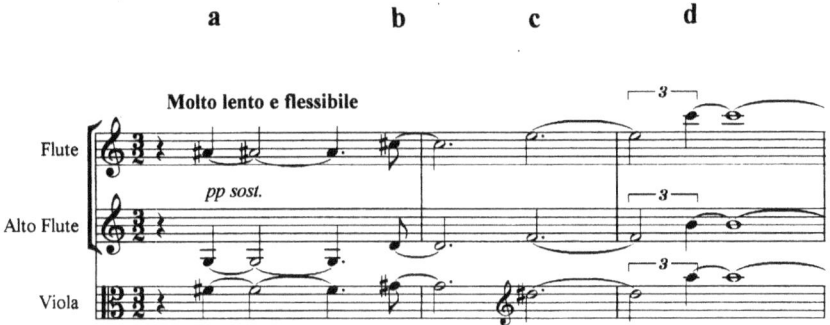

Example 5.28 (b). *Parole di San Paolo*, opening measures.

These chords recur at several points in the work, and seem to have a symbolic association with the "caritas" that is the subject of the text: they recur in mm. 32–35 ("caritatem autem non habuero"), in mm. 51–54 (on the same text), and again at the end of the work, in mm. 95–100 ("major autem horum est caritas"). As in so many other works of Dallapiccola, therefore, the row, in the form of this recurring motif, would seem to have a symbolic as well as a musical significance, and Camillo Togni pointed to two further instances of such symbolic use of the row.[47] Firstly, he pointed to the way in which the row is consistently employed in its complete form until measure 38, at which point it is divided into two hexachords as the text speaks of distributing one's goods to the poor ("Et si distribuero" (and even if I distribute all my goods to the poor). Secondly, he pointed to the passage in mm. 68–75, in which the vocal part encompasses all twelve tones by concentrating on just the fourth, fifth, and sixth pitches of the fundamental row and their inversion, together with the transpositions of both: here, the text speaks of the various characteristics of charity ("omnia suffert, omnia credit, omnia sperat, omnia sustinet"). *Parole di San Paolo* combines instrumental clarity with vocal flexibility and detailed formal design with the symbolic use of thematic and motivic units; it is one of Dallapiccola's most expressive works, one whose language seems to lead forward to that of the opera *Ulisse*, on which the composer was then working so assiduously.

Three Questions with Two Answers

Dallapiccola's music had become increasingly religious in the period under examination, and this coincided with his increasing use of musical symbolisms by means of rows or row fragments. Musical symbols played a vital role in *Three Questions with Two Answers,* the orchestral work he completed during his stay in California during the winter of 1962–63. In this case, however, the symbols embedded in the piece are so intimately related to the opera on which he was then working that it would be well nigh impossible to disentangle the close web of relationships of the two works. This is underlined by the fact that the composer did not allow the orchestral work to be published until the opera had been staged, even though the former work had already been heard in performance in New Haven in February 1963. Dallapiccola had accepted an invitation from the University of California at Berkeley to be Visiting Professor of Italian Culture in 1962, stipulating that in order to continue work on the opera, he should limit his stay in California from September 1962 until January 1963.

The libretto of *Ulisse* was to abound in questions, and three of these are embedded in the first, third, and fifth movements of *Three Questions with Two Answers,* questions the composer formulated as: "Who am I?" "Who are you?" and "Who are we?" The score of the work was published only after Dallapiccola's death, and it contains a prefatory note whose authorship is unknown. This note is remarkably specific in outlining the conception and character of *Three Questions with Two Answers*:

> Around the middle of 1960, having completed the score of *Dialoghi* for cello and orchestra, Dallapiccola began work on the opera *Ulysses.* Early in that same year he had accepted a commission from the New Haven Symphony Orchestra for an orchestral work to be completed in January 1962 (this deadline was later postponed to January 1963). Totally absorbed in the composition of *Ulysses,* Dallapiccola used material from the opera in the piece he had promised to write for the New Haven Symphony. And just because it was based on themes which he planned to develop in greater depth in *Ulysses,* the composer did not feel that the work should be published at that time, considering it a sort of preliminary sketch for *Ulysses.* For the world première at New Haven on 5 February 1963, Dallapiccola wrote a letter to Frank Brieff, conductor of the New Haven Symphony, in which he explained the meaning of the title, *Three Questions (and) Two Answers.* Unfortunately, the letter has since been lost, but it is obvious that the presentation of the work in the program notes for that concert is based on this latter and clarifies the nature of the three questions and two answers. Who am I? Who are you? Who are we? These are the three questions to which the title refers, represented by three thematic groups of three notes each. Of the two

answers, the first is peaceful, optimistic, and feminine in character (centered around a flute solo), while the second is harsh, pessimistic, and masculine (based on a descending figuration of three notes at wide intervals). The third and final answer is lacking, to be found only at the close of *Ulysses*.

Three Questions with Two Answers is in effect the only purely orchestral composition Dallapiccola wrote, since the *Partita* of 1930–32 had incorporated a soprano solo in its last movement, and both *Due pezzi* and *Variazioni* were transcriptions of works for other forces. This fact is in itself of some importance: almost all Dallapiccola's compositions are vocal, and those that do not include the voice, such as *Quaderno musicale di Annalibera, Piccola musica notturna,* and *Three Questions with Two Answers,* nonetheless incorporate extra-musical suggestions in one way or another in their musical symbolisms. *Due studi* had begun as music to accompany visual images on film, and of his other major compositions, it is only the *Ciaccona, intermezzo e adagio* for solo cello that can be regarded as free from any such external influences. This is a very important aspect of Dallapiccola's work as a whole, and although it would not be accurate to describe him as a purely vocal composer, it is true that his inspiration came in very large measure from poetic or dramatic ideas and texts, even in his relatively few purely instrumental compositions.

The context in which *Three Questions with Two Answers* can best be understood is clearly in relation to the opera *Ulisse,* for which it acted not so much as a "preliminary sketch," but rather as an essential "partner composition," complementing the opera in expression.[48] However, the work also represents the culmination of the previous decade during which, in the series of works that we have examined in this chapter, Dallapiccola gradually refined his approach to symbolic serialism, leading towards ever greater expressivity. This symbolism, together with the use of "ideograms" that we have noted at several points in his work, and the constant recourse to arch forms for a composition, created the basis of the composer's mature musical language. The orchestral work relies upon these elements to a greater extent than almost any other work Dallapiccola had previously written, and this provided a springboard with which he might launch himself into the highly self-revealing world of *Ulisse.*

The musical character of the Questions and Answers in the work follows a logical pattern, as we would expect from Dallapiccola. Each of the Question movements is based upon a motivic cell that had originally appeared in *Goethe-Lieder* ten years earlier, a cell constructed from the simplest interval relationship of major and minor seconds, arranged in a form that reflects back inwardly after its first rising interval, and is thus itself suggestive of questioning (Example 5.29).

Example 5.29. *Three Questions with Two Answers*, "Question" motif.

The Question movements of the work focus predominantly on this motif, the constituent intervals of which are subjected to contrapuntal and serial treatment. In *Ulisse,* the motif would also eventually form the initial three-tone cell of the opera's principal tone row (Sea I, see Example 6.2).

By the time that he broached the composition of *Three Questions with Two Answers,* Dallapiccola had already composed the Prologue and first act of the opera. He employs just six of the *Ulisse* rows in *Three Questions with Two Answers,* half the number that will eventually be used in the opera; the six are those that will eventually be Sea I, Sea II, Sea III, Calypso, Circe A, and Cimmerians B (see Example 6.3). However, the connections of orchestral work and opera do not end here; in addition, he gives to the orchestral percussion group a rhythmic motif that in the opera will be called "ritmo principale" (see Example 6.5): in the orchestral work, this appears at structurally important points, as for example at the end of the first and last Question movements. The two Answer movements were also to be incorporated into the musical fabric of the opera, the first becoming a fund for the scenes of Calypso (Prologue) and Circe (Act I, Scene 6), and the second providing major elements for the Scene in Hades (Act I, Scene 7).

If the nature of the Questions in the work has been clearly established by the composer himself, the nature of the two Answers remains somewhat more elusive. Given that the reworking of the two Answer movements in the opera (a reworking that involved some major alteration to important aspects of the original) appears in the two dark and somewhat gloomy scenes of Calypso and of Hades, one might be forgiven for concluding that the Answers are pessimistic ones. But it must be remembered that the transformations from orchestral to operatic contexts may not allow any such simple parallels to be drawn, and the composer himself was naturally wary of offering any clarification of the work's "meaning" that might distort its essential *musical* nature.

The five movements of *Three Questions with Two Answers* treat the row material in varied ways. The first movement (*Sostenuto; sottovoce*) is a mere fourteen measures long (the third movement is even shorter, just thirteen measures), and is based upon two rows, one operating horizontally, the other vertically. Both are derived from the row that would become the principal row of *Ulisse,* called there Sea I (Example 5.30).

Example 5.30. *Three Questions with Two Answers*. I, two rows.

In the opening measures, the placement of the two row figurations—the vertical in distinct instrumental groupings of winds contrasting with strings, the horizontal in trumpet, oboe, cello, and clarinet—has the effect of placing the latter in relief as an immediate formation, as it were, of the fundamental question "Who am I?"

In the first Answer movement (*Moderato; tranquillo*) the distinction between horizontal and vertical row groupings is maintained; the rows employed in this movement are related to the various rows that will be associated with particular characters and elements in the opera. For example, at the very opening of the movement the four string chords are related to the rows associated with Calypso and with the Cimmerians, and in this way an immediate connection is made, via the fluctuations of major and minor thirds, with the Prologue of *Ulisse* . The composer's own description of the flute sole at the heart of this movement (mm. 35–44) as "peaceful, optimistic, and feminine in character" is certainly apt, but it is perhaps surprising to find that this expressive passage does not figure in the score of the opera (Example 5.31).

Example 5.31. *Three Questions with Two Answers*. II, mm. 34–44 (flute solo).

The accompaniment to this flute melody is remarkable: a single A flat is passed at regular intervals (8 x quarter note) between wind instruments, supported by tremolos in strings and harp, thereby creating a shimmering aura surrounding the very free peregrinations of the flute melody itself.

The third movement (*Impetuoso; violento*), forming the Second Question, is developed from the first, but is even more compressed, and is of an unremitting violence of expression, the seconds of the earlier movement being replaced by their inversions in sevenths and ninths and introduced in the opening measures by a great percussion crescendo. The extreme emotional character of this movement might well have issued from the pen of one of the Viennese expressionist composers earlier in the century, rather than having the character of the "Italianate lyricism" often associated with Dallapiccola.

The fourth movement (*Largamente; sostenutissimo*) would eventually form the basis of the scene in Act I of *Ulisse* set in the Kingdom of the Cimmerians, and once again the composer's description of this Second Answer as "harsh, pessimistic, and masculine" is very apt. At mm. 15–17, the side drum whisperingly announces the rhythmic figuration which will form the "ritmo principale" of the opera. This leitmotif will be placed at the heart of the drama during the scene in Hades, underpinning the choral enunciation of death: "pianto, rimorso, eterno soffrire" (Example 5.32).

Example 5.32. *Three Questions with Two Answers*. IV, mm. 11–17.

Text and Symbol: 1954–1964 229

Example 5.32. *Continued.*

This rhythmic motif remains gently insistent in the percussion group during the ensuing part of the movement (mm. 15–28), becoming more relentless at the fortissimo climax in brass instruments (mm. 34–38), only to reappear as a continuing *ostinato* in the final part of the movement (mm. 58–65).

The final movement (*Molto sostenuto*), the "Unanswered Question" of the work, revolves around a musical figure in which two melodic ideas are presented in contrapuntal combination one with another—the "we" of the final question "Who are we?" This figure, already foreshadowed in the fourth movement in mm. 41–43 and mm. 54–55, is clearly related to elements of the initial "Sea" series that had been presented at the start of the work; here it is subjected to the kind of transpositions and elaborations that had characterized the treatment of the first question in the earlier movement (Example 5.33 (a) and (b)).

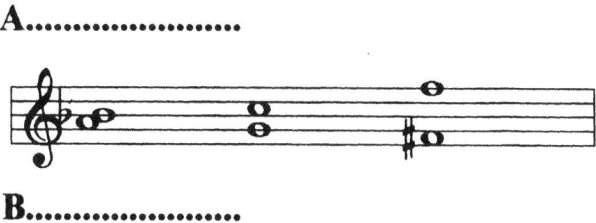

Example 5.33 (a). *Three Questions with Two Answers.* V, cell.

Example 5.33 (b). *Three Questions with Two Answers*. V, mm. 10–13.

In the course of the movement, the two principal rows of *Ulisse* (Sea I and Cimmerians) are distributed alternately through the five "cadenza" passages in the movement: Sea I in the clarinets at measure 20, Cimmerians in the cello solo at measure 25, Sea I again at measure 30 in the violin, viola, and cello, and finally Cimmerians once more at measure 37 in the violin and viola. The whole work comes to a somewhat restless conclusion with a final appearance of the "ritmo principale" in the strings.

Having examined the work in relation to the opera to which it is so intimately related, we may ask to what extent *Three Questions with Two Answers* can be said to have a life of its own independent of the opera. And how clear and unequivocal is the formulation of the "Question and Answer" components that are intended to underlie the succession of movements? Any understanding of the work that might view it purely in its own self-contained terms, as if it were Dallapiccola's attempt at a "symphonic" composition, would be misguided. Despite the intrinsic interest of the musical materials themselves, it is only through an understanding of their function within the opera that the orchestral work can fully be understood. In this sense, Dietrich Kämper's description of the work as a "preliminary study" for the opera is accurate.[49] As for the expression of the "Question and Answer" aspect, Dallapiccola clearly did not intend the orchestral work to be heard as simply an expression of the five "interpretations" in any straightforward illustrative sense. In any case, too many elements appear that would disturb such an interpretation, such as the immediate appearance of the "first question motif" in the oboe solo that begins the final movement. There inevitably remains in the listener's mind some puzzlement about the Question and Answer character of the succession of movements, but despite this, the work is a powerfully expressive example of orchestral writing by a composer not usually associated with such purely instrumental music.

The works Dallapiccola created during the 1950s, indeed his whole creative life, in some sense pointed forward to the full-scale opera *Ulisse,* finally brought to fruition in 1968. The composer's own description of it as "the result of my whole life" was undoubtedly true, in ways that we shall clarify in the final chapter of this study. It should not be thought, however, that the various compositions he penned during the period we have just examined were composed with a complete image of the later opera already in the composer's mind. Dallapiccola's creativity was one that found its most important expressivities in the frequent revisiting of previous areas, whether literary or musical, and in the gradual development of expressive tools through which poetic and musical symbols could most clearly be articulated. Without this development of expressive means, the opera that eventually saw the light would have been unthinkable.

VI

Ulysses, Wanderer and Discoverer: 1965–1975

Ulisse

It would seem inevitable that Dallapiccola should choose the Ulysses myth as the subject of his only full-scale opera; the subject had, as the composer himself said, "chosen him." In an interview he had with Leonardo Pinzauti during the last stages of preparing the opera, Dallapiccola spoke of how an artist's creation follows a path which is almost autonomous, independent of his own will, and he quoted the phrase of Nietzsche relating how "if you look for a long time into an abyss, you realize at a certain point that the abyss is looking into you."[1] Dallapiccola had lived with the myth since he first heard it from his father's lips in his early childhood:

> Since my father was a Humanist, Gods, Demi-Gods, and Goddesses sat, so to speak, at our dining table at midday and in the evening. My father told my brother and me the beautiful stories from mythology.[2]

He immersed himself in Homer's epic poems during his school days, and again in later life, but there was one event of particular significance in his childhood that had first prompted his lifelong fascination with the Ulysses myth, a silent film on the subject of the Odyssey, made by Giuseppe De Liguoro, which Dallapiccola saw in 1912. It was always a source of regret to the composer that, despite his father's position as head of a classical high school, he himself had not studied Greek. He was therefore always at a certain disadvantage in his intimacy with Greek literature through his lack of close acquaintance with the original. The Ulysses myth was to reappear in other guises at various points in his life: in 1938, Léonide Massine suggested the idea of a Ulysses ballet, an idea that was not taken up, but in 1941 Dallapiccola was asked by Mario Labroca, then Director of the Maggio Musicale Fiorentino, to make a transcription of Monteverdi's *Il ritorno d'Ulisse in patria* for the Festival. In Dallapiccola's way of working, any experience, however unimportant it might seem at the time, remained within him, waiting to have unexpected results in a quite different context many years later. We have frequently noted in this study how Dallapiccola's creativity abounded in returns—to the world of tonal and modal music, to medieval and classical literature, to texts of a religious nature, to serial symbolisms and musical ideograms. In returning to the classical myth of Ulysses the Wanderer, the composer was tracing once more a path from his childhood home on the edge of the Balkans, beyond which lay the land of Greece, and from the humanist ambience of his father's learning, towards that idealized and poetic vision of antiquity to which he constantly felt drawn.

One rather curious event that he related throws a fascinating psychological light on Dallapiccola's involvement with the Ulysses myth. This occurred in 1943, when the composer was faced with making a decision that would have enormous consequences for the whole of his future. Being married to a Jewish woman, he found himself facing the choice of a very uncertain future in an increasingly anti-Semitic Italy, or else to go into exile in Switzerland, where he had several musical friends. It is clear from the composer's own account of this momentous point in his life that it left a profound impression on him, and he seems to have summoned up classical mythology to aid his decision. The possibility of a long separation from his mother weighed heavily upon his mind, and brought to mind also the meeting of Ulysses and his mother, Anticlea, which would eventually form a central scene of the opera. During this difficult period of his life, he made a strange entry in his diary in December 1943 in which he related having met an apparition of Ulysses in the street in Florence one day.[3]

In *Ulisse*, Dallapiccola put a considerable part of his own experience as a human being, and it is therefore particularly important to understand how the work gradually took shape in his imagination. The task of unraveling the intricacies of the "work in progress" has been undertaken with admirable thoroughness by Julia van Hees, and any account of the opera must inevitably acknowledge a debt to her work.

The composer had mentioned the idea of a Ulysses opera to Domenico de'Paoli as early as 1936, and thus the Ulysses idea predated all his other operatic projects, but the real origin of the work occurred some years later. In 1945, when composing his *Quattro liriche di Antonio Machado*, Dallapiccola found a line that not only strangely echoed some words spoken by the Prisoner in *Il prigioniero*, but would ultimately find its way into the last words spoken by Ulysses in the final scene of *Ulisse*:

> Senor, ya estamos solos mi corazon y el mar (Machado)
>   (Lord, my heart and the sea are alone)
> Solo. Son solo un'altra volta. Solo coi miei pensieri (*Il prigioniero*)
>   (Alone. Alone once more. Alone with my thoughts)
> Son soli un'altra volta il tuo cuore e il mare (*Ulisse*)
>   (They are alone once more, your heart and the sea)

According to a diary entry Dallapiccola made, he first imagined the musical setting for Machado's lines as he crossed a bridge in Venice in 1947, and by 1952 he was able to sketch a plan of the various scenes of the opera, written at a restaurant table in New York. The first libretto sketches were penned during journeys between New York and Washington in December 1956, but musical ideas seem to have been sketched out some time earlier. Hans Nathan's assertion that Dallapiccola had written the first musical idea for *Ulisse,* a tone row, during a train ride from Asolo to Venice on 15 February 1960[4] is contradicted by the existence of some musical sketches dating from late1956 housed in the Dallapiccola Archive in Florence.[5]

Dallapiccola did not disguise the fact that a large part of the libretto for the opera derived from literary sources with which he had long been familiar. This was neither intended to display the composer's literary learning, nor was it simply a convenient way to construct a libretto, by creating an amalgam of quotations that seemed to suit the occasion. What he created in the libretto for *Ulisse* was a document that revealed the composer's inner life and the literature that had been most meaningful to him, and, as we shall see, this is combined with allusions to his own creative work spanning several decades. The array of literary sources is indeed vast: they come from Aeschylus (Demodocus' account of Agamemnon and Clytemnestra), from Friedrich Hölderlin's *Schicksalslied* (some parts of the Lotus-Eaters' scene), from James Joyce's *A Portrait of the Artist as a Young Man* (the "always-never" in Hades), from Thomas Mann's *Joseph and His Brothers* (Ulysses' mother's account of her death), from Gerhart Hauptmann's *Der Bogen des Odysseus* (parts concerning the figure of Melanto), from an inscription in Santa Maria Novella in Florence (parts of the text for Nausicaa), and from Kavafis' poem "Ithaca." The extent of these literary allusions, and the broad scope of literature from varying historical periods that they represent, point to a desire to create a libretto that would be all-encompassing, that would resound with the inflexions of the literary works alluded to, and that would itself be as rich and complex a document of the artist's life as the music itself. This is by no means to suggest that Dallapiccola had high literary ambitions, but nonetheless he was a remarkably "literary" composer, as our examination of his previous work has amply demonstrated. The complexity of the libretto, in terms of its origins, is, however, in no sense a barrier to the listener's immediate understanding of the drama enacted on stage, but almost every line of the text is imbued with philosophical, reflective thought. Indeed, Dallapiccola himself spoke truthfully when he described the work as "the result of my whole life."

Dallapiccola's version of the Ulysses legend is not the one that is most familiar to those who have only read Homer. The heroic Ulysses that Homer draws had been present in the libretto that Giacomo Badoaro wrote for Monteverdi's 1640 opera, the most famous operatic retelling of the story. The age in which Monteverdi's opera was composed was indeed a "heroic" one as far as operatic subject matter was concerned. The aim of composer and librettist was to project the heroic virtues of fortitude, perseverance, and compassion onto the stage through the characterization of the protagonist. By the later twentieth century, however, such a characterization would be inappropriate, if not unconvincing. Dallapiccola brings to the drama a highly significant further dimension, that of Ulysses as searcher and visionary. In this sense, Dallapiccola's protagonist is a much more potent driving force in the drama than Monteverdi's hero had been, a prime mover of events and not simply one who reacts to events. Dallapiccola's Ulysses goes in search of answers to the most urgent questions, and will never be content until he finds what his life has driven him to find. The composer, speaking about the opera, related to Leonardo Pinzauti how he had seen on the wall of a railroad station somewhere in the United States a phrase taken from the Confessions of Saint Augustine: "Thou hast made us for Thyself—and our hearts are restless until they find their rest in Thee."[6]

W. B. Stanford, in his study of the various modern versions of the Ulysses myth, investigated some of the dramatic forms in which it has appeared, including those by Gerhart Hauptmann (*Der Bogen des Odysseus*, 1912) and Jean Giraudoux (*La guerre de Troie n'aura pas lieu*, 1935), concluding that each new version often brings a fresh interpretation of the myth. He said of Dallapiccola's *Ulisse* that here Ulysses' main motivation in his Odyssean adventures is a search for his own identity and for the key to the mystery of life.[7] Dallapiccola identified with this Ulysses, and the experiences the protagonist meets on his journeys are undoubtedly symbols for elements within the composer's own life. Dallapiccola had observed in 1941, in the preface to his version of Monteverdi's *Il ritorno d'Ulisse in patria*, that for an Italian, "a Ulysses that is not filtered through Dante's thinking is inconceivable." He knew very well the reference to Ulysses that occurs in a famous passage in *La Divina Commedia*,[8] and therefore did not want the drama to conclude in Homeric manner with Ulysses the hero in triumphant return to his Kingdom of Ithaca, reclaiming his beloved Penelope from the suitors who had wrought havoc there. Ulysses the wanderer, ever in search of new lands and new experiences, had to set out once more on another final, fateful journey. At the end of this journey, he would be alone in the vastness of the ocean, meeting his death just at the moment that his questioning and visionary soul finds peace with God.

Ulisse is not only the largest in scale of all Dallapiccola's works for the stage, it is also the one in which his vision of a "dramma in musica" was most clearly presented. We saw in an earlier chapter how the possibilities for music drama had first been revealed to him in his youth when he attended some Wagner performances in Graz, and how these experiences, coming even before the operatic world of Mozart or Verdi was revealed to him, had been fundamental in shaping his dramatic ideas. From that moment on, both the musical and the dramatic aspects of opera enthralled him: he was constantly concerned, in all his stage works, with the musico-dramatic shaping of the experience. As far as *Ulisse* was concerned, this shaping was explained by the composer in an essay on the opera,[9] and once again we can see the symmetry of structure that had appeared in so many of the composer's other works. The thirteen scenes, arranged in a Prologue and two acts, reach their dramatic climax in the final scene of the first act, "In the realm of the Cimmerians," while the surrounding scenes correspond one with another on both a dramatic and a musical level. The composer himself set out the overall dramatic scheme in the shape of Ulysses' bow (Figure 6.1).

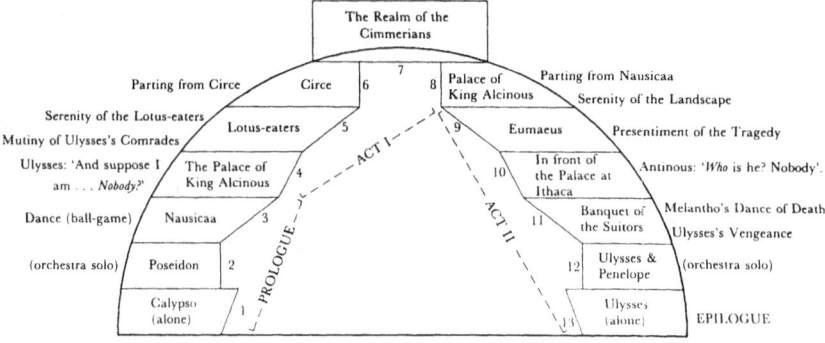

Figure 6.1. Symmetrical structural shape of *Ulisse*.

In all his works for the stage, Dallapiccola's overriding concern was to create the greatest possible network of links and correspondences between text and music, between the images present in the libretto and the musical symbols through which these images are conveyed, and his use of the leitmotif technique of Wagner clearly aided him in this. We saw in chapter 1 how, when he wrote to Wolfgang Wagner early in 1968 about his earliest experiences of Wagner's music, he mentioned in passing how he felt that "the protagonist of the third act of Tristan is the sea." In *Ulisse*, similarly, the sea is a major player, finally in the last scene being the sole companion of Ulysses as he goes to meet his end. The musical symbolization of this is drawn by means of a leitmotif that appears at the opening of the opera, as well as in its final pages: three chords, a musical image expressive of the vastness of the ocean in which Ulysses will finally find rest (Example 6.1).

Example 6.1. *Ulisse*. I, mm. 1–2.

The composer's scheme of the work (Figure 1) shows that there is a correspondence between the scenes in each half of the opera, revolving around the central Hades scene, and even if these links between scenes might appear somewhat tenuous, they are nonetheless important in establishing a framework for the opera as a whole. Thus, Episodes 2 and 12 are both purely orchestral; Episodes 3 and 11 (Nausicaa and Melanto) both present highly contrasted female dancing, the first graceful and the second earthy; Episodes 4 and 10 (Kingdoms of the Phaecians and of Ithaca) are connected by the "Nobody," as Ulysses describes himself; Episodes 5 and 9 contrast the rebellion of Ulysses' companions in the Land of the Lotus Eaters with the peacefulness of the Ithacan countryside; Episodes 6 and 8 both concern departure, first from Circe and later from Nausicaa. This leaves the central scene in Hades, the structural as well as the emotional crux of the opera. At the heart of this scene, Dallapiccola places two choruses in the form of a mirror canon "Ritmo eterno . . . ," placed between dialogues of Ulysses with his mother and with the seer Tiresias. In this way, the whole opera, in common with so many of Dallapiccola's earlier compositions, is in an overall arch form, at the center of which we find the dramatic and musical turning point, a scene of considerable emotional power with a clear structural axis at its central point. Dietrich Kämper draws a telling comparison between the bow-shaped form of *Ulisse* and the image of the bow as a symbol of life in both Aristotle and Dante.[10] In any case, the structural scheme contrasts with that of *Il prigioniero,* in which, as we saw earlier, the center of gravity is to be found in the opera's final scene, as the Prisoner's attempt to escape is finally frustrated. In contrast, the structure of *Ulisse,* with its center of gravity in the central Hades scene, is closer to that of *Job,* in which the discourse of God and Job is placed at its heart. However, it is important to realize that, even if the central Hades scene represents a centre of gravity of the drama, another important, "philosophical" axis is to be found in the Epilogue, in the final pages of which the "answer" to the fundamental questions implicit in the work is given. In this sense, *Ulisse* could be said to combine the dramatic shaping of *Il prigioniero* with that of *Job*: from the former, the emphasis on the revelation that occurs in the opera's final scene, and from the latter the central discourse that paves the way for later dramatic events.

All studies of Dallapiccola's *Ulisse,* including those of Dietrich Kämper, Julia van Hees, and Rosemary Brown, have concurred in isolating two elements that predominate in the musical language: firstly the various leitmotifs derived from its complex web of interlocking tone rows, and secondly an extensive use of allusion to Dallapiccola's earlier music. There is, indeed, every justification for stressing these two components, since any study of the sketch material for the opera housed in the Dallapiccola Archive quickly reveals that the composer himself created the work with such a framework in mind.[11] These two components, working together with the labyrinthine literary references in the libretto of the opera, serve a symbolic purpose within the drama. The fundamental row of the opera, in undulating form that already suggests the sea, is named by the composer "Sea I"; from this he derives two other rows, Sea II and Sea III (also associated with Ulysses himself); and yet again a further group of rows which are linked to specific characters or groups within the opera: Calypso, Circe (two rows), Cimmerians (two rows), Demodocus, Nausicaa. The fundamental forms of all these rows, together with their transpositions, are set out by the composer in a notebook which is available for consultation.[12] The primary element in the drama, the relationship of Ulysses to the sea itself, to which he will return in the final scene and in whose vastness he will finally be able to realize his closeness to God, is thus symbolized even in the fundamental row material. The complex interrelationship of the three fundamental rows, and the presence in all three of the major/minor second figure that had symbolized the questioning, exploratory spirit in *Three Questions with Two Answers,* already contain the germ of the whole symbolic drama (Example 6.2).

Example 6.2. *Ulisse,* rows: Sea 1, 2, 3.

A network of subsidiary rows is derived from these three, each associated with specific characters in the drama, and each containing the three-tone "Question" cell. The derivation of these rows from the initial "Sea" group is frequently complex, but the relationship of one row to another, in relation to the individual characters in the drama, is clearly of great significance. Related rows are symbolically linked to a related character: this can be seen most clearly in the rows associated with the three principal female characters in the drama, Calypso, Nausicaa, and Circe. While Nausicaa and Calypso are related by a kind of "opposition" of one row to another, that is to say with segments of the row alternating one with another, as can be seen in Example 6.3, the row associated with Circe is as it were "self-absorbed," bounded by the three-tone "Question" units.

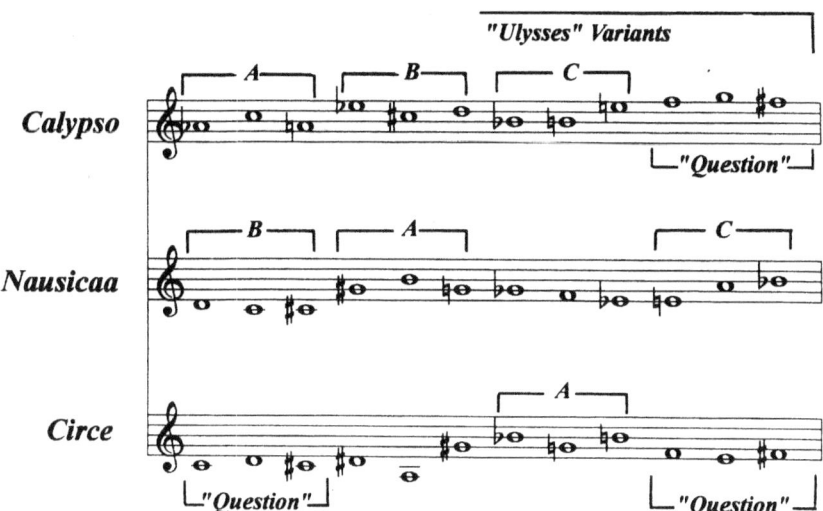

Example 6.3. *Ulisse*, "Female" rows.

This creation of a network of interconnected rows for the opera is clearly indebted to Berg's practice in *Lulu*, in which the characters who at various times come into contact with the protagonist each have an associated row derived by various means from the primary row of Lulu herself. In the case of *Ulisse*, the principal "character" in the drama is, as we have seen, the sea itself, from whose fundamental rows all others are derived. From this initial serial fabric, Dallapiccola builds a number of leitmotifs, just as he had created such leitmotifs from the various rows in *Il prigioniero,* and these become of crucial importance in the musico-dramatic formation of the opera. As we have noted, Dallapiccola here adopts a Wagnerian approach, in which the appearances of the leitmotifs function either as a memory or as a presentiment, interpreting in musical terms the drama enacted on stage. Without doubt the most important of these leitmotifs is one associated with a phrase Calypso has frequently heard Ulysses muttering to himself in his meditations upon the aim of all his actions, and she quotes this in the Prologue: "Guardare, meravigliarsi, e tornare a guardare" (Gazing, marveling, and returning once more to gaze). The leitmotif here is built from a rather expansive melodic reading of the Calypso row, finally coming to rest in the "Question" cell, repeated almost as if murmuring to oneself (Example 6.4)

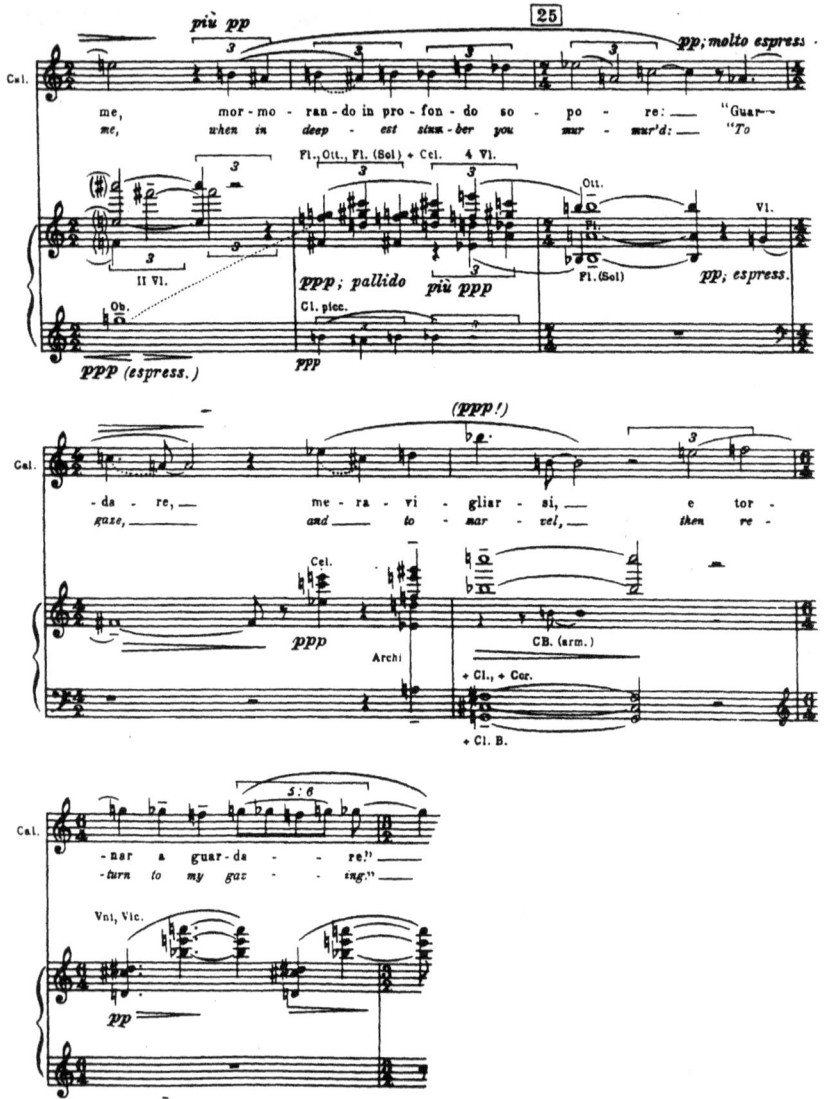

Example 6.4. *Ulisse*. I, mm. 23–29.

This leitmotif occurs twice more within the Prologue, as Calypso muses upon Ulysses' puzzling words; its final occurrence is in the Epilogue, as Ulysses himself ponders the true meaning of his life as he nears his end (Act II, mm. 998–1003). Its appearance at these points in the opera makes this, along with the triple-chord "Sea motif" one of the principal protagonists of the musical drama (Example 6.1).

Ulysses, Wanderer and Discoverer: 1965–1975   241

These two leitmotifs are made memorable by their melodic and harmonic characteristics, but on one occasion Dallapiccola employs a purely rhythmic leitmotif, as Berg had done in both his operas. Indeed, the name that Dallapiccola gives to this rhythmic theme—"ritmo principale"—is simply a translation of Berg's term "Hauptrhythmus." As we noted earlier, this motif had already made an appearance in *Three Questions with Two Answers* (see chapter 5). At its first and last appearance in the opera, it is used to suggest an overwhelming anger: it first occurs in the orchestral episode representing the fury of Poseidon (Act I, measure 92), and once more as Ulysses kills the Suitors (Act II, mm. 856–57; Example 6.5).

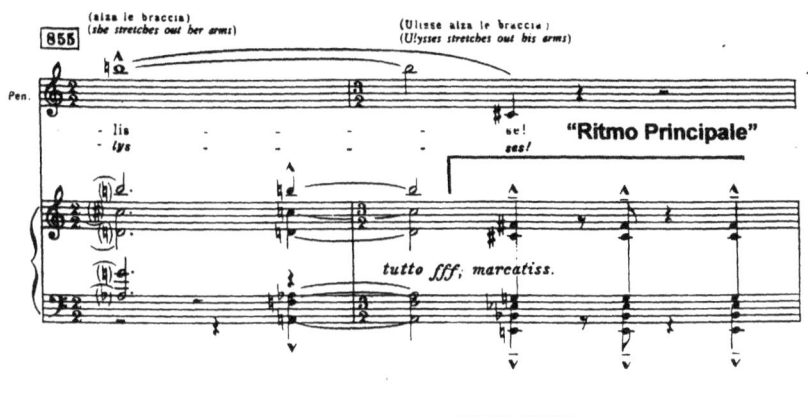

Example 6.5. *Ulisse*. II, mm. 855–58.

There is a connection here between the nervous anger of the rhythm and the mood the composer is depicting at these points in the drama, but the significance of this "ritmo principale" is not limited to a depiction of mood. It also functions in a quite different way in the crucial Hades scene of the opera, where it becomes an essential unifying element for the various canonic forms in the two big choruses. Again, its final appearance in the opera is highly significant: at Act II, measure 123, as Ulysses in a moment of illumination finally sees that he is no longer alone. He has now found companionship in the constant ebb and flow of the ocean, and the overpowering crescendo on a single tone in the orchestra at this point is built up by means of instrumental entries whose spacing also follows the "ritmo principale." The idea for such rhythmically phased instrumental entries within an orchestral crescendo was undoubtedly suggested by the similarly articulated single-tone crescendo to be found at the climactic point of Berg's *Wozzeck* (Act III, Interlude between Scenes 2 and 3).[13] Given these three distinct uses of the rhythmic motif—in depiction of anger, as a rhythmic unifier for the Hades choruses, and as a means of articulating the orchestral crescendo in the final scene—it is tempting to speculate about whether this leitmotif constitutes in effect a "fate motif" within the opera as a whole. Certainly, its connection with the anger of Poseidon in the first act, and with the killing of the Suitors in Ithaca in the second, would suggest this as a possibility, and even more so in the use of the rhythmic motif as a very clear figuration throughout the two monumental choral episodes in the Hades scene. Perhaps this motif is a symbol of the inevitability of events driving Ulysses' life towards its conclusion, and towards the revelation of the divine that will dominate the last scene of the drama.

The second building block of the musical language of *Ulisse*, the use of self-quotation (the composer spoke of "allusions"), is of no less importance than his employment of leitmotifs, but it functions in a very different way. The opera as a whole is without doubt the richest in such allusions of all Dallapiccola's work. In the course of the opera, Dallapiccola alludes to works of all periods of his creative life, from *Volo di notte, Il prigioniero, Goethe-Lieder, Canti di liberazione, An Mathilde, Cinque canti,* and *Requiescant*. We cannot really include the related orchestral work *Three Questions with Two Answers* in this list, given that this was formed very largely from musical material the composer was already planning to employ in the opera. Examples can be given from many sections of the score of *Ulisse*, and there is, without exception, a clear dramatic or textual justification for their use at that particular point. This justification is to be found in the relationship of that moment in the opera to the subject matter of the work or portion of a work to which allusion is made. One of the most important of these, for example, is to be found in the "Stars" motif of a B-major chord and twelve-tone melody which, as we pointed out in chapter 1, had first appeared in *Tre laudi* and had been reiterated in *Volo di notte* and *Il prigioniero*. In all these earlier compositions, the motif had been associated both with a vision of the starry heavens, and with a moment of poignant illumination and recognition. This metaphor clearly had its roots in Dallapiccola's great love of Dante: in the *Divina Commedia,* the word *stelle* (stars), which concludes all three parts of the poem, similarly acts as a metaphor of divine illumination. The various appearances of the "Stars" motif in *Ulisse* function not only as a reminiscence of a much earlier part of Dallapiccola's creative life, but also as a powerful symbol of Ulysses' gradual enlightenment, and its appearances in both the Prologue and Epilogue frame the drama as a whole. In the Prologue, Calypso bemoans the fact that Ulysses has spurned her offer of immortality, and as she wonders what it is that his heart desires ("What may man further wish for, if not to escape from death?"), the motif recalls the vision of the stars granted to Fabien in *Volo di notte* as the moment of his death approaches. In the Epilogue, in contrast, Ulysses ponders what his life has taught him, "merely syllables, instead of words . . . ?", and as he gazes at the stars, he asks them to show him some answer to his questioning ("Stars! . . . How many times under how many skies have I watched you and pondered your pure and tremulous beauty . . . !"; Example 6.6).

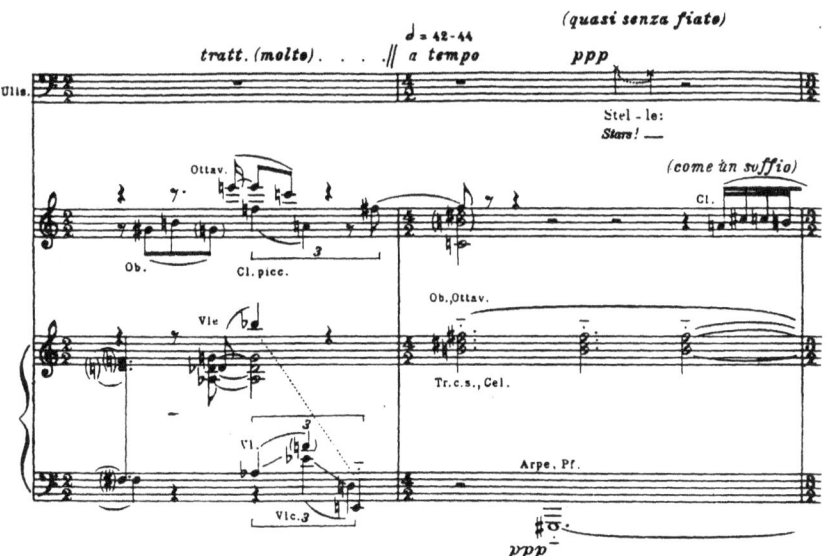

Example 6.6. *Ulisse.* "Stars" motif: II, mm. 952–54.

Example 6.6. *Continued.*

This revelation of numinous power clearly parallels in the composer's mind the revelation of overwhelming beauty that the pilot Fabien had experienced in *Volo di notte,* and Dallapiccola is simply underlining this moment with appropriate and evocative music taken from the earlier work. This was not the first occasion on which he had used an allusion to an earlier work in order to create an overwhelming emotional effect: we saw how, in the final pages of *Il prigioniero,* the allusion to the choral *Canti di prigionia* had been used to very similar effect.

It is in the Epilogue of the opera that the richest fund of allusions is to be found; they appear at regular intervals throughout the scene, almost as if Dallapiccola were reviewing the whole of his creative life. He was to refer to *Ulisse* as "the result of my whole life," and this can be understood in a double sense: not only did he place in the libretto of the opera a vast array of references to the literary works with which he had lived throughout his life, but in the Epilogue we find almost a catalogue of the composer's memories of his own work. In that same year, Luciano Berio was incorporating in part of his *Sinfonia* allusions to a dazzling array of music from both the distant and the more recent past, but in Dallapiccola's opera his field of allusion is a personalized and interior one, limited to his own musical past. If we set out the scheme of these allusions as they appear in the Epilogue, we can see that together they make up a large proportion of the material of the scene as a whole (Table 6.1).

Table 6.1. *Ulisse*: allusions in the Epilogue.

	Ulisse	Allusion
Act II:	m. 953: "Stelle": B major	*Tre laudi/Volo di notte*
	mm. 958–59: "Stelle"	*Il prigioniero*
	m. 965: "Perchè tanto diverso . . ."	*Cinque canti*
	mm. 982–88: "Trovar potessi il nome . . ."	*An Mathilde*
	m. 989: "questa mia vita . . ."	*Canti di liberazione*
	m. 1008: "se una voce . . ."	*Canti di liberazione*

If the Epilogue of *Ulisse* finally brings to light the "answer" to the fundamental questions that assail Ulysses, the central scene "in the realm of the Cimmerians" represents Ulysses' questioning and philosophical spirit in its most powerful form, and here the composer created the scene of greatest tension in the opera. As we have seen, Dallapiccola set out the ground plan of *Ulisse* in the shape of Ulysses' bow, and in this seventh episode we find the crucial turning point of both drama and music. The journey of Ulysses into the shadow world, and the ambiguous response to his questioning of those he meets there, are no doubt linked in the composer's mind with an earlier, and equally significant, operatic journey, that undertaken by Orpheus in Monteverdi's first opera. In each case the journey is undertaken in a spirit of questing and reveals to the hero some, at least, of what he is seeking. Orpheus had entered the spirit world in order to persuade the gods reigning there to release his beloved Euridice, to restore to his life the balance of which it had been robbed. In Dallapiccola's opera, Ulysses, having rejected the seductions of Circe in the previous scene ("The call of the sea is so much stronger than your threats and your seductions . . .") enters the underworld to be shown the pathways that will lead him to a full awareness of his own soul.

In Hades, Ulysses comes face-to-face with the shadows that look with perpetual sadness upon human sufferings, expressed in speaking and singing choruses relayed by loudspeaker and underpinned by the dry rattling of a side drum enunciating the "ritmo principale" (Example 6.7).

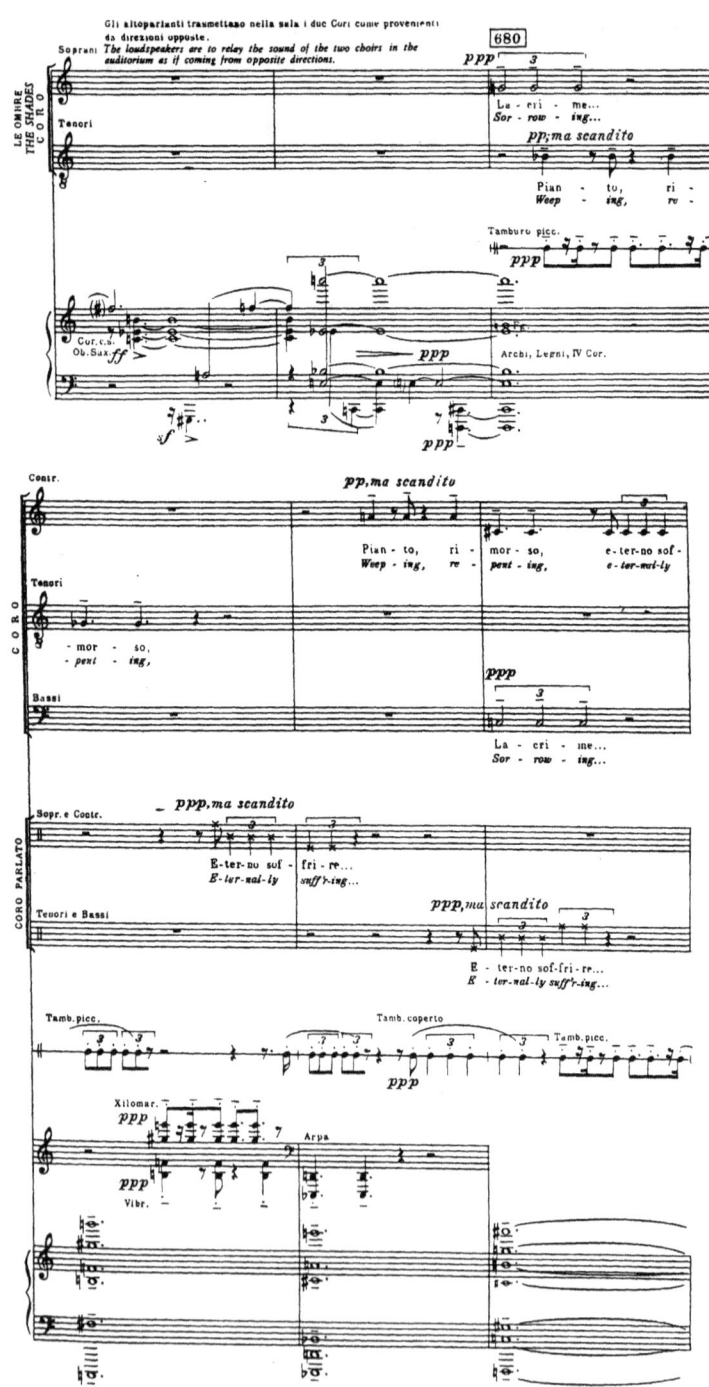

Example 6.7. *Ulisse.* I, mm. 678–83.

Tears . . .
cries, remorse, eternal suffering . . .
cries, tears . . .
Eternal darkness; never any light . . .
Eternal suffering; never any hope . . .

This rhythm is present in virtually every measure of the scene, as the choral voices of the infernal shadows enunciate the "Always! Never!" that the composer had found in his reading of James Joyce. The choral episodes, combining singing and speaking, are a further development of the choruses he had made an essential element in the drama of both *Il prigioniero* and *Job,* in all three cases as a powerful means of enunciating the "beyond." Here, however, they also have something of the sombre and serious atmosphere to be found in the Choruses of Spirits punctuating the fourth act of Monteverdi's *Orfeo*. In *Ulisse,* however, the oppression of the confined souls bound together in Hades is reflected in a taut and intense rhythmic counterpoint (Example 6.8).

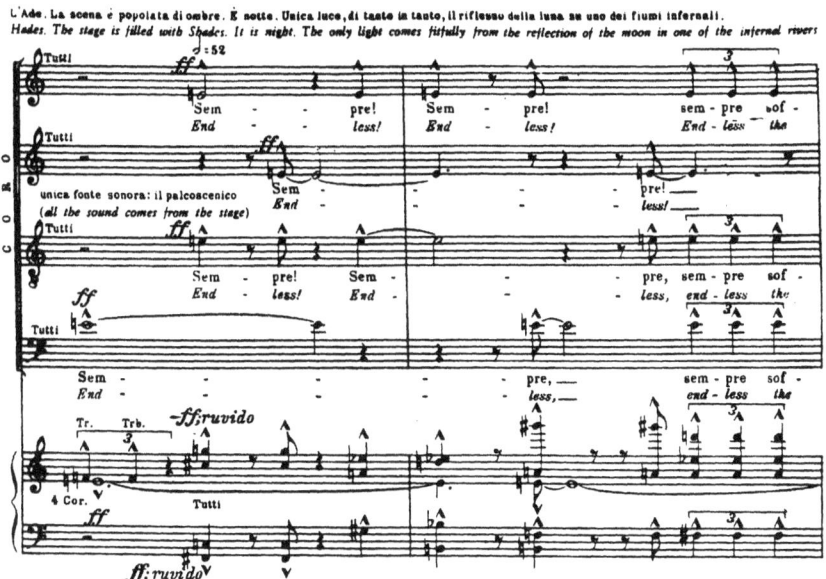

Example 6.8. *Ulisse.* I, mm. 698–701.

Example 6.8. *Continued.*

Dallapiccola commented on the overall organization of this central scene:

> This scene is parallel only to itself. And here, although I had intended to speak only about the libretto, I must make a very brief digression of a musical nature. Often in this episode chords are mirrored, and even considerably long passages are treated in the manner of Bach's mirror fugues, while rigorously adhering to the twelve-tone system.[14]

Once again in Dallapiccola's work, we see how the moments of greatest significance and power in the work are imbued with contrapuntal writing, and once again the composer seems to summon up the image of J. S. Bach to aid him. The text of the canonic choruses reflects the grandeur of the dramatic design:

> Eternal rhythm of the rivers of Hades,
> waves breaking on a rocky shore,
> seeming to say with terrible power:
> Always! Never!

The row on which the scene is based, the so-called Hades Row, now introduces into the musical drama intervals that create a wholly new perspective: major thirds, fourths, and fifths, in place of the seconds, minor thirds, and tritones that had earlier predominated (Example 6.9).

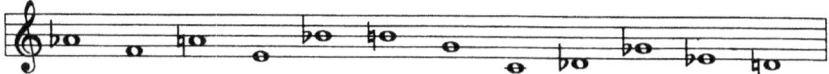

Example 6.9. *Ulisse*, "Hades" row.

The chorus of shadows asks Ulysses "Who are you? What do you seek?" to which he replies that he is seeking Tiresias, to learn from him what his final fate may be, but the shadows persist, demanding that the stranger should give his name. Ulysses recognizes the face of his mother Anticlea amongst the shadows, and as she in turn recognizes her son, her voice becomes subdued and gentle, barely rising above a secretive whisper, with many repeated-note phrases trailing off into silence as she speaks of her own death. At the exact center of the opera we find Ulysses' cry "O madre!" (Act I, mm. 860–61). From this point on, the music of the scene begins to proceed backwards. Having now reached the farthest point in his traveling of both the inner and the outer worlds, Ulysses can only retrace his steps to regain the world from which he had set out so many years earlier. This makes clear the purpose for which Dallapiccola had set out the overall form of the opera in the shape of Ulysses' bow: not only is this the turning point of both inner and outer journeys, it is also the point of greatest tension in the overall structure, demanding a release of energy to impel it towards its end.

In his conversation with his mother, it is the past that is of greatest concern to Ulysses. He questions her about her death, whereas in the dialogue with the seer Tiresias that follows, he is concerned with the future, with the fate that awaits him on his return. As Ulysses' mother disappears from view, the chorus demand that Tiresias tell them what will happen to Ulysses on his return voyage. Tiresias, the foreteller of events to come, is linked in the drama with Demodocus, who recounts the past, and they both share the same tone row in the opera. With Tiresias, however, Ulysses can have no real dialogue: the seer simply states with startling clarity what he knows of the journey to come:

> You will kiss the soil of Ithaca once more, and your son and spouse . . . but how much blood do I see around you . . . then I see you wandering alone on the ocean, your hair is white like the sea spray.

As Tiresias vanishes, unable to speak of the ultimate fate of Ulysses, there is a repetition of the canonic chorus "Ritmo eterno . . . Sempre! Mai!" that had opened the scene, and in the concluding measures the will-o'-the-wisp clarinet figures associated with the shadows inhabiting Hades trail off into a final enigmatic tritone harmony. With the return of this figure, it would seem that the scene we have witnessed, as Ulysses learns of both past and future events, is contained within parentheses, its powerful images disappearing with the return to other realities (Example 6.10).

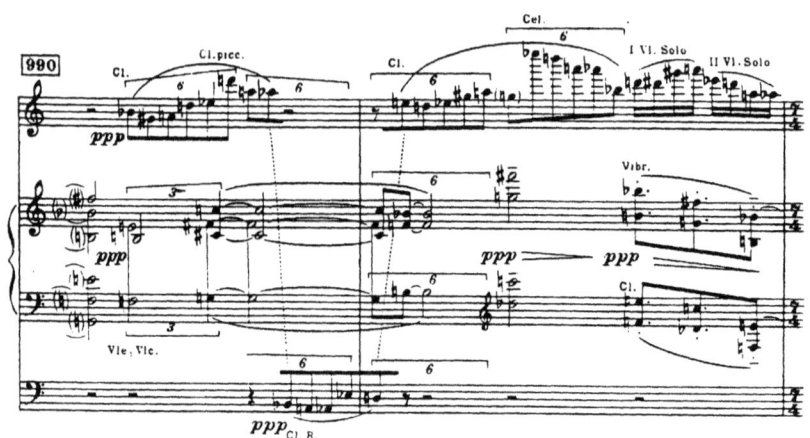

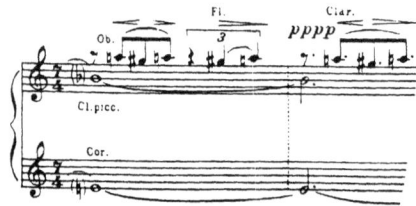

Example 6.10. *Ulisse.* I, mm. 990–92.

The two musical devices that we have examined, leitmotif and musical allusion, work together to create the musical fabric of *Ulisse,* but they operate on two very distinct levels. The leitmotifs are recognizable, recurring "public" references, while the allusions are personal and private references, to which only the composer himself and those closely bound up with his whole oeuvre could be party. Both work together, however, in suggesting the "meaning" of the opera. From a historical perspective, it is clear that *Ulisse* has roots in earlier operatic practice, and the composer's debt to three predecessors in particular is evident in various features of the work. From Claudio Monteverdi, he took aspects of the dramatic outlines of his treatment of the drama; from Wagner, whose music dramas had first led him towards music, he took the idea of a language of leitmotifs as a feature of both the dramatic conception and the thematic development of the opera; and from Alban Berg, whose work had first led him towards twelve-tone technique, he took the intricate weaving of serial constructions from which the opera draws much of its power.

Ulisse reinterprets the ancient myth of Ulysses in the light of Dante's judgment on Ulysses in the *Divina Commedia,* in the same way that Thomas Mann's novel *Joseph and His Brothers* had reinterpreted the biblical account of the Joseph story in the light of contemporary Persian versions of the legend. For both artists, the idea of an ancient myth and its universal resonance was a powerful inspiration to their creativity. When the two had met for the first time, in New York during the summer of 1952, Mann had spoken of the enormous debt he owed to James Joyce, in whose novel *Ulysses* he had sensed "the possibility of transforming 'mythologically' any event in life . . . ," and had stressed the connections between his own *Joseph and His Brothers* and Joyce's *Ulysses*. The importance of Joyce for Dallapiccola was already apparent from the two occasions, in *Tre Poemi* and in *Requiescant,* on which he had set some of Joyce's poetry, and we mentioned earlier how a fragment of the text of *A Portrait of the Artist as a Young Man* (the "Always! Never!") had been incorporated in the libretto of *Ulisse*. Despite the obvious gulf that separates Joyce's novel from Dallapiccola's opera, not least in the setting and the subject matter dealt with, it is still true that the opera would have been very different had Dallapiccola not encountered Joyce's novel at an early stage (he bought a copy in the late 1940s). Both share an interpenetration of mythology and autobiography, and equally both share a concern to "universalize" the cultural references embedded in their respective texts, whether literary or musical. One can, with some justification, say that Dallapiccola's *Ulisse* presents the myth filtered not only through the vision of it given by Dante, but also through the more modern experience of Joyce.

The first production, staged at the Berlin Opera on 29 September 1968, could hardly have occurred at a less appropriate moment. The dramatic events on the streets of Paris in May of that year, and the echoes that they provoked in many other European cities, did not bode well for the appearance at that moment of an opera on a classical theme that did not seem to have any obvious relationship to present-day events and concerns. The stage and costume designs by Ferdinando Farulli were also seen as unimaginative, simply reproducing a rather dull and conventional image of ancient Greece. Furthermore, the indisposition of Dietrich Fischer-Dieskau, who should have taken the part of Ulysses, contributed to a less than favorable climate in which the opera first saw the light. The critical reaction was, in some quarters at least, rather hostile.[15] Dallapiccola was particularly disturbed by the reaction that the German press gave to the opera's libretto, concluding that it was only to be expected that Dante's account of Ulysses should not be known in Germany, and that the last scene of the opera must therefore be a puzzle. He also commented that some people had looked at how Ulysses' intuition of a Supreme Being in this final scene and had "asked themselves whether I had wanted to present on stage a Christian Ulysses."[16] The composer had made a characteristically wry comment about this in his diary just a few days after the first performance:

> I have cast an eye over some of the critiques. I remain surprised to see how not one of them has understood that the discovery of God of my Ulysses does not by any means signify that he has become a Roman Catholic Apostolic Christian.[17]

The opera was produced at La Scala, Milan in 1970, again eliciting a very mixed response from critics and from the audience, but with the production in Düsseldorf in 1972 (repeated the same year in Florence), a greater understanding of the opera seems to have taken place. A production of the opera that might present it in such a way as to reveal the power and beauty of this, Dallapiccola's largest score still remains only a possibility.

Sicut umbra

The appearance of *Ulisse* marked an important point in Dallapiccola's creative life. Since he had contemplated the opera for a long time and had produced at the end an opera of a remarkably self-revelatory character, it would seem that he could now, with some justification, begin to work in a more relaxed manner. He was by this time sixty-four years old, and the previous decade during which he had been composing the opera had drained a good deal of his energy. He therefore began to lighten his compositional activity to some extent. Nevertheless, his activities as a whole showed no sign of slackening: he continued to give lectures, undertook some conducting of his own compositions in America, and gathered a selection of his writings for publication under the title *Appunti, incontri, meditazioni* (Notes, Encounters, Thoughts). By the summer of 1970, however, he had begun to work on a new composition commissioned by the Coolidge Foundation of Washington, *Sicut umbra* (Like unto a Shadow) for mezzo soprano and four instrumental groups, in which once again the composer's admiration for Spanish poetry was manifest in settings of three poems by Juan Ramón Jiménez.[18] Dallapiccola composed the work in reverse, beginning with the last of the four songs and ending with the first, as he commented in a letter to his publisher.[19]

The poems chosen from Jimenez' collection *Piedra y cielo* (Stone and Sky, (1917–18)) have as their subject the fragility of life, as in the texts chosen for *Requiescant*, and the title refers to a passage in the Book of Job ("Our days on earth are like unto a shadow," Job 8:9). The work bears a dedication to the memory of a friend's daughter who had recently died in a tragic accident.

The four instrumental groups of the accompanying ensemble are piccolo, flute, flute in G; E-flat clarinet, B-flat clarinet, bass clarinet; violin, viola, cello; and harp, celesta, vibraphone. The ensemble incorporates a distinct "keyboard" group, as Dallapiccola had earlier employed in *Parole di San Paolo*. The three vocal movements are preceded by an instrumental movement employing only one of the four instrumental groups (piccolo, flute, and flute in G). As in the *Goethe-Lieder* there is a clearly structured sequence in the gradual employment of the other groups as the work progresses; three clarinets and three strings in the second, three flutes, three clarinets, and three strings in the third; and adding the harp, celesta, and vibraphone group only in the fourth. Despite composing the movements of the work in reverse order, Dallapiccola created a clear-cut formal scheme in the succession of these movements: after the introductory instrumental movement, the three song settings are arranged in a slow-fast-slow sequence. It is clear that, having spent more than a decade so absorbed in the composition of his opera *Ulisse*, Dallapiccola was unable to escape from the shadow of the opera when he composed *Sicut umbra*. The presence of the opera is felt through the image of the sea which occurs both in the second poem ("El recuero") and in the third ("Epitafio ideal de un marinero"). At both of these points (mm. 116 and 182), the three-chord Sea leitmotif that had opened *Ulisse* is quoted.

The row upon which *Sicut umbra* is based begins with the three tones that had formed the "Question" motif in *Goethe-Lieder*, in *Three Questions with Two Answers*, and in *Ulisse*, and this provides a further link with the opera. Indeed, one might legitimately regard the final song of *Sicut umbra*, with its evocation of the sea as a fit tomb for a sailor lost at sea, as an epitaph for Ulysses himself. The row is present from the opening of the first movement—a mere nine measures for piccolo, flute and alto flute—in which the row is used to construct canons. The canonic form of the movement can be summarized in Table 6.2.

Table 6.2. *Sicut umbra*: the canonic form of the first movement.

	m. 1	mm. 5–6				m. 9
Voice 1:		[P: 2–12]	[P: 7–12]	[I: 1]		4–note codetta
Voice 2:	[P: 1]		[P:1–12]	[I: 2–12]		4–note codetta
Voice 3:		[P:2–12]	[P: 1–6]	[P:1	I: 2–12]	4–note codetta

From this, it can be seen that the whole piece is formed in symmetrical manner about a central axis, dividing it into two halves between measures 5 and 6. In the first half, a canon at the double octave is presented between the outer voices, whose initial tone (C sharp) is held throughout by the middle voice. At the conclusion of this, the outer voices form a row exposition divided into two hexachords, while the middle voice enunciates a complete row exposition (beginning on D) that concludes with the C sharp that had earlier been held. In the second half of the tiny movement, the lower pair of voices maintain a canon at the lower octave on a row beginning with the C now held by the upper voice. The two lower voices come to rest on the unison C sharp that had acted as a central focus of the opening part of the movement, and the piece concludes with a "codetta" in which the three four-tone groups together form another row presentation. The final three-tone chord is a verticalization of the "Question" motif that had appeared in horizontal form at the opening of the movement (Example 6.11).

Example 6.11. *Sicut umbra*. I, entire movement.

At the central point of this miniature structure (mm. 5–6), the outline of the fundamental row given by the flute (Voice II) is one that will be important at subsequent points in the work, both in the instrumental epilogue of the final piece (mm. 185–90) and also earlier in the same final song (measure 141). In the setting of the poem "Epitafio ideal de un marinero" that concludes the work, evoking a tragedy at sea, Dallapiccola once again employs the symbolism of "eye music" that had been a feature of *Cinque canti* and *Concerto per la notte di Natale dell'anno 1956*. The poet's call to look up at the starry firmament, "Hay que buscar, para saber tu tumba, por el firmamiento . . ." ("You must search the firmament to find your tomb") prompts the composer to draw in the score nine specific stellar constellations, by employing the graphic distribution of notes on the stave to suggest their placement in space, setting them out in equal-value notes, but with the precise rhythms indicated on a separate line (Example 6.12).

Example 6.12. *Sicut umbra*. IV, mm. 142–50.

Example 6.12. *Continued.*

It is clear from the sketches for *Sicut umbra*[20] that the composer had conceived these "constellation images" as an integral part of the musical workings of the piece, not as an element added later for coloristic or even idiosyncratic reasons. They appear even in early sketches of the relevant passages, and although their layout in terms of note values and instrumentation—elements that will be vital to their effect—was not yet decided, the shapes of these constellations are already present. This can be seen in a sketch for the passage (Example 6.13).

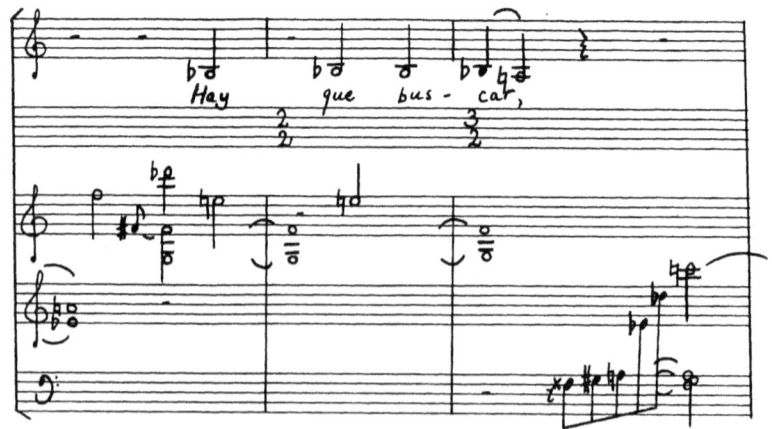

Example 6.13. *Sicut umbra*, sketch for ". . . hay que buscar . . ."

Example 6.13. Continued.

For Dallapiccola, as we have observed on many occasions in this study, the image of the starry heavens was a constant presence, appearing first in the "Stars" motif that opens both *Tre laudi* and *Volo di notte,* and providing the symbol that comes to dominate the final scene of *Ulisse.* Here in the final part of *Sicut umbra,* the composer revisits this image for one final time, on this occasion producing an effect of "eye music" that, like the cross image we observed in *Cinque canti,* is a subtle and yet telling indication of the concern with symbols that runs through Dallapiccola's work.

Tempus destruendi—Tempus aedificandi

During 1968, while he was busy preparing for the première of *Ulisse,* Dallapiccola had received a commission from the "Testimonium" Festival in Israel for a new composition, a work that should refer in some way to the city of Jerusalem. One movement of this piece, *Tempus destruendi—Tempus aedificandi,* was eventually given in the Festival in Tel Aviv in January 1971, and the completed work in Siena in August of the same year. For this work, Dallapiccola again set Latin texts, and as on so many earlier occasions, the composer turned to his wife Laura for help in finding texts that might be suitable. Laura Dallapiccola was a truly remarkable woman, and her importance in the creative, as well as the personal life of Dallapiccola could easily form the subject of a separate study. We have already remarked on many occasions about her literary and linguistic expertise coming to the aid of the composer, such as the search for texts for *Canti di prigionia* and the discovery of the short story of Villiers de L'Isle-Adam from which the composer derived the narrative of *Il prigioniero.* On the occasion of the commission from Israel for a choral work, it would seem particularly appropriate that the Catholic composer Dallapiccola and his Jewish wife Laura should work together to find a text appropriate to such a work. The text finally chosen reflected both the Jewish and Christian traditions: this was "Exhortatio," written by the eleventh-century Irish monk Dermatus, which called for the rebuilding of the Temple of Jerusalem destroyed by the Babylonians. The composer's original idea was to compose this single-movement work for unaccompanied chorus, but during its composition Dallapiccola decided that a companion piece was needed, and he therefore decided to place the "Exhortatio" alongside a setting of "Ploratus," by Paulinus of Aquileia (735–802 C.E.), a lament over the destruction of his city.

The two pieces, both for similar choral forces and both based on Latin texts, would be placed together and given the overall title *Tempus destruendi—Tempus aedificandi* (A Time of Destruction—A Time of Building).

According to Dietrich Kämper, the composer's decision to create a choral dyptich, and not simply an isolated piece, was made when Dallapiccola realized that he had neglected the composition of *a cappella* choral music since he had written the First Series of *Cori di Michelangelo* in 1933, and wished to create a contrasting piece to be placed alongside the "Exhortatio."[21] But there was, perhaps, a further reason for this decision. The "Ploratus" is concerned with the destruction of a city, indeed of a whole culture, whereas the "Exhortatio" contains a call for the rebuilding of the Temple, and thus in a sense for the creation of a whole new world. Dallapiccola was fully aware, as a Catholic composer with a Jewish wife, not only of the significance of the Temple of Jerusalem in several religious traditions, but also of the need for a harmonious and universal renewal of all those traditions within the contemporary world, and it was, almost certainly, in this spirit of renewal that *Tempus destruendi—Tempus aedificandi* was composed.

If the composition of the work represented a return to the medium of unaccompanied choral voices that Dallapiccola had last broached thirty-seven years earlier with the First Series of *Cori di Michelangelo,* it was a return which was greatly enriched by experiences he had had in the intervening years. The most important of these experiences was, undoubtedly, the assimilation of Viennese serialism, and associated with this, the greatly expanded possibilities for vocal writing that had been explored by Berg, Schoenberg, and Webern. In *Tempus destruendi—Tempus aedificandi,* the writing for the choral voices incorporates the widest possible palette of vocal sonorities: song, speech, and *bocca chiusa* are placed alongside whispered sounds, and solo voices or groupings alongside the full ensemble.

"Ploratus," the first part of the dyptich, is a highly atmospheric piece, one encompassing a certain dramatic element in its depiction of the destruction of the city of Aquileia in the text of Paulinus. The opening measures, mingling the cries of anguish in sevenths and ninths in all the choral voices with a *parlato* exclamation of the text in the upper voices, immediately suggests the tragedy. This lament will return again in mm. 16–20 and 57–61 (Example 6.14).

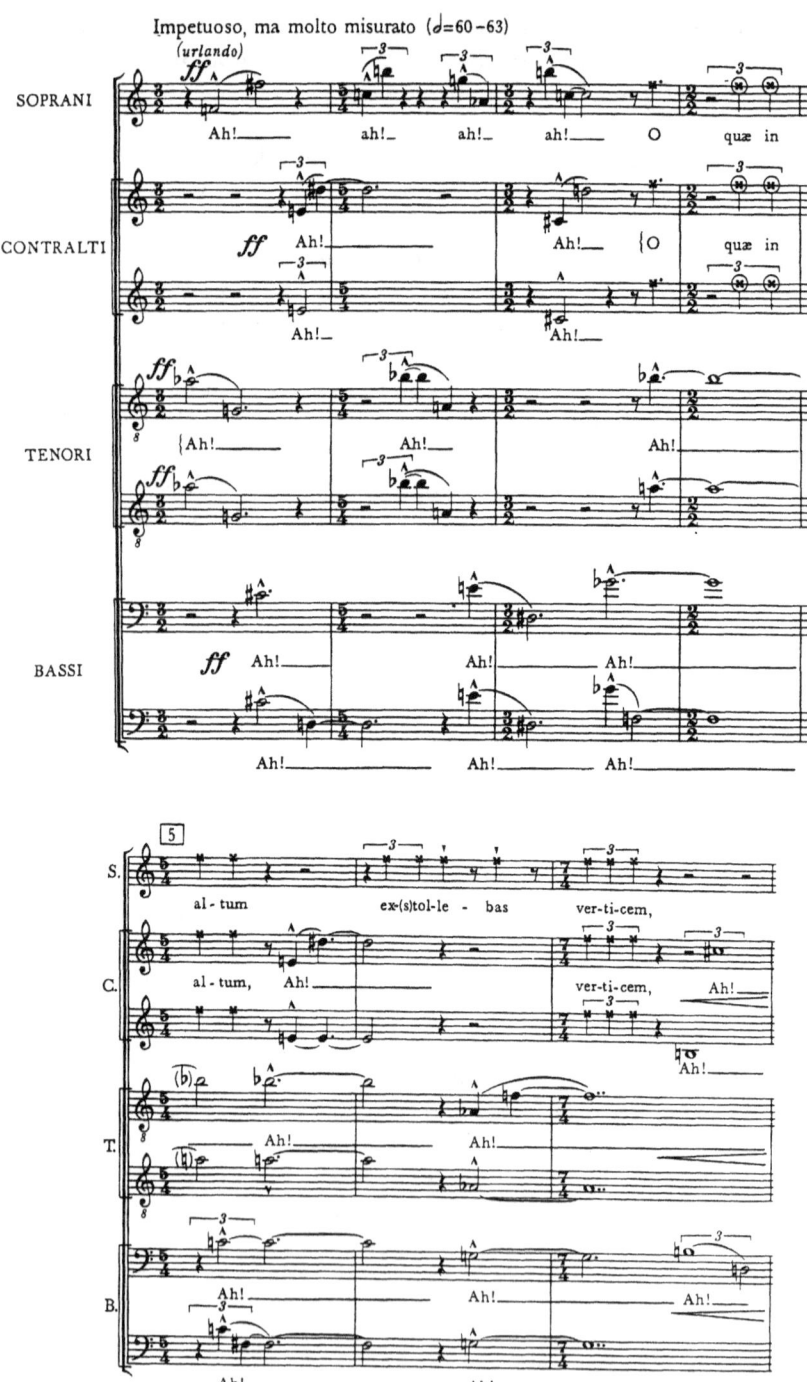

Example 6.14. *Tempus destruendi—Tempus aedificandi.* "Ploratus," mm. 1–7.

As the text describes the ruins of the city, which can never again be rebuilt, the voices gradually become hushed, and the greatest despair is expressed in a passage beginning in measure 36, with the most subdued imitation in the vocal parts, dispersed as if in a wasteland. The music of lament, with cythera and organ, is invoked by a solo soprano from measure 48; here, the fundamental row of the piece is most clearly presented, in P and transposed RI forms (Example 6.15).

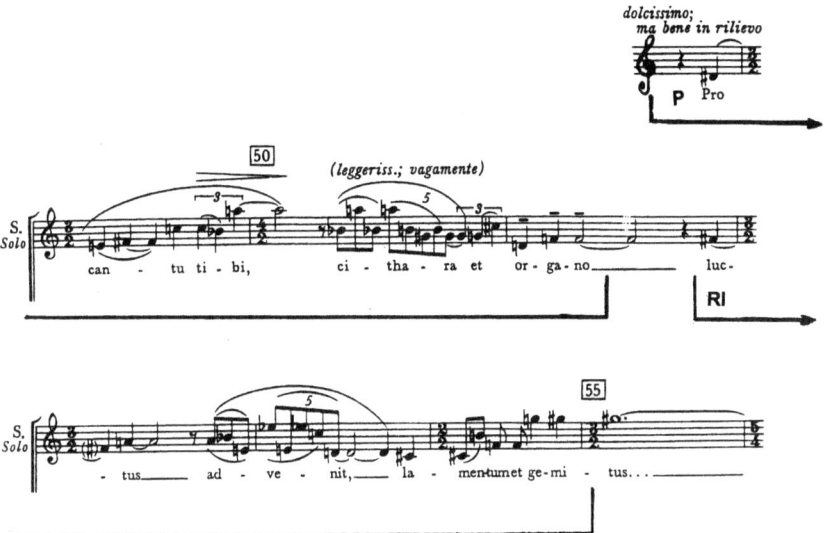

Example 6.15. *Tempus destruendi—Tempus aedificandi*. "Ploratus," mm. 48–55.

The choral voices join in the song of lament with the solo soprano from measure 62, sopranos and contraltos in prime and inverted figurations, and the piece comes to a gentle and resigned conclusion.

The second part of the dyptich, "Exhortatio," is based upon a new row, and in contrast to the preceding piece, the row is set out in unambiguous form in the opening measures, its component pitches distributed among the individual solo voices, while the remaining choral voices whisper the exhortation "Exite, Babylon" (Depart, Babylon) (Example 6.16 (a) and (b)).

Example 6.16 (a). *Tempus destruendi—Tempus aedificandi*. "Exhortatio," row.

The passage that follows (mm. 9–17), speaking of the stones and the walls of the ruined Temple of Jerusalem, isolates fragments of the melodic utterance, and the whole passage seems to recall the wasteland that the "Ploratus" had vividly depicted. The rallying cry, calling for the Babylonians to depart from the city, reappears suddenly and ferociously in the *fortissimo* from measure 18; here, as Kämper has pointed out, the composer develops a new row symmetrical row by isolating the first three pitches of the original row (Example 6.17).[22]

Ulysses, Wanderer and Discoverer: 1965–1975 263

Example 6.16 (b). *Tempus destruendi—Tempus aedificandi.* "Exhortatio," mm. 1–8.

Example 6.17. *Tempus destruendi—Tempus aedificandi.* "Exhortatio," mm. 18–22.

Example 6.17. *Continued.*

This new row formation is employed horizontally in the first measures of the passage, and is also employed vertically for the chord formations that begin to appear here and run through the remainder of the piece. The complete original row has, up to this point, not yet been presented in simple melodic form, having appeared only in the accumulation of solo voices in the opening measures of the piece. From measure 39, however, there begins a passage of haunting expressivity in which, at the very center of the piece, a solo soprano sets out this row, the final pitches 11–12 forming an accompanying harmony in the *tutti* choral voices (Example 6.18).

Example 6.18. *Tempus destruendi—Tempus aedificandi.* "Exhortatio," mm. 39–42.

This central episode, in fact, marks a parallel with the central "Hades" scene in *Ulisse*. In the opera, as we saw, Dallapiccola had placed a palindromic musical form at the farthest point of Ulysses' journey. Here, similarly, the statement of the fundamental row in P form by the solo soprano is balanced by a further statement, by the contralto solo, of the I form in mm. 50–53.[23] Once again, perhaps, placing musically symmetrical units side by side acts as a symbol of return and restoration, this time forming part of the call for the reconstruction of the Temple.

The final part of "Exhortatio," beginning in measure 57 with the crescendo to a heartfelt cry, incorporates a complex polyphony based upon the second, derived row that had first appeared from measure 18. The text here calls for the stones of the sanctuary to be gathered together once more (mm. 60–69), leading to a *pianissimo* sigh of longing (mm. 69–72) employing the first hexachord of the I form of the fundamental row, while the bass voices whisper "recolligite" (gather together). The passage from ms. 103 is an almost exact reprise of the corresponding passage earlier in the piece (mm. 18–25).

Tempus destruendi—Tempus aedificandi represents Dallapiccola's return to the composition of unaccompanied choral music that he had neglected, by his own admission, for too long, and is a remarkable example of the composer's gifts as a composer of such music. In his youth, the world of choral and madrigal composition from the Renaissance had been one of the revelations made to him by his teacher, Antonio Illersberg, and there is no doubt that the essentially polyphonic and contrapuntal nature of so much of Dallapiccola's musical inspiration can be traced back to this early influence. But by this late stage in his creative life, he is now able to enrich the polyphony with the serialism that he had acquired later, and the expressive power of the late choral work has its roots in both the earlier and the later sources of inspiration.

Commiato

Immediately after completing the choral work, Dallapiccola began to give some thought to a new project, a ballet which had been requested by the Düsseldorf Theater Ballet. He had been inspired by seeing Goya's series of paintings entitled *Los desastres de la guerra* (The Disasters of War) to create a ballet based upon this masterpiece, and he commenced work on this at the beginning of 1972, but a further commission interrupted work on the ballet. The commission was from Austrian Radio in Graz, and the work that resulted, *Commiato* (Farewell), would prove to be Dallapiccola's last composition, performed at the Styrian Autumn Festival in 1972. This completed in almost symbolic manner a whole life of musical activity: it had been in Graz, during a period of enforced exile in 1917–18, that Dallapiccola had first decided upon a musical career after seeing Wagner's *The Flying Dutchman*. The piece was written in memory of his friend Harald Kaufmann of Graz, who had died in 1970, and for the text the composer revisited once more that rich fund of popular medieval poetry to which his wife Laura had so often pointed him. The text was a *lauda* attributed to the Florentine Brunetto Latini, the thirteenth-century writer whom Dante praised as his teacher in the fifteenth canto of the *Inferno*. The choice of this text for his last completed composition was significant: not only did he return to the medieval period, from which so many of the texts of his earlier compositions had arisen, but he also invoked the name of one of the great humanists who had made of Dallapiccola's adopted city of Florence the greatest center of the humanist adventure. During the composition of *Commiato* the composer was suddenly taken seriously ill during a visit to Durham in England, and he was fully aware of the irony of the composition of what might appear to be a "farewell to life" at this time:

O fratel nostro, che se'morto e sepolto,
nelle sue braccia Iddio t'abbia raccolto.
O fratel nostro, la cui fratellanza
perduta abbiam, che morte l'ha partita,
Dio ti dia pace e vera perdonanza
di ciò che l'offendesti in questa vita:
l'anima salga, se non è salita,
dove si vede il Salvatore in volto.

O our brother, thou who now art dead and buried,
May God have gathered you into his arms.
O our brother, whose friendship
we have lost, since death did come between,
God give you peace and true forgiveness
for your offenses against Him in this life:
may your soul rise, if it is not risen already,
to where you will see the face of the Savior.

Once more, as on so many previous occasions, Dallapiccola constructed a symmetrical, paneled form for *Commiato*; the setting of the *lauda* became the central panel, with the four other movements pointing, as it were, towards this vocal movement. The first and fifth movements, each in strict retrograde one with another, have the exclamation "Ah!" as their sole text, while the purely instrumental second and fourth movements are based on canonic procedures and are also a free retrograde one of another. Even the central vocal movement based upon Latini's text, the first two verses of which are reprised at the end of the movement, exhibits a symmetrical form. In effect, therefore, the whole work, lasting fourteen minutes, is an extended palindrome, a journey away and a journey of return, a symbol of the departure of the friend who has left this life, and of the hoped-for salvation. Thus we can perhaps, without taking too much liberty, see the work as a summation of Dallapiccola's religious faith and, at the same time, as a representation in musical terms of those many "journeys and returns" with which his work had been so replete.

Sergio Sablich points to a certain relationship between *Commiato* and *Ulisse*.[24] Of particular significance here is the monosyllable "Ah!"—the sole text for the outer movements; Sablich sees this as related to the single-tone *fff* orchestral tutti which immediately precedes the revelation of God in the final scene of the opera. In *Ulisse,* this single tone had been the same G sharp with which *Commiato* begins, and the emphatic rhythmic figure consisting of rhythmic units of 5 + 3 + 2 in the ensuing instrumental parts in *Commiato* is clearly related to the rhythmic leitmotif ("ritmo principale") that had been an essential element in the opera, underpinning the instrumental entries in the orchestral crescendo (see chapter 5). The row is presented in a horizontal/vertical exposition, but the voice is here limited to the tritonal exclamation, while the instruments create the predominant rhythmic interest (Example 6.19).

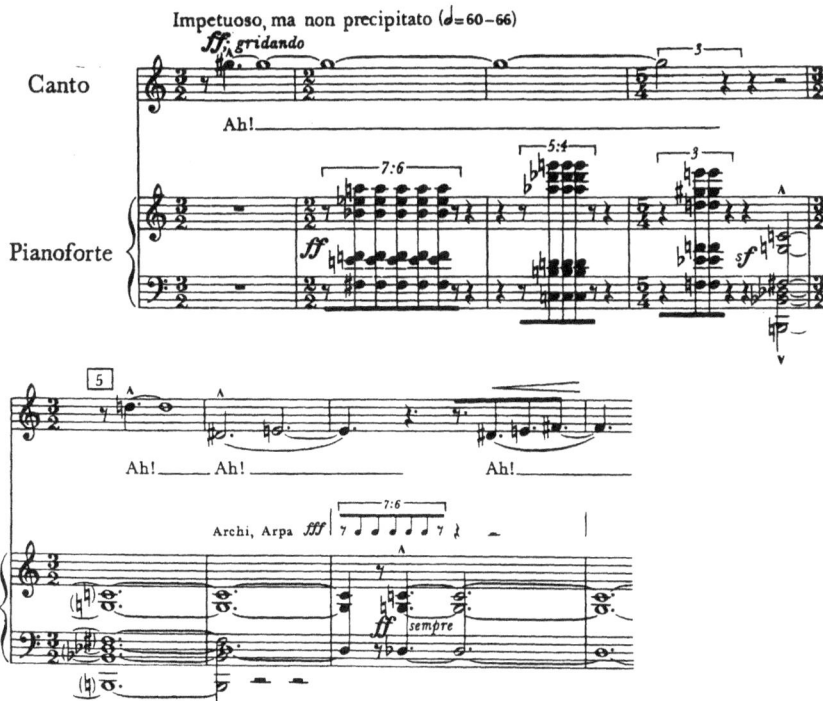

Example 6.19. *Commiato.* I, mm. 1–8.

The text Dallapiccola sets in the central lauda seems to retrace the composer's steps back to the ancient and religious texts that he had set right from the beginning of his creative life. However, as Kämper and others have noted, this movement, like the epilogue of *Ulisse*, also incorporates a number of subtler allusions to earlier works of the composer. The clearest of these, and indeed the first to appear, is the intervallic echoing of the "fratello" motif from *Il prigioniero* that is to be found at the opening of the movement on the text "O fratel nostro . . . ," a motif which is evoked through the common use of the term "brother" in both texts. This opening passage (mm. 93–98) returns once more at the end of the movement (mm. 125–30, Example 6.20).

Example 6.20. *Commiato*. III, mm. 93–96.

From the serial point of view, this movement opens with another horizontal/vertical row exposition, with the initial instrumental chord and vocal melody outlining the row, but once again the composer is not content to rely upon a single serial formation, and immediately, from measure 95 onwards, forms a secondary row from the initial three-tone group of this row. *Commiato* contains a very powerful and dramatic expression of the text, especially in the *gridando* vocalizations in the outer movements. Given the presence of this kind of writing, it seems inappropriate to regard the work as any kind of "farewell to life," despite the title it bears. Dallapiccola clearly wished it to be understood as a memorial for a friend who had recently died: to view it as a prayer on behalf of the composer himself is to impose upon it a superfluous "elegiac" ambience that it certainly does not have. At the same time, this was Dalllapiccola's last completed work, since despite the composer's endeavors to complete the ballet project based on Goya, for which a considerable amount of energy was expended, this work was not to see the light of day.

Dallapiccola traveled widely during the next couple years, but the pulmonary edema which he had suffered earlier returned once more, and having attended rehearsals for a concert of his music on the previous day, he died in Florence on the morning of 19 February 1975. On his work desk at the piano in his Florence home was a manuscript containing just eighteen measures of music. This, like so many of the compositions of his last years, would have been a work of a religious character, its text taken from chapter XIII of the *Soliloquia* of Saint Augustine,[25] and would have borne the title *Lux*. Dallapiccola had, it would seem, finally reached the illumination that had long been a potent symbol in so much of his music.

Journeyings and Returns: The Nature of Dallapiccola's Art

Those who compile musical dictionaries, in one language or in another, almost invariably work somewhat in the manner of medieval monks transcribing texts created by other hands, in many cases repeating the same formulas in their description of the work of individual composers. Thus, it is rare not to find Dallapiccola referred to in terms of one or both of two aspects: first, his position as "the first Italian twelve-tone composer," and second in terms of the "innate Italian lyricism" in his music that tempers the rigorous serialism of many of his scores. As happens so frequently with generalizations about composers, such judgments suggest fragments, but only fragments, of the artist's true significance. It cannot be denied that Dallapiccola was the first Italian composer fully to realize the possibilities of twelve-tone composition for musical expression. Furthermore, as we have frequently pointed out in this study, all three members of the Viennese circle of composers were influential on Dallapiccola's work in varying degrees and at different points in his life, in contrast to the younger generation of composers who assimilated the influence of Webern, to the almost total exclusion of Berg and Schoenberg, in the years following the end of the Second World War.

Nor can it be denied that Dallapiccola's music, whether his earlier neo-modal compositions or the later serial scores, is strongly imbued with that lyrical strain, that recourse to melodic material based upon quite simple intervals and harmonies, which has long been considered a hallmark of Italian composers from Monteverdi to Puccini and beyond. Furthermore, Dallapiccola's treatment of the basic material of a work frequently suggests a certain "Mediterranean sensuousness," a refinement and delicacy in the timbral and expressive contours of a composition to which Italian composers have frequently been prone. But such broad characteristics of the composer's work do not take us far into the nature of Dallapiccola's true importance in the music of the twentieth century. Other elements of perhaps greater significance begin to show themselves once we begin to investigate the music more carefully, elements that have been touched upon at many points in this study. These suggest that Dallapiccola is of much greater stature within twentieth-century musical culture than any neat classification as a "sensuous Italian serialist" could possibly encompass.

In the first place, Dallapiccola was an artist with a strongly developed sense of the artist's relationship to broader humanity. He was a composer in whose work we find a constant desire to forge links at every possible level with the concerns of other human beings, an element in his creative consciousness that brings him into the area occupied by such composers as Michael Tippett, Luigi Nono, and Arnold Schoenberg. Whether in those compositions he himself called his "protest music," such as *Tre laudi* and *Canti di prigionia,* or in others whose texts were chosen and arranged in order to give the clearest expression to a "philosophy," such as *Canti di liberazione* and *Requiescant,* the composer's *Weltanschauung* is always evident. But beyond this, the power of such scores as these seems to come as much from the crystalline rationality and purposefulness of their design as from the powerful emotional expression which so many of their pages exhibit. As this study has shown, the emotional power of much of Dallapiccola's music is unthinkable without this highly rational and frequently symmetrical structuring.

Dallapiccola's work as a whole is full of those "journeyings and returns" to which reference has been made on several occasions in this study. He returned at regular intervals to the same material, to particular kinds of literature from whose grip he does not seem to have been able to free himself (medieval religious verse, ancient classical texts, Spanish poetry), as well as returning to particular musical "texts," such as the music of his Italian predecessors. Indeed, the whole arena of older music, and particularly older Italian music, was one in which the composer seemed to find an endless delight, whether this is exhibited in transcriptions, re-editions, or fully creative transformations. This characteristic was of course shared with many of his fellow Italian composers during the present century (Gian Francesco Malipiero, Bruno Maderna, Luciano Berio, and Azio Corghi, to name the most obvious examples). In common with these composers, Dallapiccola found older music not only a stimulus and an inspiration, but it also guided him towards his more intimate and personal explorations as an artist.

This "circularity" in Dallapiccola's work, the return over previously explored territory in order to find new delight and fascination within it, has a great deal in common with the approach of the composer to twelve-tone serialism. The use of tone rows as symbolic entities, central images within a work's expression, goes hand in hand with a conception of musical structure in which the constant recourse to a limited, but at the same time immensely powerful, fund of basic material informs a whole composition. The row is repeated, inverted, transformed in many different ways, obeying the same laws that governed the composer's contrapuntal and canonic approach to music. Indeed, it is on occasion difficult to disentangle one from the other, the canonic from the serial, as Dallapiccola seems to allow each, whether the melodic cells of the canon or the interval cells of row formations, to proliferate according to the same principles. As we suggested early in this study, it was the inherently contrapuntal nature of Dallapiccola's musical thinking that seemed to lead him towards the later involvement with dodecaphonic and serial techniques, as a further means of refining his polyphonic ordering of musical material. Both canon and row have been seen to operate on many occasions as important symbolic entities within many compositions, most potently of all in his operatic masterpiece *Ulisse,* at whose heart lies the scene in Hades in palindromic, serial, and canonic form. This linking of basic row material and symbolic reference lay at the heart of the expression in Dallapiccola's music—an element he had studied in Berg's music early (the Chamber Concerto and the opera *Lulu,* above all, come to mind in this respect), making it his own in a truly remarkable way.

Dallapiccola was a man of wide culture, a truly European as well as an Italian composer. Born at a crossroads of several cultures, he was ready to absorb literary and musical influences coming from several directions, and his awareness of the importance of Ferruccio Busoni, with whom he shared this polyglot cultural inheritance, is significant here. The choice of texts for his compositions reflects the breadth of his literary culture: Joyce, Proust, Mann, Sappho, Antonio Machado, Michelangelo, Goethe, Heine, Oscar Wilde; and we have noted how two of these literary figures, Mann and Joyce, can be considered cornerstones of important areas of Dallapiccola's music. This "polyglot" characteristic of the composer's culture was, of course, in evidence even in some of his earlier compositions, but it became more obvious in the later period of his work.

Dallapiccola's concern with the serialism of the Viennese composers earlier in his life, at a time when virtually no other Italian composer shared such an interest, and the distance from the prevailing neoclassical trend that he assiduously maintained, placed him apart from all other Italian composers of that time. Furthermore, his creation of a highly expressive and lyrical style of serialism had a considerable influence upon younger composers, however distant his approach remained from the concerns with electronic and aleatoric music which many of the younger generation of Italian composers held during the 1950s and 1960s. The importance of

Dallapiccola's influence on the work of Luciano Berio, Sylvano Bussotti, Franco Donatoni, and Luigi Nono has perhaps still to be fully measured, but no composer, whether of his own or any younger generation, wrote music quite like that of Dallapiccola. His particular musical and human sensibility was formed from a unique set of historical circumstances and from a unique artistic personality. Like certain other twentieth-century composers (one thinks of Olivier Messiaen, of Benjamin Britten, or of Béla Bartók), he created music that is instantly recognizable and a musical language that is both highly rational and powerfully expressive. This was the point of departure from which this study of Dallapiccola's work set out, from an analogy with the work of the Renaissance painter Piero della Francesca, whose images were among the composer's most beloved artistic works, and the elements of powerful expression, vivid colorations, and rationality of design have been constant points of reference in this study.

Dallapiccola's music still awaits the recognition it undoubtedly warrants. Nonetheless, it has at least begun on the path to a more just recognition, not least through the universal admiration that it has inspired among performers. Despite the obvious problems associated with music which, in many instances, is set out for unconventional musical ensembles, performances of some of his scores occur with some frequency. Indeed, a handful of his pieces (most prominent among these are the *Goethe-Lieder*, *Quaderno musicale di Annalibera*, and *Liriche greche*) might almost by now be described as standard works of twentieth-century music. Nonetheless, there is a clear need for some of Dallapiccola's larger scores, not least his operas, to be performed more frequently, if the composer's stature and significance are fully to be assessed. As the present study has attempted to show, such an assessment would place Dallapiccola among the most important figures in the music of the twentieth century.

Appendix

List of Compositions

Dallapiccola's unpublished music, together with scores of published works, drafts and sketches, correspondence, recordings, and other archival material, is all housed in the Alessandro Bonsanti Archive, part of the Gabinetto Vieusseux, the major historical archive and library in Florence. All this material (with the exception of Dallapiccola's diaries, which will be available for consultation only seventy-five years after his death) may be viewed there, but quotation from certain material in any other context is allowed only within strict limits.

A. Original Compositions

1924–26   *Fiuri de tapo*, three songs for voice and piano; texts by Biagio Marin; unpublished.
1926   *Caligo*, for voice and piano; text by Biagio Marin; unpublished.
1927   *Due canzoni di Grado*, for small female chorus, mezzo-soprano, and small orchestra; texts by Biagio Marin; unpublished. First performance: Florence, 18 May 1929.
1928   *Dalla mia terra*, four songs for mezzo-soprano, mixed chorus, and orchestra; texts by Biagio Marin; unpublished as a whole, but third song published in *Agorà* 2, no. 3 (August 1946). First performance: Florence, 20 January 1931.
1929   *Due laudi di Iacopone da Todi*, for soprano, baritone, mixed chorus, and orchestra; unpublished.
1930   *La canzone del Quarnaro*, for tenor, male chorus, and orchestra; text by Gabriele D'Annunzio; unpublished.
1930   *Due liriche del Kalevala*, for tenor, baritone, chamber choir, and four percussion instruments; texts translated by P. E. Pavolini; unpublished, except for first song published in supplement of the *Revue Internationale de Musique* (March–April 1938); First performance: Florence, 12 June 1931.
1930–32   *Partita*, for orchestra, with soprano in fourth movement; text from *Quinquaginta Carmina Medii Aevi*; publ. Carisch, Milan. First performance: Florence, 22 January 1933.
1932   *Tre studi*, for soprano and chamber orchestra; texts from the *Kalevala*, translated by P. E. Pavolini; publ. Carisch, Milan. First performance: Venice, 12 September 1932.

1932	*Estate,* for unaccompanied male chorus; text from fragment of Alcaeus, translated by Ettore Romagnoli; publ. Zanibon, Padua. First performance: Rome, 7 April 1932.
1932–33	*Rapsodia* (Studio per *La morte del Conte Orlando*), for solo voice and chamber orchestra; text from the *Chanson de Roland,* translated by Giovanni Pascoli; unpublished. First performance: ISCM Festival, Venice, 8 September 1934.
1933–36	*Sei cori di Michelangelo Buonarroti il Giovane*: First Series, for unaccompanied mixed voices; publ. Carisch, Milan. First performance: Trieste, 17 December 1937. Second Series, for four vocal soloists (ss + aa or chamber choir, 6s + 6a) and 17 instruments; publ. Carisch, Milan. First performance: Rome, 6 April 1935. Third Series, for mixed chorus and full orchestra; publ. Carisch, Milan. First performance: Florence, 14 May 1937. First performance of complete set: Radio Prague, 26 April 1938.
1934	*Divertimento in quattro esercizi,* for soprano, flute, oboe, clarinet, viola, and cello; texts from thirteenth-century poetry; publ. Carisch, Milan. First performance: Geneva, 22 October 1934.
1935	*Musica per tre pianoforti (Inni)*; publ. Carisch, Milan. First performance: Geneva, 30 March 1936.
1936–37	*Tre laudi,* for high voice and chamber orchestra (13 instruments); texts from *Laudario dei Battuti di Modena* (1266); publ. Carisch, Milan. First performance: ISCM Festival, Venice, 8 September 1937.
1937–38	*Volo di notte,* one-act opera; libretto by composer, based on the novel *Vol de nuit* by Antoine de Saint-Exupéry; publ. Ricordi, Milan (later Universal Edition, Vienna). First performance: Florence, 18 May 1940.
1938–41	*Canti di prigionia,* in three movements: "Preghiera di Maria Stuarda," for mixed chorus and instruments; text from prayer of Mary Stuart. "Invocazione di Boezio," for female chorus and instruments; text from prayer of Boethius. "Congedo di Girolamo Savonarola," for mixed chorus and instruments; text from prayer of Savonarola. Publ. Carisch, Milan. First performance: first movement alone: Brussels, 10 April 1940; whole work: Rome, 11 December 1941.
1939–41	*Piccolo concerto per Muriel Couvreux,* for piano and chamber orchestra; publ. Carisch, Milan. First performance: Rome, 1 May 1941.
1942	*Studio sul Capriccio no. 14 di Niccolò Paganini,* for piano solo; originally written for collection of piano music published by Suvini Zerboni, later became finale of *Sonatina canonica* (see below).
1942–43	*Marsia,* one-act ballet on a subject by Aurel M. Milloss; publ. Carisch, Milan. First performance: Venice, 9 September 1948.
1942–43	*Frammenti sinfonici dal balletto 'Marsia',* for orchestra; publ. Carisch, Milan. First performance: Brussels, 12 March 1948.
1943	*Sonatina canonica in E-flat Major on 'Capricci' of Niccolò Paganini,*

	for piano solo; publ. Suvini Zerboni, Milan. First performance: Perugia, 4 March 1946.
1942–45	*Liriche greche,* consisting of: "Cinque frammenti di Saffo," for voice and chamber orchestra; texts from Sappho, translated by Salvatore Quasimodo; publ. Suvini Zerboni, Milan. First performance: Turin Radio, 7 July 1947. "Due liriche di Anacreonte," for voice, two clarinets, viola and piano; texts from Anacreon, translated by Salvatore Quasimodo; publ. Suvini Zerboni, Milan. First performance: Brussels, 24 June 1946. "Sex Carmina Alcaei," for voice and chamber ensemble; texts from Alcaeus, translated by Salvatore Quasimodo; publ. Suvini Zerboni, Milan. First performance: Rome, 10 November 1944. First complete performance of *Liriche greche*: Rome, 13 January 1949.
1945	*Ciaccona, intermezzo e adagio,* for solo cello; publ. Universal Edition, Vienna. First performance: Milan, 26 February 1946.
1946	*Rencesvals,* for baritone and piano; text consists of three fragments from the *Chanson de Roland*; publ. Suvini Zerboni, Milan. First performance: Brussels, 19 December 1946.
1946–47	*Due studi,* for violin and piano; publ. Suvini Zerboni, Milan. First performance: Basel, 9 February 1947.
1947	*Due pezzi per orchestra*; orchestral version of *Due studi* for violin and piano; publ. Suvini Zerboni, Milan. First performance: London, 3 November 1947.
1944–48	*Il prigioniero,* opera in prologue and one act; text by the composer adapted from *La torture par l'espérance* by P. A. Villiers de l'Isle-Adam and *La légende d'Ulenspigel et de Lamme Goedzak* by Charles de Coster; publ. Suvini Zerboni, Milan. First performance (radio): Turin, 1 December 1949; (staged): Florence, 20 May 1950.
1948	*Quattro liriche di Antonio Machado*; for soprano and piano; publ. Suvini Zerboni, Milan. First performance: Brussels, 2 December 1948.
1949	*Tre episodi dal balletto 'Marsia',* for piano solo; publ. Carisch, Milan. First performance: Turin, 23 January 1950.
1949	*Tre poemi,* for voice and chamber orchestra; texts by James Joyce (translated by Eugenio Montale), Michelangelo, Manuel Machado (translated by Dallapiccola); publ. Ars Viva Zurich, then Ars Viva, Schott, Mainz. First performance: Trieste, 13 March 1950.
1950	*Job,* "sacra rappresentazione"; text from The Book of Job; publ. Suvini Zerboni, Milan; First performance: Rome, 30 October 1950.
1951	*Tartiniana,* divertimento for violin and chamber orchestra on themes by G. Tartini; publ. Suvini Zerboni, Milan. First performance: Zurich, 9 March 1952.
1952	*Quaderno musicale di Annalibera,* for piano solo; publ. Suvini Zerboni, Milan. First performance: Pittsburgh, 29 November 1952.
1953	*Goethe-Lieder,* for mezzo-soprano and three clarinets; texts from Goethe, *West-Östlicher Divan*; publ. Suvini Zerboni, Milan. First performance: Boston, 28 April 1953.
1954	*Variazioni,* for orchestra; orchestral version of *Quaderno musicale di*

	Annalibera; publ. Suvini Zerboni, Milan. First performance: Louisville, 2 October 1954.
1954	*Piccola musica notturna,* for orchestra; publ. Suvini Zerboni, Milan. First performance: Hannover, 7 June 1954.
1951–55	*Canti di liberazione,* for chorus and orchestra; texts from Sébastien Castellion, Book of Exodus, Saint Augustine; publ. Suvini Zerboni, Milan. First performance: Cologne, 28 October 1955.
1955	*An Mathilde,* cantata for soprano and orchestra; texts taken from Heinrich Heine; publ. Suvini Zerboni, Milan. First performance: Donaueschingen, 16 October 1955.
1956	*Tartiniana seconda (Divertimento),* in two versions: violin and piano, violin and chamber orchestra; publ. Suvini Zerboni, Milan. First performance: (violin and piano): Vienna, 6 March 1956; (violin and orchestra): Turin, 15 March 1957.
1956	*Cinque canti,* for baritone and eight instruments; texts taken from ancient Greek poems, translated by Salvatore Quasimodo; publ. Suvini Zerboni, Milan. First performance: Washington, D.C., 30 November 1956.
1957	*Concerto per la notte di Natale dell'anno 1956,* for chamber orchestra and solo soprano; text by Iacopone da Todi; publ. Suvini Zerboni, Milan. First performance: Tokyo, 11 October 1957.
1957–58	*Requiescant,* for mixed chorus and orchestra; texts from Saint Matthew, Oscar Wilde, and James Joyce; publ. Suvini Zerboni, Milan. First performance: Hamburg, 17 November 1959.
1960	*Dialoghi,* for cello and orchestra; publ. Suvini Zerboni, Milan. First performance: Venice, 17 September 1960.
1961	*Piccola musica notturna,* version for chamber ensemble; publ. Suvini Zerboni, Milan. First performance: Flushing, N.Y., 25 March 1961.
1962	*Preghiere,* for baritone and chamber orchestra; texts by Murilo Mendes, translated Ruggero Jacobbi; publ. Suvini Zerboni, Milan. First performance: Berkeley, Calif., 10 November 1962.
1962	*Three Questions with Two Answers,* for orchestra; publ. Suvini Zerboni, Milan. First performance: New Haven, Conn., 5 February 1963.
1964	*Parole di San Paolo,* for medium voice and ensemble; texts from St Paul's First Letter to the Corinthians; publ. Suvini Zerboni, Milan; First performance: Washington, D.C., 30 October 1964.
1964	*Quattro liriche di Antonio Machado,* version for soprano and chamber orchestra; publ. Suvini Zerboni, Milan. First performance: Braunschweig, 27 November 1964.
1960–68	*Ulisse,* opera in prologue and two acts; text assembled by the composer; publ. Suvini Zerboni, Milan. First performance: Berlin, 29 September 1968.
1970	*Sicut umbra,* for mezzo-soprano and four instrumental groups; texts by Juan Ramón Jiménez; publ. Suvini Zerboni, Milan. First performance: Washington, D.C., 30 October 1970.
1970–71	*Tempus destruendi—Tempus aedificandi,* for mixed unaccompanied chorus; texts from Paul of Aquileia and Dermatus; publ. Suvini Zerboni, Milan. First performance: "Exhortatio": Tel Aviv, 4 January 1971; complete: Siena, 26 August 1971.

Appendix: List of Compositions 277

1972   *Commiato,* for soprano and chamber ensemble; text from Brunetto Latini; publ. Suvini Zerboni, Milan. First performance: Murau, Austria, 15 October 1972.

B. Music for Documentary Films

1948   *Incontri con Roma* (dir. Vittorio Carpignano)
1948   *L'esperienza del cubismo* (dir. Glauco Pellegrini)
1953   *Il miracolo della cena: il capolavoro di Leonardo da Vinci* (dir. Luigi Rognoni)

C. Transcriptions, Editions

1940   Critical edition (revised 1961) of Mussorgsky, *Pictures at an Exhibition;* publ. Carisch, Milan.
1941–42 Transcription and reduction for the modern stage of Monteverdi, *Il ritorno d'Ulisse in patria;* publ. Suvini Zerboni, Milan.
1955   Revision and realization of the figured bass of Vivaldi, Six Sonatas for cello and piano; the cello part edited by Leonard Rose; publ. International Music Company, New York.
1961   Edition and realization of the figured bass of *Italian Songs of the 17th and 18th Centuries;* publ. International Music Company, New York.

Notes

Notes to Chapter 1

1. LD, "Genesi dei *Canti di prigionia* e *Prigioniero,*" in *PM,* 400.
2. LD, "Nascita di un libretto d'opera," Lecture (given in English) at University of Michigan, Ann Arbor, October 1967; first Italian publication in *Nuova Rivista Musicale Italiana* 2, no. 4 (1968); English translation as "Birth of a Libretto" in Shackelford, *DO,* 232–62.
3. LD, letter to Wolfgang Wagner, 15 April 1968, Dallapiccola Archive, Gabinetto Vieusseux, Florence.
4. Ildebrando Pizzetti, "Di Arnold Schönberg e di altre cose," *Il Marzocco,* 17 December 1916, reprinted in Ildebrando Pizzetti, *Intermezzi critici* (Florence: Vallechi, 1921).
5. Gian Francesco Malipiero, "Orchestra e orchestrazione," *Rivista Musicale Italiana* 24, no. 1 (31 March 1917).
6. A full account of Casella's work during that period is given in Fiamma Nicolodi, *Musica e musicisti nel ventennio fascista* (Fiesole: Discanto Edizioni, 1984), 235–71. Cf. also Harvey Sachs, *Music in Fascist Italy* (London: Weidenfeld and Nicolson, 1987) and Giovanni Morelli, ed., *Alfredo Casella negli anni di apprendistato a Parigi: Atti del convegno internazionale di studi, Venezia, 13–15 maggio 1992,* Fondazione Giorgio Cini: "Studi di musica veneta" (Florence: Olschki, 1994). (Sachs, *Music in Fascist Italy* is copyright © Harvey Sachs. Reprinted by permission of PFD [Peters Fraser and Dunlop] on behalf of Harvey Sachs.)
7. The correspondence between Dallapiccola and Casella is housed in the Dallapiccola Archive, Gabinetto Vieusseux, Florence.
8. LD, letter to Arnold Schoenberg, 9 September 1949 (originally in French). Dallapiccola Archive, Gabinetto Vieusseux, Florence.
9. Vito Frazzi (San Secondo Parmense, 1888–Florence, 1975) studied in Parma, then transferred to Florence, where he was successively professor of piano, of harmony, and of composition, and also for a time Director of the Conservatory. He made editions of operas by Peri and Monteverdi for the Florence stage, and among his most important compositions are the symphonic poem *L'usignolo e la rosa* (1911), Violin Sonata (1911), *Cicilia* for chorus and orchestra (1920), Piano Quintet (1912–22) and the opera *Re Lear* (1922–28).
10. LD, "Musicisti del nostro tempo: Vito Frazzi," in *PM,* 257.
11. Olivier Messiaen, *Technique de mon langage musical* (Paris: Alphonse Leduc, 1944).
12. Michael Eckert, "Octatonic Elements in the Music of Luigi Dallapiccola," *The Music Review* 46, no.1 (1985): 35–48.
13. Fiamma Nicolodi, "Luigi Dallapiccola e la Scuola di Vienna: Note in margine ad una scelta," in *Orizzonti musicali italo-europei 1860–1980* (Rome: Bulzoni, 1990), 231–97.
14. LD, letter to Suvini Zerboni, 12 February 1955, quoted in Nicolodi, *Saggi,* 88.

15. Arnold Schoenberg, letter to Dallapiccola, 16 September 1949, Dallapiccola Archive, Gabinetto Vieusseux, Florence.

16. "Manifesto di musicisti italiani per la tradizione dell'arte romatica dell'800," *La Stampa* and other newspapers in Italy, 17 December 1932.

17. Cf. Sachs, *Music in Fascist Italy,* 23–26. (Copyright © Harvey Sachs. Reprinted by permission of PFD [Peters Fraser and Dunlop] on behalf of Harvey Sachs.)

18. LD, "Prime composizioni corali," in *Appunti,* 131–39.

19. Cf. Antony Beaumont, *Busoni the Composer* (London and Boston: Faber and Faber, 1985), 168.

20. LD, "Di un aspetto della musica contemporanea," in *Atti dell'Accademia del Reale Conservatorio di Musica 'Luigi Cherubini'* (Florence: La Stamperia, 1938), 222.

21. Cf. Volker Scherliess, "Luigi Dallapiccola über Alban Berg: Ein Brief und eine persönliche Erinnerung," in *Aspetti Musicali: Musikhistorische Dimensionen Italiens 1600 bis 2000: Festschrift für Dietrich Kämper zum 65. Geburtstag,* ed. Norbert Bolin, Christoph von Blumröder, and Imke Misch, 133–40 (Cologne: Verlag Dohr, 2001).

22. LD, "Ricordo di Hermann Scherchen," in *PM,* 174–75.

23. Kämper, *GF,* 17.

24. LD, "Praga—il XIII Festival della SIMC," *Emporium* 51, no. 12 (1935).

25. LD, "Incontro con Anton Webern (Pagine di diario 1935–1945)," first published in *Il Mondo* No. 15 (3 November 1945); English translation by John Waterhouse as "Meeting with Anton Webern (Pages from a Diary)," in *Tempo,* No. 99 (1972): 2–7; later also republished in Italian in *Appunti,* 105–9.

26. Alban Berg, letter to Dallapiccola, 20 September 1935, Dallapiccola Archive, Gabinetto Vieusseux, Florence.

27. Wladimir Vogel (Moscow, 1896–Zurich, 1984) was the son of a German father and a Russian mother. His earliest music was influenced by Scriabin, but after his family settled in Berlin after the First World War, he studied with Busoni. He taught in Berlin until 1933, but eventually fled to Switzerland, where he lived in the Ticino in very difficult circumstances. His music reflected the influence of Busoni, but during the 1930s he began to absorb twelve-tone ideas that eventually came to full fruition in his *Madrigaux* (1938–39). His cantata *Thyl Claes* (1937–45) was based upon a text taken from Charles De Coster's *La Légende de Thyl Eulenspigel et de Lamme Goedzak,* from which Dallapiccola was to take part of the idea and the text for *Il prigioniero.* Cf. Carlo Piccardi, "Wladimir Vogel: Aspetti di un'identità in divenire," in *Komponisten des 20. Jahrhunderts* (Basel: Paul Sacher Stiftung, 1986), 199–207. Cf. also Gianmario Borio: "L'emigrazione 'esterna' e 'interna' di Wladimir Vogel: Appunti per una storia sociale della musica del Novecento," in *La musica nella Germania di Hitler* (Lucca: Libreria Musicale Italiana, 1996), 79–96.

28. LD, interview in an undated broadcast by the BBC, probably in the late 1960s. This is also reported in Nicolodi, *Musica e musicisti nel ventennio fascista,* 289.

29. Ibid., 289.

30. Ibid., 289.

31. Everett Helm, "Luigi Dallapiccola in einem unveröffentlichen Gespräch," *Melos—Neue Zeitschrift für Musik* 2, no. 6 (1976): 471.

32. LD, "Prime composizioni corali," in *Appunti,* 131–39.

33. Helm, "Luigi Dallapiccola," 471.

34. LD, "My Choral Music," in *The Composer Speaks,* ed. R. S. Hines, 156–57 (Norman: Oklahoma University Press, 1963).

35. Cf. Nicolodi, "Luigi Dallapiccola e la Scuola di Vienna," 231–82.

36. LD, "L'ultimo verso (Pagine di diario)," *Campi Elisi,* August-September 1946, 58.

37. LD, "Prime composizioni corali," in *Appunti,* 131–39.

38. Helm, "Luigi Dallapiccola," 471.

39. Giulio Bertoni, "Laudario dei Battuti," *Beihefte für Romanische Philologie* (1909).

40. Interview with Hans Nathan, unpublished but recorded: recording held in Library of Congress Division of Recorded Sound, Washington D.C.

41. LD, "Job," in *PM,* 445.

42. Ibid, 445.

43. LD, "Di un aspetto della musica contemporanea," n *Atti del Reale Conservatorio "Luigi Cherubini"* (Florence: La Stamperia, 1938).

44. Joseph Gregor, *Weltgeschichte des Theaters* (Zurich: Phaidon Verlag, 1933), 15–33.

45. LD, "For the Première of *Volo di notte,*" in Shackelford, *DO,* 79–96.

46. Ibid., 96.

47. The issue of the "ideology" of *Volo di notte* is discussed in detail in Nicolodi, "Luigi Dallapiccola e la Scuola di Vienna," 263–68, and also in Raymond Fearn, "Those Magnificent Men in Their Flying Machines: The 'Ideology' of Luigi Dallapiccola's *Volo di notte,*" *Journal of Musicological Research* 16, no. 4 (1997): 283–99.

48. LD, letter to Gian Francesco Malipiero, 17 July 1938, Archivio Malipiero, Fondazione Cini, Venice.

49. LD, "Sehen was Anderen verborgen bleibt," in program book for Staatstheater, Braunschweig, No. 27, March 1965, 296–99. This item is reported in Kämper, *GF,* 32 and 201.

50. Interview with Goffredo Petrassi, from Sachs, *Music in Fascist Italy,* 146. (Copyright © Harvey Sachs. Reprinted by permission of PFD [Peters Fraser and Dunlop] on behalf of Harvey Sachs.)

51. Helm, "Luigi Dallapiccola," 471.

52. André Gide, preface to Antoine de Saint-Exupéry, *Night Flight,* trans. Stuart Gilbert (Harmondsworth: Penguin Books), 1939.

53. Saint-Exupéry, *Night Flight,* 139–40.

54. Enrico Prampolini, catalogue statement for the exhibition *Mostra futurista di aeropittura e di scenografia,* Milan, 1931.

55. Cf. Enrico Crispolti, "Second Futurism," in *Italian Art of the Twentieth Century,* 165–71 (Munich: Royal Academy of Arts/Prestel Verlag, 1989).

56. Cf. Scherliess, "Luigi Dallapiccola über Alban Berg," 133–40.

Notes to Chapter 2

1. LD, "Sulla strada della dodecafonia," in *Appunti,* 163. English translation as "On the Twelve-Tone Road," *Music Survey* 4, no. 1 (1951): 318–32.

2. LD, diary entry for 17 June 1938; published in LD, "Incontro con Anton Webern (Pagine di diario 1935–1945)," first published in *Il Mondo,* No. 15, 3 November 1945; English translation by John Waterhouse as "Meeting with Anton Webern (Pages from a Diary)," *Tempo* 99 (1972): 2–7. Later also republished in Italian in *Appunti,* 105–9.

3. The fullest account of Dallapiccola's gradual assimilation of the music of the Viennese composers is to be found in Fiamma Nicolodi, "Luigi Dallapiccola e la Scuola di Vienna: Note in margine a una scelta," in *Orizzonti musicali italo-europei, 1860–1980* (Rome: Bulzoni, 1990), 231–32.

4. LD, "Genesi dei *Canti di prigionia* e del *Prigioniero,*" in *PM,* 408.

5. Wladimir Vogel, letter to Dallapiccola, 26 November 1939, Dallapiccola Archive, Gabinetto Vieusseux, Florence.

6. LD, letter to Vogel, 18 December 1939, Dallapiccola Archive, Gabinetto Vieusseux, Florence.

7. Vogel, letter to LD, 23 December 1939, Dallapiccola Archive, Gabinetto Vieusseux, Florence.

8. LD, letter to Vogel, 3 January 1940, Dallapiccola Archive, Gabinetto Vieusseux, Florence.

9. Vogel, letter to LD, 12 January 1940, Dallapiccola Archive, Gabinetto Vieusseux, Florence.

10. LD, "Anton Webern," in *PM,* 226.

11. Vogel, letter to LD, 18 December 1939, Dallapiccola Archive, Gabinetto Vieusseux, Florence.

12. LD, "La mia protest-music," in *L'esperienza della guerra e dell'impegno sociale nella musica e nelle arti* (Florence: Maggio Musicale Fiorentino, 1971).

13. LD, letter to Vogel, 3 January 1940, Dallapiccola Archive, Gabinetto Vieusseux, Florence.

14. LD, "The Genesis of *Canti di prigionia* and *Il prigioniero,*" in Shackelford, *DO,* 43–44.

15. LD, "Credo nel teatro moderno," in the newspaper *Il Resto del Carlino,* Bologna, 2 February 1941.

16. Aurel M. Milloss, preface to the score of *Marsia* (Milan: Carisch, 1943).

17. LD, writing in the *Protokoll der XI. Dramaturgentagung* (Berlin: Dramaturgische Gesellschaft, 1963), 208. Quoted in Kämper, *GF,* 55.

18. Kämper, *GF,* 56–57.

19. Dallapiccola set out in detail his approach to the editing of the opera in LD, "Monteverdi's *Il Ritorno di Ulisse in Patria,*" in Shackelford, *DO,* 215–31.

20. A full account of Dallapiccola's work in preparing his edition of Monteverdi's opera is to be found in Fiamma Nicolodi, *Gusti e tendenze del novecento musicale in Italia* (Florence: Sansoni, 1982), 141–45.

21. Cf. Jeremy Barlow, "The Revival of Monteverdi's Operas in the Twentieth Century," in *The Operas of Monteverdi,* ed. Anne Ridler, 193–203 (Paris, London, and New York: Calder, 1992).

22. LD, "Monteverdi's *Il Ritorno di Ulisse in Patria,*" 227–28.

23. LD, letter to Fedele D'Amico, 3 August 1946, Dallapiccola Archive, Gabinetto Vieusseux, Florence.

24. LD, quoted in Sandro Perotti, *Iri da Iri: Analisi della musica strumentale di Dallapiccola* (Milan: Guerini, 1988).

25. Correspondence between LD and Paolo Giordani, Director of Suvini Zerboni, Dallapiccola Archive, Gabinetto Vieusseux, Florence. For a full account of the composition of *Sonatina canonica,* cf. Raymond Fearn: "Luigi Dallapiccola's Sonatina Canonica: Neoclassicism or . . . ?" in *Musikkonzepte—Konzepte der Musikwissenschaft: Bericht über den Internationalen Kongress der Gesellschaft für Musikforschung, Halle (Saale), 1998,* ed. Kathrin Eberl and Wolfgang Ruf, 605–10 (Kassel: Bärenreiter Verlag, 2000).

26. Dallapiccola's writing for piano is discussed in Arrigo Quattrocchi, "Il pianoforte," in *Studi su Luigi Dallapiccola: Un seminario,* ed. Arrigo Quattrocchi, 131–58 (Lucca: Libreria Musicale Italiana, 1993).

27. LD, preface to edition of Mussorgsky's *Pictures at an Exhibition* (Quadri di una esposizione) (Milan: Carisch, 1940, rev. 1970).

28. LD, letter to Fedele D'Amico, 3 August 1946, Dallapiccola Archive, Gabinetto Vieusseux, Florence.

29. LD, Diary entry for 9 March 1942, quoted in full in Kathryn Bailey, *The Life of Webern* (Cambridge: Cambridge University Press, 1998), 193–95.

30. Anton Webern, letter to LD, 3 June 1942 (original in German), Dallapiccola Archive, Gabinetto Vieusseux, Florence.

31. Salvatore Quasimodo, "Discorso sulla poesia," in *Tutte le poesie di Salvatore Quasimodo* (Milan: Mondadori, 1960), 245–55. Originally published as Appendix to *Il falso e vero verde* (Milan: Mondadori, 1956).

32. Cf. Preface to *Contemporary Italian Poetry,* ed. Carlo L. Golino (Berkeley and Los Angeles: University of California Press), 1962.

33. LD, "Birth of a Libretto," in Shackelford, *DO,* 233.

34. An admirable analysis of the components of this piece is to be found in Robert P. Morgan, *Twentieth Century Music* (New York and London: W. W. Norton, 1991), 254–56.

35. LD, "A proposito delle *Due liriche di Anacreonte,*" in *PM,* 441–42.

36. Bruno Maderna, in conversation with Leonardo Pinzauti, in *Musicisti d'oggi* (Milan: ERI, 1978). English translation in Raymond Fearn, *Bruno Maderna* (New York, London, and Chur: Harwood Academic Publishers, 1990), 315–20.

Notes to Chapter 3

1. LD, reply to a question about the state of music in Italy, *La Musica* (Rome), No. 1 (1946): 1.

2. A detailed examination of the state of Italian musical life at the end of the war can be found in Guido Salvetti and Bianca Maria Antolini, eds., *Italia millenovecentocinquanta* (Milan: Guerini e Associati, 1999).

3. Kämper, *GF,* 82.

4. LD, "Sulla strada della dodecafonia," in *Appunti,* 163. English translation as "On the Twelve-Note Road," *Music Survey* 4, no. 1 (1951): 318–32.

5. Introductory notes by Camillo Togni for the recording of works of Dallapiccola to celebrate the composer's seventieth birthday. Reprinted in Camillo Togni, *Carteggio e scritti sul novecento italiano* (Florence: Olschki, 2001), 210–11.

6. Kämper, *GF,* 82.

7. LD, letter to Alfred Frankenstein, 23 November 1962, in Dallapiccola Archive, Gabinetto Vieusseux, Florence.
8. Cf. Togni, *Carteggio e scritti sul novecento italiano,* 212.
9. Ibid., 213.
10. LD, "Sulla strada della dodecafonia," 458.
11. Letter of Poulenc to Dallapiccola, 15 October 1938, in *Francis Poulenc: Correspondance 1910–1963,* ed. Myriam Chimènes (Paris: Fayard, 1991), 471.
12. LD, letter to Paul Collaer, 6 October 1946, in Dallapiccola Archive, Gabinetto Vieusseux, Florence.
13. Original in *La Chanson de Roland,* Cantos 55, 56, and 66; English translation in *The Song of Roland: Done in English, in the Original Measure* by Charles Scott Moncrieff (London: Chapman and Hall, 1919), 24 and 28.
14. Hans Nathan, "On Dallapiccola's Working Methods," *Perspectives of New Music* 15, no. 2 (1979): 34–57.
15. Kämper, *GF,* 84.
16. LD, "Die moderne Musik und ihre Beziehungen zu den übrigen Künsten," in *Die neue Weltschau: Zweite internationale Aussprache über den Anbruch eines aperspektivischen Zeitalters* (Stuttgart: Deutsche Verlags-Anstalt, 1953), 42.
17. Kämper, *GF,* 85.
18. LD, letter to P. M. Sauerbrei, March 1973, in Dallapiccola Archive, Gabinetto Vieusseux, Florence.
19. Camillo Togni, "Luigi Dallapiccola," in *Enciclopedia Musicale Ricordi* (Milan: Ricordi, 1964); reprinted in Togni, *Carteggio e scritti di Camillo Togni sul novecento italiano,* 198–207.
20. Kämper, *GF,* 85.
21. Interview of LD by Camillo Togni, 27 December 1960. Reported in "Rendiconto di una conversazione con Luigi Dallapiccola," in Togni, *Carteggio e scritti di Camillo Togni sul novecento italiano,* 205–7.
22. LD, "Birth of a Libretto," in Shackelford, *DO,* 239.
23. Kämper, *GF,* 65–67.
24. Villiers de L'Isle-Adam, "La torture par l'espérance," in his *Contes cruels* (Paris: Calmann-Lévy, 1883); Charles de Coster, *La légende d'Ulenspiegel et de Lamme Goedzak,* first published 1868.
25. Cf. Dietrich Kämper, "Uno sguardo nell'officina: Gli schizzi e gli abbozzi del *Prigioniero,*" *Nuova Rivista Musicale Italiana* 14, no. 2 (1980): 227ff.
26. In Music Appendix of *Polyphonie* 1 (1947–48).
27. LD, "Notes sur mon opéra," *Polyphonie* 1 (1947–48): 139ff.
28. Lisa Pevarello, *È arrivato il cantastorie* (The storyteller has arrived) (Florence: Marzocco, 1941).
29. LD, "Per la prima rappresentazione di *Volo di notte,*" in *PM,* 421. In English as "For the first performance of *Volo di notte,*" in Shackelford, *DO,* 79–96.
30. Shackelford, *DO,* 80.
31. Kämper, *GF,* 74.
32. Massimo Mila, "*Il prigioniero* di Luigi Dallapiccola," *La Rassegna Musicale* 4 (1950): 303–11.
33. LD, letter to Suvini Zerboni, quoted in Nicolodi, *Saggi,* 92.

34. LD, "What is the Answer to *The Prisoner?*" *San Francisco Sunday Chronicle,* 2 December 1962.

35. LD, "Comments on Contemporary Opera," in Shackelford, *DO,* 104.

Notes to Chapter 4

1. The first Italian composers to incorporate elements of serialism into their musical language, alongside Dallapiccola himself, were Luigi Cortese, Roman Vlad, and, especially, Camillo Togni. The motivation for these composers' move in this direction is fully examined, and a detailed account given of this Italian serialism of the wartime and immediate post-war years, in Roberto Zanetti, *La musica italiana nel novecento* (Busto Arsizio: Bramante, 1985), 1221–64.

2. For a full account of this, cf. Hans Keller and Milein Kosman: *Stravinsky Seen and Heard* (London: Toccata Press, 1982), 7–29.

3. Igor Stravinsky and Robert Craft, *Conversations with Igor Stravinsky* (London: Faber and Faber, 1958), 25.

4. René Leibowitz, "Luigi Dallapiccola," *L'Arche* 23, no. 3 (1947): 118–24.

5. Olivier Messiaen, *Technique de mon langage musical* (Paris: Alphonse Leduc, 1944), 58–63.

6. LD, "13 Settembre," in *PM,* 237ff.

7. Cf. Pierluigi Petrobelli, radio talk on *Tre poemi* (London: BBC, 1978).

8. Kämper, *GF,* 94.

9. Sketches in the Dallapiccola Archive, Gabinetto Vieusseux, Florence (File: LD Mus. 51).

10. The poem by James Joyce is reproduced with the permission of the Estate of James Joyce. © Copyright, the Estate of James Joyce.

11. Sketches in the Dallapiccola Archive, Gabinetto Vieusseux, Florence, LD Mus. 51.

12. LD, letter to Schoenberg, 2 December 1949 (Original in French), Dallapiccola Archive, Gabinetto Vieusseux, Florence.

13. LD, letter to Schoenberg, 9 January 1950 (Original in French), Dallapiccola Archive, Gabinetto Vieusseux, Florence.

14. Sketches in the Dallapiccola Archive, Gabinetto Vieusseux, Florence, LD Mus. 51.

15. Cf. Patrick Carnegy, *Faust as Musician: A Study of Thomas Mann's novel 'Doctor Faustus'* (London: Chatto and Windus), 1973.

16. LD, "Birth of a Libretto," in Shackelford, *DO,* 233.

17. Letter of Thomas Mann to Lavinia Mazzuchetti, 14 March 1949, in *Thomas Mann: Briefe 1937–1947* (Frankfurt: S. Fischer Verlag, 1961); English translation in *Letters of Thomas Mann 1889–1945,* trans. Richard and Clara Winston (London: Secker and Warburg, 1970), 2:572–73.

18. LD, "What is the Answer to *The Prisoner?*" *San Francisco Sunday Chronicle,* 2 December 1962.

19. LD, "Intorno a *Ulisse,*" Talk recorded by RAI (Italian Radio), September 1968.

20. Cf. Kämper, *GF,* 96.

21. LD, "Dichiarazioni sul mio *Job*," Introductory essay written for the première of the opera, in *ESZ News* (1950), 5.

22. LD, Interview with Piero Santi, Milan 1967, in the Dallapiccola Archive, Gabienetto Vieusseux, Florence.

23. LD, Interview with Piero Santi on *Job*, in *La Scala*, 29 May 1967; cf. also *PM,* 442 n. 1.

24. Ute Schomerus, *Ecce Homo: Die Sacra Rapperesentazione "Job" von Luigi Dallapiccola* (Hamburg: Von Bockel Verlag, 1998). Cf. also Rosemary Brown, "Continuity and Recurrence in the Creative Development of Luigi Dallapiccola" (Ph.D. thesis, University of North Wales, Bangor), 1977.

25. Camillo Togni, "Luigi Dallapiccola," in *Enciclopedia Musicale Ricordi* (Milan: Ricordi, 1964); reprinted in Togni, *Carteggio e scritti di Camillo Togni sul novecento italiano* (Florence, Leo Olschki, 2001), 198–207.

26. Togni, *Carteggio,* 202.

27. LD, letter to Hans Nathan, Dallapiccola Archive, Gabinetto Vieusseux, Florence. Cf. Hans Nathan, "The Twelve-Tone Compositions of Luigi Dallapiccola," *The Musical Quarterly* 45, no. 3 (1958): 291 n. 3. Cf. also Joachim Noller, *Wird das gesungene Wort auf der Bühne eine Konvention bleiben?: Zum italienischen Musiktheater des 20. Jahrhunderts* (Hamburg: Von Bockel Verlag, 1997).

28. Schomerus, *Ecce Homo,* 170.

29. Brown, "Continuity and Recurrence," 285ff.

30. Sketches for the libretto are to be found in the Dallapiccola Archive, Gabinetto Vieusseux, Florence, LD Mus. LI.6.

31. LD, letter to his wife, 6 July 1951, in Nicolodi, *Saggi,* 126.

32. LD, letter to his wife, 28 June 1952, in Nicolodi, *Saggi,* 127.

33. Hans Nathan, "Luigi Dallapiccola: Fragments from Conversations," *The Music Review* 27, no. 4 (November 1966): 296.

34. Sketches in the Dallapiccola Archive, Gabinetto Vieusseux, Florence, LD Mus. 56.

35. Charles Burney, *A General History of Music from the Earliest Ages to the Present Period* (London, 1789, reprint, New York: Dover Publications, 1957), 448–50.

36. Sandro Perotti, *Iri da Iri: Analisi della musica strumentale di Dallapiccola* (Milan: Guerini, 1988), 88–90.

37. Anne Phillips Basart, "The Twelve-Tone Compositions of Luigi Dallapiccola" (M.A. thesis, University of California, Berkeley), 1960.

38. This film, directed by the eminent musicologist Luigi Rognoni, was produced by Rizzoli Film in 1953. For further information on *Il cenacolo,* cf. Mila De Santis, ed., *Dallapiccola: Letture e prospettive* (Lucca: Ricordi/Libreria Musicale Italiana, 1997), 431–71. Also cf. Mario Ruffini, *L'opera di Luigi Dallapiccola: Catalogo ragionato* (Milan: Suvini Zerboni, 2002), 221–25.

39. In an earlier draft of the work, the composer called No. 2 "Ritmi" ("Rhythms"), not "Accenti" ("Accents"); the final movement was called "Sogni" ("Dreams"), not "Quartina" ("Quatrain"); also included was some material that would not eventually find its way into the final version of the work, including a "Contrapunctus secundus," which became incorporated in *Canti di liberazione,* retained at the original pitch-level and ending with a verticalization of the B-A-C-H motif, clearly marked as such in the sketch.

40. David Lewin, "Serial Transformation Networks in Dallapiccola's 'Simbolo,'"

in his *Musical Form and Transformation: Four Analytic Essays* (New Haven, Conn.: Yale University Press, 1993), chapter 1.

41. Olivier Messiaen, *Technique de mon langage musical*, 24–26.

42. Olivier Messiaen, letter to Dallapiccola, 27 April 1947, Dallapiccola Archive, Gabinetto Vieusseux, Florence.

43. Milton Babbitt, "Contextual Counterpoint," in *Words about Music*, ed. Stephen Dembski and Joseph N. Straus, 38–42 (Madison: University of Wisconsin Press, 1987).

44. LD, "Words and Music in 19th-Century Italian Opera," in Shackelford, *DO*, 133–63.

45. Ibid., 134.

46. Cf. Kämper, *GF*, 109.

47. Michael Eckert, "Text and Form in Dallapiccola's *Goethe-Lieder*," *Perspectives of New Music* (Spring-Summer 1979): 98–111.

48. Kämper, *GF*, 110.

49. Eckert, "Text and Form."

50. Nathan, "Luigi Dallapiccola: Fragments from Conversations," 296.

Notes to Chapter 5

1. Cf. Rudolf Stephan, *Von Kranichstein zur Gegenwart: 50 Jahre Darmstädter Ferienkurse* (Stuttgart: DACO Verlag Günter Bläse), 1996.

2. Kämper, *GF*, 113.

3. Ibid., 114.

4. Sandro Perotti, *IRI da IRI: Analisis della musica strumentale di Dallapiccola* (Milan: Guerini e Associati, 1988), 154–57.

5. Letter of LD to René Leibowitz, 4 March 1955, Dallapiccola Archive, Gabinetto Vieusseux, Florence.

6. Cf. Kämper (1984), 118.

7. LD, "Note per un'analisi dei *Canti di liberazione*," in *PM*, 473. Cf. also Kämper, *GF*, 120–21.

8. Kämper, *GF*, 123–25. Cf. also Dietrich Kämper, "Ricerca ritmica e metrica: Beobachtungen am Spätwerk Dallapiccolas," *Neue Zeitschrift für Musik* 135 (1974): 94ff. Cf. also Rosemary Brown "La sperimentazione ritmica in Dallapicccola tra libertà e determinazione," *Rivista Italiana di musicologia* 13 (1978): 142ff.

9. LD, letter to Suvini Zerboni, 22 May 1955, Dallapiccola Archive, Gabinetto Vieusseux, Florence.

10. An admirable full account of *An Mathilde* is to be found in Peter Kiesewetter, "Luigi Dallapiccola: *An Mathilde*," *Melos* 50, no.1 (1988): 2–30. Cf. also Massimo Mila, "L'incontro Heine-Dallapiccola," *La Rassegna Musicale* 27 (1957): 301ff.

11. Roman Vlad, *Storia della dodecafonia* (Milan: Suvini Zerboni, 1958), 310.

12. Kämper, *GF*, 117.

13. Hans Nathan, "The Twelve-Tone Composition of Luigi Dallapiccola," *The Musical Quarterly* 44, no. 3 (1958): 294–95 and 299.

14. LD, interview with Josef Rufer during the interval of a concert broadcast by "Sender Freies Berlin," January 1961.

15. The originals for the sonatas of Tartini used as the basis of *Tartiniana seconda* can be found in the collection *La raccolta di sonate autografe per violino: Manoscritto 1888 Fasc. dell'Archivio Musicale della Veneranda Arca del Santo in Padova* (Padua: Edizioni dell'Accademia Tartiniana, 1976). For a full investigation of *Tartiniana* and *Tartiniana seconda*, cf. Thomas Gartmann, *Klassizistische Moderne: Eine Begleitpublikation zur Konzertreihe im Rahmen der Veranstaltungen '10 Jahre Paul Sacher Stiftung'* (Winterthur: Amadeus Verlag, 1996), 324–27.

16. The work had originally borne the title *Improvisation (after Tartini) for Violin and Piano* when it was published in *The Score* 15 (March 1956): 56ff.

17. LD, "Tartiniana seconda," in *PM*, 486ff., originally published in program book of the *Unione Musicale di Torino, March 1975*.

18. Jacques Wildberger, "Dallapiccolas *Cinque canti*," *Melos* 26 (1959): 7ff. Cf. also LD, "A proposito dei *Cinque Canti*, in *PM*, 493.

19. Quoted in Roberto Zanetti, *La musica italiana nel novecento* (Busto Arsizio: Bramante, 1985), 1174 n. 44.

20. Kämper, *GF,* 131.

21. Igor Stravinsky and Robert Craft: *Conversations with Igor Stravinsky* (London: Faber and Faber, 1959), 120.

22. LD, letter to Suvini Zerboni, 25 May 1957, Dallapiccola Archive, Gabinetto Vieusseux, Florence.

23. Cf. Kämper, *GF,* 133–34.

24. LD, "Note sul *Concerto per la notte di Natale 1956*," in *PM,* 498.

25. Hans Nathan, "On Dallapiccola's working methods," *Perspectives of New Music* 15, no.2 (1977): 34–52.

26. Kämper, *GF,* 135.

27. Ibid., 139.

28. LD, "*Requiescant,*" in *PM,* 501.

29. Hans Nathan, "Luigi Dallapiccola: Fragments from Conversations," *The Music Review* 27 (1966): 307.

30. Kämper, "Ricerca ritmica e metrica," 95ff.; Brown: "La sperimentazione ritmica in Dallapiccola," 151.

31. Cf. C. H. Bachmann: "Dallapiccola's *Requiescant*," *Musica* 14 (1960): 31.

32. Dallapiccola Archive, Gabinetto Vieusseux, Florence: LD Mus 84.

33. LD, letters to Suvini Zerboni, 15 April 1959 and 29 April 1959, Dallapiccola Archive, Gabinetto Vieusseux, Florence.

34. LD, letters to Suvini Zerboni, 23 December 1958 and 9 January 1959, Dallapiccola Archive, Gabinetto Vieusseux, Florence.

35. LD, "Sui miei *Dialoghi*," in *PM,* 504.

36. Ibid.

37. Cf. Perotti, *IRI da IRI,* 163–81.

38. Kämper, *GF,* 142.

39. LD, letter to David Lepine, 2 June 1964, Dallapiccola Archive, Gabinetto Vieusseux, Florence.

40. After he began as a modernist, the religious faith of Murilo Mendes (Brazil 1901–Lisbon 1975) began to emerge in *Tempo e Eternidade* (Time and Eternity) in 1935. Later books of poetry included *A poesia em panico* (Poetry in Panic), 1938; *Poesia libertade* (Poetry Liberty), 1947; and *Tempo español* (Spanish Time), 1959. His poetry combined his deep religiosity with an often tormented feeling for contemporary social and political events.

41. Kämper, GF, 145–47.
42. Ibid., 147.
43. Michael Eckert, in a review of Kämper, GF, in *The Journal of Musicology* 4 (1987): 567.
44. PM 509; also mentioned in a letter of LD to Asher Zlotnik, in Fiamma Nicolodi, *Fondo Dallapiccola,* in *Catalogo della Mostra dell'Archivio Contemporaneo,* Gabinetto Vieusseux, Florence, 20 May–30 June 1978 (Florence: tip. Mori, 1978), 61.
45. Kämper, GF, 148.
46. Pierre Michel, *Luigi Dallapiccola* (Geneva: Editions Contrechamps, 1996), 67.
47. Camillo Togni, sleeve-note for the recording *Dallapiccola,* November-December 1973, on the occasion of Dallapiccola's seventieth birthday, CBS S 61490 (1974). Reprinted in Camillo Togni, *Carteggi e scritti di Camillo Togni sul novecento italiano* (Florence: Leo Olschki, 2001), 215–16.
48. Cf. Pierluigi Petrobelli, "Dallapiccola's last orchestral piece," *Tempo,* no. 123 (1977): 2; cf. also Kämper, GF, 156–57.
49. Kämper, GF, 156.

Notes to Chapter 6

1. Leonardo Pinzauti, *Musicisti d'oggi: Venti colloqui* (Turin: ERI [Edizioni Rai], 1978), 35.
2. LD, press conference, 26 June 1968, quoted in Julia van Hees, *Luigi Dallapiccolas Bühnenwerk 'Ulisse': Untersuchungen zu Werk und Werkgenese* (Kassel: Gustav Bosse Verlag, 1994), 5.
3. Van Hees, *Luigi Dallapiccolas Bühnenwerk 'Ulisse,'* 5–6.
4. Hans Nathan, "On Dallapiccola's Working Methods," *Perspectives of New Music* (1977): 46.
5. Mila De Santis, ed., *Fondo Luigi Dallapiccola: Autografi, scritti a stampa, bibliografia critica, con un elenco dei corrispondenti* (Florence: Edizioni Polistampa, 1995), 59, items 115 and 116.
6. Pinzauti, *Musicisti d'oggi,* 34.
7. W. B. Stanford, "Ulysses in Modern Times," in *The Quest for Ulysses,* ed. W. B. Stanford and J. V. Luce, 213–35 (London: Phaidon, 1974).
8. Dante Alighieri, *La Divina Commedia: Inferno,* Canto 26, lines 76–142. Cf. also W. B. Stanford and J. V. Luce, eds., *The Quest for Ulysses,* 186–89. Aspects of the literary background to Dallapiccola's *Ulisse* are discussed in Raymond Fearn, "Homer-Dante-Joyce-Dallapiccola: Four Artists in Search of Ulysses," in *Irish Musical Studies: The Maynooth International Musicological Conference, 1995,* ed. Patrick F. Devine and Harry White, 411–21 (Dublin: Four Courts Press, 1996).
9. LD, "Birth of a Libretto," in Shackelford, DO, 232–62.
10. Kämper, GF, 159.
11. The sketch material for *Ulisse* is listed in Mila De Santis, ed., *Fondo Luigi Dallapiccola,* 59–69.
12. Item LD. Mus. 99, Dallapiccola Archive, Gabinetto Vieusseux, Florence. Cf. Mila De Santis, ed., *Fondo Luigi Dallapiccola,* 61.

13. Cf. Berg's lecture on "Wozzeck," in H. F. Redlich, *Alban Berg: The Man and His Music* (London: John Calder, 1957), 261–85. Cf. also Douglas Jarman, *The Music of Alban Berg* (London and Boston: Faber and Faber, 1979/1983), 189–98.

14. LD, "Birth of a Libretto," in Shackelford, *DO*, 1:232–62.

15. Kämper, *GF*, 154.

16. LD, "Note per il programma della prima esecuzione italiana di Ulisse al Teatro alla Scala," in *PM*, 532. English Translation in Shackelford, *DO*, 263–66.

17. LD, quoted in Nicoloci, *Saggi*, 136.

18. Juan Ramón Jiménez (1881–1958) was born in Andalusia and was awarded the Nobel Prize for Literature in 1956. His early poetry had been influenced by French poets, but later he developed towards modernism, with a strong religious element that increased in his later years.

19. LD, letter to Suvini Zerboni, 26 August 1970, Dallapiccola Archive, Gabinetto Vieusseux, Florence.

20. Dallapiccola Archive, Gabinetto Vieusseux, Florence, LD. Mus. 123.

21. Kämper, *GF*, 175.

22. Ibid., 176.

23. Cf. Franco Bruni, "Musica visiva," in *Studi su Luigi Dallapiccola*, ed. Arrigo Quattrocchi, 23–25 (Lucca: Libreria Musicale Italiana, 1993).

24. Sergio Sablich, "*Commiato*: Opera ultima, ultima opera," In *Dallapiccola: Letture e prospettive*, ed. Mila De Santis (Lucca: Ricordi/Libreria Musicale Italiana, 1997).

25. Dallapiccola Archive, Gabinetto Vieusseux, Florence, LD Mus. 154 and 155.

Select Bibliography

A. Writings by Dallapiccola

Two selections of Dallapiccola's writings have been published in Italian, one made by the composer himself, the other made by Fiamma Nicolodi after the composer's death. Only some of these writings have so far been published in English, although several of Dallapiccola's articles have appeared in English-language journals. One collection of articles translated into English has been edited by Rudy Shackelford, and a fu rther volume is to be published in 2004.

Dallapiccola, Luigi. *Appunti, incontri, meditazioni.* Milan: Suvini Zerboni, 1970.
———. *Parole e musica.* Ed. Fiamma Nicolodi. Milan: Il Saggiatore, 1980.
———. "Di un aspetto della musica contemporanea." *Atti dell'Accademia del Reale Conservatorio di Musica "Luigi Cherubini."* Florence: La Stamperia, 1938.
———. "Credo nel teatro moderno." Bologna: *Il Resto del Carlino,* 2 Feb. 1941.
———. "Dichiarazioni sul mio 'Job.'" [Essay written for the première of the opera.] *ESZ News,* Milan (1950): 5.
———. "Intorno a Ulisse." Talk recorded by RAI (Radiotelevisione Italiana), September 1968.
———. "Meeting with Anton Webern (Pages from a Diary)." *Tempo* 99 (1972): 2–7. This is a translation by John Waterhouse of an article by Dallapiccola that also appears in Italian in PM.
———. "What is the answer to 'The Prisoner.'" *San Francisco Sunday Chronicle,* 2 Dec. 1962, 27.
Shackelford, Rudy, ed. *Dallapiccola on Opera: Selected Writings of Luigi Dallapiccola.* Vol. 1. London: Toccata Press, 1987.

B. Writings about Dallapiccola

Amato, Joseph. "The Works for Voice and Piano of Luigi Dallapiccola: An Eclectic Analysis." Ph.D. diss., New York University, 1998.
Babbitt, Milton. *Milton Babbitt: Words about Music.* Ed. Stephen Dembski and Joseph N. Straus. Madison: University of Wisconsin Press, 1987, 38–42.
Bachmann, C. H. "Dallapiccola's 'Requiescant.'" *Musica,* No. 14 (1960): 31.
Basart, Anne Philips. "The Twelve-Tone Compositions of Luigi Dallapiccola." M.A. thesis, University of California, Berkeley, 1960.
Biondi, Michel. "Compositional Process in Dallapiccola's 'Ulisse': A Survey and Analysis of New Findings in the Dallapiccola Archive, Florence, Italy." Ph.D. diss., City University of New York, 1994.
Brown, Rosemary. "Continuity and Recurrence in the Creative Development of Luigi Dallapiccola." Ph.D. diss., University of Wales, 1977.
———. "Dallapiccola's Use of Symbolic Self-Quotation." *Studi musicali* 4 (1975): 277 ff.

———. "La sperimentazione ritmica in Dallapiccola tra libertà e determinazione." *Rivista italiana di musicologia* 13 (1978): 142–73.
Ciarpaglini, Giorgio, ed. "Conversazione con Luigi Dallapiccola." *L'Approdo Letterario* 61 (March 1975): 93–99.
Dapogny, James Elliott. "Style and Method in Three Compositions of Luigi Dallapiccola." D.M.A. diss., University of Illinois, 1971.
DeLio, Thomas. "A Proliferation of Canons: Luigi Dallapiccola's *Goethe Lieder* No. 2." *Perspectives of New Music* 23, no. 2 (1985): 185–95.
De Santis, Mila, ed. *Dallapiccola: Letture e prospettive: Atti del Convegno internazionale di studi, Empoli-Firenze, 16–19 February 1995*. Lucca: Ricordi/Libreria Musicale Italiana, 1997.
———, ed. *Fondo Luigi Dallapiccola: Autografi, scritti astampa, bibliografia critica con un elenco dei corrispondenti*. Florence: Edizioni Polistampa, 1995.
Dwelley, Robert. "An Analysis of Luigi Dallapiccola's 'Piccola Musica Notturna.'" Ph.D. diss., University of Rochester, 1985.
Eckert, Michael. "Between Tradition and Avant-Garde: The Music of Luigi Dallapiccola." *The European Legacy: Toward New Paradigms* 2, no. 1 (1997): 86–91.
———. "Myth and Modernity in Dallapiccola's *Ulisse*." *The European Legacy: Toward New Paradigms* 1, no. 4 (1996): 1585–90.
———. "Octatonic Elements in the Music of Luigi Dallapiccola." *Music Review* 46, no. 1 (1985): 35–48.
———. "Text and Form in Dallapiccola's *Goethe-Lieder*." *Perspectives of New Music*, ___ (1979): 98–111.
Fearn, Raymond. "Homer–Dante–Joyce–Dallapiccola: Four Artists in Search of Ulysses." In *Irish Musical Studies*, vol. 4, ed. Gerard Graves and Harry White. Dublin: Irish Academic Press, 1996. Also given as a paper at the International Musicological Conference, Maynooth, Ireland, 1995.
———. *Italian Opera since 1945*. London: Harwood Academic Publishers, 1997.
———. "Luigi Dallapiccola's *Sonatina Canonica*: Neoclassicism . . . Or?" In *Musikkonzepte—Konzepte der Musikwissemschaft: Bericht über den Internationalen Kongress der Gesellschaft für Musikforschung, Halle (Saale) 1998*, ed. Kathrin Eberl and Wolfgang Ruf, 605–10. Kassel: Bärenreiter, 2000.
———. *Selected Letters of Luigi Dallapiccola*. Basingstoke: Ashgate Publishers, in preparation.
———. "Those Magnificent Men in Their Flying Machines: The 'Ideology' of Luigi Dallapiccola's *Volo di notte*." *Journal of Musicological Research* 16, no. 4 (1997): 283–99.
Gartmann, Thomas. "Aus dem Weg zur Dodekaphonie: Die *Tartiniana* und *Tartiniana seconda* von Luigi Dallapiccola." In *Klassizistische Moderne: Eine Begleitpublikation zur Konzertreihe im Rahmen der Veranstaltungen "10 Jahre Paul Sacher Stiftung": Werkeinführungen, Essays, Quellentexte*, ed. Felix Meyer, 324–27. Winterthur: Amadeus, 1996.
Gatti, Guido. "L'opera di Luigi Dallapiccola." *Quaderni della Rassegna Musicale* 2 (1965).
Gould, Glen H. "A Stylistic Analysis of Selected Twelve-Tone Works by Luigi Dallapiccola." Ph.D. diss., Indiana University, 1964.
Hees, Julia van. *Luigi Dallapiccolas Bühnenwerk "Ulisse": Untersuchungen zu Werk und Werkgenese*. Kassel: Gustav Bosse, 1994.

Helm, Everett. "Luigi Dallapiccola in einem unveröffentlichen Gespräch." *Melos—Neue Zeitschrift für Musik* 2, no. 6 (1976).
Hines, R. S., ed. *The Composer Speaks*. Norman: University of Oklahoma Press, 1963.
Kämper, Dietrich. "*Commiato*: Bemerkungen zu Dallapiccolas letztem Werk." *Schweizerische Musikzeitung—Revue Musicale Suisse* 4 (1975): 194–200.
———. "Dallapiccola und der Schönberg-Kreis." In *Bericht über den 2. Kongress derInternationalen Schönberg-Gesellschaft: "Die Wiener Schule in der Musikgeschichte des 20. Jahrhunderts,"* ed. Rudolph Stephan and Sigrid Wiesmann, 83–92. Publikationen der Internationalen Schönberg-Gesellschaft, Bd. 2. Vienna: E. Lafite, 1986.
———. *Gefangenschaft und Freiheit: Leben und Werk des Komponisten Luigi Dallapiccola*. Cologne: Gitarre und Laute, 1984. Italian Edition as *Luigi Dallapiccola: La vita e l'opera*. Florence: Sansoni, 1985.
———. "Ricerca ritmica e metrica: Beobachtungen am Spätwerk Dallapiccolas." *Neue Zeitschrift für Musik* 135 (1974): 94–99.
———. "Uno sguardo nell'officina: Gli schizzi e gli abbozzi del *Prigioniero*." *Nuova Rivista Musicale Italiana* 14, no. 2 (1980): 227l.
Kiesewetter, Peter. "Luigi Dallapiccola: *An Mathilde*." *Melos* 50, no. 1 (1988): 2–30.
Leibowitz, René. "Luigi Dallapiccola." *L'Arche* 23, no. 3 (1947): 118–24.
Lewin, David. "Serial Transformation Networks in Dallapiccola's 'Simbolo.'" In David Lewin, *Musical Form and Transformation: Four Analytical Essays*, chap. 1. New Haven, Conn.: Yale University Press, 1993.
MacDonald, Calum. "Dallapiccola: A Programme-Planner's Guide." *Tempo*, No. 115 (December 1975).
———. "Dallapiccola: The Complete Works." *Tempo*, No. 116 (March 1976).
Mancini, David. "Form and Polarity in Late Works of Luigi Dallapiccola." Ph.D. diss., Yale University, 1987.
———. "Twelve-Tone Polarity in Late Works of Luigi Dallapiccola." *Journal of Music Theory* 30, no. 2 (1986): 203–24.
Mason, Colin. "Dallapiccola and the Twelve-Note Method." *The Listener* (London, BBC), 29 April 1954, 757.
Michel, Pierre. *Luigi Dallapiccola*. Geneva: Contrechamps, 1996.
Mila, Massimo. "Il *Prigioniero* di Luigi Dallapiccola." *La Rassegna Musicale* 4 (1950): 303–11.
———. "Sulla dodecafonia di Dallapiccola." *Annali della Scuola Normale Superiore di Pisa*, series 3, vol. 6, no. 3 (1976).
Montecchi, Giordano."Rigore seriale e poetica della memoria in Dallapiccola." *Musica/Realtà* 3, no. 9 (1982): 37–54.
Nathan, Hans. "Luigi Dallapiccola: Fragments from Conversations." *Music Review* 27, no. 4 (1966): 294.
———. "On Dallapiccola's Working Methods." *Perspectives of New Music* 15, no. 2 (1977): 34–57.
———. "The Twelve-Tone Compositions of Luigi Dallapiccola." *Musical Quarterly* 44, no. 3 (1958): 289–310.
Neumann, Peter Horst, and Jürg Stenzl. "Luigi Dallapiccolas *Goethe-Lieder*." *Schweizerische Beiträge zur Musikwissenschaft* 4 (1980): 171.

Nicolodi, Fiamma, "Fondo Dallapiccola." In *Catalogo della mostra dell'Archivio Contemporaneo, Gabinetto Vieusseux*. Florence: tip. Mori, 1978.

———. *Gusti e tendenze del novecento musicale in Italia*. Florence: Sansoni, 1982.

———. "Luigi Dallapiccola e la Scuola di Vienna: Note in margine ad una scelta." In *Orizzonti musicali italo-europei, 1860–1980*. Rome: Bulzoni, 1990.

———. *Musica e musicisti nel ventennio fascista*. Fiesole: Discanto Edizioni, 1984.

Nicolodi, Fiamma, ed. *Luigi Dallapiccola: Saggi, testimonianze, carteggio, biografia e bibliografia*. Milan: Suvini Zerboni, 1975.

Noller, Joachim. *Wird das gesungene Wort auf der Bühne eine Konvention bleiben?: Zum italienischen Musiktheater des 20. Jahrhunderts*. Hamburg: Von Bockel Verlag, 1997.

Perkins, John McIvor. "Dallapiccola's Art of Canon." *Perspectives of New Music* 1, no. 2 (1963): 95–106.

Perotti, Sandro. *Iri da Iri: Analisi della musica strumentale di Dallapiccola*. Milan: Guerini e Associati, 1988.

Petito, Sue Burnett. "The Piano Works of Luigi Dallapiccola (1904–1975): An Analysis for Performance." Ph.D. diss., New York University, 1989.

Petrobelli, Pierluigi. "Dallapiccola's Last Orchestral Piece." *Tempo*, No. 123 (December 1977): 2–6.

———. "On Dante and Italian Music: Three Moments. Lectures Given at the University of California, Berkeley, Autumn 1988." *Cambridge Opera Journal* 2, no. 3 (November 1990): 219–49.

Piccardi, Carlo. "La musica italiana verso il Fascismo." In *Aspetti Musicali: Musikhistorische Dimensionen Italiens 1600 bis 2000: Festschrift für Dietrich Kämper zum 65. Geburtstag*, ed. Norbert Bolin, Christoph von Blumröder, and Imke Misch, 111–20. Cologne: Verlag Dohr, 2001.

Pinzauti, Leonardo. *Musicisti d'oggi: venti colloqui*. ERI (Edizioni RAI Radiotelevisione Italiana) (1978): 31–41.

Quattrocchi, Arrigo, ed. *Studi su Luigi Dallapiccola: Un seminario*. Lucca: Libreria Musicale Italiana, 1993.

Ruffini, Mario. *L'opera di Luigi Dallapiccola: Catalogo ragionato*. Milan: Suvini Zerboni, 2002.

Sachs, Harvey. *Music in Fascist Italy*. London: Weidenfeld and Nicolson, 1987.

Scherliess, Volker. "Luigi Dallapiccola über Alban Berg: Ein Brief und eine persönliche Erinnerung." In *Aspetti Musicali: Musikhistorische Dimensionen Italiens 1600–2000: Festschrift für Dietrich Kämper zum 65. Geburtstag*, ed. Norbert Bolin, Christoph von Blumröder, and Imke Misch, 133–40. Cologne: Verlag Dohr, 2001.

Schomerus, Ute. *Ecce Home: Die Sacra Rappresentazione "Job" von Luigi Dallapiccola*. Hamburg: Von Bockel, 1998.

Shackleford, Rudy. "Dallapiccola and the Organ." *Tempo*, No. 111 (December 1974): 15–22.

Shirley, Wayne. "Luigi Dallapiccola's Sketch for *Ulisse*." In *Music History from Primary Sources*, ed. Jon Newsom and Alfred Mann, 201–5. Washington: Library of Congress, 2000.

Togni, Camillo. *Carteggi e scritti di Camillo Togni sul novecento italiano*. Florence: Leo Olschki, 2001.

Venuti, Massimo. *Il teatro di Dallapiccola*. Milan: Suvini Zerboni, 1985.

Vlad, Roman. "A Footnote to 'Dallapiccola and the Organ.'" *Tempo*, No. 116 (March 1976): 21–23.
———. *Luigi Dallpiccola*. Translated by Cynthia Jolly. Milan: Suvini Zerboni, 1957. Reprint, Irvine, California: Reprint Services Corporation, 1987.
———. *Modernità e tradizione nella musica contemporanea*. Turin: Einaudi, 1955.
———. *Storia della dodecafonia*. Milan: Suvini Zerboni, 1958, 275–311.
Waterhouse, John C. G. "Dallapiccola." In *New Grove Dictionary of Music*, ed. Stanley Sadie. 2nd edition. vol. 10. London: Macmillan, 1981.
Weber, Horst. "Dallapiccola—Maderna—Nono: Tradition in der itanienischen Moderne." In *Bericht über den 2. Kongress der Internationalen Schönberg-Gesellschaft: "Die Wiener Schule in der Musikgeschichte des 20. Jahrhunderts,"* ed. Rudolph Stephan and Sigrid Wiesmann, 93–98. Publikationen der Internationalen Schönberg-Gesellschaft, Bd. 2. Vienna: E. Lafite, 1986.
Wildberger, Jaques. "Dallapiccolas *Cinque Canti*." *Melos* 26 (1959): 7.
Wilkinson, Edward N. "Theory and Practice: An Interpretation of Serialism in the Music of Luigi Dallapiccola." Ph.D. diss., Royal Holloway College, University of London, 1982.
Zanetti, Roberto. *La musica italiana nel novecento*. Busto Arsizio: Bramante, 1985.
Zanolini, Bruno. *Luigi Dallapiccola: Conquista di un linguaggio (1928–1941)*. Padova: Zanibon, 1974. Reprint, Milan: Suvini Zerboni, 1997.

C. Writings about Twelve-Tone Music

Adorno, Theodor Wiesengrund. *Alban Berg*. Cambridge: Cambridge University Press, 1991.
Bailey, Kathryn. *The Life of Webern*. Cambridge: Cambridge University Press, 1998.
———. *The Twelve-Note Music of Anton Webern*. Cambridge: Cambridge University Press, 1991.
The Berg-Schoenberg Correspondence. Edited by Juliane Brand, Christopher Hailey, and Donald Harris. Basingstoke: Macmillan, 1987.
Boretz, B., and E. Cone, eds. *Perspectives on Schoenberg and Stravinsky*. Princeton, N.J.: Princeton University Press, 1968.
Boulez, Pierre. *Boulez on Music Today*. London: Faber and Faber, 1971.
Brindle, Reginald Smith. *Serial Composition*. Oxford: Oxford University Press, 1966.
Carner, Mosco. *Alban Berg: The Man and the Work*: London: Faber and Faber, 1979.
Dahlhaus, Carl. *Schoenberg and the New Music*. Cambridge: Cambridge University Press, 1987.
Haimo, Ethan. *Schoenberg's Serial Odyssey*. Oxford: Clarendon Press, 1990.
Jarman, Douglas. *The Berg Companion*. Basingstoke: Macmillan, 1989.
———. *The Music of Alban Berg*. London: Faber and Faber, 1979.
Keller, Hans, and Milein Cosman. *Stravinsky Seen and Heard*. London: Toccata Press, 1982.
Kolneder, Walter. *Anton Webern: An Introduction to His Works*. London: Faber and Faber, 1968.
Leibowitz, René. *Schoenberg and His School: The Contemporary Stage of the Lan-*

guage of Music. New York: Philosophical Library, 1949. Reprint, New York: Da Capo Press, 1970.

Manzoni, Giacomo. *Arnold Schoenberg: L'uomo, l'opera i testi musicati.* Milan: Feltrinelli, 1975.

Moldenhauer, Hans. *Anton Webern: A Chronicle of His Life and Work.* London: Victor Gollancz, 1978.

Neighbour, Oliver, Paul Griffiths, and George Perle. *Second Viennese School.* London: Macmillan, 1983.

Payne, Anthony. *Schoenberg.* Oxford: Oxford University Press, 1968.

Perle, George. *The Operas of Alban Berg: I. Wozzeck, II. Lulu.* 2 vols. Berkeley: University of California Press, 1980 and 1985.

———. *Serial Composition and Atonality.* Berkeley: University of California Press, 1962. Reprint, 1981.

Redlich, Hans Ferdinand. *Alban Berg: The Man and His Music.* London: John Calder, 1957.

Reich, Willi. *The Life and Work of Alban Berg.* London: Thames and Hudson, 1965.

———. *Schoenberg: A Critical Biography.* London: Longman, 1971.

Rognoni, Luigi. *La scuola musicale di Vienna.* Turin: Einaudi, 1966.

Rosen, Charles. *Schoenberg.* London: Marion Boyars, 1976.

Rufer, Josef. *Composition with Twelve Notes Related Only One with Another.* London: Rockliff, 1954.

———. *The Works of Arnold Schoenberg.* London: Faber and Faber, 1962.

Schoenberg, Arnold. *Style and Idea.* London: Faber and Faber, 1975. Includes essay "Composition with Twelve Tones," 214–45.

Stein, Erwin. *Orpheus in New Guises.* London: Rockliff, 1953.

Straus, Joseph N. *Introduction to Post-Tonal Theory.* 2nd edition. Upper Saddle River, N.J.: Prentice Hall, 2000.

Stuckenschmidt, H. H. *Arnold Schoenberg: His Life, World and Work.* London: John Calder, 1977.

Webern, Anton. *The Path to the New Music.* London: Universal Edition, 1975.

Wildgans, Friedrich. *Anton Webern.* London: Calder and Boyars, 1966.

Wuorinen, Charles. *Simple Composition.* New York: Longman, 1979.

Index

Accademia Musicale Chigiana (Siena), 98
Aeropittura (Aerial Painting), 44
Aeschylus, 234
Albeniz, Isaac, 6
Alberti, Domitilla (mother of Dallapiccola), 3
Alcaeus, 14
Altenberg, Peter, 85
Ambrosi, Alfredo, 44
Anbruch (magazine), 58
Augustine (Saint), 187, 235, 269
   Confessions, 187, 235
   Soliloquia, 269

Bacci, Baccio Maria, 8
B-A-C-H motif, 36, 158–59, 187, 192, 204
Bach, J. S., 1, 14, 20, 63, 101, 152, 192, 248
   Art of Fugue, 157
   Chaconne (Partita for solo violin), 101
   Goldberg Variations, 20, 158
   Musical Offering, 94, 154, 158
   Notebook for Anna Magdalena, 157
   Three-Part Inventions, 196
   Two-Part Inventions, 162
   Well-Tempered Clavier, 14, 158
Badoaro, Giacomo, 234
Balbo, Italo, 44
Balla, Giacomo, 44
Barbieri, Corrado, 5
Bartók, Béla, 5, 16, 24, 75, 272
   Music for Strings, Percussion, and Celesta, 183–85
Basart, Anne, 157
Baudelaire, Charles, 85
Beach, Amy, 6
Beethoven, Ludwig van, 6, 7, 43, 59, 75, 180
   Diabelli Variations, 75
   "Eroica" Symphony, 59
   Fidelio, 43
   "Pastoral" Symphony, 180

Berg, Alban, 1, 16, 17, 20, 21, 30–33, 38, 45–49, 50, 58, 60, 85, 103, 114, 129, 179, 212, 239, 241, 250, 259, 269, 271
   Chamber Concerto, 271
   Four Pieces for clarinet and piano, 17
   Lulu, 38, 45, 123, 149, 239, 271
   Lulu Symphony, 20, 46
   Lyric Suite, 17
   Violin Concerto, 33, 48, 108
   Der Wein, 17
   Wozzeck, 17, 30, 38, 45, 66, 103, 104, 124, 125
Berio, Luciano, 20, 73, 81, 142, 151–52, 179, 244, 270, 272
   Folk Songs, 20
   Sinfonia, 244
Berkeley, University of California at, 217, 220–21, 224
Bernac, Pierre, 110
Boethius, 56–57, 60
   The Consolation of Philosophy, 56–57, 60
Bonsanti, Alessandro, 8
Bontempelli, Massimo, 10
Bosso, Renato di, 44
Boulanger, Nadia, 73
Boulez, Pierre, 214
Brahms, Johannes, 82, 151
   Symphony No. 3, 151
Brecht, Bertolt, 142
Britten, Benjamin, 21, 272
Brown, Rosemary, 150, 189, 207, 237
Büchner, Georg, 21
   Woyzeck, 21
Busoni, Ferruccio, 14, 72, 84, 153, 271
   Doktor Faust, 126–27
   Fantasia Contrappuntistica, 14, 153
   Sonatina, 14
Bussotti, Sylvano, 272

Campanella, Tommaso, 56
Carillon Music Society (Geneva), 22

Casella, Alfredo, 5–6, 8, 10, 11, 12, 16, 28, 29, 51, 278 n. 6
   Partita, 11
Casiraghi, Roberto, 5
Cassadó, Gaspar, 98, 99, 212–13, 216
Castellion, Sébastien, 56, 186
Cavalieri, Emilio de', 14
   Rappresentazione di Anima e di Corpo, 14
(Il) cenacolo (film), 157
Chanson de Roland, 16
Charles V, 122
Cimarosa, Domenico, 9
Consolo, Ernesto, 5, 9
Coolidge, Elizabeth Sprague, 221
Corelli, Antonio, 9
Corghi, Azio, 270
Couvreux, Lucienne, 53
Couvreux, Muriel, 53
Crali, Tullio, 44

Dallapiccola, Annalibera, 135, 211–12
Dallapiccola, Laura (Coen-Luzzato), 33, 41, 52, 186, 193, 258
Dallapiccola, Luigi
   An Mathilde, 193–97
   Appunti, incontri, meditazioni, 252
   Caligo, 8*Canti di liberazione*, 36, 56, 64, 130, 140, 152, 153, 157, 158, 161, 171, 182, 185–93, 204, 209, 270
   Canti di prigionia, 2, 8, 18, 33, 36, 41, 49, 50, 53, 56–65, 68, 71–72, 83, 86, 100, 116, 117, 119, 126, 146, 153, 186, 187, 192, 209, 217, 244, 258, 270
   Canzone del Quarnaro, 7, 85
   Ciaccona, intermezzo e adagio, 98, 99–105, 157, 193, 225
   Cinque canti, 30, 197, 200–204, 205, 206, 254, 258
   Commiato, 200, 207, 265–69
   Concerto per la notte di Natale dell'anno 1956, 30, 36, 197, 200, 203, 204–5, 206, 254
   Cori di Michelangelo, 14, 28–33, 35, 46, 259
   Dalla mia terra, 13

   Dialoghi, 99, 212–16
   Divertimento in quattro esercizi, 17–20, 130
   Due canzoni di Grado, 8
   Due laudi di Iacopone da Todi, 9, 17, 130, 200
   Due liriche del Kalevala (Frammento del Kalevala), 10–11, 13
   Due pezzi, 105, 221, 225
   Due studi, 98, 105–10, 111, 180, 182, 221, 225
   Estate, 13–14
   Fiuri de tapo, 8
   Goethe-Lieder, 35, 140, 171–78, 180, 182, 194, 196, 203, 225, 252, 253, 272
   Job, 68, 115, 130, 140–52, 209, 221, 237, 244, 247
   Liriche greche, 14, 33, 41, 50, 51, 81, 82, 83, 84–96, 97, 99, 128, 130, 193, 200, 206, 272
   Lux, 269
   Marsia, 66–72, 115
   Musica per tre pianoforti (Inni), 8, 17, 22–28
   Parole di San Paolo, 113, 221–23, 252
   Partita, 11–13, 65, 130, 225
   Piccola musica notturna, 180–85, 221, 222, 225
   Piccolo concerto per Muriel Couvreux, 53–55, 70, 83, 84
   Preghiera di Maria Stuarda, 53, 56, 59, 60, 62, 186
   Preghiere, 216–21
   Il prigioniero, 2, 4, 16, 33, 35, 41, 43, 50, 51, 62, 64, 65, 66, 86, 96, 97, 99, 115–27, 128, 131, 140, 141, 143, 151, 182, 186, 203, 233, 237, 239, 243, 247, 258, 268
   Quaderno musicale di Annalibera, 36, 75, 152, 153, 157–71, 178, 182, 185, 187, 188, 189, 204, 212, 221, 225, 272, 285 n. 39
   Quattro liriche di Antonio Machado, 131–34, 193, 233
   Rappresentazione di Anima e di Corpo, 14–16

Rapsodia (Studio per la morte del Conte Orlando), 17, 110–11
Rencesvals, 99, 110–14
Requiescant, 206–12, 251, 270
Sex carmina Alcaei, 130
Sicut umbra, 30, 252–58
Sonatina canonica, 74–78, 83, 84, 95, 96, 153, 154, 198
Studio sul Capriccio no. 14 di Niccolò Paganini, 74
Tartiniana, 152–57
Tartiniana seconda, 153, 197–200
Tempus destruendi—Tempus aedificandi, 209, 258–65
Three Questions with Two Answers, 173, 178, 213, 224–31, 238, 241, 253
Tre episodi dal balletto "Marsia," 75
Tre laudi, 32, 33–38, 41, 43, 45, 52, 55, 83, 87, 93, 100, 126, 130, 153, 178, 200, 204, 243, 258, 270
Tre poemi, 134–40, 206, 251
Ulisse, 4, 14, 16, 34, 39, 43, 86, 115, 127, 131, 139, 141, 151, 173, 178, 196–97, 209, 216, 223–31 passim, 232–52, 253, 258, 265, 267, 268, 271
Volo di notte, 4, 8, 16, 31, 33, 34, 36, 38–49, 50, 53, 55, 60, 66, 68, 71, 83, 100, 115, 116, 123, 124, 126, 141, 243, 244, 258
D'Annunzio, Gabriele, 15, 85
Dante Alighieri, 1, 4, 5, 16, 34, 171, 237, 243, 251, 266
  La Divina Commedia, 4, 235, 243, 251, 266
Darmstadt (Summer School of Music), 139, 179
Debussy, Claude, 5, 8, 45, 75, 85
  Iberia, 5
  Pelléas et Mélisande, 124
  Prélude à l'après-midi d'un faune, 68
De Coster, Charles, 116
  La légende d'Ulenspiegel et de Lamme Goedzak, 116
Dent, Edward J., 168
De'Paoli, Domenico, 233

Depero, Fortunato, 44
Dermatus, 258–65
Des Knaben Wunderhorn, 12
Dies Irae, 59, 62, 145
Donatoni, Franco, 272
Dottori, Gerardo, 44
Dukas, Paul, 6
Düsseldorf Theater Ballet, 265

Eckert, Michael, 7, 172, 218
Eisler, Hanns, 152
Eliot, T.S., 8
Enescu, Georges, 5
Epstein, Jacob, 143
  Ecce Homo, 143
L'esperienza del cubismo (film), 98

Falla, Manuel de, 6
Farulli, Ferdinando, 251
Fauré, Gabriel, 5
Fillia (Luigi Colombo), 44
Fischer-Dieskau, Dietrich, 251
Florio, Alice Andrich, 4
Fortner, Wolfgang, 212
Frankenstein, Alfred, 105
Frazzi, Vito, 6–7, 50, 278 n. 9
  Re Lear, 7
  Scale alternate, 7
  Studio dell'armonia cromatica ultratonale, 7
Frescobaldi, Girolamo, 9

Gabrieli, Giovanni, 9, 22, 24
Gatti, Guido, 16, 72, 142
Ghedini, Giorgio Federico, 11
  Concerto dell'albatro, 150
  Partita, 11
Gide, André, 42
Giordani, Paolo, 74–75, 282 n. 25
Giraud, Albert, 85
Giraudoux, Jean, 253
  La guerre de Troie n'aura pas lieu, 253
Giubbe Rosse Café, 7
Goethe, Johann Wolfgang von, 15, 130, 171–78, 271
  Faust, 15
  West-Östlicher Divan, 171
Goya, Francisco, 265

Index

Graz (Austria), 3, 43
Gregor, Joseph, 39
Grevenberg, Julius, 4

Haas, Robert, 72
Hába, Aloys, 20, 58
   Matka, 20
Hauptmann, Gerhart, 234, 235
   Der Bogen des Odysseus, 234, 235
Haydn, Joseph, 95
Heine, Heinrich, 130, 193–97, 271
Herbert, George, 203
Hindemith, Paul, 73
Hitler, Adolf, 56
Hoare, Samuel, 56
Hölderlin, Friedrich, 234
   Schicksalslied, 234
Homer, 232, 234
Hugo, Victor,
   Légende des siècles, 66

Iacopone da Todi, 16, 200, 204
Ibert, Jacques, 151
Ibsen, Henrik, 15–16
   Peer Gynt, 15–16
Ideograms, 30
Illersberg, Antonio, 4, 32, 265
Incontri con Roma (film), 98
Indy, Vincent d', 72, 154,
International Musical Congress
   (Florence 1937), 16
I.S.C.M. (International Society for
   Contemporary Music)
   Prague 1935, 20, 21, 38, 51
   London 1938, 51
   London 1946, 130
Istria, 1, 2, 8

Jalowetz, Heinrich, 21
Janacek, Leos, 20
Jenufa, 20
Jiménez, Juan Ramon, 130, 252–58, 289 n. 18
Jone, Hildegard, 85
Joyce, James, 1, 130, 135, 136, 139, 152, 206–12, 247, 251, 271
   A Portrait of the Artist as a Young Man, 234, 251

Ulysses, 152, 251

Kafka, Franz, 8
Kämper, Dietrich, 70, 99, 103, 113, 114, 116, 125, 135, 180, 189, 196, 205, 207, 216, 217, 218, 221, 231, 237, 259, 262, 268
Kaufmann, Harald, 265
Kavafis, Constantine
   Ithaka, 234
King, Martin Luther, 186
Kodaly, Zoltan, 16
Kolisch Quartet, 17, 58
Koussevitzky, Serge, 151, 154, 157
Krenek, Ernst
   Über neue Musik, 58
Kreutzberg, Harald, 142–43

Labroca, Mario, 72
Ladri di biciclette (film), 98
La Méri, 9
Latini, Brunetto, 266–69
Laudario dei Battuti, 33
Leibowitz, René, 129–30, 138
Léonard, Hubert, 154
Leonardo da Vinci, 157
Lepine, David, 216
Lewin, David, 158
Liebermann, Rolf, 206
Liguoro, Giuseppe de, 3, 232
   The Odyssey of Homer (L'odissea di Omero) (film), 3
Lönnrot, Elias, 10
Lorca, Federico Garcia, 96
Loria, Arturo, 8
Loriod, Yvonne, 162

Maazel, Lorin, 212
Machado, Antonio, 130, 131–34, 180, 271
Machado, Manuel, 135
Machaut, Guillaume de, 204
   Ma fin est mon commencement, 204
Maderna, Bruno, 73, 81, 96, 179, 270
Maggio Musicale Fiorentino (Festival), 16, 17, 72, 232
Magnani, Luigi, 105
Mahler, Gustav, 5, 9, 12, 15, 82, 207

Kindertotenlieder, 207
Symphony No. 1, 9
Symphony No. 3, 15, 207
Symphony No. 4, 12
Malipiero, Gian Francesco, 10, 28, 29, 40, 72–73, 81, 213, 270
  Dialoghi, 213
  Sette canzoni, 28
  Torneo notturno, 28
Mallarmé, Stéphane, 85
"Manifesto of Italian Musicians for the Tradition of Nineteenth-Century Romantic Art," 9–10, 13
Mann, Monika, 140
Mann, Thomas, 139, 140, 152, 171, 191, 234, 251, 271
  Doktor Faustus, 139, 140
  Joseph and His Brothers, 140, 142, 152, 171–72, 234, 251
  The Tables of the Law, 191
  The Tales of Jacob, 140
Marin, Biagio, 8
Marinetti, Benedetta, 44
Marinetti, Filippo, 44
Massine, Léonide, 232
Materassi, Sandro, 9, 99, 105, 153, 154, 197
Melville, Hermann, 150
  Moby Dick, 150
Mendes, Murilo, 130, 216–21, 287 n. 40
Messiaen, Olivier, 7, 132, 151, 272
  Cantéodjayâ, 161
  Oiseaux exotiques, 162
  Quatre études de rhythme, 161
  Technique de mon langage musical, 7
  "Turangalila" Symphony, 162
Michel, Pierre, 222
Michelangelo (Buonarroti), 110, 130, 135, 137, 271
Mila, Massimo, 125
Milhaud, Darius, 16, 22
  Christophe Colomb, 124
  Mort d'un tyran, 59
Milloss, Aurel, 66–72
Moissi, Alexander, 143
Monachesi, Sante, 44
Montale, Eugenio, 8, 85, 130, 135
Monteverdi, Claudio, 9, 50, 72–73, 74, 169, 245, 250, 269
  Il combattimento di Tancredi e Clorinda, 115
  Orfeo, 245, 247
  Il ritorno d'Ulisse in patria, 72–73, 81, 232, 234, 235
Montgomery (Alabama), 186
Mozart, Wolfgang Amadeus, 3, 235
  Don Giovanni, 3
Mussolini, Benito, 28, 33, 41, 52, 57
Mussorgsky, Modest, 6, 22, 75
  Pictures at an Exhibition, 6, 22, 72, 75–76

Nathan, Hans, 112, 149, 196, 204, 232
Nicolodi, Fiamma, 7, 24
Nietzsche, Friedrich, 15, 232
  Also sprach Zarathustra, 15
Nono, Luigi, 73, 96, 142, 179, 212, 270, 272
  Epitaffio, 96

Ojetti, Paola, 24

Paganini, Niccolò, 153, 154
  Caprices, 74–81
Paisà (film), 98
Paisiello, Giovanni, 9
Palestrina, Giovanni Pierluigi da, 9
Pappenheim, Marie, 85
Paulinus (of Aquileia), 258–65
Perotti, Sandro, 183,
Persichetti, Vincent, 170, 221,
Petrassi, Goffredo, 11, 12, 24, 41, 67, 98
  La follia di Orlando, 67
  Morte dell'aria, 142
  Partita, 11
  Ritratto di Don Chisciotte, 67
  Salmo IX, 150–51
Peyron, Guido, 8
Philip II, 118, 121
Piero della Francesca, 1, 105, 106, 110, 111, 180, 272
Pinzauti, Leonardo, 235
Pirandello, Luigi, 10
Pischiutta, 3
Pisino (Pazin, Mitterburg) (Istria), 1, 2, 151

Pizzetti, Ildebrando, 5, 7, 9, 10
Poulenc, Francis, 110
Prampolini, Enrico, 44
Proust, Marcel, 8, 113, 139, 271
Puccini, Giacomo, 3, 6, 9, 45, 269

Quasimodo, Salvatore, 8, 84–96, 200,
  Discourse on Poetry, 85
Queen's College, New York, 204, 206

Rameau Chamber Music Society of
  Tokyo, 204
Rassegna Musicale (journal), 58–59
Ravel, Maurice, 4, 5, 6, 8, 18
  Chansons madécasses, 18
  L'heure espagnole, 4
Reich, Willi, 16, 21
Respighi, Ottorino, 9, 12, 180
  Lauda per la Natività del Signore,
  12
Rilke, Rainer Maria, 8
Rimsky-Korsakov, Nicolai, 5
Rossi, Mario, 33
Rossini, Gioacchino, 9
  Il Turco in Italia, 142
Rostropovich, Mstislav, 99
Rückert, Friedrich, 207

Sablich, Sergio, 267
Sagra Musicale Umbra (Perugia), 98
Saint-Exupéry, Antoine de,
  Vol de nuit, 39–43, 44, 53
Sappho, 271
Satie, Erik, 6
Savinio, Alberto, 142
Savonarola, Girolamo, 56–57, 60, 62
Scarlatti, Alessandro, 9
Scherchen, Hermann, 180, 212
Schlee, Alfred, 58, 81
Schoenberg, Arnold, 4, 5, 9, 16, 17,
  18, 20, 21, 31, 32, 38, 50, 58, 71,
  82, 85, 99, 107, 125, 138, 139,
  167, 179, 186, 187, 192, 259,
  269, 270
  Chamber Symphony, 5, 32, 38
  Five Orchestral Pieces, Op. 16, 167
  Gurrelieder, 4, 5
  Harmonielehre, 5, 32

  Moses und Aron, 31, 127, 143
  Ode to Napoleon Bonaparte, 59
  Pelleas und Melisande, 38
  Pierrot Lunaire, 5, 6, 16, 18, 38,
  185
  Six Little Piano Pieces, Op. 19, 16,
  162, 170
  String Quartet No. 1, 17
  String Quartet No. 2, 5
  String Quartet No. 3, 58
  String Quartet No. 4, 58
  Suite, Op. 25, 58
  A Survivor from Warsaw, 59
  Three Piano Pieces, Op. 11, 5, 38
  Three Satires, 38, 58
  Variations for Orchestra, 20, 38
  Violin Concerto, 107
Schubert, Franz, 82
  Lied der Suleika, 171
Schumann, Robert, 80
  Dichterliebe, 193
  Kinderszenen, 158
Schwarz, Hanna, 17
Sibelius, Jean, 10
Sindacato Nazionale di Musicisti
  (National Musicians' Union), 13–
  14
Skriabin, Alexander, 6
Società Nazionale di Musica (National
  Music Society), 5
Socrates, 56
Solaria, 7–8
Somenzi, Mimo, 44
Sophocles, 143
Stanford, W. B., 235
Stein, Erwin, 138
Stockhausen, Karlheinz, 214
Strauss, Richard, 9
  Alpensinfonie, 38
  Elektra, 9
  Salome, 9
Stravinsky, Igor, 5, 6, 8, 22, 63
  Chorale Variations on "Vom Himmel
  hoch da komm'ich her," 81
  Dumbarton Oaks Concerto, 154
  Les noces, 8, 22
  Petrushka, 5
Strehler, Giorgio, 142

Strobel, Heinrich, 193
Stuart, Mary, 52–53, 60, 117
Styrian Autumn Festival, 265

Tanglewood Summer School, 151, 154, 179
Tartini, Giuseppe, 81, 152–57, 197–200, 287 n. 15
Tasso, Torquato, 115
   Gerusalemme liberata, 115
Tato, Guglielmo, 44
Te Deum, 144, 148, 149
Testimonium Festival (Israel), 258
Tippett, Michael, 270
   A Child of Our Time, 59
Todi, Iacopone da
Togni, Camillo, 109, 114, 148, 149

Ungaretti, Giuseppe, 8, 85

Van Hees, Julia, 232, 237
Vecchi, Orazio, 142
   L'anfiparnaso, 142
Venice Festival of Contemporary Music, 17, 98
   1934, 17, 57
Verdi, Giuseppe, 3, 9, 20, 29, 168, 169, 235
   Otello, 20
   Simon Boccanegra, 9
Veretti, Antonio, 11
   Partita, 11
Verlaine, Paul, 85
Villiers de L'Isle-Adam, 65, 258
   Contes cruels, 65
   L'enjeu, 151
   La torture par l'espérance, 116
Vivaldi, Antonio, 73, 180
Vlad, Roman, 195
Vogel, Wladimir, 13, 21, 31, 46, 57–59, 60, 279 n. 27
   Madrigaux, 57
   Thyl Claes, 32, 59, 143
   Wagadus Untergang durch die Eitelkeit, 31

Wagner, Richard, 3, 4, 5, 7, 235, 236, 239, 250
   The Flying Dutchman, 3, 265
   Die Meistersinger von Nürnberg, 3, 4, 152
   Parsifal, 4
   The Ring of the Nibelungs, 3
   Tristan und Isolde, 4, 5, 20, 236
   Die Walküre, 196
Wagner, Wolfgang, 236
Weber, Carl Maria von,
   Der Freischütz, 3
Webern, Anton, 1, 16, 17, 20–21, 50, 51, 52, 81–83, 85, 93, 128, 129, 130, 139, 162, 179, 195, 259, 269
   Das Augenlicht, 51–52, 58–59, 82
   Canons, Op. 16, 172, 205
   Cantata No. 1, Op. 29, 201
   Concerto, Op. 24, 20–21, 51,
   Ricercare from Bach's *The Musical Offering,* 154
   Six Bagatelles, 21
   String Quartet, Op. 28, 58, 201, 221
   Variations, Op. 21, 82
   Variations, Op. 27, 58, 138, 162
Weill, Kurt, 82
Wellesz, Egon, 16
Wildberger, Jacques, 201
Wilde, Oscar, 130, 206–12, 271
Wolf, Hugo, 82

Xenakis, Iannis, 212

Zandonai, Riccardo, 9
Zweig, Stefan, 52

The Music of Luigi Dallapiccola

Luigi Dallapiccola (1904–1975) was one of the most important Italian composers of the twentieth century. His music is admired by performers and listeners as much for its lyrical expressivity and emotional power as for its clarity of form and construction. As well as writing several operas (including the one-act *The Prisoner* and the later full-length *Ulysses*), Dallapiccola composed a large number of works in which the human voice, whether solo or in chorus, plays an important role. Most prominent of these is the three-movement *Canti di prigionia* (Songs of imprisonment), in which the composer created a powerful piece of "protest music" against the oppressions of fascism by setting prayers by three prisoners awaiting execution: Mary Stuart, Boethius, and Savonarola. Dallapiccola also set texts by writers as diverse as James Joyce, Salvatore Quasimodo, Antonio Machado, Goethe, and Heine.

The Music of Luigi Dallapiccola is the first book in English which deals with the work of Dallapiccola as a whole, offering a survey of his development as a composer from the first, hesitant vocal compositions of his student years up to the works of his last decade, in which Italian lyricism is combined with great formal and constructional rigor. Dallapiccola was the first Italian to adopt the twelve-tone techniques of Schoenberg, but he placed them within a "Mediterranean" ambience of sensuousness and sharply contoured formal outlines. Raymond Fearn suggests that Dallapiccola should be understood not only as an influential figure in the postwar development of Italian music, but also as one who renewed and revitalized the older traditions of Italian music.

Raymond Fearn is Senior Lecturer in Music at Keele University, Staffordshire. He is the author of two other books on twentieth-century Italian music, one on Italian opera since 1945 and one on the composer Bruno Maderna.

Praise for *The Music of Luigi Dallapiccola*:

"The life and works of Luigi Dallapiccola have finally received the presentation they deserve. Raymond Fearn's *The Music of Luigi Dallapiccola* includes a detailed analysis of the creative process in all its aspects. Superbly researched, it places Dallapiccola in the complex context of his times."
—Dietrich Kämper, University of Köln and author of *Gefangenschaft und Freiheit: Leben und Werk des Komponisten Luigi Dallapiccola*

"This book is well researched and well written. It is highly informative and provides a great deal of insight into one of the twentieth century's finest composers."
—Brian Alegant, Oberlin College Conservatory of Music

www.ingramcontent.com/pod-product-compliance
Lightning Source LLC
Chambersburg PA
CBHW071231230426
43668CB00011B/1392